华东师范大学第二附属中学

NO.2 HIGH SCHOOL OF EAST CHINA NORMAL UNIVERSITY

国际课程导学

——AP Mathematics 数学基础

（代数与分析初步）

吴 森 汪 健◎编著

谢欢欣 姚道路 肖文娟 岳燕梅 张宋菲 杜昌敏 姚 瑶◎参编

上海交通大学出版社

SHANGHAI JIAO TONG UNIVERSITY PRESS

内容提要

　　本书针对美国大学先修课程 AP 课程的相关要求编写,内容包括集合与命题、不等式、函数、三角、三角函数及数列与数学归纳法等,旨在为 AP 微积分 AB/BC 提供前序基础课程。本书采用了双语写作,重点知识部分强化了数学术语以及一些习惯用语的英文表述,同时设置了大量源于科学情境及生活情境的例题。另外,全书配套了相当数量的习题,并附有答案,可供读者自我检测之用。本书基于华东师范大学第二附属中学国际课程班的配套参考资料编写,适合以本科留学为目标的中国高中学生阅读使用。

图书在版编目(CIP)数据

　　国际课程导学. AP 数学基础 代数与分析初步/ 吴森,
汪健编著. —上海: 上海交通大学出版社,2023.7
　　ISBN 978 - 7 - 313 - 25745 - 1

　　Ⅰ. ①国… Ⅱ. ①吴…②汪… Ⅲ. ①中学数学课-
高中-美国-升学参考资料 Ⅳ. ①G634

　　中国国家版本馆 CIP 数据核字(2023)第 047680 号

国际课程导学——AP 数学基础(代数与分析初步)
GUOJI KECHENG DAOXUE——AP SHUXUE JICHU(DAISHU YU FENXI CHUBU)

编　　著:吴 森 汪 健
出版发行:上海交通大学出版社　　　　　　　　地　　址:上海市番禺路 951 号
邮政编码:200030　　　　　　　　　　　　　　电　　话:021 - 64071208
印　　制:上海景条印刷有限公司　　　　　　　经　　销:全国新华书店
开　　本:889 mm×1194 mm　1/16　　　　　　印　　张:15.25
字　　数:437 千字
版　　次:2023 年 7 月第 1 版　　　　　　　　　印　　次:2023 年 7 月第 1 次印刷
书　　号:ISBN 978 - 7 - 313 - 25745 - 1
定　　价:82.00 元

总　序

　　华东师范大学第二附属中学（以下简称"二附中"）是教育部直属的重点中学，以办成世界一流高中为目标，致力于培养创造未来的人。二附中一贯重视教育国际化，早在20世纪80年代就曾在联合国开发计划署资助下开展国际教师交流研学活动。1999年获上海市教育主管部门批准成立国际部，成为上海为数不多的公办外籍人员子女学校之一。2014年，依照上海市教委《关于开展普通高中国际课程试点工作的通知》精神，二附中申请国际课程试点项目获批。二附中国际课程试点项目追求三大目标：锻炼一支具有国际视野、追求卓越的高素质教师团队；建设一套中西融通、未来可对外输出的国际课程体系；培养一批具有全球胜任力和中国核心价值观的学生。本套丛书就是二附中国际课程试点项目的重要学术研究成果。

　　早在20世纪90年代，二附中就曾在理科实验班系统开展大学先修课程的试点。2008以来，北大、清华等高校发起的中国大学先修课程项目也在二附中开展试点。针对AP课程（Advanced Placement Courses），二附中先后派出10多位教师前往国际姐妹学校（如加拿大多伦多大学附中、美国新泽西培德学校等）进行学习交流。二附中开设的国内外大学先修课，均不要求学生购买境外教材，而是由教师根据学生的实际情况，结合国内外高中和大学本科基础课程资料，自主设计教学大纲，编写适用于本校学生的教学资料。

　　二附中国际课程项目属于公办国际课程项目，是中国教师用中国语言教授中国学生，基本定位就是借鉴大学课程与国际课程来深化高中课程教学改革，实现中西大学先修课程的融合，实现本土化、校本化。二附中国际课程项目团队自2015年成立以来，积极承接上海市基础教育国际课程比较研究所的课题，其中《高中数学融合研究——以中美课程为例》和《AP物理课程与国内课程的融合》两项课题已发表于2018年7月出版的《高中国际课程本土化实践研究》。国际课程项目团队经过六年多时间的课程研究、研修学习和教学实践，依托本校教师团队，已经在国际课程班独立开设14—16门AP课程。特别是数学、物理和化学三门学科，二附中拥有很强的师资以及很高的教学水平，学生整体理科素养也较高，因此国际课程项目团队率先对这三门学科进行了校本AP课程的系统开发。这三门课程以二附中理科校本教材为蓝本，优化教学内容，强化大学中学衔接，凸显学科核心素养，努力培养学生的全球胜任力。以数学课程为例，学校组织专业教师团队，对比中外多种数学教材，参照国内课程标准，保留中国传统教材重视基础知识和基本能力的特色，适当加入国际高中教材中与生活相联系的案例，编写完成高中数学国际课程大纲和导学，既保证了国际高中数学的知识广度和应用性，又兼顾了国内高中数学的教学强度和难度。

　　本套丛书既着眼于校本应用，也关注市场，供有兴趣参与AP课程的读者学习参考。编写组每月召开研讨会商讨疑难问题，依据自编课程大纲，以中英双语的形式呈现。编写的教学资料应用于多年的教学实践过程中，围绕参与国际课程学习学生的需求进行了多轮修订，颇受好评。我们希望能坚持试点，深化改革，共同为二附中教育国际化和上海基础教育国际化闯出一条新路。

施洪亮

前　言

AP课程(Advanced Placement Courses)项目于1955年在美国设立,是在高中阶段开设达到大学学术标准和学业水平的课程,由美国大学理事会负责开发和管理。AP考试成绩将作为大学录取学生的参考标准之一,有些大学还可将AP考试成绩转换为相应大学课程的学分。

虽然美国的AP课程已经走过了60多年的历程,形成了一套比较成熟的课程体系,可为我国的高中国际课程设计提供参考,但是由于AP课程在难度、知识量、教材体系等方面并不完全适合我国的高中国际课程教学需求,需要在实践中建立更适合中国学生的国际课程。同时,作为AP课程的预备知识,相应高中课程的开发也是高中国际课程的一项重要任务,如何在保有我国基础教育特色的前提下实现与AP课程的对接是一个亟待解决的问题。

华东师范大学第二附属中学自2014年启动国际课程项目以来,便以AP微积分的相关课程为抓手,开始寻找上述问题的解决方案,进而催生了现在呈现在大家面前的校本融合数学教材。本书脱胎于华东师范大学第二附属中学数学校本教材,并融入了一定的国际课程元素,集中表现在以下几个方面:(1)双语文本的使用;(2)数学问题与实际应用背景的结合;(3)对信息技术应用于数学学习的强化。经过在2017届国际课程班和国际部境外班的实践,编者又对教材的使用进行了优化,突出"从特殊到一般"的逻辑主线,调整了部分章节的顺序,为学生的后续学习和备考提供了支持。

在本书的编写和修订期间,恰逢《普通高中数学课程标准》出台,这也成为后续调整修订的主要依据。众所周知,数学是一门以问题来驱动的学科,历史上有不少著名的问题推动了数学学科本体知识体系的发展。同样地,驱动问题在数学学习的过程中也扮演了重要的角色。因此,在融合教材的发展过程中,编者不仅广泛参考了国内外经典教材,也借鉴了以高考为代表的一系列大型考试中出现的具有启发性的问题,以求在宽度和深度两方面同时拓展学生的数学能力。

此外,编者也关注到从2020年起陆续出版的沪教版数学新教材。该教材一改二期课改教材演绎式的逻辑主线,转而强调以运算来串联知识体系,并且在此基础上形成了归纳式的逻辑主线。这一改动使得新教材更加注重逻辑思维的训练,同时加大了数学建模、概率统计等应用数学的比重,弥补了二期课改教材在知识板块方面的不足同时,也强化了融合教材在推理方面的弱项。同时,沪教版新教材在时隔近二十年之后首次迎回微积分的单元,国内外高中教材实现真正的接轨。这些变化都与编写本书时的初衷不谋而合。

长期以来,华东师范大学第二附属中学的理科教学都是学校的特色,特别在拔尖人才培养方面独树一帜。能够在竞争激烈的中国高中教育界屹立不倒,和学校的教研团队锐意进取,始终走在课程改革的前沿是密不可分的。自国际课程项目创立以来,数学课程继承了这一传统,特别是在本书的编写过程中,改变了二期课改教材中"从一般到特殊"的演绎式的逻辑主线。这一点在沪教版新教材中也得到了印证,充分证明了融合教材的引领作用。

编者在欣喜地看到新教材变化的同时,也针对日趋复杂的国际形势作了现实的思考。当今的出国升学方向已经呈现出多元化态势,除了美国、加拿大、英国、新加坡,包括一些其他欧洲大陆国家也开始纳入升学人群的考虑方向。而这些国家的升学通道对数学学术水平的要求与美国的 SAT 不同,更接近于我国高考要求。因此本书也从现实考虑,力求保障学生得到足够的训练,从而为将来提供更多的可能。

感谢华师大二附中对于国际课程项目的大力支持,为本书的编写和出版提供了坚实的保障。感谢华师大二附中国际课程班和国际部的学生,在本书的使用过程中提出了许多建设性意见。

由于编者自身水平有限,书中难免会有一些错误和不妥之处,还望读者指正。相关建议和意见可发邮件至 gjkcdxapsxjc@163.com,编者不胜感激。

Contents

第 1 章

集合与命题 Sets and Propositions

1.1 ◈ 集合 Sets

在现实生活和数学中,我们常常把一些对象放在一起,作为一个整体来研究.例如:

(1) 某校高中一年级的所有学生.

(2) 某次篮球比赛的所有参赛队.

(3) 平面上到定点距离等于定长的点的全体.

(4) 所有锐角三角形.

我们把能够确切指定的一些对象所组成的整体叫作**集合**,简称**集**(set),用大写字母 A,B,C 表示.集合中的各个对象叫作这个集合的**元素**(element),用小写字母 a,b,c 表示.

如果 a 是集合 A 的元素,那么就说 a 属于 A,记作 $a \in A$.

如果 a 不是集合 A 的元素,那么就说 a 不属于 A,记作 $a \notin A$.

A **set** is a collection of distinct objects. Sets are conventionally denoted by capital letters,such as set A,B,C. Each object is called an **element** of the set. Elements are conventionally denoted by lowercase letters,such as a,b,c.

If a is an element of set A,the notation $a \in A$ is used. If a is not an element of set A,the notation $a \notin A$ is used.

我们把含有有限个元素的集合叫作**有限集**(finite set).

无限个元素的集合叫作**无限集**(infinite set).

A **finite set** is a set containing a finite number of elements.

An **infinite set** is a set containing an infinite number of elements.

数的集合简称**数集**(**number sets**),我们把常用的数集用特定的字母表示,见 Table 1-1.

Table 1-1

数 集 的 名 称	字 母 的 表 示	数 集 的 名 称	字 母 的 表 示
自然数集(set of natural numbers)	**N**	有理数集(set of rational numbers)	**Q**
正整数集(set of positive integers)	**N***	实数集(set of real numbers)	**R**
整数集(set of integers)	**Z**		

集合的性质 Properties of Sets

(1) 确定性：一个元素要么在这个集合内，要么不在这个集合内，两者必居其一．

(2) 互异性：集合中的元素是互不相同的．

(3) 无序性：集合中的元素没有一定的顺序．

Properties of sets

(1) Whether an element is in a set or not is determined.

(2) The elements of a set are mutually distinct.

(3) The order of the elements in a set does not matter.

集合的表示方法 Representation of Sets

(1) 列举法：将集合中的元素一一列举出来，写在大括号内，适用于元素不太多的有限集．

(2) 描述法：将集合中的元素所具有的共同性质描述出来，其形式为｛元素的一般形式 | 所有元素的共性｝，适用于无限集或元素较多的有限集．

(3) 图示法：用图形围成的区域来表示集合，所用图叫作**文氏图**（**Venn diagrams**）．

Three typical ways to represent sets

(1) Roster form, in which the elements of the sets are enclosed in curly brackets separated by commas. For example, set $A = \{-2, -1, 0, 1, 2, 3\}$.

(2) Set builder form, which describes the common feature of all the elements of a set. For example, set $A = \{x \in \mathbf{Z} \mid -3 < x < 4\}$.

(3) Venn Diagram, which consists of a universal set U represented by a rectangle and sets within it represented by circles. For example, $U = \mathbf{Z}$ and $A = \{-2, -1, 0, 1, 2, 3\}$ are shown in Figure 1-1.

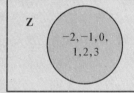

Figure 1-1

1 Determine whether the following objects can form a set:

(1) The names of students in Grade 10.

(2) The fractions with denominator 3.

(3) Numbers very close to 0.

Solution: (1) The names of students in Grade 10 can form a set.

(2) The fractions with denominator 3 can form a set.

(3) Numbers very close to 0 can not form a set.

2 Describe the sets by suitable representations:

(1) Set A: All positive factors of 30.

(2) Set B: All natural numbers with remainder 3 when divided by 5.

(3) Set C: All the points on the graph of function $y = x^2 + 2x - 3$.

Solution:

(1) $A = \{1, 2, 3, 5, 6, 10, 15, 30\}$.

(2) $B = \{x \mid x = 5n + 3, n \in \mathbf{N}\}$.

(3) $C = \{(x, y) \mid y = x^2 + 2x - 3\}$.

3 If there is no more than one element in set $A = \{x \mid ax^2 - 2x - 1 = 0, x \in \mathbf{R}\}$, find the range of a.

Solution: If $a = 0$, the equation $-2x - 1 = 0$ has only one root $-\dfrac{1}{2}$. Thus, $a = 0$ works.

If $a \neq 0$, the quadratic equation $ax^2 - 2x - 1 = 0$ has two identical real roots or no real root, so $\Delta =$

$4+4a \leqslant 0$, thus $a \leqslant -1$.

Therefore, the range of a is $\{a \mid a=0 \text{ or } a \leqslant -1\}$.

集合之间的关系 Relations between Sets

观察下列集合：

$$A=\{1, 2\}, B=\{1, 2, 3, 4\}, C=\{x \mid x^2-3x+2=0\}.$$

可发现，集合 A 中的任何一个元素都是集合 B 的元素，集合 C 中的元素和集合 A 中的元素完全相同.

一般地，对于两个集合 A 与 B，如果集合 A 中的任何一个元素都是集合 B 的元素，那么我们就说集合 A 是集合 B 的**子集(subset)**，记作 $A \subseteq B$ 或 $B \supseteq A$，读作 A 包含于 B 或 B 包含 A.

对于两个集合 A 与 B，如果 $A \subseteq B$ 且 $B \subseteq A$，那么叫作集合 A 与集合 B **相等(equal sets)**，记作 $A=B$，读作"集合 A 等于集合 B".因此，如果两个集合所含的元素完全相同，那么这两个集合相等.

一般地，对于 A 与 B 两个集合，如果 $A \subseteq B$，并且集合 B 中至少有一个元素不属于 A，那么集合 A 是集合 B 的**真子集(proper subset)**.记作 $A \subset B$ 或 $B \supset A$，读作 A 真包含于 B 或 B 真包含 A.

If every element of set A is also in set B, then set A is a **subset** of set B, written as $A \subseteq B$ or $B \supseteq A$.

Sets A and B are equal if and only if they contain exactly the same elements, written as $A=B$.

If set A is a subset of set B, and set B contains at least one element that is not in set A, then set A is called a proper subset of set B, written as $A \subset B$ or $B \supset A$.

图示法 Venn diagrams：

For example：$U=Z$, $A=\{1, 2\}$, $B=\{1, 2, 3, 4\}$, then $A \subseteq B$. As shown in Figure 1-2, the circle representing set A is placed within the circle representing set B. Figure 1-2 can also show that $A \subset B$.

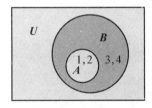

Figure 1-2

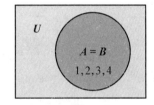

Figure 1-3

$U=Z$, $A=\{1, 2, 3, 4\}$, $B=\{1, 2, 3, 4\}$, then $A=B$. As shown in Figure 1-3, the set A and set B are represented by the same circle.

我们规定**空集(empty set)**不含任意元素，记作 $\varnothing$.

The **empty set** is a set which contains no elements. It is represented by $\varnothing$.

4 Let x and y be integers, set $A=\{2x, x+y\}$, set $B=\{7, 4\}$. If $A=B$, find the values of x and y.

Solution： As $\{2x, x+y\}=\{7, 4\}$, we have the following two cases.

(1) $\begin{cases} 2x=7 \\ x+y=4 \end{cases}$. Solving the system of equations, we get $\begin{cases} x=\dfrac{7}{2} \\ y=\dfrac{1}{2} \end{cases}$. As x, y are not integers, this case is discarded.

(2) $\begin{cases} 2x=4 \\ x+y=7 \end{cases}$. Solving the system of equations, we get $\begin{cases} x=2 \\ y=5 \end{cases}$. Then, $A=\{4, 7\}$ and $B=\{7, 4\}$ satisfy $A=B$.

Therefore $x=2$ and $y=5$.

5 Let set $A=\{a, b, c\}$, find all the subsets and proper subsets of A.

Solution: The subsets of set A are: $\varnothing$, $\{a\}$, $\{b\}$, $\{c\}$, $\{a, b\}$, $\{b, c\}$, $\{a, c\}$, $\{a, b, c\}$.

The proper subsets of set A are: $\varnothing$, $\{a\}$, $\{b\}$, $\{c\}$, $\{a, b\}$, $\{b, c\}$, $\{a, c\}$.

6 Let set $A=\{a, a^2, ab\}$, set $B=\{1, a, b\}$. If $A=B$, find the values of a and b.

Solution: As $\{a, a^2, ab\}=\{1, a, b\}$, we have the following two cases.

(1) $\begin{cases} a^2=b \\ ab=1 \end{cases}$, then $\begin{cases} a=1 \\ b=1 \end{cases}$. As the elements of a set must be distinct, this case is discarded.

(2) $\begin{cases} a^2=1 \\ ab=b \end{cases}$ and $a\neq 1$, then $\begin{cases} a=-1 \\ b=0 \end{cases}$. We have $A=\{-1, 1, 0\}$, $B=\{-1, 1, 0\}$.

Therefore $a=-1$ and $b=0$.

集合的运算 Operations on Sets

观察下列集合：

$A=\{x \mid 0<x<3\}$, $B=\{x \mid 1<x<4\}$, $C=\{x \mid 1<x<3\}$，易知集合 C 是由所有既属于集合 A 又属于集合 B 的元素组成的.

一般地，由所有属于集合 A 且属于集合 B 的元素组成的集合叫作 A 与 B 的**交集（intersection）**，记作 $A \bigcap B$，读作"A 交 B"，即 $A \bigcap B=\{x \mid x \in A \text{ 且 } x \in B\}$.

The **intersection** of two sets A and B is the set of all the elements that are common in both set A and set B. The intersection of sets A and B is written as $A \bigcap B$.

Two sets A and B are disjoint or mutually exclusive if they have no elements in common. In this case $A \bigcap B=\varnothing$.

一般地，由所有属于集合 A 或者属于集合 B 的元素组成的集合叫作 A 与 B 的**并集（union）**，记作 $A \bigcup B$，读作"A 并 B"，即 $A \bigcup B=\{x \mid x \in A \text{ 或 } x \in B\}$.

The **union** of two sets A and B is the set of all the elements that are in either set A or set B. The union of sets A and B is written as $A \bigcup B$.

在给定的问题中，若研究的所有集合都是某一给定集合的子集，那么称这个给定的集合为**全集（universal set）**.

一般地，若集合 A 是全集 U 的子集，由全集 U 中不属于集合 A 的元素组成的集合叫作集合 A 在全集 U 中的**补集（complementary set）**，记作 $\bar{A}$，读作"A 补"，即 $\bar{A}=\{x \mid x \in U \text{ 且 } x \notin A\}$.

The universal set U is the set of all elements under consideration. The complement of set A is the set of all the elements of universal set U that are not elements of set A. The complement of set A is written as set $\bar{A}$.

We can make two immediate observations about complementary sets. For any set A and set $\bar{A}$:

(1) The intersection of sets A and $\bar{A}$ is the empty set, written as $A \cap \bar{A} = \varnothing$.

(2) The union of sets A and $\bar{A}$ is the universal set, written as $A \cup \bar{A} = U$.

用文氏图（Venn Diagram）可以直观地表示 $A \cap B$、$A \cup B$ 以及 $\bar{A}$ 的一般情况，见 Figure 1 - 4.

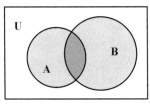
$A \cup B$ is shaded

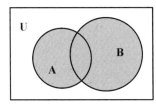
$A \cap B$ is shaded

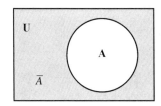
$\bar{A}$ is shaded

Figure 1 - 4

7 Let set $A = \{(x, y) \mid 3x - y = 7\}$, set $B = \{(x, y) \mid 2x + y = 3\}$, find set $A \cap B$.

Solution： $A \cap B = \{(x, y) \mid 3x - y = 7 \text{ and } 2x + y = 3\} = \{(x, y) \mid x = 2 \text{ and } y = -1\} = \{(2, -1)\}$.

8 Let set $A = \{x \mid -2 < x < 2\}$, set $B = \{x \mid x > 1 \text{ or } x < -1\}$, find sets $A \cap B$ and $A \cup B$.

Solution： $A \cap B = \{x \mid -2 < x < -1 \text{ or } 1 < x < 2\}$.

$A \cup B = R$.

9 Let set $U = \{a, b, c, d, e\}$, set $A = \{a, b\}$, set $B = \{b, c, d\}$.

(1) Find the sets $\bar{A} \cap \bar{B}$, $\bar{A} \cup \bar{B}$, $\overline{A \cap B}$, $\overline{A \cup B}$.

(2) What do we know from the solution (1)?

Solution： (1) Since $U = \{a, b, c, d, e\}$ and $A = \{a, b\}$, we know $\bar{A} = \{c, d, e\}$.

As $B = \{b, c, d\}$, we have $\bar{B} = \{a, e\}$.

So $\bar{A} \cap \bar{B} = \{e\}$, $\bar{A} \cup \bar{B} = \{a, c, d, e\}$.

Since $A = \{a, b\}$ and $B = \{b, c, d\}$, we have $A \cap B = \{b\}$ and $A \cup B = \{a, b, c, d\}$.

So $\overline{A \cap B} = \{a, c, d, e\}$, $\overline{A \cup B} = \{e\}$.

(2) $\bar{A} \cap \bar{B} = \overline{A \cup B}$, $\bar{A} \cup \bar{B} = \overline{A \cap B}$.

练习 Exercise

1. Express the following sets in set builder form.

(1) Set $A = \{1, 4, 7, 10, 13\}$.

(2) Set $B = \{-2, -4, -6, -8, -10\}$.

(3) Set $C = \{1, 5, 25, 125, 625 \cdots\}$.

(4) Set $D = \left\{0, \pm\dfrac{1}{2}, \pm\dfrac{2}{5}, \pm\dfrac{3}{10}, \pm\dfrac{4}{17} \cdots\right\}$.

2. Let set $A = \{2, 4, 6\}$. If $a \in A$ and $6 - a \in A$, find the value of a.

3. Let set $A=\{x \mid x^2+(a-1)x+b=0\}$. If there is only one element a in set A, find the values of a and b.

4. Let set $A=\{2, 3, a^2+2a-3\}$, set $B=\{a+3, 2\}$. If $5 \in A$ and $5 \notin B$, find the value of a.

5. Let set $A=\{x \mid 0 \leqslant x < 3, x \in \mathbf{Z}\}$. How many proper subsets does set A have?

　A. 5　　　　　　　　B. 6　　　　　　　　C. 7　　　　　　　　D. 8

6. Let set $A=\{x \mid -1 < x < 2\}$, set $B=\{x \mid 0 < x < 1\}$, then (　　).

　A. $A > B$　　　　　　　　　　　　　　B. $A \subseteq B$

　C. $A \subset B$　　　　　　　　　　　　　D. $B \subset A$

7. Let set $A=\{x \mid x-1=0\}$, set $B=\{x \mid x^2-ax-2=0\}$. If $A \subseteq B$, find the value of a.

8. Let set $A=\{x \mid a-2 < x < a+2\}$, set $B=\{x \mid -2 < x < 3\}$.

　(1) If $A \subseteq B$, find the value of a.

　(2) If a is a real number that satisfies $B \subseteq A$, find the value of a.

9. Let set $A=\{(x, y) \mid y=-x+1\}$, set $B=\{(x, y) \mid y=x^2-1\}$. Find the set $A \bigcap B$.

10. Let set $A=\{x \mid x^2+px+15=0\}$, set $B=\{x \mid x^2-5x+q=0\}$, and $A \bigcap B=\{3\}$.

　(1) Find the values of p, q.

　(2) Find set $A \bigcup B$.

11. Let universal set $U=\{2, 3, a^2+2a-3\}$. If $A=\{b, 2\}$, $\bar{A}=\{5\}$, find the values of a and b.

12. Let universal set $U=\{(x, y) \mid x, y \in \mathbf{R}\}$, set $A=\left\{(x, y) \,\middle|\, \dfrac{y-3}{x-2}=1, x, y \in \mathbf{R}\right\}$.

　(1) If set $B=\{(x, y) \mid y=x+1, x, y \in \mathbf{R}\}$, find the set $A \bigcap \bar{B}$.

　(2) If set $B=\{(x, y) \mid y \neq x+1, x, y \in \mathbf{R}\}$, find the set $\overline{A \bigcup B}$.

1.2 ◆ 命题的形式及等价关系
The Forms of Proposition and Equivalent Relationship

命题与推出关系 Proposition and Implication

下列语句哪些是命题,哪些不是命题? 如果是命题,哪些命题是真命题? 哪些命题是假命题? 为什么?

(1) 个位数是 5 的正整数能被 5 整除.

(2) 上课请不要讲话.

(3) 互为补角的两个角不相等.

(4) 如果两个三角形的三条边对应相等,这两个三角形全等吗?

上述语句中,(1)和(3)是可以判断真假的陈述句,它们是命题. (2)不是判断语句,(4)是问句,不是表示判断的陈述句,因此(2)和(4)都不是命题.那么,怎样判断命题的真假呢?

(1)中个位数是 5 的自然数可以写成 $10k+5(k \in \mathbf{N})$ 的形式,而 $10k+5=5(2k+1)$,所以 $10k+5$ 能被 5 整除,即"个位数是 5 的正整数能被 5 整除"是一个真命题.

(3)中取一个角为90°,另一个角也为90°,它们是互补的,但它们相等了,所以"互为补角的两个角不相等"是一个假命题.

一般地说,如果命题 α 成立可以推出命题 β 也成立,那么我们说由 α 可以推出 β,并用"$\alpha \Rightarrow \beta$"表示,读作"α 推出 β".换句话说,$\alpha \Rightarrow \beta$ 表示以 α 为条件,β 为结论的命题是真命题.

如果命题 α 成立,而命题 β 不成立,即 α 成立不能推出 β 成立,可记作 $\alpha \not\Rightarrow \beta$,即 $\alpha \not\Rightarrow \beta$ 表示以 α 为条件,β 为结论的命题是假命题.

如果 $\alpha \Rightarrow \beta$,而且 $\beta \Rightarrow \alpha$,那么记作 $\alpha \Leftrightarrow \beta$,叫作 α 与 β 等价.

A proposition is a statement whose validity can be determined. For example: the statement "if $2x = 4$, then $x = 2$" is a proposition, which can be written as $2x = 4 \Rightarrow x = 2$. Here " $\Rightarrow$ " is the symbol of implication.

Note that the implication in the example above can also be reversed, which leads to the fact that the implication is both ways. This is written as $x = 2 \Leftrightarrow 2x = 4$. The symbol " $\Leftrightarrow$ " is read as "if and only if" or simply as "iff". " $\Leftrightarrow$ " is the symbol of equivalence.

But not every implication works both ways in this manner. If $x = 2$, it follows that $x^2 = 4$. However, the reverse is not true. The proposition is false because x might be -2. We would write this statement as $x^2 = 4 \not\Rightarrow x = 2$.

推出关系满足传递性:如果 $\alpha \Rightarrow \beta$,$\beta \Rightarrow \gamma$,那么 $\alpha \Rightarrow \gamma$. 例如(1)的证明过程可以写成:$\alpha$:自然数 n 的个位数是 $5 \Rightarrow \alpha_1$:$n = 10k + 5(k \in \mathbf{N}) \Rightarrow \alpha_2$:$n = 5(2k + 1)(k \in \mathbf{N}) \Rightarrow \beta$:$n$ 能被 5 整除,即 $\alpha \Rightarrow \alpha_1 \Rightarrow \alpha_2 \Rightarrow \beta$.

> The transitivity of implication relationships: given propositions α, β and γ, if $\alpha \Rightarrow \beta$ and $\beta \Rightarrow \gamma$, it follows that $\alpha \Rightarrow \gamma$.

四种命题形式(Four Propositional Forms)

一个命题的条件和结论分别是另一个命题的结论和条件,这样的两个命题叫作**互逆命题**,把其中的一个命题叫作**原命题**(original proposition),另一个命题叫作**逆命题**(converse proposition). 一个命题的条件和结论分别是另一个命题条件的否定和结论的否定,这样的两个命题叫作**互否命题**,把其中的一个命题叫作**原命题**,另一个命题叫作**否命题**(inverse proposition). 一个命题的条件和结论分别是另一个命题结论的否定和条件的否定,这样的两个命题叫作**互为逆否命题**,把其中的一个命题叫作**原命题**,另一个命题叫作原命题的**逆否命题**(contrapositive proposition).

交换原命题的条件和结论,所得的命题是逆命题;同时否定原命题的条件和结论,所得的命题是否命题;交换原命题条件和结论,并且同时否定,所得的命题是逆否命题.

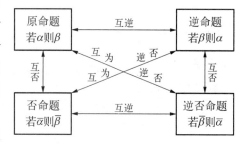

Figure 1 - 5

> Given a proposition such as "if $x^2 - 3x + 2 > 0$, then $x^2 - 3x > 0$." The converse proposition is "if $x^2 - 3x > 0$, then $x^2 - 3x + 2 > 0$." The inverse proposition is "if $x^2 - 3x + 2 \leqslant 0$, then $x^2 - 3x \leqslant 0$." The contrapositive proposition is "if $x^2 - 3x \leqslant 0$, then $x^2 - 3x + 2 \leqslant 0$."

反证法(Proof by contradiction)是一种论证方式,其方法是首先假设某命题的否命题成立(即在原命题的条件下,结论不成立),然后推理出明显矛盾的结果,从而下结论说原假设不成立,原命题成立,得证.

> Proof by contradiction works by assuming that the proposition is false and then proving that this assumption leads to a contradiction.

证明步骤:

(1)反设:假设命题结论不成立,即假设结论的反面成立.

(2) 归谬：从这个命题出发,经过推理证明得出矛盾.

(3) 结论：由矛盾判断假设不成立,从而肯定命题的结论正确.

1 True or false:

(1) If $A = \{1, 2, 3\}$, $B = \{1, 2, 3\}$, then A is the proper subset of B. (   )

(2) If $A \subseteq B$, then $A \bigcup B = A$. (   )

(3) If $A \bigcap B = A$, then $A \subseteq B$. (   )

(4) If $A \bigcap B = \varnothing$, then $A = B = \varnothing$. (   )

> **Solution**：(1) False. (2) False. (3) True. (4) False.

2 Determine the relationship between propositions α and β.

(1) Given proposition γ, and $\alpha \Rightarrow \beta$, $\beta \Rightarrow \gamma$, $\gamma \Rightarrow \alpha$.

(2) α：$x^2 > y^2$, β：$x > y > 0$.

(3) α：$a \in A \bigcup B$, β：$a \in A$.

> **Solution**：
>
> (1) Given $\beta \Rightarrow \gamma$, $\gamma \Rightarrow \alpha$, then $\beta \Rightarrow \alpha$. Since $\alpha \Rightarrow \beta$ and $\beta \Rightarrow \alpha$, we get $\alpha \Leftrightarrow \beta$.
>
> (2) $\beta \Rightarrow \alpha$.
>
> (3) $\beta \Rightarrow \alpha$.

3 Given the proposition "If $a > c$ and $b > d$, then $a + b > c + d$, a, b, c, $d \in \mathbf{R}$". Find the converse proposition, inverse proposition and contrapositive proposition.

> **Solution**：Converse proposition：If $a + b > c + d$, then $a > c$ and $b > d$.
>
> Inverse proposition：If $a \leqslant c$ or $b \leqslant d$, then $a + b \leqslant c + d$.
>
> Contrapositive proposition：If $a + b \leqslant c + d$, then $a \leqslant c$ or $b \leqslant d$.

4 (1) Given the proposition：if the origin is on the parabola $y = x^2 + bx + c$, then $c = 0$. Find the converse proposition.

(2) Given the proposition：if $a \neq 1$ or $b \neq 2$, then $a^2 + b^2 - 2a - 4b + 5 \neq 0$. Find the inverse proposition.

(3) Given the proposition：if $a > \dfrac{1}{a}$, then $| a | > 1$. Find the contrapositive proposition.

> **Solution**：
>
> (1) If $c = 0$, then the origin is on the parabola $y = x^2 + bx + c$.
>
> (2) If $a = 1$ and $b = 2$, then $a^2 + b^2 - 2a - 4b + 5 = 0$.
>
> (3) If $| a | \leqslant 1$, then $a \leqslant \dfrac{1}{a}$.

5 Given the proposition：if $x = 0$, then $xy = 0$. Find the contrapositive proposition and determine whether it is true or false.

> **Solution**：Contrapositive proposition：If $xy \neq 0$, then $x \neq 0$. As the original proposition and its contrapositive proposition are equivalent, and the original proposition is true, so the contrapositive proposition is true.

6 Prove: $\sqrt{2}$ is irrational.

Prove: Assume that $\sqrt{2}$ is rational, then $\sqrt{2} = \dfrac{p}{q}$, where p and q are co-prime positive integers. Hence, $\dfrac{p}{q} = \sqrt{2} \Rightarrow \dfrac{p^2}{q^2} = 2 \Rightarrow p^2 = 2q^2 \Rightarrow p^2$ is even $\Rightarrow p$ is even.

If p is even, there must be another integer r that is half of p. Then

$$p = 2r \Rightarrow p^2 = 4r^2 \Rightarrow 2q^2 = 4r^2 \Rightarrow q^2 = 2r^2 \Rightarrow q^2 \text{ is even} \Rightarrow q \text{ is even}.$$

Since p and q are co-prime, p and q cannot both be even. So $\sqrt{2}$ is irrational.

充分条件，必要条件 Sufficient Condition，Necessary Condition

在日常生活中，我们做事情需要具备一定的条件，有的条件能够保证我们完成这件事，而有的条件虽然不能保证完成这件事，但却是完成它必不可少的. 例如：

(1) 用 20 元钱买一本 19.80 元的书，那么就书价而言，"20 元钱"就是"买一本 19.80 元的书"的充分条件；

(2) 用水将生米煮成熟饭，那么"水"就是"生米煮成熟饭"的必不可少的条件.

一般地，用 α、β 分别表示两个命题，如果命题 α 成立，可以推出命题 β 也成立，即 $\alpha \Rightarrow \beta$，那么 α 叫作 β 的**充分条件**(sufficient condition)，β 叫作 α 的**必要条件**(necessary condition).

如果既有 $\alpha \Rightarrow \beta$，又有 $\beta \Rightarrow \alpha$，即 $\alpha \Leftrightarrow \beta$，那么 α 既是 β 的充分条件，又是 β 的必要条件，这时我们称 α 是 β 的**充分而且必要条件**(sufficient and necessary condition)，简称**充要条件**.

Given two propositions α and β, if α is true and $\alpha \Rightarrow \beta$, then proposition α is called a sufficient condition for β and β is called a necessary condition for α. If $\alpha \Rightarrow \beta$ and $\beta \Rightarrow \alpha$, that is $\alpha \Leftrightarrow \beta$, then α is sufficient and necessary for β.

7 Fill in the blanks with *sufficient*, *necessary*, *sufficient and necessary* or *neither sufficient nor necessary*.

(1) If $p: a^2 > b^2$, $q: a > b$, then p is _____ for q.

(2) If $p: \{x \mid x > -2 \text{ or } x < 3\}$, $q: \{x \mid x^2 - x - 6 < 0\}$, then p is _____ for q.

(3) If $p: a$ and b are both odd numbers, $q: a + b$ is even number, then p is _____ for q.

(4) If $p: 0 < m < \dfrac{1}{3}$, $q:$ the quadratic equation $mx^2 - 2x + 3 = 0$ has two distinct real roots with the same sign, then p is _____ for q.

Solution:

(1) As $a^2 > b^2 \not\Rightarrow a > b$ and $a > b \not\Rightarrow a^2 > b^2$, p is neither sufficient nor necessary for q.

(2) As $\{x \mid x > -2 \text{ or } x < 3\} \not\Rightarrow \{x \mid x^2 - x - 6 < 0\}$, and $\{x \mid x^2 - x - 6 < 0\} \Rightarrow \{x \mid x > -2 \text{ or } x < 3\}$, p is necessary for q.

(3) As a and b are both odd numbers $\Rightarrow a + b$ is even number, and $a + b$ is even number $\not\Rightarrow a$ and b are both odd numbers, p is sufficient for q.

(4) As the quadratic equation $mx^2 - 2x + 3 = 0$ has two distinct real roots with the same sign, we have $\begin{cases} \Delta = 2^2 - 4 \cdot m \cdot 3 > 0 \\ x_1 x_2 = \dfrac{3}{m} > 0 \end{cases}$. Solving the system of inequalities gives $0 < m < \dfrac{1}{3}$. So p is sufficient and necessary for q.

8 (1) Given the proposition p: $x < 0$, find a sufficient condition and a necessary condition for p.

(2) Given the proposition p: the function $y = (m^2 - 4)x^{2n^2 - 3n}$ is an inverse proportional function. Find a sufficient condition for p.

Solution:

(1) Sufficient condition: $x < -1$.

Necessary condition: $x < 2$. (The answer is not unique.)

(2) $m = 3$, $n = 1$. (The answer is not unique.)

9 Given the proposition p: $x_1 > 3$ and $x_2 > 3$. Find a sufficient and necessary condition for p.

Solution: $x_1 + x_2 > 6$ and $(x_1 - 3)(x_2 - 3) > 0$.

10 Given α: $x < 1$, β: $x < 3a + 2$. If α is sufficient for β, find the range of a.

Solution: As α is sufficient for β, $\alpha \Rightarrow \beta$.

Thus $1 < 3a + 2$.

Therefore $a > -\dfrac{1}{3}$.

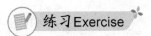 练习 Exercise

1. True or false:

(1) The empty set $\varnothing$ is a proper subset of any set. (   )

(2) If $a \in A \cap B$, then $a \in B$. (   )

(3) If $a \in A \cup B$, then $a \in A \cap B$. (   )

(4) If $ax + b = 0$, then $x = -\dfrac{b}{a}$. (   )

2. Proposition A: if $x < 3$, then $x < 5$;

Proposition B: if $x \geqslant 3$, then $x \geqslant 5$;

Proposition C: if $x \geqslant 5$, then $x \geqslant 3$.

Determine the relationship between A, B and C.

3. Given α: $-1 \leqslant x \leqslant 3$, β: $x \leqslant m - 1$. If $\alpha \Rightarrow \beta$, find the range of m.

4. Given the proposition "If $c < 0$ and $ac > bc$, then $a < b$". Find the converse proposition, inverse proposition and contrapositive proposition.

5. Given the proposition "If $mn < 0$, then the quadratic equation $mx^2 - x + n = 0$ has two distinct real roots." Find the contrapositive proposition and determine whether it is true or false.

6. Let $A = \{x \mid x = m^2 - n^2, \ m \in \mathbf{Z}, \ n \in \mathbf{Z}\}$,

(1) Prove: $11 \in A$, $12 \in A$, $2k + 1 \in A$.

(2) Prove: $10 \notin A$.

7. Fill in the blanks with *sufficient*, *necessary* or *sufficient and necessary*.

(1) If p: $x = 0$, q: $xy = 0$, then p is _____ for q.

(2) If p: $x < 2$, q: $0 < x < 2$, then p is _____ for q.

(3) If p: the four sides of a quadrilateral are equal, q: the quadrilateral is a rhombus, then p is _____ for q.

8. (1) Given the proposition p: $x^2 = y^2$. Find a sufficient condition for p.

   (2) Given the proposition p: $a + b = 2$. Find a necessary condition for p.

9. (1) Given the proposition p: $xy > 0$, proposition q: $|x + y| = |x| + |y|$ ($x, y \in \mathbf{R}$). Is p sufficient and necessary for q?

   (2) Given $\alpha \Rightarrow \bar{\beta}$ and $\bar{\gamma} \Rightarrow \beta$, is proposition γ necessary for proposition α?

10. Given α: $-1 \leqslant x \leqslant 3$, β: $x < m - 1$ or $x > m + 1$. If α is sufficient for β, find the range of m.

第 2 章

不等式 Inequalities

2.1 ◆ 不等式的性质 Properties of Inequalities

不等关系与相等关系都是客观事物的基本数量关系,是数学研究的重要内容.建立不等观念、处理不等关系与处理等量问题是同样重要的.我们如何利用不等关系来解决问题呢?

例如:一间房子地面面积为 a 平方米,窗子面积为 b 平方米,如果地面和窗子面积同时增加 m 平方米.问房子采光效果与原来相比,是变好了还是变差了? 解决此问题就需要用到不等式性质。

两个实数 a,b 的大小关系具有以下特性:

(1) 设 $a,b \in \mathbf{R}$, $\begin{cases} a-b>0 \Leftrightarrow a>b, \\ a-b=0 \Leftrightarrow a=b, \\ a-b<0 \Leftrightarrow a<b. \end{cases}$

(2) 设 $a,b \in \mathbf{R}^+$, $\begin{cases} \dfrac{a}{b}>1 \Leftrightarrow a>b, \\ \dfrac{a}{b}=1 \Leftrightarrow a=b, \\ \dfrac{a}{b}<1 \Leftrightarrow a<b. \end{cases}$

我们曾学习过以下不等式性质:

(1) 如果 $a>b$,那么 $a+c>b+c$.

(2) 如果 $a>b$,$c>0$,那么 $ac>bc\left(\text{或} \dfrac{a}{c}>\dfrac{b}{c}\right)$;如果 $a>b$,$c<0$,那么 $ac<bc\left(\text{或} \dfrac{a}{c}<\dfrac{b}{c}\right)$.

利用以上性质证明性质(2):

证明:由题 $ac-bc=(a-b)c$,因为 $a>b$,所以 $a-b>0$.

当 $c>0$,$(a-b)c>0$,即 $ac>bc$;当 $c<0$,$(a-b)c<0$,即 $ac<bc$.

由此性质可以推导得到:如果 $a>b>0$,$c>d>0$,那么 $ac>bd$.

很明显,这一推论可以推广到任意有限个两边都是正数的同向不等式两边分别相乘.这就是说,两个或者更多个两边都是正数的同向不等式两边分别相乘,所得不等式与原不等式同向.由此,我们得到以下不等式性质:

如果 $a>b>0$,那么 $a^n>b^n(n \in \mathbf{N}, n \geqslant 2)$.

因此,基于以上不等式性质(1)、(2),我们能推导出以下一系列不等式基本性质:

不等式基本性质 Properties of Inequalities

性质定理 1:对称性,$a>b \Leftrightarrow b<a$.

性质定理 2：传递性，$a > b$，$b > c \Rightarrow a > c$.

性质定理 3：加法单调性，$a > b \Rightarrow a + c > b + c$.

推论 3.1：$a + b > c \Leftrightarrow a > c - b$.

推论 3.2：$a > b$，$c > d \Rightarrow a + c > b + d$. 可推广至任意有限个同向不等式相加.

推论 3.3：$a > b$，$c < d \Rightarrow a - c > b - d$.

性质定理 4：乘法单调性，$a > b$，$c > 0 \Rightarrow ac > bc$.

$$a > b，c < 0 \Rightarrow ac < bc.$$

推论 4.1：$a > b > 0$，$c > d > 0 \Rightarrow ac > bd$. 同向不等式可乘原则

推论 4.2：$a > b > 0$，$0 < c < d \Rightarrow \dfrac{a}{c} > \dfrac{b}{d}$. 异向不等式可除原则

推论 4.3：$a > b$，$ab > 0 \Rightarrow \dfrac{1}{a} < \dfrac{1}{b}$.

推论 4.4：$a > b > 0 \Rightarrow 0 < \dfrac{1}{a} < \dfrac{1}{b}$.

推论 4.5：$a > b > 0 \Rightarrow a^n > b^n (n \in \mathbf{N}^*)$. $(a > b \Rightarrow a^{2n-1} > b^{2n-1} (n \in \mathbf{N}^*))$

推论 4.6：$a > b > 0 \Rightarrow \sqrt[n]{a} > \sqrt[n]{b} (n \in \mathbf{N}^*)$. $(a > b \Rightarrow \sqrt[2n-1]{a} > \sqrt[2n-1]{b} (n \in \mathbf{N}^*))$

掌握不等式的性质，应注意条件与结论间的对应关系，是" $\Rightarrow$ "符号还是" $\Leftrightarrow$ "符号.运用不等式性质的关键是对不等号方向的把握，条件与不等号方向是紧密相连的.

1. Property of Inequality

Let a and b be real numbers.

If $a > b$, then $b < a$.

When solving linear equations, we often perform the same operations on both sides and the equation remains valid. This is not always the case when solving an inequality. In particular, the following questions arise.

(1) If we add or subtract a number on both sides of an inequality, will the inequality hold?

(2) If we multiply or divide both sides of an inequality by a number, will the inequality hold?

2. Addition and Subtraction Property of Inequality

Let a, b and c be real numbers.

If $a > b$, then $a + c > b + c$.

3. Multiplication and Division Property of Inequality

(1) Let a, b and c be real numbers with $c > 0$.

If $a > b$, then $ac > bc$.

If $a > b$, then $\dfrac{a}{c} > \dfrac{b}{c}$.

(2) Let a, b and c be real numbers with $c < 0$.

If $a > b$, then $ac < bc$.

If $a > b$, then $\dfrac{a}{c} < \dfrac{b}{c}$.

Just as we use the properties of equality to solve equations, we can use the properties of inequality to solve inequalities.

1 Solve the inequality $5 < -3(x-7)$.

> **Solution:** $-3(x-7) > 5$ Swap the left side and the right side.
>
> $x - 7 < -\dfrac{5}{3}$ Divide both sides by -3.
>
> $x < 7 - \dfrac{5}{3}$ Add 7 to both sides.
>
> $x < \dfrac{16}{3}$ Simplify.

2 True or False:

(1) If $ax > b$, then $x > \dfrac{b}{a}$. (   )

(2) If $ac^2 < bc^2$, then $a < b$. (   )

> **Solution:**
>
> (1) Multiply both sides by $\dfrac{1}{a} < 0$. If $\dfrac{1}{a} < 0$, then $ax > b \Rightarrow ax \cdot \dfrac{1}{a} < b \cdot \dfrac{1}{a} \Rightarrow x < \dfrac{b}{a}$. So the statement is false.
>
> (2) As we know $c^2 \geqslant 0$. If $ac^2 < bc^2$, then $c^2 > 0$. Multiply both sides by $\dfrac{1}{c^2} > 0$.
>
> Since $\dfrac{1}{c^2} > 0$, then $ac^2 < bc^2 \Rightarrow ac^2 \cdot \dfrac{1}{c^2} < bc^2 \cdot \dfrac{1}{c^2} \Rightarrow a < b$. So the statement is true.

3 If $a < b < 0$, then which one is true? (   )

A. $a^2 < b^2$ B. $c - a < c - b$ C. $|a| < |b|$ D. $a^3 < b^3$

> **Solution:**
>
> Since $a < b < 0 \Rightarrow -a > -b > 0$, we have $(-a)^2 > (-b)^2 \Rightarrow a^2 > b^2$.
>
> Similarly, $(-a)^3 > (-b)^3 \Rightarrow -a^3 > -b^3 \Rightarrow a^3 < b^3$, so A is false and D is true.
>
> As $-a > -b > 0 \Rightarrow c - a > c - b$, B is false.
>
> By definition of absolute values, C is false, so we choose D.

4 If $a > b$, $c < d$, prove: $a - c > b - d$.

> **Proof:**
>
> If $a > b$, $c < d$, then $a - b > 0$, $d - c > 0$.
>
> Since $(a - c) - (b - d) = (a - b) + (d - c) > 0$, we have $a - c > b - d$.

5 (1) If $24 < a \leqslant 25$, $5 < b \leqslant 12$, what are the ranges of $a + b$, $a - b$, ab, $\dfrac{a}{b}$?

(2) If $-\dfrac{\pi}{2} < \beta < \alpha < \dfrac{\pi}{2}$, what is the range of $2\alpha - \beta$?

> **Solution:**
>
> (1) Since $24 < a \leqslant 25$, $5 < b \leqslant 12$, then $29 < a + b \leqslant 37$, $120 < ab \leqslant 300$.
>
> And also $-12 \leqslant -b < -5$, so we get $12 < a - b < 20$.

As $\dfrac{1}{12} \leqslant \dfrac{1}{b} < \dfrac{1}{5}$, $24 < a \leqslant 25$, we get $2 < \dfrac{a}{b} < 5$.

So $29 < a+b \leqslant 37$, $12 < a-b < 20$, $120 < ab \leqslant 300$, $2 < \dfrac{a}{b} < 5$.

(2) Since $-\pi < 2\alpha < \pi$, $-\dfrac{\pi}{2} < -\beta < \dfrac{\pi}{2}$, we get $-\dfrac{3\pi}{2} < 2\alpha - \beta < \dfrac{3\pi}{2}$.

And as $\beta < \alpha$, so $0 < 2\alpha - \beta < \dfrac{3}{2}\pi$.

6 If a, b, c are positive real numbers and $b < c$, compare ab and $ac+bc$.

Solution： Take the difference between the two： $ab - (ac+bc) = a(b-c) - bc$.

Since $b < c \Rightarrow b - c < 0$ and $a > 0$, $a(b-c) < 0$.

Since $b > 0$, $c > 0 \Rightarrow bc > 0 \Rightarrow -bc < 0$, $a(b-c) - bc < 0$.

So $ab < ac+bc$.

7 If a, b are positive real numbers and $a \neq b$, compare $a^a b^b$ and $a^b b^a$.

Solution： Note that all numbers are positive. Take the quotient of the two：

$$\frac{a^a b^b}{a^b b^a} = \frac{a^{a-b}}{b^{a-b}} = \left(\frac{a}{b}\right)^{a-b}.$$

(a) If $a > b > 0$, then $\dfrac{a}{b} > 1$, $a - b > 0$ and $\left(\dfrac{a}{b}\right)^{a-b} > 1$, so $a^a b^b > a^b b^a$.

(b) If $0 < a < b$, then $0 < \dfrac{a}{b} < 1$, $a - b < 0$ and $\left(\dfrac{a}{b}\right)^{a-b} > 1$, so $a^a b^b > a^b b^a$.

So $a^a b^b > a^b b^a$.

8 If a, b are positive real numbers, compare $\left(\dfrac{a^2}{b}\right)^{\frac{1}{2}} + \left(\dfrac{b^2}{a}\right)^{\frac{1}{2}}$ and $\sqrt{a} + \sqrt{b}$.

Solution 1： Take the difference between the two：

$$\left[\left(\frac{a^2}{b}\right)^{\frac{1}{2}} + \left(\frac{b^2}{a}\right)^{\frac{1}{2}}\right] - (\sqrt{a} + \sqrt{b}) = \frac{a}{\sqrt{b}} + \frac{b}{\sqrt{a}} - \sqrt{a} - \sqrt{b} = \frac{a-b}{\sqrt{b}} + \frac{b-a}{\sqrt{a}} = (a-b)\left(\frac{1}{\sqrt{b}} - \frac{1}{\sqrt{a}}\right)$$

$$= \frac{(a-b)(\sqrt{a} - \sqrt{b})}{\sqrt{ab}} = \frac{(\sqrt{a} + \sqrt{b})(\sqrt{a} - \sqrt{b})^2}{\sqrt{ab}}$$

As a, b are positive real numbers, we get $\sqrt{ab} > 0$, $\sqrt{a} + \sqrt{b} > 0$, $(\sqrt{a} - \sqrt{b})^2 \geqslant 0$,

So $\dfrac{(\sqrt{a} + \sqrt{b})(\sqrt{a} - \sqrt{b})^2}{\sqrt{ab}} \geqslant 0$. So $\left(\dfrac{a^2}{b}\right)^{\frac{1}{2}} + \left(\dfrac{b^2}{a}\right)^{\frac{1}{2}} \geqslant \sqrt{a} + \sqrt{b}$.

Solution 2： As $\left(\dfrac{a^2}{b}\right)^{\frac{1}{2}} + \left(\dfrac{b^2}{a}\right)^{\frac{1}{2}}$ and $\sqrt{a} + \sqrt{b}$ are both positive, we could compare them by squaring both.

Since $\left(\left(\dfrac{a^2}{b}\right)^{\frac{1}{2}} + \left(\dfrac{b^2}{a}\right)^{\frac{1}{2}}\right)^2 = \dfrac{a^2}{b} + \dfrac{b^2}{a} + 2\sqrt{ab}$, $(\sqrt{a} + \sqrt{b})^2 = a + b + 2\sqrt{ab}$, we get $\left(\left(\dfrac{a^2}{b}\right)^{\frac{1}{2}}+\left(\dfrac{b^2}{a}\right)^{\frac{1}{2}}\right)^2-(\sqrt{a}+\sqrt{b})^2=\dfrac{a^2}{b}+\dfrac{b^2}{a}-a-b=\dfrac{(a+b)\,(a-b)^2}{ab}.$

As a, $b \in \mathbf{R}^+$, $\dfrac{(a+b)\,(a-b)^2}{ab} \geqslant 0$. So we have $\left(\dfrac{a^2}{b}\right)^{\frac{1}{2}}+\left(\dfrac{b^2}{a}\right)^{\frac{1}{2}} \geqslant \sqrt{a}+\sqrt{b}$.

Solution 3: Take the quotient of the two positive numbers:

$$\dfrac{\left(\dfrac{a^2}{b}\right)^{\frac{1}{2}}+\left(\dfrac{b^2}{a}\right)^{\frac{1}{2}}}{\sqrt{a}+\sqrt{b}}=\dfrac{\dfrac{a}{\sqrt{b}}+\dfrac{b}{\sqrt{a}}}{\sqrt{a}+\sqrt{b}}=\dfrac{(\sqrt{a})^3+(\sqrt{b})^3}{\sqrt{a}\,\sqrt{b}\,(\sqrt{a}+\sqrt{b})}=\dfrac{(\sqrt{a}+\sqrt{b})(a+b-\sqrt{ab})}{\sqrt{a}\,\sqrt{b}\,(\sqrt{a}+\sqrt{b})}=\dfrac{a+b-\sqrt{ab}}{\sqrt{ab}}$$

$$=\dfrac{(\sqrt{a}-\sqrt{b})^2+\sqrt{ab}}{\sqrt{ab}}=1+\dfrac{(\sqrt{a}-\sqrt{b})^2}{\sqrt{ab}}\geqslant 1.$$

As $\left(\dfrac{a^2}{b}\right)^{\frac{1}{2}}+\left(\dfrac{b^2}{a}\right)^{\frac{1}{2}}>0$, $\sqrt{a}+\sqrt{b}>0$,

we have $\left(\dfrac{a^2}{b}\right)^{\frac{1}{2}}+\left(\dfrac{b^2}{a}\right)^{\frac{1}{2}}\geqslant \sqrt{a}+\sqrt{b}$.

9 If we dissolve a grams of sugar into a cup of water, the mass of the sugar water is b grams. If we put another m grams of sugar into it, it will be sweeter than before. Please convert the situation into an inequality, and prove it.

Solution:

As the question says, we may get the inequality $\dfrac{a}{b}<\dfrac{a+m}{b+m}\;(b>a>0, m>0)$.

Proof:

Take the difference between the two sides $\dfrac{a+m}{b+m}-\dfrac{a}{b}=\dfrac{b(a+m)-a(b+m)}{b(b+m)}=\dfrac{m(b-a)}{b(b+m)}.$

Since $b>a>0$, $m>0$, $b-a>0$, $b+m>0$, then $\dfrac{m(b-a)}{b(b+m)}>0$.

So we have $\dfrac{a+m}{b+m}>\dfrac{a}{b}$.

10 If 4 tulips and 5 roses cost you less than 22 yuan, 6 tulips and 3 roses cost you more than 24 yuan, then which will cost you more, 2 tulips or 3 roses?

Solution:

Suppose every tulip costs x yuan, every rose costs y yuan, then $\begin{cases}4x+5y<22\\6x+3y>24\end{cases}$.

Let $2x-3y=a(4x+5y)+b(6x+3y)=(4a+6b)x+(5a+3b)y$, then $\begin{cases}4a+6b=2\\5a+3b=-3\end{cases}$.

Solving the systems of the equation, we have $\begin{cases}a=-\dfrac{4}{3}\\b=\dfrac{11}{9}\end{cases}$, then $2x-3y=-\dfrac{4}{3}(4x+5y)+\dfrac{11}{9}(6x+3y)$.

So we get $2x - 3y > -\dfrac{4}{3} \times 22 + \dfrac{11}{9} \times 24 = 0$, which means 2 tulips cost more than 3 roses.

11 Let $a_1 > 0$, $a_1 \neq \sqrt{2}$, $a_2 = 1 + \dfrac{1}{a_1 + 1}$.

(1) Prove: $\sqrt{2}$ is between a_1 and a_2.

(2) Which one is closer to $\sqrt{2}$, a_1 or a_2?

Solution:

(1) It suffices to prove $(\sqrt{2} - a_1)(\sqrt{2} - a_2) < 0$.

Since $(\sqrt{2} - a_1)(\sqrt{2} - a_2) = (\sqrt{2} - a_1)\left(\sqrt{2} - 1 - \dfrac{1}{a_1 + 1}\right) = \dfrac{(1 - \sqrt{2})(\sqrt{2} - a_1)^2}{a_1 + 1} < 0$, $\sqrt{2}$ is between a_1 and a_2.

(2) It amounts to compare: $\left|\sqrt{2} - a_1\right|$, $\left|\sqrt{2} - a_2\right|$.

Since $\left|\sqrt{2} - a_2\right| = \left|\dfrac{(1 - \sqrt{2})(\sqrt{2} - a_1)}{a_1 + 1}\right| = \dfrac{\sqrt{2} - 1}{a_1 + 1}\left|\sqrt{2} - a_1\right| < \left|\sqrt{2} - a_1\right|$, we get the conclusion that a_2 is closer to $\sqrt{2}$ than a_1.

12 If $f(x) = ax^2 - c(a \neq 0)$, $-4 \leqslant f(1) \leqslant -1$, $-1 \leqslant f(2) \leqslant 5$, what is the range of $f(3)$?

Determine if the following solution is true or false:

As $-4 \leqslant f(1) \leqslant -1$, $-1 \leqslant f(2) \leqslant 5$, then $-4 \leqslant a - c \leqslant -1$ ①; $-1 \leqslant 4a - c \leqslant 5$ ②;

②-① to get $0 \leqslant 3a \leqslant 9$, so $0 \leqslant a \leqslant 3$. Similarly, $1 \leqslant c \leqslant 7$. So $-7 \leqslant 9a - c \leqslant 26$, and $-7 \leqslant f(3) \leqslant 26$.

Solution:

If $0 \leqslant a \leqslant 3$, $1 \leqslant c \leqslant 7$, when $a = 3$, $c = 1$, $4a - c = 11 \notin [-1, 5]$, but $-1 \leqslant 4a - c \leqslant 5$, the statements are contradictory. So the solution is false.

The correct answer is as follows:

Let $f(3) = mf(1) + nf(2)$, then $9a - c = m(a - c) + n(4a - c)$.

We simplify it as $9a - c = (m + 4n)a - (m + n)c$, so $\begin{cases} m + 4n = 9 \\ m + n = 1 \end{cases}$.

Solving the system of equation, we have $\begin{cases} m = -\dfrac{5}{3} \\ n = \dfrac{8}{3} \end{cases}$. So we get $f(3) = -\dfrac{5}{3}f(1) + \dfrac{8}{3}f(2)$.

Since $-4 \leqslant f(1) \leqslant -1$, $-1 \leqslant f(2) \leqslant 5$, we get the conclusion: $-1 \leqslant f(3) \leqslant 20$.

13 If a and b are real numbers, prove: $a^2 + b^2 \geqslant 2ab$.

Proof:

If a and b are real numbers, then $(a - b)^2 \geqslant 0$. So $a^2 - 2ab + b^2 \geqslant 0$. Therefore $a^2 + b^2 \geqslant 2ab$.

14 If a and b are positive real numbers, prove: $\sqrt{ab} \leqslant \dfrac{a + b}{2}$.

Proof：

If a and b are positive real numbers，then $(\sqrt{a} - \sqrt{b})^2 \geqslant 0$. So $a - 2\sqrt{ab} + b \geqslant 0$.

Therefore $\sqrt{ab} \leqslant \dfrac{a+b}{2}$.

Remark：This inequality is the two variables case of the Arithmetic Mean-Geometric Mean (AM-GM) inequality.

If a and b are real numbers，$a^2 + b^2 \geqslant 2ab$. $a^2 + b^2 = 2ab$，if and only if $a = b$,

If a and b are positive real numbers，$\sqrt{ab} \leqslant \dfrac{a+b}{2}$. $\sqrt{ab} = \dfrac{a+b}{2}$ if and only if $a = b$.

 练习 Exercise

1. Solve the inequality.

   (1) $3 - 4x < -2$.　　　　　　　(2) $3 - 4x < -2x + 1$.

   (3) $\dfrac{3-4x}{7} < \dfrac{-2x+1}{2}$.

2. True or false：

   (1) If $a < b$，$c < 0$, then $\dfrac{c}{a} < \dfrac{c}{b}$.

   (2) If $ac^{-3} > bc^{-3}$, then $a > b$.

   (3) If $a > b$，$b > c$, then $a - b > b - c$.

3. If $n > -1$，$n \neq 1$, prove：$n^3 + 1 > n^2 + n$.

4. If $a > b > c$，$a + b + c = 0$, prove：(1) $ac < 0$; (2) $-2 < \dfrac{c}{a} < -\dfrac{1}{2}$.

5. If $m > 1$, let $A = \sqrt{m+1} - \sqrt{m}$，$B = \sqrt{m} - \sqrt{m-1}$, which one is bigger, A or B?

6. If $x \in \mathbf{R}$, compare these two expressions：$x^6 + 1$ and $x^4 + x^2$.

7. If x，y，$z \in \mathbf{R}$, compare these two expressions：$5x^2 + y^2 + z^2$ and $2xy + 4x + 2z - 2$.

8. If a，$b \in \mathbf{R}^+$，$b^2 = ac$, compare these two expressions：$a^2 - b^2 + c^2$ and $(a - b + c)^2$.

9. Compare these two expressions：$\left(1 + \dfrac{\sqrt{2}}{a}\right)^3$ and $2 - \left(1 - \dfrac{\sqrt{2}}{a}\right)^3$.

10. If the origin is on the graph of the quadratic function $y = f(x)$，$1 \leqslant f(-1) \leqslant 2$，$3 \leqslant f(1) \leqslant 4$, what is the range of $f(-2)$?

11. Prove：$a^2 + b^2 + c^2 \geqslant ab + bc + ca$.

12. If $ab \neq 0$, find the range of $\dfrac{a}{b} + \dfrac{b}{a}$.

2.2 ◈ 一元二次不等式的解法　Quadratic Inequalities

一元二次不等式 Quadratic Inequalities

形如 $ax^2 + bx + c > 0$ 或 $ax^2 + bx + c < 0 \ (a \neq 0)$ 的不等式叫作**一元二次不等式**.

Let $f(x)$ be a quadratic function. Then $f(x) < 0$ and $f(x) > 0$ are called **quadratic inequalities.**

There are two ways to solve a quadratic inequality $f(x) < 0$ (or $f(x) > 0$): factorization or graph analysis, as is shown in the examples below.

1 Solve $x^2 - 2x - 3 > 0$.

Solution 1: Factorize the quadratic $x^2 - 2x - 3 = (x-3)(x+1)$.

Then, $x^2 - 2x - 3 > 0 \Leftrightarrow (x-3)(x+1) > 0$,

which means $\begin{cases} x-3>0 \\ x+1>0 \end{cases}$ (1) or $\begin{cases} x-3<0 \\ x+1<0 \end{cases}$ (2).

The solution to (1) is $x > 3$, and the solution to (2) is $x < -1$. Hence, the solution set is $(-\infty, -1) \cup (3, +\infty)$.

Solution 2: Sketch the graph of the function $y = x^2 - 2x - 3$, in the Figure 2-1, you can see that the graph lies above the x-axis when x is greater than 3 or less than -1. So the solution set is $(-\infty, -1) \cup (3, +\infty)$.

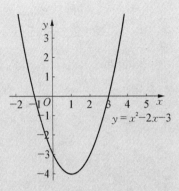

Figure 2-1

2 Solve $x^2 - x < 6$.

Solution 1: Collect the terms to find: $x^2 - x - 6 < 0$. Factorize the quadratic $x^2 - x - 6 = (x-3)(x+2)$. Then, $x^2 - x - 6 < 0 \Leftrightarrow (x-3)(x+2) < 0$, which means $\begin{cases} x-3>0 \\ x+2<0 \end{cases}$ (1) or $\begin{cases} x-3<0 \\ x+2>0 \end{cases}$ (2).

The solution set of (1) is $\varnothing$, and the solution set of (2) is $-2 < x < 3$. Then, combining (1) and (2) the solution set is $(-2, 3)$.

Solution 2: Collect the terms to find $x^2 - x - 6 < 0$.

Sketch the graph of the function $y = x^2 - x - 6$,

then in the Figure 2-2, you can see that the graph is below the x-axis when x is greater than -2 and less than 3.

So the solution set is $(-2, 3)$.

REMARK: When solving inequalities, pay attention to whether the inequality sign contains equal sign or not. If the inequality is $x^2 - x \leqslant 6$, then the solution set of the inequality is a closed interval $[-2, 3]$.

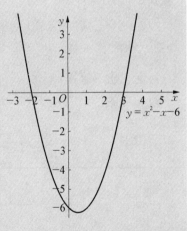

Figure 2-2

3 Solve the following inequalities.

(1) $x^2 + 2x + 4 > 0$.　　(2) $x^2 + 2x + 1 \leqslant 0$.　　(3) $x^2 + 3x + 5 < 0$.　　(4) $x^2 - 4x + 4 > 0$.

Solution: (1) The solution set of $x^2 + 2x + 4 > 0$ is $(-\infty, +\infty)$.

(2) The solution set of $x^2 + 2x + 1 \leqslant 0$ is $\{-1\}$.

(3) The solution set of $x^2 + 3x + 5 < 0$ is $\varnothing$.

(4) The solution set of $x^2 - 4x + 4 > 0$ is $(-\infty, 2) \cup (2, +\infty)$.

探究一般的一元二次不等式的解法

一般地,怎样确定一元二次不等式 $ax^2 + bx + c > 0$ 与 $ax^2 + bx + c < 0 (a \neq 0)$ 的解集呢?

确定一元二次不等式的解集,关键要考虑以下两点:

(1) 抛物线 $y = ax^2 + bx + c$ 与 x 轴的位置关系,也就是一元二次方程 $ax^2 + bx + c = 0$ 的根的情况.

(2) 抛物线 $y = ax^2 + bx + c$ 的开口方向,也就是 a 的符号.

由于 $a < 0$ 可以转化为 $a > 0$,下面就 $a > 0$ 情况作讨论.

4 Solve the inequality $ax^2 + bx + c > 0 (a > 0)$.

Solution: If $\Delta = b^2 - 4ac > 0$, the two different roots of $ax^2 + bx + c = 0$ are x_1, x_2 (let $x_1 < x_2$), then the solution set of $ax^2 + bx + c > 0 (a > 0)$ is $(-\infty, x_1) \bigcup (x_2, +\infty)$.

If $\Delta = b^2 - 4ac = 0$, the two repeated roots of $ax^2 + bx + c = 0$ are $x_1 = x_2 = -\dfrac{b}{2a}$, then the solution set of $ax^2 + bx + c > 0 (a > 0)$ is $\left(-\infty, -\dfrac{b}{2a}\right) \bigcup \left(-\dfrac{b}{2a}, +\infty\right)$.

If $\Delta = b^2 - 4ac < 0$, there are no real roots of $ax^2 + bx + c = 0$, then the solution set of $ax^2 + bx + c > 0 (a > 0)$ is **R**.

5 Solve the inequality $ax^2 + bx + c < 0 (a > 0)$.

Solution: If $\Delta = b^2 - 4ac > 0$, the two different roots of $ax^2 + bx + c = 0$ are x_1, x_2 (let $x_1 < x_2$), then the solution set of $ax^2 + bx + c < 0 (a > 0)$ is (x_1, x_2).

If $\Delta = b^2 - 4ac = 0$, the two repeated roots of $ax^2 + bx + c = 0$ are $x_1 = x_2 = -\dfrac{b}{2a}$, then the solution set of $ax^2 + bx + c < 0 (a > 0)$ is $\varnothing$.

If $\Delta = b^2 - 4ac < 0$, there are no real roots of $ax^2 + bx + c = 0$, then the solution set of $ax^2 + bx + c < 0 (a > 0)$ is $\varnothing$.

一元二次不等式 $ax^2 + bx + c > 0$ 或 $ax^2 + bx + c < 0 (a > 0)$ 的解集

设相应的一元二次方程 $ax^2 + bx + c = 0 (a > 0)$,$\Delta = b^2 - 4ac$,则不等式的解的各种情况见下表 (Table 2 - 1):

Table 2 - 1

	$\Delta > 0$	$\Delta = 0$	$\Delta < 0$
二次函数 $y = ax^2 + bx + c$ $(a > 0)$ 的图像	$y = ax^2 + bx + c$	$y = ax^2 + bx + c$	$y = ax^2 + bx + c$
一元二次方程 $ax^2 + bx + c = 0$ $(a > 0)$ 的根	有两相异实根 x_1, $x_2 (x_1 < x_2)$	有两相等实根 $x_1 = x_2 = -\dfrac{b}{2a}$	无实根

续 表

	$\Delta > 0$	$\Delta = 0$	$\Delta < 0$
$ax^2 + bx + c > 0$ ($a > 0$) 的解集	$(-\infty, x_1) \bigcup (x_2, +\infty)$	$\left\{ x \mid x \neq -\dfrac{b}{2a} \right\}$	$\mathbf{R}$
$ax^2 + bx + c < 0$ ($a > 0$) 的解集	(x_1, x_2)	$\varnothing$	$\varnothing$

6 If the solution set of $ax^2 + bx + c > 0 (a > 0)$ is $(-\infty, -2) \bigcup \left(-\dfrac{1}{2}, +\infty\right)$, find the solution set of $ax^2 - bx + c > 0$.

Solution: As we know -2 and $-\dfrac{1}{2}$ are the two roots of $ax^2 + bx + c = 0$, then $\begin{cases} -\dfrac{b}{a} = -\dfrac{5}{2} \\ \dfrac{c}{a} = 1 \end{cases}$. Let $a = 2$, $b = 5$, $c = 2$.

The solution set of $2x^2 - 5x + 2 > 0$ is $\left(-\infty, \dfrac{1}{2}\right) \bigcup (2, +\infty)$.

7 If the solution set of $ax^2 - 3x + 6 > 4$ is $\{x \mid x < 1 \text{ or } x > b\}$.

(1) Find a and b.

(2) Solve $(x - c)(ax - b) < 0$ (c is a constant).

Solution: (1) As we know 1 and b are the two roots of $ax^2 - 3x + 2 = 0$, then $\begin{cases} b = \dfrac{2}{a} \\ 1 + b = \dfrac{3}{a} \end{cases}$. So $a = 1$, $b = 2$.

(2) Substituting $a = 1$ and $b = 2$ into $(x - c)(ax - b) < 0$, we have $(x - c)(x - 2) < 0$.

When $c > 2$, the solution set is $(2, c)$; when $c < 2$, the solution set is $(c, 2)$; when $c = 2$, the solution set is $\varnothing$.

8 If a is a real number, the two roots of $7x^2 - (a + 13)x + (a^2 - a - 2) = 0$ is in the section $(0, 1)$ and $(1, 2)$, find value range of a.

Solution: Let $f(x) = 7x^2 - (a + 13)x + (a^2 - a - 2)$, then according to the graph, we have $\begin{cases} f(0) > 0 \\ f(1) < 0. \\ f(2) > 0 \end{cases}$ Hence, $\begin{cases} a^2 - a - 2 > 0 \\ a^2 - 2a - 8 < 0. \\ a^2 - 3a > 0 \end{cases}$ Solving the system of inequalities gives $-2 < a < -1$ or $3 < a < 4$.

So the value range of a is $(-2, -1) \bigcup (3, 4)$.

练习Exercise

1. Find the solution sets of the following inequalities.

(1) $x^2 - x + 1 > 0$ (2) $x^2 + x + 1 \leqslant 0$

(3) $3x^2 - 4\sqrt{3}x + 4 > 0$ (4) $289x^2 + 510x + 225 \leqslant 0$

2. Find the solution sets of the following systems of inequalities.

(1) $\begin{cases} x^2 - 2x - 8 < 0 \\ x^2 - 2x \geqslant 0 \end{cases}$ (2) $\begin{cases} x^2 + x - 12 > 0 \\ x^2 - x - 30 \leqslant 0 \end{cases}$

(3) $\begin{cases} x^2 - 9x + 18 < 0 \\ x^2 - 5x - 6 \geqslant 0 \end{cases}$

3. For a certain brand of car, the relationship between the braking distance s (m) and the speed x (km/h) of the car is:

$$s = \frac{1}{20}x + \frac{1}{180}x^2$$

In a traffic accident, the braking distance of this car was measured to be greater than 39.5 m. What is the smallest speed of this car before braking? (Accurate to 0.01 km/h)

4. What is the range of a, when the solution set of $x^2 + (a-1)x + 4 > 0$ is **R**?

5. For any x, the value of $mx^2 + (m-1)x + (m-1)$ is always less than 0. Find the range of m.

6. Solve the inequality about x: $ax^2 - (a+1)x + 1 > 0$.

2.3 ◆ 多项式除法、余式定理和因式定理
The Divisions of Polynomials; The Remainder and Factor Theorems

求多项式函数的零点是代数中非常重要的问题之一.

When $f(x)$ is a polynomial function and a is a real number, the following statements are equivalent.

1. $x = a$ is a zero of the function $f(x)$.

2. $x = a$ is a solution of the polynomial equation $f(x) = 0$.

3. $x - a$ is a factor of the polynomial $f(x)$.

4. $(a, 0)$ is an x-intercept of the graph of $f(x)$.

多项式除法 The Division of Polynomials

带余除法：任意非零多项式 $g(x)$ 去除 $f(x)$，则存在唯一的商式 $q(x)$ 和余式 $r(x)$，使得 $f(x) = g(x)q(x) + r(x)$，其中 $r(x) = 0$ 或 $r(x)$ 的次数小于 $g(x)$ 的次数. 当 $r(x) = 0$ 且 $f(x) \neq 0$ 时，$g(x)$ 是 $f(x)$ 的一个因式.

The Division Algorithm

If $f(x)$ and $g(x)$ are polynomials such that $g(x) \neq 0$, then there exist unique polynomials $q(x)$ and $r(x)$ such that $f(x) = g(x)q(x) + r(x)$, where $r(x) = 0$ or the degree of $r(x)$ is less than the degree of $g(x)$. If the remainder $r(x) = 0$ and $f(x) \neq 0$, then $g(x)$ is a factor of $f(x)$.

长除法 Long Division

多项式长除法是常见的算数技巧长除法的推广版本,是指用一个同次或低次的多项式去除以另一个多项式.多项式除以多项式一般用竖式进行演算,步骤如下:

(1) 把被除式、除式按某个字母作降幂排列,并把所缺的项用零补齐.

(2) 用被除式的第一项除以除式的第一项,得到商式的第一项.

(3) 用商式的第一项去乘除式,把积写在被除式下面(同类项对齐),消去相等项,把不相等的项结合起来.

(4) 把减得的差当作新的被除式,再按照上面的方法继续演算,直到余式为零或余式的次数低于除式的次数时为止.即,被除式=除式×商式+余式.

综合除法 Synthetic Division

当除式为 $x-c$ 的形式时,多项式长除法可以用一种简便的方法代替,称为**综合除法**.

设被除式为 $f(x)=a_n x^n+a_{n-1}x^{n-1}+\cdots+a_1 x+a_0$,除式为 $x-c$,商式为 $q(x)=b_{n-1}x^{n-1}+b_{n-2}x^{n-2}+\cdots+b_1 x+b_0$,余数为 r,则由 $f(x)=(x-c)q(x)+r$,比较系数得 $a_n=b_{n-1}$,$a_{n-1}=b_{n-2}-cb_{n-1}$,$\cdots$,$a_0=r-cb_0$,即得 $b_{n-1}=a_n$,$b_{n-2}=a_{n-1}+cb_{n-1}$,$\cdots$,$r=a_0+cb_0$,我们得到综合除法:

c	a_n	a_{n-1}	a_{n-2}	$\cdots$	a_1	a_0
		cb_{n-1}	cb_{n-2}	$\cdots$	cb_1	cb_0
	b_{n-1}	b_{n-2}	b_{n-3}	$\cdots$	b_0	r

1 Use long division to divide the polynomial $2x^4-10x+5-15x^2$ by x^2+x+1.

Solution: Begin by writing the dividend in descending powers of x. Because there is no x^3-term in the dividend $2x^4-10x+5-15x^2$, we need to rewrite the dividend as $2x^4+0x^3-15x^2-10x+5$ before taking the Long division.

$$
\begin{array}{r}
2x^2-2x-15 \\
x^2+x+1{\overline{\smash{\big)}\,2x^4+0x^3-15x^2-10x+5}} \\
\underline{2x^4+2x^3+2x^2} \\
-2x^3-17x^2-10x \\
\underline{-2x^3-2x^2-2x} \\
-15x^2-8x+5 \\
\underline{-15x^2-15x-15} \\
7x+20
\end{array}
$$

In fractional form,we can write this result as follows.

$$\frac{2x^4-10x^2-15x+5}{x^2+x+1}=2x^2-2x-15+\frac{7x+20}{x^2+x+1}$$

This implies that

$$2x^4-10x^2-15x+5=(x^2+x+1)(2x^2-2x-15)+7x+20.$$

2 Divide $f(x)=x^4-10x^2-2x+4$ by $x+2$.

Solution 1：Use long division

$$
\begin{array}{r}
x^3 - 2x^2 - 6x + 10 \\
x+2\overline{\smash{\big)}\ x^4 + 0x^3 - 10x^2 - 2x + 4} \\
\underline{x^4 + 2x^3} \\
-2x^3 - 10x^2 \\
\underline{-2x^3 - 4x^2} \\
-6x^2 - 2x \\
\underline{-6x^2 - 12x} \\
10x + 4 \\
\underline{10x + 20} \\
-16
\end{array}
$$

So，we have $f(x) = x^4 - 10x^2 - 2x + 4 = (x+2)(x^3 - 2x^2 - 6x + 10) - 16$.

Solution 2：Use synthetic division

We should set up the array as Figure 2 - 3. A zero is included for the missing x^3-term in the dividend. Rewrite $x + 2$ as $x - (-2)$.

The synthetic division works by adding terms in columns and multiplying the results by -2.

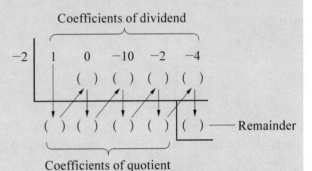

Figure 2 - 3

$$
\begin{array}{r|rrrrr}
-2 & 1 & 0 & -10 & -2 & 4 \\
   &   & -2 & 4 & 12 & -20 \\
\hline
   & 1 & -2 & -6 & 10 & -16
\end{array}
$$

So，$f(x) = x^4 - 10x^2 - 2x + 4 = (x+2)(x^3 - 2x^2 - 6x + 10) - 16$.

3 Divide the polynomial $6x^3 - 25x^2 + 23x - 6$ by $x - 3$ and use the result to factor the polynomial completely.

Solution： Use synthetic division

$$
\begin{array}{r|rrrr}
3 & 6 & -25 & 23 & -6 \\
  &   & 18 & -21 & 6 \\
\hline
  & 6 & -7 & 2 & 0
\end{array}
$$

From this division, we can conclude that $6x^3 - 25x^2 + 23x - 6 = (x-3)(6x^2 - 7x + 2)$ and by factoring the quadratic $6x^2 - 7x + 2$, we have $6x^3 - 25x^2 + 23x - 6 = (x-3)(2x-1)(3x-2)$.

余式定理、因式定理 The Remainder Theorem and Factor Theorem

在例 2 中，$f(-2) = -16$ 就是 $f(x)$ 被 $x - (-2)$ 除所得的余式.

一般地，当一个多项式 $f(x)$ 除以 $(x-c)$ 时，所得的余数等于 $f(c)$. 这就是**余式定理**.

余式定理 The Remainder Theorem

If a polynomial $f(x)$ is divided by $x - c$, then the remainder is $f(c)$.

Proof： From the Division Algorithm，we have $f(x)=(x-c)q(x)+r(x)$,

And because either $r(x)=0$ or the degree of $r(x)$ is less than the degree of $x-c$，we know that $r(x)$ must be a constant. That is，$r(x)=r$. Now，by evaluating $f(x)$ at $x=c$，we have $f(c)=(c-c)q(c)+r=r$.

另一个重要的定理是**因式定理**：

一个多项式有因式 $x-c$ 当且仅当 $f(c)=0$。

因式定理 The Factor Theorem

A polynomial $f(x)$ has a factor $x-c$ if and only if $f(c)=0$.

Proof： By the Remainder Theorem，if $f(c)=0$，then $f(x)=(x-c)q(x)$，and $x-c$ is a factor of $f(x)$. Conversely，if $x-c$ is a factor of $f(x)$，then division of $f(x)$ by $x-c$ yields a remainder of 0. So，by the Remainder Theorem，$f(c)=0$.

4 Use the Remainder Theorem to evaluate $f(x)=3x^3+8x^2+5x-6$ when $x=-2$.

Solution： Using synthetic division，we obtain the following.

$$
\begin{array}{r|rrrr}
-2 & 3 & 8 & 5 & -6 \\
   &   & -6 & -4 & -2 \\
\hline
   & 3 & 2 & 1 & -8
\end{array}
$$

Because the remainder is $r=-8$，we can conclude that $f(-2)=-8$.

We can check this by substituting $x=-2$ in the original function.

5 If $f(x)=2x^4+5x^3-8x^2-17x-6$，determine whether each of the following is a factor of $f(x)$.
(1) $x-1$；   (2) $x-2$.

Solution： (1) Use direct substitution to find $f(1)$：

$$f(1)=2\times1^4+5\times1^3-8\times1^2-17\times1-6=2+5-8-17-6=-24.$$

Since $f(1)\neq0$，$x-1$ is not a factor of $f(x)$.

(2) Use synthetic division to find $f(2)$：

$$
\begin{array}{r|rrrrr}
2 & 2 & 5 & -8 & -17 & -6 \\
  &   & 4 & 18 & 20 & 6 \\
\hline
  & 2 & 9 & 10 & 3 & 0
\end{array}
$$

Since $f(2)=0$，$x-2$ is a factor of $f(x)$.

6 Show that $x-2$ and $x+3$ are factors of $f(x)=2x^4+3x^3-14x^2-9x+18$. Then find the remaining factors of $f(x)$.

Solution： Using synthetic division with the factor $(x-2)$ we obtain the following.

$$
\begin{array}{r|rrrrr}
2 & 2 & 3 & -14 & -9 & 18 \\
  &   & 4 & 14 & 0 & -18 \\
\hline
  & 2 & 7 & 0 & -9 & 0
\end{array}
$$

The remainder is 0，so $f(2)=0$ and $(x-2)$ is a factor.

Take the result of this division and perform synthetic division again using the factor $x+3$.

$$\begin{array}{c|cccc} -3 & 2 & 7 & 0 & -9 \\ & & -6 & -3 & 9 \\ \hline & 2 & 1 & -3 & 0 \end{array}$$

The remainder is 0, so $f(-3)=0$ and $(x+3)$ is a factor.

Because the resulting quadratic expression factors as $2x^2+x-3=(2x+3)(x-1)$,

we get the complete factorization of $f(x)$ is $f(x)=(x-2)(x+3)(2x+3)(x-1)$.

多项式函数的零点 Real Zeros of Polynomial Functions

对于一次函数和二次函数的零点,我们容易通过解方程来求得. 一些特殊的高次多项式,如果能够进行因式分解,使问题转化为解一次方程或二次方程的问题,则它的零点也能够求出.

对于整系数多项式函数 $f(x)=a_nx^n+a_{n-1}x^{n-1}+\cdots+a_2x^2+a_1x+a_0(a_0\neq 0)$,在利用因式分解的方法求零点时,如果 $qx-p(p,q\in \mathbf{Z}$,且 p,q 互素)是多项式 $f(x)$ 的一个因式$\Big($也就是说 $x=\dfrac{p}{q}$ 是函数的一个零点,$x=\dfrac{p}{q}$ 是方程 $f(x)=0$ 的一个根$\Big)$,那么存在一个整系数多项式 $g(x)$,使得 $a_nx^n+a_{n-1}x^{n-1}+\cdots+a_1x+a_0=(qx-p)g(x)$.

由上面式子可以发现,q 能够被 a_n 整除,p 能够被 a_0 整除.

这个结论就是著名的**有理根定理**(**The Rational Root Theorem**)

The Rational Root Theorem

Let $f(x)$ be a Polynomial of degree n with integral coefficients and a nonzero constant term:$f(x)=a_nx^n+a_{n-1}x^{n-1}+\cdots+a_2x^2+a_1x+a_0$, where $a_0\neq 0$.

If one of the roots of the equation $f(x)=0$ is $x=\dfrac{p}{q}$ where p and q are nonzero integers with no common factor other than 1, then p must be a factor of a_0, and q must be a factor of a_n.

尽管我们可以利用有理根定理以及因式分解的方法求部分多项式函数的零点,但并不能解决所有多项式函数求零点的问题. 我们可以借助电脑或图形计算器,找出多项式函数的零点.

此外,我们也可以根据多项式函数的图像的连续性,以及零点存在定理,近似估计出多项式函数的零点所在的区间.

零点存在定理 The Location Principle

如果函数 $f(x)$ 在定义区间 $[a,b]$ 上的图像是一条连续不断的曲线,且有 $f(a)f(b)<0$,那么在区间 (a,b) 内至少存在一个实数 c,使 $f(c)=0$,即函数 $f(x)$ 在区间 (a,b) 上至少存在一个零点,这就是**零点存在定理**.

The Location Principle

If $f(x)$ is continuous function and a and b are real numbers such that $f(a)$ and $f(b)$ have opposite signs, then there is at least one real root $x=c$ of the equation $f(x)=0$ between a and b. See Figure 2-4.

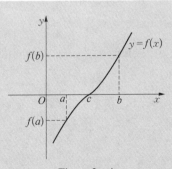

Figure 2-4

7 Find all the real zeros of $f(x) = x^3 + 5x^2 + 5x - 2$.

Solution:

According to the rational root theorem, the possible rational zeros could be ± 1, ± 2. Since $f(1) = 9$, $f(-1) = -3$, $f(2) = 36$, $f(-2) = 0$, we can see -2 is the zero of $f(x)$. Use synthetic division:

$$
\begin{array}{r|rrrr}
-2 & 1 & 5 & 5 & -2 \\
   &   & -2 & -6 & 2 \\
\hline
   & 1 & 3 & -1 & 0
\end{array}
$$

We have $f(x) = x^3 + 5x^2 + 5x - 2 = (x+2)(x^2 + 3x - 1)$.

Solve the quadratic equation $x^2 + 3x - 1 = 0$, then $x = \dfrac{-3 \pm \sqrt{13}}{2}$.

So the zeros of $f(x)$ are $x = -2$ and $x = \dfrac{-3 \pm \sqrt{13}}{2}$.

8 According to the rational root theorem, what are the possible rational zeros of $P(x) = 3x^4 + 13x^3 + 15x^2 - 4$? Then find all the real zeros of $f(x)$.

Solution:

$x = \dfrac{p}{q}$ is a possible rational root if p divides -4 and q divides 3. Thus p could equal ± 1, ± 2, or ± 4, and q could equal ± 1 or ± 3. Therefore, $\dfrac{p}{q}$ could equal ± 1, ± 2, ± 4, $\pm \dfrac{1}{3}$, $\pm \dfrac{2}{3}$, or $\pm \dfrac{4}{3}$.

Since $P(1) = 27$, $P(-1) = 1$, $P(2) = 208$, $P(-2) = 0$, $x = -2$ is a root. Apply the synthetic division:

$$
\begin{array}{r|rrrrr}
-2 & 3 & 13 & 15 & 0 & -4 \\
   &   & -6 & -14 & -2 & 4 \\
\hline
   & 3 & 7 & 1 & -2 & 0
\end{array}
$$

So $P(x) = (x+2)(3x^3 + 7x^2 + x - 2)$.

To find the other root of $P(x) = 0$, solve the equation $3x^3 + 7x^2 + x - 2 = 0$.

Picking up where we left off in our list of possible rational roots, we can check $x = -2$ again because it may be a double root:

$$
\begin{array}{r|rrrr}
-2 & 3 & 7 & 1 & -2 \\
   &   & -6 & -2 & 2 \\
\hline
   & 3 & 1 & -1 & 0
\end{array}
$$

So, $x = -2$ is indeed a double root, and the resulting equation is quadratic, which we can solve using the quadratic formula:

$$3x^2 + x - 1 = 0, \quad x = \frac{-1 \pm \sqrt{13}}{6}.$$

Therefore，$P(x) = (x+2)^2 \left(x - \dfrac{-1+\sqrt{13}}{6}\right)\left(x - \dfrac{-1-\sqrt{13}}{6}\right)$, the real zeros of $P(x)$ are

$x = -2$ and $x = \dfrac{-1 \pm \sqrt{13}}{6}$.

9 Use a graphing calculator to estimate the zeros of $f(x) = 4x^3 - 52x^2 + 153x - 119$.

Solution：

Use graphing calculator to sketch the graph of $f(x) = 4x^3 - 52x^2 + 153x - 119$. The x-intercepts of the graph are the zeros of $f(x)$.

We can use TRACE to find the x-intercept of the graph (see Figure 2 - 5).

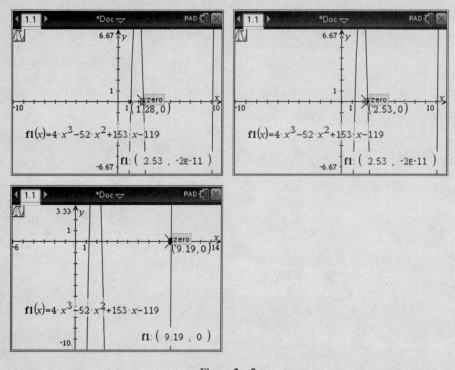

Figure 2 - 5

Therefore，the zeros of $f(x)$ are about $x_1 = 1.28$, $x_2 = 2.53$, $x_3 = 9.19$.

10 Use bisection method to estimate the zero of $f(x) = 4x^3 - 52x^2 + 153x - 119$，$x \in$ (1, 2). (Round your answer to the first decimal place.)

Solution：

Step 1：Find the midpoint $x_1 = \dfrac{1+2}{2} = 1.5$ of the interval (1, 2). Since $f(x_1) = f(1.5) = 7$，$f(1)f(1.5) < 0$，according to location principle, there exists at least one real root of $f(x) = 0$ in the interval (1, 1.5).

Step 2：Find the midpoint $x_2 = \dfrac{1+1.5}{2} = 1.25$ of the interval (1, 1.5). Since $f(x_2) = f(1.25) = -1.1875$，$f(1.25)f(1.5) < 0$，according to location principle, there exists at least one real root of $f(x) = 0$ in the interval (1.25, 1.5).

Step 3: Find the midpoint $x_3 = \dfrac{1.25 + 1.5}{2} = 1.375$ of the interval $(1.25, 1.5)$. Since $f(x_3) = f(1.375) = 3.460\,94$, $f(1.25)f(1.375) < 0$, according to location principle, there exists at least one real root of $f(x) = 0$ in the interval $(1.25, 1.375)$.

Step 4: Find the midpoint $x_4 = \dfrac{1.25 + 1.375}{2} = 1.312\,5$ of the interval $(1.25, 1.375)$. Since $f(x_4) = f(1.312\,5) = 1.278\,32$, $f(1.25)f(1.312\,5) < 0$, according to location principle, there exists at least one real root of $f(x) = 0$ in the interval $(1.25, 1.312\,5)$.

Step 5: Round the endpoints of the interval $(1.25, 1.312\,5)$ to the first decimal place, $1.25 \approx 1.3$, $1.312\,5 \approx 1.3$.

Therefore, the estimated real zero of $f(x) = 4x^3 - 52x^2 + 153x - 119$ in the interval $x \in (1, 2)$ is 1.3.

练习 Exercise

1. Apply the long division algorithm to calculate.

   (1) $(4x^3 - 7x^2 - 11x + 5) \div (4x + 2)$.　　　　(2) $(x^3 - 9x + 1) \div (x^2 + 1)$.

2. Apply the synthetic division algorithm to calculate.

   (1) $(3x^3 - 17x^2 + 15x - 23) \div (x - 4)$.　　　　(2) $(5x^3 + 6x + 7) \div (x + 2)$.

3. Apply the Remainder Theorem and synthetic division to find each value. Verify your answers using another method.

   (1) $f(x) = 2x^3 - 5x + 3$, find $f(1)$, $f(-2)$, $f\left(\dfrac{1}{2}\right)$.

   (2) $f(x) = 4x^4 - 16x^3 + 7x^2 + 10$, find $f(-1)$, $f(2)$, $f(3)$.

4. Verify the given factors of $f(x)$, find the remaining factor(s) of $f(x)$, and use your results to write the complete factorization of $f(x)$.

   (1) Function: $f(x) = 2x^3 + 3x^2 - 3x - 2$, factors: $(x + 2)$, $(x - 1)$.

   (2) Function: $f(x) = x^4 - 2x^3 - 11x^2 + 6x + 24$, factors: $(x + 2)$, $(x - 4)$.

   (3) Function: $f(x) = 6x^3 + 17x^2 - 5x - 6$, factors: $(2x + 1)$, $(3x - 2)$.

5. There is a demand for certain type of gift boxes. Based on cost calculations, the volume V, of each box to be constructed can be modeled by the polynomial function $V(x) = x^3 + 6x^2 + 11x + 6$, where x is a positive integer such that $10 \leqslant x \leqslant 20$. The height h, of each box is a linear function of x such that $h(x) = x + 2$. Can you use this information to determine the dimensions of the boxes in terms of polynomials?

6. Perform the division by assuming that n is a positive integer: $\dfrac{x^{3n} + 9x^{2n} + 27x^n + 27}{x^n + 2}$.

7. Find the value of k such that $x - 4$ is a factor of $x^3 - kx^2 - 3kx - 8$.

8. According to the rational root theorem, what are the possible rational roots of each equation?

   (1) $2x^3 - 3x^2 + 9x - 4 = 0$.　　　　(2) $6x^4 - 2x^2 + 9x + 5 = 0$.

9. Find all the real zeros of the following functions.

   (1) $f(x) = 2x^3 - 5x^2 - 2x + 5$.

(2) $f(x) = 6x^4 - 7x^3 - 15x^2 + 14x + 6$.

10. Use a graphing calculator to estimate the zeros of the following functions (round your answer to the first decimal place).

(1) $f(x) = 2x^3 + x^2 + 4x - 14$.   (2) $f(x) = 0.23x^4 - 0.5x^3 - 3.4$.

11. Use bisection method to estimate the zero of the following functions (round your answer to the first decimal place).

(1) $f(x) = 2x^3 - 3x^2 - 18x + 28$, $x \in (1, 2)$.

(2) $f(x) = x^3 - 5x + 3$, $x \in (0, 1)$.

12. A wooden block is in the shape of a rectangular prism with dimensions $(a-3)$ cm, a cm, $(a+6)$ cm, for some integer a. The surface of the block is painted and the block is cut into 1 cm cubes by cuts parallel to the faces. If exactly half of these cubes have no paint on them, find the dimensions of original block.

13. If $ax^2 + bx + c = 0$ has roots r_1 and r_2, then: $r_1 + r_2 = -\dfrac{b}{a}$, $r_1 r_2 = \dfrac{c}{a}$. For the equation $a_n x^n + a_{n-1}x^{n-1} + a_{n-2}x^{n-2} + \cdots + a_0 = 0 (a_n \neq 0)$, can you state a similar relationship between the roots of a polynomial equation and the coefficients of the polynomial?

2.4 ◆ 多项式函数和多项式不等式
Polynomial Functions and Polynomial Inequalities

多项式函数是一类简单的初等函数.在实际问题中,遇到研究的两个变量 y 与 x 之间的依赖关系,往往需要通过实验或观测可得到这两个变量的对应数值.我们通常希望找到能尽量准确地反映 y 与 x 之间的依赖关系,且计算又比较简单的函数.如果我们知道 y 与 x 之间的依赖关系是一个很"光滑的"函数,则常常使用多项式函数来描述 y 与 x 之间的关系.

我们已经学过一次函数 $f(x) = 2x - 1$ 和二次函数 $g(x) = x^2 - 3x + 5$. 一次函数和二次函数都属于多项式函数.

多项式函数 Polynomial Functions

形如 $f(x) = a_n x^n + a_{n-1}x^{n-1} + \cdots + a_2 x^2 + a_1 x + a_0$,其中 $a_n, a_{n-1}, \cdots, a_2, a_1, a_0 \in \mathbf{R}, a_n \neq 0, n \in \mathbf{N}$,这样的函数叫作 **$n$ 次多项式函数**.

> A function $f(x)$ is called a **polynomial function of x with degree n**, if $f(x) = a_n x^n + a_{n-1}x^{n-1} + \cdots + a_2 x^2 + a_1 x + a_0$, where n is a non-negative integer and $a_n, a_{n-1}, \cdots, a_2, a_1, a_0$ are real numbers with $a_n \neq 0$.

The expressions $a_n x^n$, $a_{n-1}x^{n-1}$, $\cdots$, $a_2 x^2$, $a_1 x$, a_0 are called the **terms** of the polynomial, and the numbers a_n, a_{n-1}, $\cdots$, a_2, a_1, a_0 are called the coefficients of the polynomial.

We usually write them in descending powers of x. The term containing the highest power of x is called the **leading term**. The coefficient of the leading term is called the **leading coefficient**, and the power of x contained in the leading term is called the **degree** of the polynomial. Polynomials of the first few degrees have special names, as indicated in Table 2 - 2.

Table 2 - 2

Degree	Name	Degree	Name
0	Constant	3	Cubic
1	Linear	4	Quartic
2	Quadratic	5	Quintic

多项式函数的图像 Graphs of Polynomial Functions

多项式函数的图像都是连续的、光滑的. 在进一步认识多项式函数的图像时,我们重点关注以下两个方面:

1. 首项系数和次数

随着自变量 x 的向左或向右变化,多项式函数的图像都最终无限上升或无限下降. 图像最终上升或下降由函数的次数(奇次或者偶次)以及它的首项系数(正或者负)来决定.

As x moves without bound to the left or to the right, the graph of the polynomial function $f(x) = a_n x^n + a_{n-1} x^{n-1} + \cdots + a_2 x^2 + a_1 x + a_0$ eventually rises or falls in the following manner.

(1) When n is *odd*:

If the leading coefficient is positive ($a_n > 0$), then the graph falls to the left and rises to the right; If the leading coefficient is negative ($a_n < 0$), then the graph rises to the left and falls to the right.

(2) When n is *even*:

If the leading coefficient is positive ($a_n > 0$), then the graph rises to the left and to the right;

If the leading coefficient is negative ($a_n < 0$), then the graph falls to the left and to the right.

2. 零点

一般地,若 $(x-a)^k$,$k \geqslant 1$,$k \in \mathbf{N}$ 是多项式函数 $f(x)$ 的一个因式,则 $x = a$ 是一个 k 重零点:

当 k 是奇数时,函数图像在 $x = a$ 处穿过 x 轴;

当 k 是偶数时,函数图像在 $x = a$ 处与 x 轴相切.

A factor $(x-a)^k$,$k \geqslant 1$,$k \in \mathbf{N}$,yields a repeated zero $x = a$ of multiplicity k.

1. When k is odd, the graph crosses the x-axis at $x = a$.

2. When k is even, the graph touches the x-axis (but does not cross the x-axis) at $x = a$.

根据多项式函数只有在零点处可能改变符号这个事实,我们可以画出函数的大致图像. 在相邻两个零点之间,一个多项式函数一定完全是正的或者完全是负的. 也就是说,我们把多项式函数的零点按大小顺序排列,它们把数轴划分成若干区间,在每个区间上,函数的符号是确定的. 我们可以在每个区间上选取一个 x 的值,根据它所对应的函数值确定这个区间上函数值的符号.

1 Describe the right-hand and left-hand behavior of the graph of each function.

(1) $f(x) = -x^3 + 3x$.　　　　(2) $f(x) = x^4 - 4x^2 + 1$.　　　　(3) $f(x) = 2x^5 - x$.

Solution:

(1) Because the degree is odd and the leading coefficient is negative, the graph rises to the left and falls to the right, as shown in Figure 2 - 6.

(2) Because the degree is even and the leading coefficient is positive, the graph rises to the left

and to the right, as shown in Figure 2 - 7.

(3) Because the degree is odd and the leading coefficient is positive, the graph falls to the left and rises to the right, as shown in Figure 2 - 8.

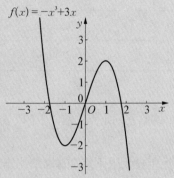

Figure 2 - 6

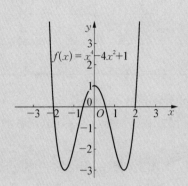

Figure 2 - 7

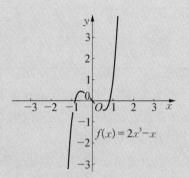

Figure 2 - 8

2 Sketch the graph of $f(x) = (x+2)(x-1)(x-2)$.

Solution：

Step 1. Find the real zeros of the function: The real zeros of $f(x)$ are $x = -2$, $x = 1$ and $x = 2$. So, the x-intercepts are $(-2, 0)$, $(1, 0)$ and $(2, 0)$. Plot the zeros on a number line. See Figure 2 - 9.

Step 2. Form a sign chart of $f(x)$. See Table 2 - 3.

Figure 2 - 9

Table 2 - 3

Test Interval	$(-\infty, -2)$	$(-2, 1)$	$(1, 2)$	$(2, +\infty)$
Sign of $f(x)$	$-$	$+$	$-$	$+$

Step 3. Sketch the graph: Draw a continuous curve through the x-intercepts. Step 1 gives you the x-intercepts of the graph, and Step 2 tells you where the graph is above or below the x-axis. Because the leading coefficient is positive and the degree is odd, you know that the graph eventually falls to the left and rises to the right. As indicated by the multiplicities of the zeros, the graph should cross the x-axis at $x = -2$, $x = 1$ and $x = 2$. See Figure 2 - 10.

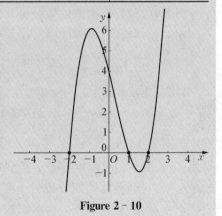

Figure 2 - 10

3 Sketch the graph of $f(x) = -2x^3 + 10x^2 - \dfrac{25}{2}x$.

Solution：

Step 1. Find the real zeros of the function. By factoring

$$f(x) = -2x^3 + 10x^2 - \frac{25}{2}x = -\frac{1}{2}x(4x^2 - 20x + 25) = -\frac{1}{2}x(2x-5)^2.$$

The real zeros of $f(x)$ are $x=0$ and $x=\dfrac{5}{2}$. So, the x-intercepts are $(0, 0)$ and $\left(\dfrac{5}{2}, 0\right)$.

Step 2. Form the sign chart of $f(x)$. See Table 2 – 4.

Table 2 – 4

Test Interval	$(-\infty, 0)$	$\left(0, \dfrac{5}{2}\right)$	$\left(\dfrac{5}{2}, +\infty\right)$
Sign of $f(x)$	$+$	$-$	$-$

Step 3. Sketch the graph: Draw a continuous curve through the x-intercepts. Step 1 gives you the x-intercepts of the graph, and Step 2 tells you where the graph is above or below the x-axis. Because the leading coefficient is negative and the degree is odd, you know that the graph eventually rises to the left and falls to the right. As indicated by the multiplicities of the zeros, the graph crosses the x-axis at $x=0$ but does not cross the x-axis at $x=\dfrac{5}{2}$. See Figure 2 – 11.

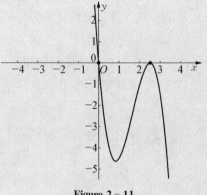

Figure 2 – 11

4 Sketch the graph of $f(x)=x^6-7x^5+16x^4-12x^3$.

Solution:

Step 1. Find the real zeros of the function:
$$f(x)=x^6-7x^5+16x^4-12x^3=x^3(x^3-7x^2+16x-12)=x^3(x-2)^2(x-3).$$

The real zeros of $f(x)$ are $x=0$, $x=2$ and $x=3$. So, the x-intercepts are $(0, 0)$, $(2, 0)$ and $(3, 0)$.

Step 2. Form the sign chart of $f(x)$. See Table 2 – 5.

Table 2 – 5

Test Interval	$(-\infty, 0)$	$(0, 2)$	$(2, 3)$	$(3, +\infty)$
Sign of $f(x)$	$+$	$-$	$-$	$+$

Step 3. Sketch the graph: Draw a continuous curve through the x-intercepts. Step 1 gives you the x-intercepts of the graph, and Step 2 tells you where the graph is above or below the x-axis. Because the leading coefficient is negative and the degree is odd, you know that the graph eventually rises to the left and falls to the right. As indicated by the multiplicities of the zeros, the graph crosses the x-axis at $x=0$ and $x=3$, but does not cross the x-axis at $x=2$. See Figure 2 – 12.

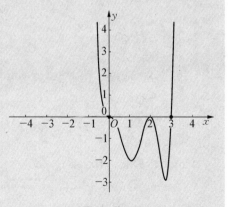

Figure 2 – 12

Notes: If a polynomial $f(x)$ has a squared factor $(x-a)^2$, then $x=a$ is a double root of $f(x)=0$. In this case, the graph of $y=f(x)$ is tangent to the x-axis at $x=a$.

If a polynomial $f(x)$ has a cubed factor $(x-a)^3$, then $x=a$ is a triple root of $f(x)=0$. In this case, the graph of $y=f(x)$ flattens out around $(a, 0)$ and crosses the x-axis at $x=a$.

多项式不等式 Polynomial Inequalities

如果 $f(x)$ 是一个多项式,则不等式 $f(x)>0$ 和 $f(x)<0$ 叫作**多项式不等式**.

Let $f(x)$ be any polynomial. Then $f(x)>0$ and $f(x)<0$ are called **polynomial inequalities.**

解高次多项式不等式的步骤如下:

把不等式等价变形为不等号一边是零,一边是各因式的积的形式,把各因式的根标在数轴上(通常将未知数的最高次项系数转化正数).

对多项式函数零点所形成的各个区间进行符号判断. 可以采取在各个区间任取一个点测试其函数值符号的方法,也可以采用**曲线穿根法**,即当未知数的最高次项系数为正时,由右至左,由上至下,逐一经过各根,在奇次根处穿过轴,在偶次根处不穿过轴,根据曲线在轴的上方或下方,判断区间函数值为正或负.

5 Solve $x^3 - x^2 - 2x < 0$.

Solution:

Step 1. Find zeros of the polynomial:
$$f(x) = x^3 - x^2 - 2x = x(x^2 - x - 2) = x(x-2)(x+1).$$

The zeros are $x=-1$, $x=0$ and $x=2$.

Plot the zeros on a number line. Use open dots since $f(x)$ is strictly less than zero. See Figure 2-13.

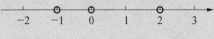

Figure 2-13

Step 2. Find the sign of $f(x)$ in each interval. See Table 2-6 and Figure 2-14.

Table 2-6

Test Interval	$(-\infty, -1)$	$(-1, 0)$	$(0, 2)$	$(2, +\infty)$
Sign of $f(x)$	$-$	$+$	$-$	$+$

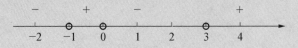

Figure 2-14

The solution set of $f(x) < 0$ is $(-\infty, -1) \bigcup (0, 2)$.

6 Solve $(x^2 - 1)(x-3)^2 \geqslant 0$.

Solution:

Step 1. Find zeros of the polynomial: $f(x) = (x^2 - 1)(x-3)^2 = (x+1)(x-1)(x-3)^2$.

The zeros are $x=-1$, $x=1$ and $x=3$.

Since $f(x)$ is greater than or equal to zero, use solid dots to plot zeros.

Step 2. Find the sign of $f(x)$ in each interval. See Table 2-7 and Figure 2-15.

Table 2 - 7

Test Interval	$(-\infty, -1)$	$(-1, 1)$	$(1, 3)$	$(3, +\infty)$
Sign of $f(x)$	+	−	+	+

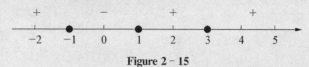

Figure 2 - 15

The solution set of $f(x) \geqslant 0$ is $(-\infty, -1] \cup [1, +\infty)$.

Notes: A polynomial $f(x)$ will change sign at a zero a if a corresponds to the factor $(x-a)^k$ where k is odd, and $f(x)$ will not change sign at a zero a if a corresponds to the factor $(x-a)^k$ where k is even.

7 Solve $(x+1)^2(-x+2)(x-1)^3(x-3) \leqslant 0$.

Solution:

Step 1. The inequality $(x+1)^2(-x+2)(x-1)^3(x-3) \leqslant 0$ is equivalent to $(x+1)^2(x-2)(x-1)^3(x-3) \geqslant 0$.

The zeros of $f(x) - (x+1)^2(x-2)(x-1)^3(x-3)$ are $x=-1$, $x=1$, $x=2$ and $x=3$.

Since $f(x)$ is greater than or equal to zero, use solid dots to plot zeros.

Step 2. Find the sign of $f(x)$ in each interval. Draw a continuous curve from the upper right side of the axis, through all the dots. As indicated by the multiplicities of the zeros, the curve crosses the axis at $x=1$, $x=2$ and $x=3$, but tangent to the axis at $x=$ −1. See Figure 2 - 16.

The solution set is $\{-1\} \cup [1, 2] \cup [3, +\infty)$.

Figure 2 - 16

练习 Exercise

1. Match the polynomial function with its graph.

(1) $f(x) = -2x^2 - 3x$.

(2) $f(x) = 2x^3 - 4x + 1$.

(3) $f(x) = -\dfrac{1}{3}x^4 + 2x^2$.

(4) $f(x) = -\dfrac{1}{3}x^3 + x^2 - \dfrac{4}{3}$.

(5) $f(x) = x^4 + \dfrac{5}{2}x^3$.

(6) $f(x) = \dfrac{1}{4}x^5 - 2x^3 + \dfrac{7}{4}x$.

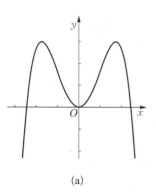

(a)

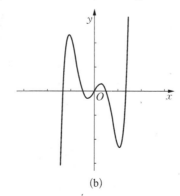

(b)

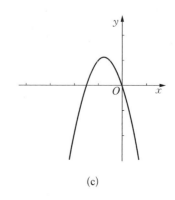

(c)

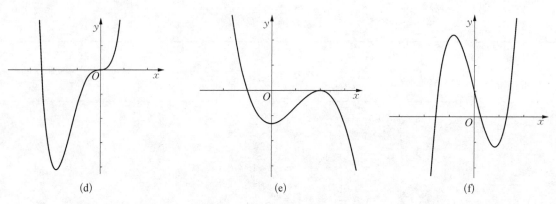

(d)　　　　　(e)　　　　　(f)

Figure 2 - 17

2. Determine whether the statement is True or False. Justify your answer.

　(1) If $f(x)$ is a polynomial function of x such that $f(1)=-6$ and $f(5)=6$, then $f(x)$ has at most one real zero between $x=1$ and $x=5$.

　(2) If the graph of a polynomial function falls to the right, then its leading coefficient is negative.

　(3) If the graph of a polynomial function rises to the left, then its leading coefficient is positive.

　(4) A sixth degree polynomial function has at most six real zeros.

3. Sketch the graph of the following function.

　(1) $f(x)=x^3-9x$. 　　　　(2) $f(x)=-x^3+3x^2$.

　(3) $g(x)=x^3(x-3)^2$. 　　　　(4) $h(x)=-\dfrac{1}{5}(x+3)^2(x-3)^2$.

4. Sketch the graph of the function $f(x)=-\dfrac{1}{2}x^6-\dfrac{5}{2}x^5-3x^4+2x^3+4x^2$.

5. Give an equation of each polynomial graph shown.

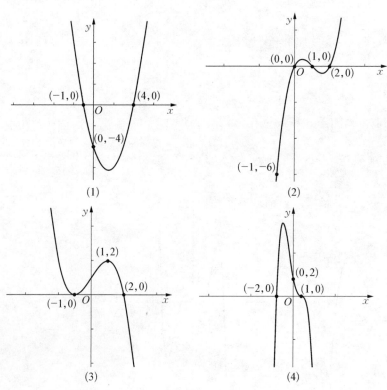

(1)　　　　　(2)

(3)　　　　　(4)

Figure 2 - 18

6. Find an equation of the quartic function whose graph goes through the point $(0, 3)$ and is tangent to the x-axis at $(-3, 0)$ and $(2, 0)$.

7. If $f(x)$ is a cubic polynomial such that $f(0)=0$, $f(3)=-4$ and $f(x)$ is positive only when $x > 5$, find $f(x)$.

8. Solve the polynomial inequalities：
   (1) $x^3 + 3x^2 > 2x + 6$.

   (2) $(x^2 - 4x - 5)(x^2 + x - 2) < 0$.

   (3) $(x+2)^2 (-x+1)^3 (x+1)(x-2) > 0$.

   (4) $2x^3 + 13x^2 - 8x \geqslant 52$.

9. Growth of a Yeast Culture：The data in Table $2-8$ represent the population of a yeast cells in a culture measured over time (in hours)：

Table 2 - 8

Time	0	3	6	9	12	15	18
Population	9.6	47.2	174.6	441	594.8	651.1	661.8

(1) Use a graphing utility to create a scatter plot of the data.

(2) Use the regression feature of the graphing utility to find a cubic model for the data. (A cubic model has the form $ax^3 + bx^2 + cx + d$ where a, b, c and d are constant and x is variable.)

(3) According to the model，the when did the population of a yeast cells in the culture exceed 300?

2.5 ◆ 分式不等式 & 绝对值不等式的解法
Rational Inequalities & Absolute Value Inequalities

分式不等式 Rational Inequalities

像 $\dfrac{f(x)}{g(x)} < 0$ 或 $\dfrac{f(x)}{g(x)} > 0$(其中 $f(x)$、$g(x)$ 为整式且 $g(x)$ 不为 0)这样,分母中含有未知数的不等式称为分式不等式.

> A **rational function** is a quotient of polynomial functions. It can be written in the form of $f(x) = \dfrac{N(x)}{D(x)}$, where $N(x)$ and $D(x)$ are polynomials and $D(x)$ is not the zero polynomial.
>
> Let $f(x)$ be any rational function. Then $f(x) > 0$ or $f(x) < 0$ are called **rational inequalities.**

实际上, 由于 $\dfrac{f(x)}{g(x)} > 0$ (or < 0)$\Leftrightarrow f(x)g(x) > 0$ (or < 0), $\dfrac{f(x)}{g(x)} \geqslant 0$ (or $\leqslant 0$)$\Leftrightarrow$ $\begin{cases} f(x)g(x) \geqslant 0 \text{ (or } \leqslant 0) \\ g(x) \neq 0 \end{cases}$, 我们可以把分式不等式转化为多项式不等式求解.

1 Solve $\dfrac{2x-3}{3x-2} < 0$.

Solution 1：

$\dfrac{2x-3}{3x-2} < 0$ is equivalent to (1) $\begin{cases} 2x-3 > 0 \\ 3x-2 < 0 \end{cases}$, or (2) $\begin{cases} 2x-3 < 0 \\ 3x-2 > 0 \end{cases}$.

Then the solution set of (1) is $\varnothing$ and the solution set of (2) is $\left(\dfrac{2}{3}, \dfrac{3}{2}\right)$, so the solution set of

$\dfrac{2x-3}{3x-2} < 0$ is $\left(\dfrac{2}{3}, \dfrac{3}{2}\right)$.

Solution 2:

We can know the solution set of $\dfrac{2x-3}{3x-2} < 0$ is equivalent to the solution set of $(2x-3)(3x-$

$2) < 0$. The solution set of $(2x-3)(3x-2) < 0$ is $\left(\dfrac{2}{3}, \dfrac{3}{2}\right)$, whence the solution set of $\dfrac{2x-3}{3x-2} < 0$ is

$\left(\dfrac{2}{3}, \dfrac{3}{2}\right)$.

2 Solve $\dfrac{2x-7}{x-5} \leqslant 3$.

Solution:

Rewrite the inequality as $\dfrac{2x-7-3(x-5)}{x-5} \leqslant 0$, or equivalently $\dfrac{x-8}{x-5} \geqslant 0$.

Since the rational inequality $\dfrac{x-8}{x-5} \geqslant 0$ has the same solution set as the system of polynomial

inequalities $\begin{cases} (x-8)(x-5) \geqslant 0 \\ x-5 \neq 0 \end{cases}$, the solution set of the inequality is $(-\infty, 5) \cup [8, +\infty)$.

3 Solve $\dfrac{(x+2)(x-5)^2}{x-4} \leqslant 0$.

Solution:

Since the inequality is equivalent to the system of polynomial inequalities $\begin{cases} (x+2)(x-5)^2(x-4) \leqslant 0, \\ x-4 \neq 0 \end{cases}$

we can construct a curve as we did when solving the polynomial inequalities. See Figure 2‑19.

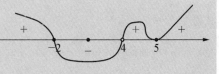

Therefore, the solution set of $\dfrac{(x+2)(x-5)^2}{x-4} \leqslant 0$ is

$[-2, 4) \cup \{5\}$.

Figure 2‑19

4 Solve $\dfrac{x^2-9x+11}{x^2-2x+1} \geqslant 7$.

Solution:

Rewrite the inequality as $\dfrac{x^2-9x+11-7(x^2-2x+1)}{x^2-2x+1} \geqslant 0$, equivalently $\dfrac{6x^2-5x-4}{x^2-2x+1} \leqslant 0$.

Since the inequality is equivalent to the system of polynomial inequalities

$\begin{cases} (2x+1)(3x-4)(x-1)^2 \leqslant 0 \\ (x-1)^2 \neq 0 \end{cases}$, the solution set of the inequality is $\left[-\dfrac{1}{2}, 1\right) \cup \left(1, \dfrac{4}{3}\right]$.

5 What is the range of k such that the inequality $\dfrac{2x^2+2kx+k}{4x^2+6x+3} < 1$ holds for all $x \in \mathbf{R}$?

Solution：

Rewrite the inequality as $\dfrac{2x^2+(6-2k)x+(3-k)}{4x^2+6x+3}>0$. Since $4x^2+6x+3>0$, the rational

inequality $\dfrac{2x^2+(6-2k)x+(3-k)}{4x^2+6x+3}>0$ has the same solution set as the inequality $2x^2+(6-2k)x+(3-k)>0$. As $\Delta=(6-2k)^2-4\times2\times(3-k)<0$, we have $1<k<3$.

Therefore, the range of k is $(1,3)$.

绝对值不等式 Absolute Value Inequalities

The absolute value of a real number x, denoted $|x|$, can be interpreted geometrically as the distance from x to zero in either direction on the number line.

$$|x|=\begin{cases} x & (x>0) \\ 0 & (x=0) \\ -x & (x<0) \end{cases}$$

The distance on the number line between the numbers a and b is $|a-b|$.

由绝对值的几何意义可知，求不等式 $|x|<a(a>0)$ 的解集就是求在数轴上到原点的距离小于 a 的点所对应的实数 x 的集合. 所以不等式 $|x|<a(a>0)$ 的解集为 $(-a,a)$. 类似地，可以得到不等式 $|x|>a(a>0)$ 的解集为 $(-\infty,-a)\cup(a,+\infty)$. 见 Table 2-9.

Table 2-9

Inequality	Meaning	Graph	Solution
$|x|<a(a>0)$	The distance from x to 0 is less than a units.		$-a<x<a$
$|x|>a(a>0)$	The distance from x to 0 is greater than a units.		$x<-a$ or $x>a$

Absolute value inequalities $|f(x)|<a(a>0)$ and $|f(x)|>a(a>0)$ can be transformed as shown in Table 2-10.

Table 2-10

Inequality	Equivalent Inequality
$|f(x)|<a(a>0)$	$-a<f(x)<a$
$|f(x)|>a(a>0)$	$f(x)<-a$ or $f(x)>a$

6 Solve $|3-2x|<5$.

Solution： $|3-2x|<5$ is equivalent to $-5<3-2x<5$, then $-1<x<4$. Therefore, the solution set is $(-1,4)$.

7 Solve $|2x-1|+3\geqslant8$.

Solution: From $|2x-1|+3\geqslant 8$, we can get $|2x-1|\geqslant 5$, which is equivalent to $2x-1\leqslant -5$ or $2x-1\geqslant 5$. So the solution set is $(-\infty,-2]\cup[3,+\infty)$.

8 Solve $\left|\dfrac{2x-3}{x+2}\right|>1$.

Solution：

$\left|\dfrac{2x-3}{x+2}\right|>1$ is equivalent to $|2x-3|>|x+2|$ and $x+2\neq 0$.

Equivalently, $\begin{cases}(2x-3)^2>(x+2)^2\\x+2\neq 0\end{cases}$. So the solution set is $(-\infty,-2)\cup\left(-2,\dfrac{1}{3}\right)\cup(5,+\infty)$.

9 Solve $|x^2-5x+5|<1$.

Solution 1：

$|x^2-5x+5|<1$ is equivalent to $\begin{cases}x^2-5x+5<1\\x^2-5x+5>-1\end{cases}$.

So the solution set of $|x^2-5x+5|<1$ is $(1,2)\cup(3,4)$.

Solution 2：

From $|x^2-5x+5|<1$, we can get $(x^2-5x+5)^2<1$. By writing the inequality in general form and factoring it, we have $(x-2)(x-3)(x-4)(x-1)<0$. So the solution set of $|x^2-5x+5|<1$ is $(1,2)\cup(3,4)$.

10 Solve $2<|x^2-2x-1|<7$.

Solution 1：

Rewrite $2<|x^2-2x-1|<7$ as $\begin{cases}|x^2-2x-1|>2\\|x^2-2x-1|<7\end{cases}$, which is equivalent to $\begin{cases}x^2-2x-1<-2\text{ or }x^2-2x-1>2\\-7<x^2-2x-1<7\end{cases}$.

So the solution set of $2<|x^2-2x-1|<7$ is $(-2,-1)\cup(3,4)$.

Solution 2：

$2<|x^2-2x-1|<7$ is equivalent to $2<x^2-2x-1<7$ or $-7<x^2-2x-1<-2$.

So the solution set of $2<|x^2-2x-1|<7$ is $(-2,-1)\cup(3,4)$.

11 Solve $|x+2|+|x-1|<4$.

Solution 1： The real numbers are divided into three parts by $x=-2$ and $x=-1$：$x<-2$, $-2\leqslant x<1$ and $x\geqslant 1$.

When $x<-2$, $|x+2|+|x-1|<4$ is equivalent to $-x-2-x+1<4$, so $-\dfrac{5}{2}<x<-2$.

When $-2\leqslant x<1$, $|x+2|+|x-1|<4$ is equivalent to $x+2-x+1<4$, so $-2\leqslant x<1$.

When $x\geqslant 1$, $|x+2|+|x-1|<4$ is equivalent to $x+2+x-1<4$, so $1\leqslant x<\dfrac{3}{2}$.

Therefore, the solution set of $|x+2|+|x-1|<4$ is $\left(-\dfrac{5}{2},\dfrac{3}{2}\right)$.

Solution 2: The geometric meaning of the inequality $|x+2|+|x-1|<4$ is that the sum of the distances from x to -2 and 1 is less than 4 units.

As shown in Figure 2-20, we can get the points A_1 and B_1, and the sum of the distances from each point on the line segment A_1B_1 (exclude the endpoints) to -2 and 1 is less than 4 units.

So the solution set of $|x+2|+|x-1|<4$ is $\left(-\dfrac{5}{2}, \dfrac{3}{2}\right)$.

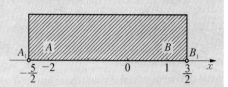

Figure 2-20

12 Solve $|2x-1|<2m-1(m\in \mathbf{R})$.

Solution:

If $2m-1\leqslant 0$, $|2x-1|<2m-1$ does not hold. So the solution set of $|2x-1|<2m-1$ is $\varnothing$ when $m\leqslant \dfrac{1}{2}$.

If $2m-1>0$, $|2x-1|<2m-1$ is equivalent to $-(2m-1)<2x-1<2m-1$, then $1-m<x<m$. So the solution set of $|2x-1|<2m-1$ is $(1-m, m)$, when $m>\dfrac{1}{2}$.

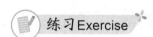

练习 Exercise

1. Solve the following rational inequalities.

   (1) $\dfrac{(x-3)(x-4)}{(x-5)(x-6)^2}<0$.

   (2) $\dfrac{(2x-5)^3}{x^2-3x-28}\geqslant 0$.

   (3) $x>\dfrac{1}{x}$.

   (4) $\dfrac{(x-2)^2(x+1)^3}{x^2+x+1}>0$.

   (5) $\dfrac{15x^2-11x+2}{-2x^2+3x+2}<0$.

   (6) $\dfrac{5-x}{x^2-2x-3}<-1$.

2. If $m>n>0$, find the solution set of the inequality $\dfrac{(mx-n)(x-2)}{x-1}\geqslant 0$.

3. What is the range of k such that the inequality $\dfrac{2x^2+2kx+k}{4x^2+6x+3}<1$ always holds?

4. Solve the following inequalities.

   (1) $|6-3x|<12$.

   (2) $|3x-9|\geqslant 9$.

5. Solve the following inequalities.

   (1) $2<|x-6|\leqslant 5$.

   (2) $0<|x-3|<1$.

6. Solve the following inequalities.

   (1) $|x|+|x-2|>5$.

   (2) $|x-1|+|x-5|<7$.

7. Solve the following inequalities.

   (1) $|x-3|<x-2$.

   (2) $x-1<|x^2+x+1|$.

   (3) $\dfrac{1}{|2x-3|}\leqslant 2$.

   (4) $\left|\dfrac{2x+3}{3x-2}\right|\geqslant 1$.

8. If the inequality $|x+1|+|x+2| \geqslant m$ holds for all $x \in \mathbf{R}$, find the range of m.

9. (1) Give three examples illustrating the triangle inequality: $|a+b| \leqslant |a|+|b|$.

   (2) Use the triangle inequality stated in (1) to prove $|a-b| \leqslant |a|+|b|$ and $|a|-|b| \leqslant |a+b|$.

第 3 章

函数 Functions

3.1 ◇ 函数的概念与函数关系的建立
Functions and Modeling

函数 Function

设 A、B 是非空数集,如果按照某个确定的对应关系 f,使得对于集合 A 中的任意一个数 x,在集合 B 中都有唯一确定的数 y 与之对应,那么就称 $f: A \rightarrow B$ 为集合 A 到集合 B 的一个**函数**,记作 $y = f(x)$,$x \in A$,其中,x 叫作自变量,x 的取值范围 A 叫作函数的**定义域**;与 A 的值相对应的 y 值叫作函数值,函数值的集合 $\{y \mid y = f(x), x \in A\}$ 叫作函数的**值域**,值域是集合 B 的子集.

> **Definition of Function**
>
> A **function** f is a mapping that assigns to each element in a set A a unique element in a set B. The set A is the **domain** (or set of inputs) of the function, and the set B contains the **range** (or set of outputs).

The Figure 3 – 1 shows a function f mapping, or pairing, a domain element x to a range element $f(x)$, read "the value of f at x" or "f of x". Although f names the function and $f(x)$ gives its value at x, we sometimes refer to the function $f(x)$, thereby indicating both the function f and the variable x of its domain.

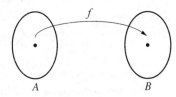

Figure 3 – 1

> **Characteristics of a Function from Set A to Set B**
>
> Each element in A must be matched with an element in B.
>
> An element in A can not be matched with two different elements in B.
>
> Some elements in B may not be matched with any element in A.
>
> Two or more elements in A may be matched with the same element in B.

We can treat a function f as a set of ordered pairs (x, y) such that x is an element of the domain of f and y is the corresponding element of the range. This is written formally as $\{(x, y) \mid y = f(x)\}$ or more simply as $y = f(x)$.

f is the name of the function.

x is the **independent variable**.

y is the **dependent variable**.

$f(x)$ is the value of the function at x.

Although the letters f, x and y are commonly used in general discussions of functions, other letters can be used.

Four common ways to represent functions are as follows.

Four Ways to Represent a Function

① **Verbally** by a sentence that describes how the input variable is related to the output variable.

② **Numerically** by a table or a list of ordered pairs that matched input values with output values.

③ **Graphically** by points on a graph in a coordinate plane in which the horizontal axis represents the input and the vertical axis represents the output values.

④ **Algebraically** by an equation in two variables.

1 Which of the equations represents y as a function of x?

(1) $2x^2 + y = 2$ (2) $2x + y^2 = 2$

Solution:

To determine whether y is a function of x, try to solve for y in terms of x.

(1) Solving for y yields $y = -2x^2 + 2$.

To each value of x there corresponds exactly one value of y.

So y is a function of x.

(2) Solving for y yields $y = \pm\sqrt{2 - 2x}$.

The $\pm$ indicates that to certain value of x there are two corresponding values of y. So, y is not a function of x.

2 (1) Let $f(x) = x^2 + 2x - 3$. Find the value of $f(-3)$, $f(a)$ and $f(a-1)$.

(2) Given $f(a-2) = a^2 + 1$, $a \in \mathbf{R}$. Find the expression of $f(x)$.

Solution:

(1) Replacing x with 3 in $f(x)$ yields $f(3) = (-3)^2 + 2 \times (-3) - 3 = 0$.

Replacing x with a yields $f(a) = a^2 + 2a - 3$.

Replacing x with a yields $f(a-1) = (a-1)^2 + 2(a-1) - 3 = a^2 - 2a + 1 + 2a - 2 - 3 = a^2 - 4$.

(2) Let $t = a - 2$, then $a = t + 2$. Since $a \in \mathbf{R}$, we can conclude $t \in \mathbf{R}$.

$f(t) = (t+2)^2 + 1 = t^2 + 4t + 5$.

So, $f(x) = x^2 + 4x + 5$, $x \in \mathbf{R}$.

3 Evaluate the piece-wisely defined function at $x = -1$, 0 and 1.

$$f(x) = \begin{cases} 2x^2 + x - 1 & x < 0 \\ 3x - 4 & x \geqslant 0 \end{cases}.$$

Solution:

Because $x = -1$ is less than 0, use $f(x) = 2x^2 + x - 1$ to obtain $f(-1) = 2 \times (-1)^2 + (-1) - 1 = 0$.

For $x = 0$, use $f(x) = 3x - 4$ to obtain $f(0) = 0 - 4 = -4$.

For $x = 1$, use $f(x) = 3x - 4$ to obtain $f(1) = 3 - 4 = -1$.

Remark: A function is fully described in terms of a rule and a domain. The domain of a function can be described explicitly or it can be implied by the expression used to define the function. If a domain is not described explicitly, we use the natural domain, which is the set of all real numbers for which the expression is defined.

4 Find the domain of each function.

(1) $g(x) = \dfrac{1}{2x - 6}$.

(2) $h(x) = \sqrt{4 + 5x}$.

Solution:

(1) Since $\dfrac{1}{2x - 6}$ is not defined when the denominator is 0, the domain of g is the set of all real number except for 3, which is $\{x \mid x \neq 3\} = (-\infty, 3) \cup (3, +\infty)$.

(2) This function is defined only for x-values for which $4 + 5x \geqslant 0$. By solving the inequality, we can conclude that $x \geqslant -\dfrac{4}{5}$. So, the domain is the interval $\left[-\dfrac{4}{5}, +\infty \right)$.

5 An isosceles triangle ABC has two equal sides with the lengths of 4 cm and a variable altitude. Let the altitude be denoted by x cm. See Figure 3 - 2.

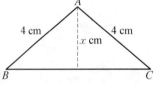

Figure 3 - 2

(1) Write the perimeter P as a function of the altitude x.

(2) Write the area A as a function of the altitude x.

Solution: (1) $P(x) = 8 + 2\sqrt{16 - x^2}$, $x \in (0, 4)$.

(2) $A(x) = x\sqrt{16 - x^2}$, $x \in (0, 4)$.

6 A company produces a product for which the variable cost is \$20.53 per unit and the fixed costs are \$79 800. The product sells for \$27.98. Let x be the number of units produced and sold.

(1) The total cost for a business is the sum of the variable cost and the fixed costs. Write the total cost C as a function of the number of units produced.

(2) Write the revenue R as a function of the number of units sold.

(3) Write the profit P as a function of the number of units sold. (Note: $P = R - C$)

Solution: (1) $C = 20.53x + 79\,800$, $x \in [0, +\infty)$.

(2) $R = 27.98x$, $x \in [0, +\infty)$.

(3) $P = R - C = 27.98x - (20.53x + 98\,000) = 7.45x - 98\,000$, $x \in [0, +\infty)$.

7 The Individual Income Tax Law (IIT Law) 2018 clearly stipulate that a tax resident shall pay Chinese IIT on his or her income derived from China and overseas. For comprehensive income, the progressive tax rate ranging from 3% to 45% shall be applied.

"Taxable Income" in Table 3 - 1 is the balance of monthly salary minus CNY 5 000. For example, if the monthly salary or the wage is CNY 9 000, the taxable income is CNY 4 000. It can be seen from the tax rate table that the tax rate of RMB 3 000 is 3% and the tax rate of RMB 1 000 is 10%, so the individual income tax is $3\,000 \times 3\% + 1\,000 \times 10\% = 190$ yuan.

Table 3 - 1 Tax Rate Table for Comprehensive Income

Bracket	Taxable Income (Tax Included)	Rate(%)
1	Not over CNY 3 000	3
2	Over CNY 3 000 to 12 000	10
3	Over CNY 12 000 to 25 000	20
4	Over CNY 25 000 to 35 000	25
5	Over CNY 35 000 to 55 000	30
6	Over CNY 55 000 to 80 000	35
7	Over CNY 80 000	45

(1) Find the function of individual income tax (y) about salary and wage income x ($0 \leqslant x \leqslant 50\,000$).

(2) The individual income tax paid by a person is 1 500 yuan a month. How much is his salary in that month?

Solution: (1) The function expression is:

$$y = \begin{cases} 0 & x \in [0,\ 5\,000] \\ (x - 5\,000) \times 3\% & x \in (5\,000,\ 8\,000] \\ 90 + (x - 8\,000) \times 10\% & x \in (8\,000,\ 17\,000] \\ 990 + (x - 17\,000) \times 20\% & x \in (17\,000,\ 30\,000] \\ 3\,590 + (x - 30\,000) \times 25\% & x \in (30\,000,\ 40\,000] \\ 6\,090 + (x - 40\,000) \times 30\% & x \in (40\,000,\ 60\,000] \end{cases}$$

(2) Suppose the salary is x, when the tax paid is 1 500 yuan, by the expression above, we have the range of x, which is (17 000, 30 000). By solving the equation $990 + (x - 17\,000) \times 20\% = 1\,500$, we get $x = 19\,550$.

So, the salary in that month is 19 550 yuan.

8 A shopping mall launched a promotion during the festival, "For every 100 yuan, you'll have 30 yuan off.", for example, the consumption amount is 180 yuan and the deduction is 30 yuan, and the actual payment is 150 yuan; the consumption amount of 200 yuan is deducted by 60 yuan, and the actual payment is 140 yuan. And so on.

(1) Find the function for the actual payment y and the consumption amount x.

(2) If the amount of consumption is different, can the actual payment be the same?

Solution:

(1) Let x be the consumption amount, y be the actual payment.

We use $[x]$ to express the largest integer which is no more than x, for example $[3.1] = 4$, $[4] = 4$, $[-0.5] = -1$.

Then $y = x - \left[\dfrac{x}{100}\right] \times 30$, $x \in [0,\ +\infty)$.

(2) If the consumption amount is different, the actual payment can be the same. For example, for the consumption amount is 170 yuan, the actual payment is 140 yuan; and for the consumption amount is 200 yuan, the actual payment is also 140 yuan.

9 There is a cylindrical cup with no lid, its inner surface area is 100 cm². Find the function of its capacity V (cm³) about the radius of the inner base x (cm).

Solution: Let height of the cup be h cm, then we have

$$100 = \pi x^2 + 2\pi x h.$$

Solving for h yields $h = \dfrac{100 - \pi x^2}{2\pi x}$.

Therefore, $V = \pi x^2 h = \pi x^2 \cdot \dfrac{100 - \pi x^2}{2\pi x} = 50x - \dfrac{\pi x^3}{2}$.

By $x > 0$ and $\pi x^2 < 100$, we get $0 < x < \dfrac{10\sqrt{\pi}}{\pi}$.

So the function is $V = 50x - \dfrac{\pi x^3}{2}$, $x \in \left(0, \dfrac{10\sqrt{\pi}}{\pi}\right)$.

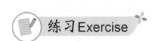

1. Determine whether the relation or equation represents y as a function of x.

(1)

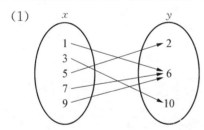

(2)

(3) $y + \pi = 0$.

(4) $x - 2 = 0$.

(5) $y = |x - 2|$.

(6) $|y| = x - 2$.

(7) $x^2 + y - 3 = 0$.

(8) $(x - 2)^2 + (y + 2)^2 = 4$.

2. For the numbers 2 through 9 on the phone keyboard (see the picture), create two relations: one that maps numbers to letters, and one that maps letters to numbers. Are both relations functions? Explain.

3. Evaluate functions. Complete the following table.

(1) $f(x) = -x^2 + 2$.

x	-2	-1	0	1	2
$f(x)$					

(2) $g(t) = \dfrac{1}{3} \mid t - 3 \mid$.

t	-3	0	3	6	9
$g(t)$					

(3) $h(s) = \begin{cases} 5 - s^2 & s < 1 \\ s + 3 & s \geqslant 1 \end{cases}$.

s	-2	-1	0	1	2
$h(s)$					

4. Finding the domain for the following functions:

(1) $f(x) = -4x^2 + 5x - 7$.　　　　　(2) $f(x) = \dfrac{1}{x} - 1$.

(3) $f(x) = \sqrt{2x - 5}$.　　　　　(4) $f(x) = \dfrac{1}{x - 2} - \dfrac{5}{x + 2}$.

(5) $f(x) = \dfrac{2\sqrt{x - 1}}{3x - 4}$.　　　　　(6) $f(x) = \dfrac{2x + 3}{\sqrt{x - 6}}$.

5. A rectangle is bounded by the x-axis and the semicircle $y = \sqrt{4 - x^2}$ (see Figure 3-3). Write the area S of the rectangle as a function of x and graphically determine the domain of the function.

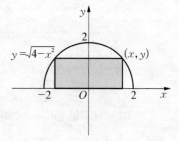

Figure 3-3

6. A cake factory produces a cake for which the cost is 40 yuan per piece while the price is 60 yuan per piece with a daily sale of 1 000 pieces. In order to meet the market demand, they plan to improve the cake's grade and increase the cost moderately. If the percentage increase in the cost of each cake is x ($0 < x < 1$), the percentage increase in the factory price of each cake is $0.5x$, while the expected percentage increase in daily sales is $0.8x$. Given that "daily profit = (factory price $-$ cost) $\times$ daily sales", let the daily profit after cost increased be y.

(1) Write the expression of y about x;

(2) In order to increase the daily profit, find the range of x.

7. Let $ABCD$ be an isosceles trapezoid with base angle $45°$. The length of BC is 7 cm, while the length of legs is $2\sqrt{2}$ cm. When a line l, perpendicular to BC with foot F, move from left to

right，the line l cut the trapezium into two parts (see Figure 3 - 4). Let $BF = x$，write the function expression of the area of left part y about x.

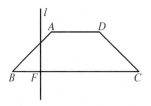

Figure 3 - 4

8. (1) Think about what it means for two functions to be **equal**.

(2) Would you say that the functions $f(x) = |x|$ and $g(x) = \sqrt{x^2}$ are equal?

(3) Are the functions $f(x) = |x|$ and $g(x) = (\sqrt{x})^2$ equal?

3.2 ◇ 函数的运算与反函数
Operations on Functions and Inverse Functions

函数的四则运算 Arithmetic Combinations of Functions

我们已经学习了一些基本函数的性质与图像.在实际应用中,我们遇到的函数往往并不是基本函数,而是由它们组合而成的.与实数的运算一样,函数也有四则运算.

Sums, Differences, Products and Quotients of Functions

Let f and g be two functions with overlapping domains. Then，for all x common to both domains，the **sum, difference, product, and quotient** of f and g are defined as follows.

1. Sum：$\quad (f + g)(x) = f(x) + g(x)$

2. Difference：$(f - g)(x) = f(x) - g(x)$

3. Product：$\quad (f \cdot g)(x) = f(x) \cdot g(x)$

4. Quotient：$\left(\dfrac{f}{g}\right)(x) = \dfrac{f(x)}{g(x)}, \; g(x) \neq 0$

值得注意的是,函数组合的定义域是两个函数定义域的公共部分.

1 Let $f(x) = \sqrt{x+1} + \sqrt{1-x}$，$g(x) = \sqrt{x+1} - \sqrt{1-x}$，find $(f+g)(x)$、$(f-g)(x)$、$(f \cdot g)(x)$、$\left(\dfrac{f}{g}\right)(x)$，and write down their domains.

Solution：

Obviously，

$$(f + g)(x) = 2\sqrt{x+1}$$
$$(f - g)(x) = 2\sqrt{x-1}$$
$$(f \cdot g)(x) = 2x$$
$$\left(\frac{f}{g}\right)(x) = \frac{1 + \sqrt{1-x^2}}{x}$$

Since the domains of f, g are both $[-1, 1]$, the domains of $f \pm g$ and $f \cdot g$ are both $[-1, 1]$.

There are additional requirements for the domain $\dfrac{f}{g}$：$g(x) \neq 0$, so its domain is $[-1, 0) \bigcup (0, 1]$.

函数组合的图像 Graphs of Combined Functions

我们知道函数的图像是认识函数性质的一个重要运算途径,现在,我们简要分析一下两个函数算术组合的图像.

2 Let $f(x) = x$, $g(x) = \dfrac{1}{x}$, sketch the graph of $(f \pm g)(x)$.

Solution: Noticed that the common domain of the two functions is: $(-\infty, 0) \bigcup (0, \infty)$ (see Figure 3-5). We can plot the sum function (difference function) in this domain by the method of superposition, as is shown in the diagram.

As shown in Figure 3-6, draw vertical "arrows" from the x-axis to the graph $y = \dfrac{1}{x}$ (that is, draw vectors starting from $(x, 0)$ and ending at $\left(x, \dfrac{1}{x}\right)$). These "arrows" are then superimposed on the image of $y = x$, the resulting curve is the graph of $y = x + \dfrac{1}{x}$.

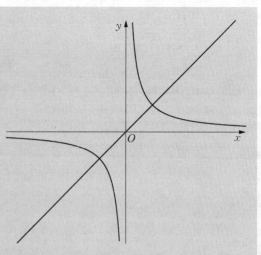

Figure 3-5

Similarly, we can get the graph of $y = x - \dfrac{1}{x}$, as shown in Figure 3-7.

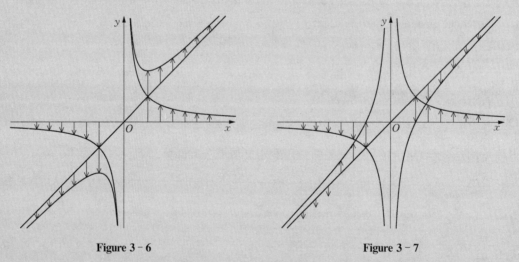

Figure 3-6   Figure 3-7

3 The graphs of $f(x)$ and $g(x)$ are shown in Figure 3-8:

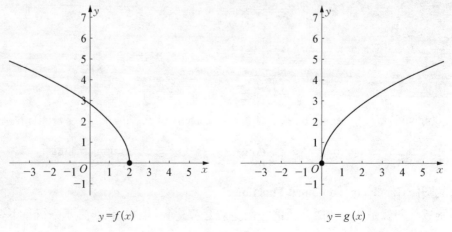

$y = f(x)$ $y = g(x)$

Figure 3-8

The graphs of $f \pm g$, $f \cdot g$ and $\dfrac{f}{g}$ are shown in Figure 3-9. Try to match the graphs with their corresponding functions:

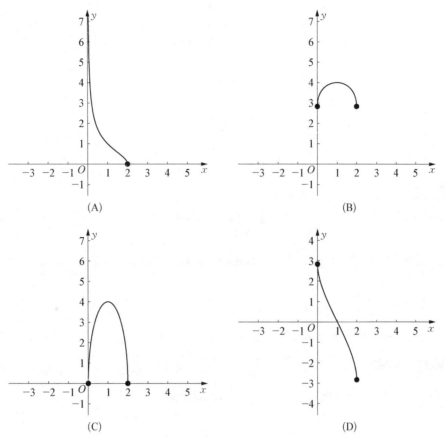

Figure 3-9

Solution: We noticed that $f(2) = g(0) = 0$, so $(f+g)(2) > 0$ and $(f-g)(2) < 0$. Therefore, (B) is the graph of $f+g$, (D) is the graph of $f-g$. By $(f \cdot g)(0) = (f \cdot g)(2) = 0$, and $\left(\dfrac{f}{g}\right)(x)$ is not defined at $x = 0$. Thus (C) is the graph of $f \cdot g$, and (A) is the graph of $\dfrac{f}{g}$.

In the above example, by analyzing the zeros of the function, we determined the property of the graph of the arithmetic of functions, and this method is to solve the problem by plugging in special value which is valuable.

函数的复合 The Composition of the Two Functions

The composite function of f and g, denoted by $f \circ g$, is a function such that:

(1) $(f \circ g)(x) = f(g(x))$ which is read "f circle g of x equals f of g of x";

(2) x is in the domain of g and $g(x)$ is in the domain of f.

函数复合以后,若 x 的取值范围非空,结果仍是函数,则我们称之为两个函数的复合函数.

我们将通过下面的例子来学习如何求复合函数.

4 Let $f(x) = \dfrac{1}{x}$ and $g(x) = \sqrt{x+2}$.

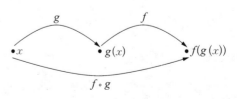

Figure 3-10

(1) Find a rule for $(f \circ g)(x)$ and state the domain of the composite function.

(2) Find a rule for $(g \circ f)(x)$ and state the domain of the composite function.

Solution: (1) $(f \circ g)(x) = f(g(x)) = f(\sqrt{x+2}) = \dfrac{1}{\sqrt{x+2}}$.

Solving $\sqrt{x+2} \neq 0$, we can get the domain of the composite function $f \circ g$, which is $\{x \mid x > -2\}$.

(2) $(g \circ f)(x) = g(f(x)) = g\left(\dfrac{1}{x}\right) = \sqrt{\dfrac{1}{x} + 2}$.

Solving $\dfrac{1}{x} + 2 \geqslant 0$, we can get the domain of the composite function $g \circ f$, which is $\left\{x \mid x \leqslant -\dfrac{1}{2} \text{ or } x > 0\right\}$.

5 (1) Given the domain of $y = f(x)$ is $[0, 2]$, and $g(x) = 2x + 2$, find the domain of $(f \circ g)(x)$.

(2) Given $g(x) = 2x + 2$, and the domain of $(f \circ g)(x)$ is $[0, 2]$, find the domain of $y = f(x)$.

Solution: (1) The domain of the function $y = f(g(x))$ is determined by $0 \leqslant g(x) \leqslant 2$, solving the inequality, we get $-1 \leqslant x \leqslant 0$. Thus, the domain of $y = f(g(x))$ is $[-1, 0]$.

(2) Since the domain of $y = f(g(x))$ is $[0, 2]$, then $0 \leqslant x \leqslant 2$, so we have $2 \leqslant 2x + 2 \leqslant 6$. Thus, the domain of $y = f(x)$ is $[2, 6]$.

6 Given $g(x) = 1 - 2x$, $f(g(x)) = \dfrac{1 - x^2}{x^2}$, find the value of $f\left(\dfrac{1}{2}\right)$.

Solution: By $g(x) = \dfrac{1}{2}$, we get $x = \dfrac{1}{4}$. Substitute $x = \dfrac{1}{4}$ into the function $f(g(x)) = \dfrac{1 - x^2}{x^2}$, thus

$$f\left(g\left(\dfrac{1}{4}\right)\right) = \dfrac{1 - \dfrac{1}{16}}{\dfrac{1}{16}} = 15.$$

7 If a linear function $f(x)$ is such that $f(f(x)) = 4x + 1$, find $f(x)$.

Solution: Let $f(x) = ax + b$ $(a \neq 0)$, then $f(f(x)) = a(ax + b) + b = 4x + 1$. Since $\begin{cases} a^2 = 4 \\ ab + b = 1 \end{cases}$,

we get $\begin{cases} a = 2 \\ b = \dfrac{1}{3} \end{cases}$ or $\begin{cases} a = -2 \\ b = -1 \end{cases}$. Therefore, $f(x) = 2x + \dfrac{1}{3}$ or $f(x) = -2x - 1$.

8 (1) Given $f(2x - 1) = x^2$ $(x \geqslant 0)$, find $f(x)$.

(2) Given $f(x + x^{-1}) = x^2 + x^{-2}$, find $f(x)$.

Solution:

(1) **Method 1:** Let $t = 2x - 1$. Since $x \geqslant 0$, we have $t \geqslant -1$ and $x = \dfrac{t+1}{2}$.

Thus, $f(t) = \left(\dfrac{t+1}{2}\right)^2$, $t \geqslant -1$.

Therefore, $f(x) = \left(\dfrac{x+1}{2}\right)^2$, $x \geqslant -1$.

Method 2: Noticed $f(2x-1) = x^2 = \left(\dfrac{2x-1}{2} + \dfrac{1}{2}\right)^2$, $x \geqslant 0$.

Therefore $f(x) = \left(\dfrac{x}{2} + \dfrac{1}{2}\right)^2 = \left(\dfrac{x+1}{2}\right)^2$, $x \geqslant -1$.

(2) Given that $f(x + x^{-1}) = x^2 + x^{-2}$, then the domain of $f(x + x^{-1})$ is $(0, +\infty)$, that is $x + x^{-1} \in [\sqrt{2}, +\infty)$. Therefore, the domain of $f(x)$ is $[\sqrt{2}, +\infty)$.

Since $f(x + x^{-1}) = x^2 + x^{-2} = (x + x^{-1})^2 - 2$, we have $f(x) = x^2 - 2$.

So $f(x) = x^2 - 2$, $x \in [\sqrt{2}, +\infty)$.

反函数 Inverse Functions

一般地，对于函数 $y = f(x)$，设它的定义域为 D，值域为 A.如果对 A 中任意一个值 y，在 D 中总有唯一确定的 x 值与它对应，且满足 $y = f(x)$，这样得到的 x 关于 y 的函数叫作 $y = f(x)$ 的反函数，记作 $x = f^{-1}(y)$. 在习惯上，自变量常用 x 表示，而函数用 y 表示，所以把它改写为 $y = f^{-1}(x)(x \in A)$.

A function f defined for some domain D is one-one if, for each number y in the range A of f there is only one number $x \in$ D such that $y = f(x)$. The function with domain A defined by $x = f^{-1}(y)$ is the inverse function of $y = f(x)$. Usually x represents the independent variable, and y represents the dependent variable, then we rewrite the inverse function as $y = f^{-1}(x)$, $x \in A$.

将 $y = f(x)$ 和 $y = f^{-1}(x)$ 的关系，总结如下：

(1) 若 $f(a) = b$，则 $f^{-1}(b) = a$.

(2)

	$y = f(x)$	$y = f^{-1}(x)$
定义域	D	A
值域	A	D

(3) $f^{-1}(f(x)) = x$, $x \in D$; $f(f^{-1}(x)) = x$, $x \in A$.

9 The graphs of the functions are given as below. Which of them has an inverse function? （　　）

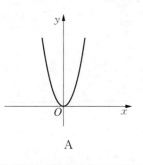

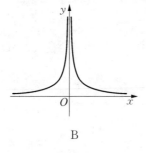

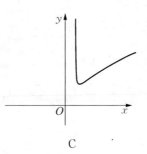

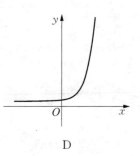

| A | B | C | D |

Solution: According to the definition of inverse function, the function $f(x)$ must be a one-to-one function, which means no horizontal line can meet the graph more than once. Therefore, D is the correct answer.

10 Given $f(x) = x^2 + 1$, does the function $y = f(x)$ have an inverse?

Solution: When $y=2$, we have $x=\pm 1$. Therefore $y=f(x)$ is not one-to-one, whence has no inverse.

11 Find the inverse function of $f(x)=\dfrac{4-3x}{2x-5}$.

Solution: Because $y=\dfrac{4-3x}{2x-5}$, solve for x, then $x=\dfrac{5y+4}{2y+3}$. Interchange x and y, then $y=\dfrac{5x+4}{2x+3}$.

So the inverse function is $f^{-1}(x)=\dfrac{5x+4}{2x+3}$, $x\neq -\dfrac{3}{2}$.

12 Given $f(x)=\dfrac{3x+1}{4x+2}$, find $f^{-1}(0.7)$.

Solution 1: Given $f(x)=\dfrac{3x+1}{4x+2}$, then $f^{-1}(x)=\dfrac{-2x+1}{4x-3}$, therefore $f^{-1}(0.7)=2$.

Solution 2: Let $f^{-1}(0.7)=t$, then $f(t)=0.7$. Solving for t from $\dfrac{3t+1}{4t+2}=0.7$, we get $t=2$.
Therefore $f^{-1}(0.7)=2$.

13 Graph the function and its inverse in the same coordinate system.
(1) $y=x^2+2x-1$ ($x\geqslant 0$);   (2) $y=x^3$.

Solution: The graph of question (1) is shown as Figure 3-11, and the graph of question (2) is shown as Figure 3-12.

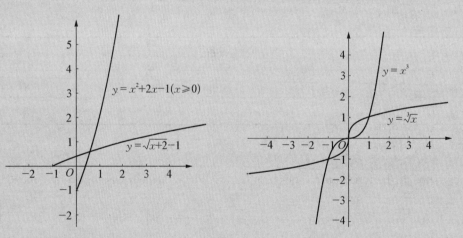

Figure 3-11   Figure 3-12

Remark: The graphs of $y=f(x)$ and $y=f^{-1}(x)$ are symmetric with respect to the line $y=x$.

练习 Exercise

1. For the following functions $f(x)$ and $g(x)$, find $(f+g)(x)$、$(f-g)(x)$、$(f\cdot g)(x)$、$\left(\dfrac{f}{g}\right)(x)$, and find their domains.

(1) $f(x)=x^2$, $g(x)=4x-5$.   (2) $f(x)=\sqrt{x^2+6}$, $g(x)=\dfrac{x^2}{x^2+1}$.

(3) $f(x) = 2\sqrt{x} + \sqrt{1-x}$, $g(x) = \sqrt{x} - \sqrt{1-x} + 2$.

(4) $f(x) = \dfrac{1}{x^3 + 4x^2}$, $g(x) = \dfrac{x+4}{x}$.

2. For the following functions $f(x)$ and $g(x)$, sketch the graph of $(f \pm g)(x)$.

(1) $f(x) = x^2$, $g(x) = 2x$.   (2) $f(x) = x^2$, $g(x) = \dfrac{1}{x}$.

3. Let $f(x) = \sqrt{x}$, $g(x) = 2x - 1$, and $h(x) = \dfrac{x}{3}$. Find the answer of each of the following.

(1) $f(g(h(9)))$.   (2) $h(f(g(5)))$.   (3) $h(g(f(36)))$.   (4) $g(h(f(16)))$.

4. Given $f(x) = \sqrt{x}$, $g(x) = 3x^2 - 8x + 4$, find the domain of $(f \circ g)(x)$.

5. Find each of the following $f(x)$.

(1) $g(x) = 2x$, $(f \circ g)(x) = (1 - \sqrt{2}x)(1 + \sqrt{2}x)$.

(2) $g(x) = \sqrt{x} + 1$, $(f \circ g)(x) = x + 2\sqrt{x}$.   (3) $g(x) = \dfrac{1}{x}$, $(f \circ g)(x) = \dfrac{x}{1-x^2}$.

6. If $f(x+1) = 2x^2 + 1$, find $f(x-1)$.

7. Find the inverse function of the following functions.

(1) $y = 3x + 2$.   (2) $y = -\dfrac{3}{x}$.   (3) $y = x^2 (x \leqslant 0)$.   (4) $y = \sqrt{x} + 1 (x \geqslant 0)$.

8. If $f(x) = \dfrac{x-1}{x}$, find $f^{-1}(\sqrt{2})$.

9. Given that $f(x) = \left(\dfrac{x-1}{x+1}\right)^2 (x > 1)$, then

(1) Find the inverse function $f^{-1}(x)$.

(2) If the inequality $(1 - \sqrt{x})f^{-1}(x) > a(a - \sqrt{x})$ is true for $x \in \left[\dfrac{1}{16}, \dfrac{1}{4}\right]$, find the range of a.

10. Given that $f(x) = 2\left(\dfrac{1}{2} - \dfrac{1}{a^x + 1}\right) (a > 0$, and $a \neq 1)$.

(1) Find the inverse function $y = f^{-1}(x)$.   (2) Solve the inequality $f^{-1}(x) > 1$.

11. Is $y = f^{-1}(x+1)$ the inverse function of $y = f(x+1)$? Explain.

3.3 ◆ 函数的性质 Properties of Functions

增函数和减函数 Increasing and Decreasing Functions

对于函数 $y = f(x)$ 在给定的区间上任意两个不相等的值 x_1，x_2，当 $x_1 < x_2$ 时，如果总有 $f(x_1) < f(x_2)$，则称函数 $y = f(x)$ 在这个区间上是增函数；而如果总有 $f(x_1) > f(x_2)$ 时，就称函数在这个区间上是减函数.

> **Increasing, Decreasing, and Constant Functions**
>
> When a function is (strictly) increasing on an interval, for any x_1 and x_2 in the interval, $x_1 < x_2$ implies $f(x_1) < f(x_2)$.
>
> When a function is (strictly) decreasing on an interval, for any x_1 and x_2 in the interval, $x_1 < x_2$ implies $f(x_1) > f(x_2)$.
>
> When a function is constant on an interval, for any x_1 and x_2 in the interval, $f(x_1) = f(x_2)$.

单调性和单调区间 Monotonicity and Intervals of Monotonicity

如果一个函数在某个区间上是增函数或减函数,就说此函数在这个区间上具有**单调性**,它是函数在某个区间上的性质,这个区间就称为此函数的**单调递增或递减区间**.

If a function is increasing or decreasing on an interval, we say these functions are monotonic. It's the property of the function for all x in the interval, and the interval is called an interval on which the function is increasing/decreasing.

1 The domain for the function as shown in Figure 3-13 is $[-10, 10]$, find intervals on which $y = f(x)$ is increasing or decreasing.

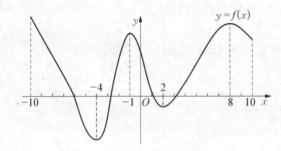

Figure 3-13

Solution: $f(x)$ is increasing for $x \in (-4, -1)$ and $x \in (2, 8)$.
$f(x)$ is decreasing for $x \in (-10, -4)$, $x \in (-1, 2)$ and $x \in (8, 10)$.

2 Show that $f(x) = x + \dfrac{2}{x}$ is increasing on the interval $(\sqrt{2}, +\infty)$.

Proof: For any $x_1, x_2 \in (\sqrt{2}, +\infty)$, $x_1 < x_2$, we have

$$
\begin{aligned}
f(x_1) - f(x_2) &= \left(x_1 + \frac{2}{x_1}\right) - \left(x_2 + \frac{2}{x_2}\right) \\
&= (x_1 - x_2) + \left(\frac{2}{x_1} - \frac{2}{x_2}\right) \\
&= (x_1 - x_2) + \frac{2(x_2 - x_1)}{x_1 x_2} \\
&= (x_1 - x_2)\left(1 - \frac{2}{x_1 x_2}\right) \\
&= (x_1 - x_2)\frac{x_1 x_2 - 2}{x_1 x_2}
\end{aligned}
$$

Since $\sqrt{2} < x_1 < x_2$, we know $x_1 - x_2 < 0$, $x_1 x_2 > 2$.

Then we have $f(x_1) - f(x_2) < 0$, $f(x_1) < f(x_2)$, therefore, $f(x) = x + \dfrac{2}{x}$ is increasing on the interval $(\sqrt{2}, +\infty)$.

3 (1) If $f(x) = \begin{cases} x^2 - ax, & x \geqslant 1 \\ (4a-1)x - 1, & x < 1 \end{cases}$ is increasing on the interval $(-\infty, +\infty)$, find the range of a.

(2) If $f(x) = \dfrac{ax+1}{x+2}$ is increasing on the interval $(-2, +\infty)$, find the range of a.

Solution: (1) As $f(x) = x^2 - ax$ is increasing on $x \geqslant 1$, we have $\dfrac{a}{2} \leqslant 1$, $a \leqslant 2$.

As $f(x) = (4a-1)x - 1$ is increasing on $x < 1$, we have $4a - 1 > 0$, $a > \dfrac{1}{4}$.

When $x = 1$, from $(4a-1) \times 1 - 1 \leqslant 1^2 - a \times 1$, we have $a \leqslant \dfrac{3}{5}$.

Therefore, $a \in \left(\dfrac{1}{4}, \dfrac{3}{5} \right]$.

(2) $f(x) = \dfrac{ax+1}{x+2} = \dfrac{a(x+2)+1-2a}{x+2} = \dfrac{1-2a}{x+2} + a$, for any x_1, $x_2 \in (-2, +\infty)$, $x_1 < x_2$,

$f(x_1) - f(x_2) = \dfrac{1-2a}{x_1+2} - \dfrac{1-2a}{x_2+2} = \dfrac{(1-2a)(x_2-x_1)}{(x_1+2)(x_2+2)}$.

As $f(x) = \dfrac{ax+1}{x+2}$ is increasing on $x \in (-2, +\infty)$, $f(x_1) - f(x_2) < 0$,

and since $x_2 - x_1 > 0$, $x_1 + 2 > 0$, $x_2 + 2 > 0$, we have $1 - 2a < 0$.

Therefore, $a \in \left(\dfrac{1}{2}, +\infty \right)$.

4 If $g(x)$ is decreasing on the interval $[m, n]$, $a \leqslant g(x) \leqslant b$, while $f(x)$ is increasing on $x \in [a, b]$, show that $(f \circ g)(x)$ is decreasing on $[m, n]$.

Proof: For any $m \leqslant x_1 < x_2 \leqslant n$,

As $g(x)$ is decreasing on $x \in [m, n]$ and $a \leqslant g(x) \leqslant b$, we have $a \leqslant g(x_2) < g(x_1) \leqslant b$.

Since $f(x)$ is increasing on $[a, b]$, we have $(f \circ g)(x_1) > (f \circ g)(x_2)$.

Therefore, $(f \circ g)(x)$ is decreasing on the interval $[m, n]$.

Remark: We could draw conclusions as follows:

If $g(x)$ is increasing on $x \in D_1$, and $g(x) \in D_2$, $f(x)$ is increasing on $x \in D_2$, then $(f \circ g)(x)$ must be increasing on $x \in D_1$.

If $g(x)$ is decreasing on $x \in D_1$, and $g(x) \in D_2$, $f(x)$ is decreasing on $x \in D_2$, then $(f \circ g)(x)$ must be increasing on $x \in D_1$.

If $g(x)$ is increasing on $x \in D_1$, and $g(x) \in D_2$, $f(x)$ is decreasing on $x \in D_2$, then $(f \circ g)(x)$ must be decreasing on $x \in D_1$.

If $g(x)$ is decreasing on $x \in D_1$, and $g(x) \in D_2$, $f(x)$ is increasing on $x \in D_2$, then $(f \circ g)(x)$ must be decreasing on $x \in D_1$.

5 Find the interval on which the function $f(x) = \sqrt{-x^2 + 4x - 3}$ is decreasing.

Solution: Solving the inequality $-x^2 + 4x - 3 \geqslant 0$, gives $1 \leqslant x \leqslant 3$.

So, the domain of the function $f(x)$ is $[1, 3]$.

Let $u = -x^2 + 4x - 3$, then $y = \sqrt{u}$. We know that $y = \sqrt{u}$ is increasing on $u \in [0, +\infty)$, and $u = -x^2 + 4x - 3$ is decreasing on $x \in [2, 3]$.

Therefore, $f(x) = \sqrt{-x^2 + 4x - 3}$ is decreasing on $[2, 3]$.

6 The domain of the function $f(x)$ is $(0, +\infty)$. For any $x \in (1, +\infty)$, $f(x) > 0$, and for any $x, y \in (0, +\infty)$, $f\left(\dfrac{x}{y}\right) = f(x) - f(y)$.

(1) Show that $f(x)$ is increasing on the interval $(0, +\infty)$.

(2) Given $f(2) = 1$, solve the inequality $f(x) - f\left(\dfrac{1}{x-3}\right) \leqslant 2$.

Solution: (1) For any x_1, x_2 in the interval $(0, +\infty)$, $x_1 < x_2$, we have $\dfrac{x_2}{x_1} > 1$.

Then $f(x_2) - f(x_1) = f\left(\dfrac{x_2}{x_1}\right) > 0$, which means $f(x_1) < f(x_2)$.

Therefore, $f(x)$ is increasing on $(0, +\infty)$.

(2) Since $f\left(\dfrac{x}{y}\right) = f(x) - f(y)$ for any x, $y \in (0, +\infty)$,

We have $f\left(\dfrac{4}{2}\right) = f(4) - f(2) = f(2)$, then $f(4) = 2f(2) = 2$.

The inequality $f(x) - f\left(\dfrac{1}{x-3}\right) \leqslant 2$ can be written as $f(x(x-3)) \leqslant f(4)$.

Given that $f(x)$ is increasing on $(0, +\infty)$, we have $\begin{cases} x > 0 \\ \dfrac{1}{x-3} > 0 \\ x(x-3) \leqslant 4 \end{cases}$.

Solving the system of inequalities, gives $3 < x \leqslant 4$.

Therefore, the solution set of the inequality $f(x) - f\left(\dfrac{1}{x-3}\right) \leqslant 2$ is $(3, 4]$.

函数的奇偶性 Even and Odd Functions

如果对于函数 $f(x)$ 的定义域 D 内任意一个 x，都有 $f(-x) = f(x)$，那么函数 $f(x)$ 就叫作**偶函数**.
如果对于函数 $f(x)$ 的定义域 D 内任意一个 x，都有 $f(-x) = -f(x)$，那么函数 $f(x)$ 就叫作**奇函数**.
偶函数的图像关于 y 轴对称，奇函数的图像关于原点对称.

Even and Odd Functions

A function is said to be even when its graph is symmetric with respect to the y-axis and odd when its graph is symmetric with respect to the origin.

A function $y = f(x)$ is **even** when, for each x in the domain of $f(x)$, $f(-x) = f(x)$.

A function $y = f(x)$ is **odd** when, for each x in the domain of $f(x)$, $f(-x) = -f(x)$.

理解函数的奇偶性需注意以下几点：

(1) 函数的奇偶性与单调性的差异.奇偶性是函数在定义域上的对称性，单调性是反映函数在某一区间上函数值的变化趋势.

(2) 定义域关于原点对称是函数具有奇偶性的前提条件.换言之，若所给函数的定义域不关于原点对称，则函数一定不具有奇偶性.

(3) 既奇又偶函数的表达式是 $f(x) = 0$，$x \in A$，定义域 A 是关于原点对称的非空数集.

(4) 若奇函数在原点处有定义，则有 $f(0) = 0$.

7 Determine whether the following functions are even, odd or neither：

(1) $f(x) = x^3 + 2x$.

(2) $f(x) = 2x^4 + 3x^2$.

(3) $f(x) = x^2 + 2x + 5$.

(4) $f(x) = \dfrac{x^3 - x^2}{x - 1}$.

(5) $f(x) = \sqrt{1 - x^2} + \sqrt{x^2 - 1}$.

(6) $f(x) = \begin{cases} (x+5)^2 - 4 & x \in (-6, -1] \\ (x-5)^2 - 4 & x \in [1, 6) \end{cases}$.

Solution:

(1) The domain of $f(x) = x^3 + 2x$ is all real numbers.

Since $f(-x) = (-x)^3 + 2(-x) = -(x^3 + 2x) = -f(x)$, we know that $f(x) = x^3 + 2x$ is odd.

(2) The domain of $f(x) = 2x^4 + 3x^2$ is all real numbers.

Since $f(-x) = 2(-x)^4 + 3(-x)^2 = 2x^4 + 3x^2 = f(x)$, we know that $f(x) = 2x^4 + 3x^2$ is even.

(3) $f(x) = x^2 + 2x + 5$ is neither even nor odd because $f(1) = 8$, $f(-1) = 4$, $f(-1) \neq \pm f(1)$.

(4) $f(x) = \dfrac{x^3 - x^2}{x - 1}$ is neither even nor odd because $\dfrac{x^3 - x^2}{x - 1}$ is not defined at $x = 1$, while $f(-1) = 1$.

(5) $f(x) = \sqrt{1 - x^2} + \sqrt{x^2 - 1}$ is both odd and even because the domain of $f(x)$ is $\{1, -1\}$, and $f(x) = 0$.

(6) $f(x) = \begin{cases} (x+5)^2 - 4 & x \in (-6, -1] \\ (x-5)^2 - 4 & x \in [1, 6) \end{cases}$ is even because $f(-x) = f(x)$, as follows:

When $x \in (-6, -1]$, $-x \in [1, 6)$, $f(-x) = (-x-5)^2 - 4 = (x+5)^2 - 4 = f(x)$.

When $x \in [1, 6)$, $-x \in (-6, -1]$, $f(-x) = (-x+5)^2 - 4 = (x-5)^2 - 4 = f(x)$.

8 The domain of function $f(x)$ is $[-5, 5]$. The graph in Figure 3 - 14 shows part of the graph of function $f(x)$ on the interval $[0, 5]$.

(1) If $f(x)$ is odd, solve the inequality $f(x) < 0$.

(2) If $f(x)$ is even, solve the inequality $f(x) < 0$.

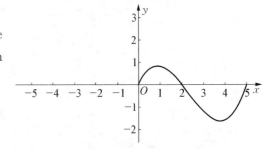

Figure 3 - 14

Solution: (1) Since the function $f(x)$ is odd, its graph is symmetric with respect to the origin. We can draw the other half graph of $f(x)$ on the interval $[-5, 0]$ as shown in Figure 3 - 15.

So, the solution set of $f(x) < 0$ is $(-2, 0) \cup (2, 5)$.

(2) Since the function $f(x)$ is even, its graph is symmetric with respect to the y-axis. We can draw the other half graph of $f(x)$ on the interval $[-5, 0]$ as shown in Figure 3 - 16.

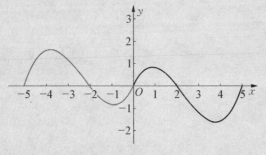

Figure 3 - 15

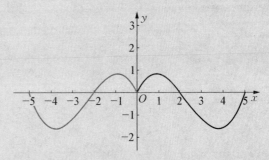

Figure 3 - 16

So, the solution set of $f(x) < 0$ is $(-5, -2) \cup (2, 5)$.

9 $f(x)$ is an odd function whose domain is **R**. When $x > 0$, $f(x) = x^2 + 3x - 1$.

(1) Find the expression of $f(x)$ when $x < 0$.

(2) $f(x)$ is an odd function and $g(x)$ is an even function. If $f(x) + g(x) = x^2 + x + 1$, find $f(x)$ and $g(x)$.

Solution: (1) Since $f(x)$ is an odd function, $f(-x) = -f(x)$.

When $x < 0$, $-x > 0$, $f(x) = -f(-x) = -[(-x)^2 + 3(-x) - 1] = -x^2 + 3x + 1$.

So, when $x < 0$, $f(x) = -x^2 + 3x + 1$.

(2) $f(x) + g(x) = x^2 + x + 1$ ①, $f(-x) + g(-x) = (-x)^2 - x + 1 = x^2 - x + 1$ ②.

Since $f(x)$ is an odd function and $g(x)$ is an even function, $f(-x) = -f(x)$, $g(-x) = g(x)$,

from ② we have $-f(x) + g(x) = x^2 - x + 1$ ③.

① + ③ gives $2g(x) = 2x^2 + 2$, so $g(x) = x^2 + 1$.

① − ③ gives $2f(x) = 2x$, so $f(x) = x$.

10 Let $f(x)$ be an even function whose domain is $[-2, 2]$, and $f(x)$ is decreasing on the interval $[-2, 0]$. Solve the inequality $f(1-x) < f(x)$.

Solution: Since $f(x)$ is an even function whose domain is $[-2, 2]$, from $f(1-x) < f(x)$ we

have $\begin{cases} |1-x| < |x| \\ -2 \leqslant x \leqslant 2 \\ -2 \leqslant 1-x \leqslant 2 \end{cases}$.

Solving the system of inequalities, gives $\dfrac{1}{2} < x \leqslant 2$.

Therefore, the solution set of the inequality $f(1-x) < f(x)$ is $\left(\dfrac{1}{2}, 2 \right]$.

11 $f(x) = \dfrac{ax+b}{1+x^2}$ is an odd function whose domain is $(-1, 1)$, and $f\left(\dfrac{1}{2}\right) = \dfrac{2}{5}$.

(1) Find the value of a and b.

(2) Show that $f(x)$ is increasing for all $x \in (-1, 1)$.

(3) Solve the inequality $f(x-1) + f(x) < 0$.

Solution: (1) Since $f(x)$ is an odd function whose domain is $(-1, 1)$, $f(0) = -f(0)$ gives $f(0) = 0$.

Then we have $b = 0$.

Since $f\left(\dfrac{1}{2}\right) = \dfrac{2}{5}$, $\dfrac{\dfrac{1}{2}a}{1 + \dfrac{1}{4}} = \dfrac{2}{5}$, then we have $a = 1$.

(2) $f(x) = \dfrac{x}{1+x^2}$ $(-1 < x < 1)$.

For any x_1, $x_2 \in (-1, 1)$, $x_1 < x_2$, $f(x_1) - f(x_2) = \dfrac{x_1}{1+x_1^2} - \dfrac{x_2}{1+x_2^2} = \dfrac{(x_1 - x_2)(1 - x_1 x_2)}{(1+x_1^2)(1+x_2^2)}$.

Since $-1 < x_1 < x_2 < 1$, we have $x_1 - x_2 < 0$, $1 - x_1 x_2 > 0$, $(1+x_1^2)(1+x_2^2) > 0$.

So $f(x_1) - f(x_2) < 0$.

Therefore, $f(x)$ is increasing for $x \in (-1, 1)$.

(3) $f(x-1) + f(x) < 0$, $f(x-1) < -f(x)$.

As $f(-x) = -f(x)$, the inequality is equivalent to $f(x-1) < f(-x)$.

Since $f(x)$ is increasing for all $x \in (-1, 1)$, we have $\begin{cases} -1 < x-1 < 1 \\ -1 < -x < 1 \\ x-1 < -x \end{cases}$,

Solving the system of inequalities gives $0 < x < \dfrac{1}{2}$.

Therefore, the solution set of the inequality $f(x-1) + f(x) < 0$ is $\left(0, \dfrac{1}{2}\right)$.

函数的最值 Extreme Values of a Function

一般地,设函数 $y = f(x)$ 在 x_0 处的函数值是 $f(x_0)$,如果对于定义域内任意的 x,不等式 $f(x_0) \leqslant f(x)$ 都成立,那么 $f(x_0)$ 叫作函数 $y = f(x)$ 的最小值,记作 $y_{\min} = f(x_0)$. 如果对于定义域内任意的 x, 不等式 $f(x_0) \geqslant f(x)$ 都成立,那么 $f(x_0)$ 叫作函数 $y = f(x)$ 的最大值.记作 $y_{\max} = f(x_0)$.

Extreme Values of a Function

Let $y = f(x)$ be defined on the domain D containing x_0.

$f(x_0)$ is called the **minimum** of f on the domain D if $f(x_0) \leqslant f(x)$ for all x in D. The notation is $y_{\min} = f(x_0)$.

$f(x_0)$ is called the **maximum** of f on the domain D if $f(x_0) \geqslant f(x)$ for all x in D. The notation is $y_{\max} = f(x_0)$.

The minimum and maximum of a function on the domain D are also called the **absolute minimum** and **absolute maximum**, or the **global minimum** and **global maximum**.

12 Find the maximum or minimum value of the following quadratic function.

(1) $f(x) = 3x^2 - 4x + 1$.

(2) $f(x) = -x^2 - x + 1$.

Solution: (1) Since $f(x) = 3x^2 - 4x + 2 = 3\left(x - \dfrac{2}{3}\right)^2 - \dfrac{1}{3} \geqslant -\dfrac{1}{3}$, $f(x)$ has the minimum at $x = \dfrac{2}{3}$. The minimum value is $f\left(\dfrac{2}{3}\right) = -\dfrac{1}{3}$.

(2) Since $f(x) = -x^2 - x + 1 = -\left(x + \dfrac{1}{2}\right)^2 + \dfrac{5}{4} \leqslant \dfrac{5}{4}$, $f(x)$ has the maximum at $x = -\dfrac{1}{2}$. The maximum value is $f\left(-\dfrac{1}{2}\right) = \dfrac{5}{4}$.

Remark: By completing the square of the quadratic function $f(x) = ax^2 + bx + c$, we can rewrite the function as $f(x) = a\left(x + \dfrac{b}{2a}\right)^2 + \left(c - \dfrac{b^2}{4a}\right)$, which implies the following.

When $a > 0$, $f(x)$ has a minimum at $x = -\dfrac{b}{2a}$. The minimum value is $f\left(-\dfrac{b}{2a}\right)$.

When $a < 0$, $f(x)$ has a maximum at $x = -\dfrac{b}{2a}$. The maximum value is $f\left(-\dfrac{b}{2a}\right)$.

13 Find the extreme values of the following functions:

(1) $f(x) = x^2 - 3x + 1$, $x \in [0, 5]$.

(2) $f(x) = x + \dfrac{2}{x}$, $x \in [1, 4]$.

(3) $f(x) = 2x + \sqrt{1 - 2x}$.

(4) $f(x) = \dfrac{2x^2 + x + 1}{x + 1}$, $x \in [1, 4]$.

Solution: (1) Since $f(x) = x^2 - 3x + 1 = \left(x - \dfrac{3}{2}\right)^2 - \dfrac{5}{4}$, the function $f(x)$ is decreasing for $x \in \left[0, \dfrac{3}{2}\right]$ and increasing for $x \in \left[\dfrac{3}{2}, 5\right]$.

So, $f(x)$ has the minimum at $x = \dfrac{3}{2}$, the minimum value is $f\left(\dfrac{3}{2}\right) = -\dfrac{5}{4}$.

As $f(0) = 1$, $f(5) = 11$, $f(x)$ has the maximum at $x = 5$. So the maximum value is $f(5) = 11$.

(2) When $x > 0$, using AM-GM inequality we can have $x + \dfrac{2}{x} \geqslant 2\sqrt{x \cdot \dfrac{2}{x}} = 2\sqrt{2}$, and $x + \dfrac{2}{x} = 2\sqrt{2}$ implies $x = \sqrt{2}$.

Since the domain of $f(x)$ is $[1, 4]$ and $\sqrt{2} \in [1, 4]$, $f(x)$ has the minimum at $x = \sqrt{2}$. So the minimum value is $f(\sqrt{2}) = 2\sqrt{2}$.

As the function $f(x)$ is decreasing for $x \in [1, \sqrt{2}]$ and increasing for $x \in [\sqrt{2}, 4]$, $f(1) = 3$, $f(4) = \dfrac{9}{2}$, we know that $f(x)$ has the maximum at $x = 4$ and the maximum value is $f(4) = \dfrac{9}{2}$.

(3) Let $t = \sqrt{1 - 2x}$ ($t \geqslant 0$), then $x = \dfrac{1 - t^2}{2}$, $2x + \sqrt{1 - 2x} = -t^2 + t + 1$.

The function $g(t) = -t^2 + t + 1 = -\left(t - \dfrac{1}{2}\right)^2 + \dfrac{5}{4}$ has the maximum value $g(t)_{\max} = g\left(\dfrac{1}{2}\right) = \dfrac{5}{4}$ and has no minimum value.

From $t = \dfrac{1}{2}$ we can obtain $x = \dfrac{3}{8}$.

Therefore, the function $f(x) = 2x + \sqrt{1 - 2x}$ has the maximum at $x = \dfrac{3}{8}$, and the maximum value is $\dfrac{5}{4}$. $f(x)$ has no minimum.

(4) The function $f(x) = \dfrac{2x^2 + x + 1}{x + 1}$ can be written as $f(x) = \dfrac{2(x + 1)^2 - 3(x + 1) + 2}{x + 1} = 2(x + 1) + \dfrac{2}{x + 1} - 3$.

Let $t = x + 1$, then $2(x + 1) + \dfrac{2}{x + 1} - 3 = 2t + \dfrac{2}{t} - 3$, $t \in [2, 5]$.

The function $g(t) = 2t + \dfrac{2}{t} - 3$ is increasing for $t \in [2, 5]$, then $g(t)_{\min} = g(2) = 2$ and $g(t)_{\max} = g(5) = \dfrac{37}{5}$.

Since $t=2$ implies $x=1$, and $t=5$ implies $x=4$, the function $f(x)=\dfrac{2x^2+x+1}{x+1}$, $x \in [1, 4]$ has its minimum at $x=1$, and the minimum value is 2. $f(x)$ has its maximum at $x=4$, and the maximum value is $\dfrac{37}{5}$.

14 Find the range of the following functions:

(1) $y=\dfrac{3x+1}{x-2}$.　　　(2) $y=\sqrt{-x^2-x+2}$.　　　(3) $y=\dfrac{2x^2+4x-7}{x^2+2x+3}$.

Solution:

(1) **Method 1:** Rearranging the function $y=\dfrac{3x+1}{x-2}$ gives $x=\dfrac{2y+1}{y-3}$, then we know that $y \neq 3$.

So the range of $y=\dfrac{3x+1}{x-2}$ is $(-\infty,3) \cup (3, +\infty)$.

Method 2: The function can be written as $y=\dfrac{3x+1}{x-2}=\dfrac{3(x-2)+7}{x-2}=3+\dfrac{7}{x-2}$.

Since $\dfrac{7}{x-2} \neq 0$, $3+\dfrac{7}{x-2} \neq 3$. So the range of $y=\dfrac{3x+1}{x-2}$ is $(-\infty, 3) \cup (3, +\infty)$.

(2) Solving $-x^2-x+2 \geqslant 0$ gives $-2 \leqslant x \leqslant 1$. So, the domain of the function is $[-2, 1]$.

Since $-x^2+x+2=-\left(x+\dfrac{1}{2}\right)^2+\dfrac{9}{4} \in \left[0, \dfrac{9}{4}\right]$, we have $0 \leqslant \sqrt{-x^2-x+2} \leqslant \dfrac{3}{2}$.

Therefore, the range of the function $y=\sqrt{-x^2-x+2}$ is $\left[0, \dfrac{3}{2}\right]$.

(3) As $x^2+2x+3 \neq 0$, x can be any real numbers.

Rearranging the function gives $(y-2)x^2+2(y-2)x+3y+7=0$　①.

When $y \neq 2$, ① is a quadratic equation with variable x.

As the equation ① has real solution, we have $\Delta \geqslant 0$, which is $[2(y-2)]^2-4(y-2)(3y+7) \geqslant 0$.

Solving the inequality gives $-\dfrac{9}{2} \leqslant y \leqslant 2$, so $-\dfrac{9}{2} \leqslant y < 2$.

Substituting $y=2$ into ① gives $6+7=0$, which is not true.

Therefore, the range of the function $y=\dfrac{2x^2+4x-7}{x^2+2x+3}$ is $\left[-\dfrac{9}{2}, 2\right)$.

15 A leasing company owns 100 cars for rent. All cars could be rent out while the rent is set at 3 000 yuan per month. One more car will be idle once rising in price for each 50 yuan. The management fee for renting out a car is 150 yuan per month while 50 yuan for a car laying idle.

(1) How many cars will be rent out once the rent is set at 3 600 yuan per month?

(2) What's the maximum monthly profit of the leasing company? Indicate the corresponding monthly rent.

Solution:

(1) Once the rent is set at 3 600 yuan per month, the number of cars laying idle is $\dfrac{3\,600-3\,000}{50}=$ 12. So, 88 cars can be rent out.

(2) Let the rent be x yuan per month, then the total monthly profit for the company would be

$$f(x) = \left(100 - \frac{x - 3\,000}{50}\right)(x - 150) - \frac{x - 3\,000}{50} \times 50$$

$$= -\frac{x^2}{50} + 162x - 21\,000$$

$$= -\frac{1}{50}(x - 4\,050)^2 + 307\,050$$

So, when $x = 4\,050$, $f(x)_{max} = f(4\,050) = 307\,050$.

Therefore, the maximum profit is 307 050 yuan and the corresponding rent 4 050 yuan per month.

16 Find the extreme values of the following function

(1) $f(x) = |\,x + 1\,| - |\,x - 2\,|$.

(2) $f(x) = \sqrt{x^2 + 4x + 5} + \sqrt{x^2 - 4x + 8}$.

Solution:

(1) **Method 1:**

The function $f(x) = |\,x + 1\,| - |\,x - 2\,|$ can be written as $f(x) = \begin{cases} -3, & x \leqslant -1 \\ 2x - 1, & -1 < x < 2 \\ 3, & x \geqslant 2 \end{cases}$.

When $-1 < x < 2$, $-3 < 2x - 1 < 3$.

Therefore, the minimum value of $f(x)$ is -3, and the maximum value of $f(x)$ is 3.

Method 2:

$|\,x + 1\,|$ is the distance between the point x and the point -1 on the number axis while $|\,x - 2\,|$ is the distance between the point x and the point 2.

When $x \leqslant -1$, $|\,x + 1\,| - |\,x - 2\,| = -3$; when $-1 < x < 2$, $-3 < |\,x + 1\,| - |\,x - 2\,| < 3$; when $x \geqslant 2$, $|\,x + 1\,| - |\,x - 2\,| = 3$.

Therefore, the minimum value of $f(x)$ is -3 and the maximum value of $f(x)$ is 3.

(2) Draw a rectangle with length 4 and width 3 and divide it into 12 unit squares, as shown in Figure 3-17.

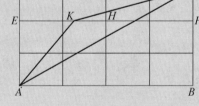

Let $HK = x$, then $EK = 2 - x$, $KF = 2 + x$, $AK = \sqrt{(x-2)^2 + 2^2}$, $KC = \sqrt{(x+2)^2 + 1}$.

Figure 3-17

Hence, $AK + KC \geqslant AC = 5$ with equation holds if and only if the points A, K, C are co-linear.

So the minimum value of the function is 5.

17 A wooden frame is shown in Figure 3-18. The bottom of the frame is a rectangle with sides x m and y m, and the top is an isosceles right triangle. The total area of the frame is 8 m². When does the amount of material reach its minimum? Find the corresponding values of x and y. (Round to 0.001 m)

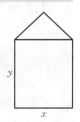

Figure 3-18

Solution: Since the area is $x \cdot y + \dfrac{1}{2} \cdot x \cdot \dfrac{x}{2} = 8$, $y = \dfrac{8 - \dfrac{x^2}{4}}{x} = \dfrac{8}{x} - \dfrac{x}{4} \, (0 < x < 4\sqrt{2})$.

So the total length of the wooden frame is $L = 2x + 2y + 2\left(\dfrac{\sqrt{2}x}{2}\right) = \left(\dfrac{3}{2} + \sqrt{2}\right)x + \dfrac{16}{x}$.

By using AM-GM inequality, we have $\left(\dfrac{3}{2} + \sqrt{2}\right)x + \dfrac{16}{x} \geqslant 2\sqrt{16\left(\dfrac{3}{2} + \sqrt{2}\right)} = 4\sqrt{6 + 4\sqrt{2}}$, and

$L = 4\sqrt{6 + 4\sqrt{2}}$ if and only if $\left(\dfrac{3}{2} + \sqrt{2}\right)x = \dfrac{16}{x}$.

Solving the equation gives $x = \dfrac{4}{\sqrt{\dfrac{3}{2} + \sqrt{2}}} = 8 - 4\sqrt{2} \approx 2.343$, then we have $y = 2\sqrt{2} \approx 2.828$.

Therefore, when the amount of material reaches its minimum, x is 2.343 m and y is 2.828 m.

练习 Exercise

1. Given that $f(x)$ is decreasing on $(-2, 2)$, and $f(m-1) - f(1-2m) > 0$, find the range of m.

2. Find intervals on which the function $y = \sqrt{x^2 - 4x - 5}$ is increasing/decreasing.

3. If $f(x) = \begin{cases} ax^2 - x + 1, & x \leqslant 1 \\ (2a-1)x + \dfrac{3}{4}, & x > 1 \end{cases}$ is decreasing for all x, find the range of a.

4. If $f(x) = \dfrac{x^2 + a}{x} \, (a > 0)$ is increasing on $(2, +\infty)$, find the range of a.

5. The domain of the function $f(x)$ is $\mathbf{R}$. For any x_1, x_2, we have $f(x_1) > 0$, $f(x_2) > 0$, $f(x_1 + x_2) = f(x_1) \cdot f(x_2)$. When $x < 0$, $f(x) < 1$. $f(1) = 2$.

   (1) Show that $f(x)$ is increasing for $x \in \mathbf{R}$.

   (2) Solve the inequality $f(x^2) \cdot f(x) < 4$.

6. Determine whether the following functions are even, odd, both or neither:

   (1) $f(x) = (x-1)\sqrt{\dfrac{1+x}{1-x}}$.

   (2) $f(x) = \dfrac{1}{x} - x$.

   (3) $f(x) = \sqrt{4 - x^2} + \sqrt{x^2 - 4}$.

   (4) $f(x) = |x+1| + |x-1|$.

   (5) $f(x) = \begin{cases} x+1, & x > 0 \\ 1, & x = 0 \\ -x+1, & x < 0 \end{cases}$.

7. The domain of the function $f(x)$ is $[-3, 3]$. The graph in Figure 3 - 19 shows half graph of the function $f(x)$ on the interval $[0, 3]$.

   (1) If $f(x)$ is even, draw the graph and solve the inequality $f(x) < 0$.

   (2) If $f(x)$ is odd, draw the entire graph and solve the inequality $f(x) < 0$.

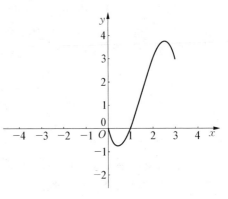

Figure 3 - 19

8. The domain of the odd function $f(x)$ is **R**. When $x > 0$, $f(x) = -2x^2 + 3x + 1$.

    (1) Find $f(x)$ when $x < 0$.

    (2) Draw the graph of $f(x)$.

9. The function $f(x) = x^5 + ax^3 + bx - 8$, where a, b are constants. If $f(-2) = 10$, find $f(2)$.

10. The domain of the even function $f(x)$ is **R.** If $f(x)$ is increasing on $[0, +\infty)$, solve the inequality $f(x) \geqslant f(-2)$.

11. The domain of the odd function $f(x)$ is $[-1, 1]$ and $f(1) = 1$. For any a, $b \in [-1, 1]$, $a + b \neq 0$, $\dfrac{f(a) + f(b)}{a + b} > 0$.

    (1) Determine whether $f(x)$ is increasing or decreasing on $[-1, 1]$ and prove it.

    (2) Solve the inequality $f\left(x + \dfrac{1}{2}\right) - f\left(\dfrac{1}{x-1}\right) < 0$.

    (3) If $f(x) \leqslant m^2 - 2pm + 1$ for any $x \in [-1, 1]$, $p \in [-1, 1]$, find the value set of m.

12. Find the maximum and minimum of the following functions.

    (1) $y = -2x^2 + 5x + 6$.   (2) $y = x^2 + x + 1$, $x \in [-1, 3]$.

    (3) $y = x^2 + x + 1$, $x \in (1, 5]$.   (4) $y = x^2 + x + 1$, $x \in [-5, -1]$.

13. Find the maximum and minimum of the following functions：

    (1) $y = |-x^2 + 4| - 2$.   (2) $y = x + \sqrt{2x - 1}$.

    (3) $y = 2 - \sqrt{-x^2 + 4x}$, $x \in [0, 4]$.   (4) $y = \dfrac{2x}{x+1}$, $x \in [0, 2]$.

    (5) $y = \dfrac{1 - x^2}{1 + x^2}$.

14. Find the range of the following functions：

    (1) $y = \dfrac{x^2 + 2x + 2}{x + 1}$.   (2) $y = \dfrac{x + 2}{\sqrt{x + 1}}$.

    (3) $f(x) = \dfrac{x^2 + 5}{\sqrt{x^2 + 4}}$.   (4) $y = \dfrac{\sqrt{x + 2}}{x + 3}$.

    (5) $y = \dfrac{2x^2 - x + 2}{x^2 + x + 1}$.   (6) $y = |x + 1| + |x - 2|$.

15. Given a cylindrical metal container with constant volume. When the total quantity of materials reaches its minimum, what are the height and radius of the can?

16. Given that a is a constant real number, $f(x) = x^2 + |x - a| + 1$, $x \in$ **R.**

    (1) Determine for what values of a is $f(x)$ odd, even or neither；

    (2) Find the minimum of $f(x)$.

3.4 ◆ 函数图像的变换
Transformations of the Functions

    数学里的变换,指一个图形(或表达式)到另一个图形(或表达式)的演变.图像变换是函数的一种作图方法.已知一个函数的图像,通过某种方式变换,得到另一个与之相关的函数的图像,这样的作图方法叫作图像变换.

平移变换 Translations

1. 左右平移变换

将函数 $y = f(x)$ 的图像沿 x 轴方向平移 $|m|$ 个单位,得到函数 $y = f(x+m)$ $(m \neq 0)$ 的图像.当 $m > 0$ 时,向左平移;当 $m < 0$ 时,向右平移.

2. 上下平移变换

将函数 $y = f(x)$ 的图像沿 y 轴方向平移 $|n|$ 个单位,得到函数 $y = f(x) + n$ $(n \neq 0)$ 的图像.当 $n > 0$ 时,向上平移;当 $n < 0$ 时,向下平移.

Vertical and Horizontal Shifts

Let c be a positive real number. **Vertical and horizontal shifts** in the graph of $y = f(x)$ are represented as follows:

1. Vertical shift c units *up*: $h(x) = f(x) + c$

2. Vertical shift c units *down*: $h(x) = f(x) - c$

3. Horizontal shift c units to the *right*: $h(x) = f(x - c)$

4. Horizontal shift c units to the *left*: $h(x) = f(x + c)$

❶ Graph the two functions on the same coordinate plane, and explain how to obtain the graph of $g(x)$ by translating the graph of $f(x)$.

(1) $f(x) = x^2$, $g(x) = x^2 + 2$.

(2) $f(x) = x^2$, $g(x) = (x - 2)^2$.

Solution: (1) As shown in Figure 3 - 20, the graph of $g(x) = x^2 + 2$ can be obtained by shifting the graph of $f(x) = x^2$ two units up. Actually, $g(x) = x^2 + 2 = f(x) + 2$.

(2) As shown in Figure 3 - 21, the graph of $h(x) = (x - 2)^2$ can be obtained by shifting the graph of $f(x) = x^2$ two units to the right. Actually, $g(x) = (x - 2)^2 = f(x - 2)$.

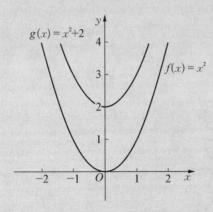

Figure 3 - 20

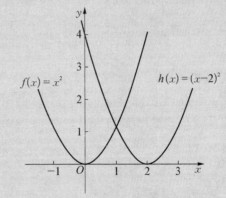

Figure 3 - 21

❷ Use the graph of $f(x) = x^3$ to sketch the graph of following function.

(1) $g(x) = x^3 - 2$.

(2) $h(x) = (x + 2)^3 + 2$.

Solution: The graph of $g(x) = x^3 - 2$ is obtained from that of $f(x) = x^3$ by shifting two units downward, as shown in Figure 3 - 22.

The graph of $h(x) = (x+2)^3 + 2$ is obtained from that of $f(x) = x^3$ by shifting two units to the left and two units upward, as shown in Figure 3-23.

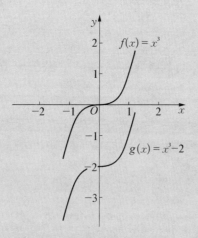

Figure 3-22

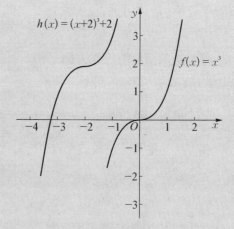

Figure 3-23

3 (1) The graph of $g(x)$ is obtained from that of $y = (x-1)^2 + 3$ by shifting one unit to the right and one unit down. Find $g(x)$.

(2) If the graph of $y = f(x)$ goes through the point $(1, 1)$, find its corresponding point on the graph of $y = f(x+4) - 2$.

(3) How can you obtain the graph of $y = f(2x+3)$ by translating the graph of $y = f(2x-3)$?

Solution: (1) By shifting the graph of $y = (x-1)^2 + 3$ one unit to the right, you can obtain $y = (x-2)^2 + 3$. Then shifting the graph of $y = (x-2)^2 + 3$ one unit down, you can obtain $y = (x-2)^2 + 2$. So, $g(x) = (x-2)^2 + 2$.

(2) The corresponding point on the graph of $y = f(x+4) - 2$ is $(-3, -1)$.

(3) As $y = f(2x-3) = f[2(x-3)+3]$, the graph of $y = f(2x+3)$ can be obtained from that of $y = f(2x-3)$ by shifting three units to the left.

对称变换 Reflections

(1) 函数 $y = f(x)$ 的图像与 $y = -f(x)$ 的图像关于 **x** 轴对称.

(2) 函数 $y = f(x)$ 的图像与 $y = f(-x)$ 的图像关于 **y** 轴对称.

(3) 函数 $y = f(x)$ 的图像与 $y = -f(-x)$ 的图像关于**原点**对称.

Reflections

Reflections in the coordinate axes or the origin of the graph of $y = f(x)$ are represented as follows:

1. Reflection in the x-axis: $y = -f(x)$

2. Reflection in the y-axis: $y = f(-x)$

3. Reflection in the origin: $y = -f(-x)$

4 Use the graph of $f(x) = \dfrac{1}{x}$ $(x > 0)$ to sketch the graph of the functions $y = -f(x)$, $y = f(-x)$ and $y = -f(-x)$.

Solution:

The graph of $y = -f(x)$ is the mirror image (or reflection) of the graph of $y = f(x)$ as shown in Figure 3 – 24. Notice that each point (x, y) on the original graph becomes the point $(x, -y)$ on the reflected graph.

The graph of $y = f(-x)$ is obtained by reflecting the graph of $y = f(x)$ in the y-axis as shown in Figure 3 – 25. Notice that each point (x, y) on the original graph becomes the point $(-x, y)$ on the reflected graph.

The graph of $y = -f(-x)$ is obtained by reflecting the graph of $y = f(x)$ in the origin as shown in Figure 3 – 26. Notice that each point (x, y) on the original graph becomes the point $(-x, -y)$ on the reflected graph.

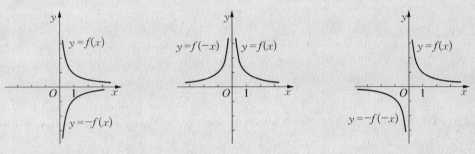

Figure 3 – 24   Figure 3 – 25   Figure 3 – 26

5 The graph of the function $f(x) = x^4$ is shown in Figure 3 – 27. Each of the graphs below is a transformation of the graph of f. Write an equation for each of these functions.

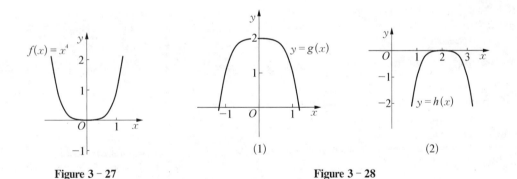

Figure 3 – 27   Figure 3 – 28

Solution:

(1) The graph of g is a reflection in the x-axis followed by an upward shift of two units of the graph of $f(x) = x^4$. So, the equation for g is $g(x) = -x^4 + 2$.

(2) The graph of h is a horizontal shift of three units to the right followed by a reflection in the x-axis of the graph of $f(x) = x^4$. So, the equation for h is $h(x) = -(x - 2)^4$.

6 Reflections and Translations

Compare the graph of each function with the graph of $f(x) = \sqrt{x}$.

(1) $g(x) = -\sqrt{x}$.   (2) $h(x) = \sqrt{-x}$.   (3) $k(x) = -\sqrt{x+3}$.

Algebraic Solution:

(1) The graph of g is a reflection of the graph of f in the x-axis because $g(x) = -\sqrt{x} = -f(x)$.

(2) The graph of h is a reflection of the graph of f in the y-axis because $h(x) = \sqrt{-x} = f(-x)$.

(3) The graph of k is a left shift of three units followed by a reflection in the x-axis because $k(x) = -\sqrt{x+3} = -f(x+3)$.

Graphical Solution:

(1) Graph f and h on the same coordinate plane (Figure 3 - 29). From the graph, we can see that the graph of h is a reflection of the graph of f in the x-axis.

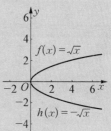

Figure 3 - 29

(2) Graph f and g on the same coordinate plane (Figure 3 - 30). From the graph, we can see that the graph of g is a reflection of the graph of f in the y-axis.

(3) Graph f and k on the same coordinate plane (Figure 3 - 31). From the graph, we can see that the graph of k is a left shift of three units of the graph of f, followed by a reflection in the x-axis.

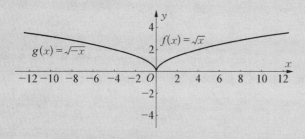

Figure 3 - 30

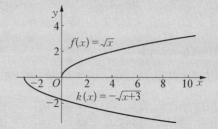

Figure 3 - 31

7 Compare the graph of each function with the graph of $f(x) = \sqrt{x}$.

(1) $g(x) = \sqrt{2-x}$.　　　　(2) $h(x) = 4 - \sqrt{2-x}$.

Solution:

(1) Graph them on the same coordinate plane (Figure 3 - 32). From the graph, you can see that the graph of $y = \sqrt{2-x}$ is a reflection of the graph of $y = \sqrt{x}$ in the line $x = 1$.

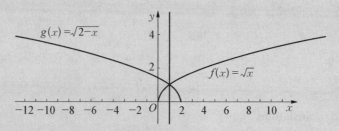

Figure 3 - 32

(2) Graph them on the same coordinate plane (Figure 3-33). From the graph, you can see that the graph of $y=4-\sqrt{2-x}$ is a reflection of the graph of $y=\sqrt{x}$ in the point $(1, 2)$.

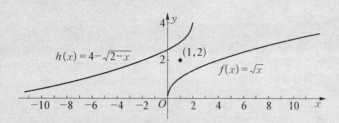

Figure 3-33

翻折变换 Flipping

(1) 上下翻折：$y=|f(x)|=\begin{cases}f(x), & f(x)\geqslant 0 \\ -f(x), & f(x)<0\end{cases}$.

函数 $y=f(x)$ 的图像保留 x 轴上方的图像不变，将 x 轴下方的图像沿 x 轴翻折上去，得到 $y=|f(x)|$ 的图像.

(2) 左右翻折：$y=f(|x|)=\begin{cases}f(x), & x\geqslant 0 \\ f(-x), & x<0\end{cases}$.

函数 $y=f(x)$ 的图像保留 y 轴右侧的图像不变，去掉 y 轴左侧的图像，将 y 轴右侧的图像沿 y 轴翻折过去，得到 $y=f(|x|)$ 的图像.

(1) Vertical Flipping：

To obtain the graph of $y=|f(x)|$ from the graph of $y=f(x)$：
- keep the part of graph lying above and on the x-axis;
- reflect the part of graph lying below the x-axis, discarding what was there.

(2) Horizontal Flipping：

To obtain the graph of $y=f(|x|)$ from the graph of $y=f(x)$：
- keep the part of graph lying to right of and on the y-axis;
- reflect the part of graph lying to the left of the y-axis, discarding what was there.

8 (1) Graph $y=|x^2-3|$ and $y=x^2-3$ on the same coordinate plane, and compare the two graphs.

(2) Graph $y=|x|^2-3|x|$ and $y=x^2-3x$ on the same coordinate plane, and compare the two graphs.

Solution：

The graph of $y=|f(x)|$ is identical to the graph of $y=f(x)$ when $f(x)\geqslant 0$ and is identical to the graph of $y=-f(x)$ when $f(x)<0$. This principle is applied to produce the graph of $y=|x^2-3|$ by using the graph of $y=x^2-3$, as shown in Figure 3-34.

The graph of $y=f(|x|)$ is identical to the graph of $y=f(x)$ when $x\geqslant 0$ and is identical to the graph of $y=f(-x)$ when $x<0$. This principle is applied to produce the graph of $y=|x|^2-3|x|$ by using the graph of $y=x^2-3x$, as shown in Figure 3-35.

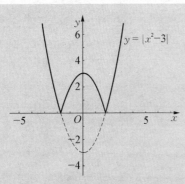

Figure 3 - 34

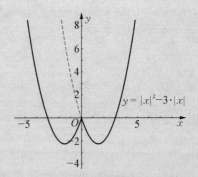

Figure 3 - 35

9 (1) Sketch the graph of $f(x) = |(2x+4)^2 - 5|$.

(2) Discuss the number of points at which the two functions $y = f(x)$ and $y = a$ intersect.

Solution:

(1) The graph of $f(x) = |(2x+4)^2 - 5|$ is shown in Figure 3 - 36.

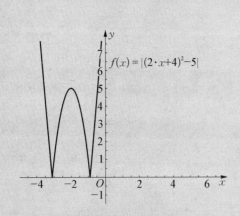

Figure 3 - 36

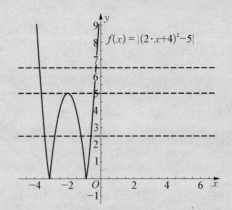

Figure 3 - 37

(2) As shown in Figure 3 - 37,

When $a < 0$, there is no intersection;

When $0 < a < 5$, there are 4 intersections of $y = f(x)$ and $y = a$;

When $a = 5$, there are 3 intersections of $y = f(x)$ and $y = a$;

When $a = 0$ or $a > 5$, there are 2 intersections of $y = f(x)$ and $y = a$.

伸缩变换 Stretching and Shrinking Graphs

(1) 竖直伸缩变换.

函数 $y = cf(x)$ ($c > 0$) 的图像,可将 $y = f(x)$ 图像上每一点的纵坐标伸 ($c > 1$) 缩 ($0 < c < 1$) 到原来的 c 倍,横坐标不变而得到.

(2) 水平伸缩变换.

函数 $y = f(cx)$ ($c > 0$) 的图像,可将 $y = f(x)$ 图像上每一点的横坐标伸 ($0 < c < 1$) 缩 ($c > 1$) 到原来的 $\dfrac{1}{c}$,纵坐标不变而得到.

The graph of $y = cf(x)$ while c is positive (and not equal to 1) is obtained by vertically stretching or shrinking the graph of $y = f(x)$. The points on the x-axis remain fixed, while all the other points move away from the x-axis for $c>1$ (a vertical stretch) or toward the x-axis for $0<c<1$ (a vertical shrink).

The graph of $y=f(cx)$ while c is positive (and not equal to 1) is obtained by horizontally stretching or shrinking the graph of $y=f(x)$. The points on the y-axis remain fixed, while all the other points move away from the y-axis for $c>1$ (a horizontal shrink) or toward the y-axis for $0<c<1$ (a horizontal stretch).

10 (1) Compare the graph of $g(x)=\dfrac{1}{3}\mid x\mid$ and $h(x)=3\mid x\mid$ with the graph of $f(x)=\mid x\mid$.

(2) Compare the graph of $g(x)=1-8x^3$ and $h(x)=1-\dfrac{1}{8}x^3$ with the graph of $f(x)=1-x^2$.

Solution:

(1) As shown in Figure 3 – 38, the graph of $g(x)=\dfrac{1}{3}\mid x\mid=\dfrac{1}{3}f(x)$ can be obtained by

vertically shrinking the graph of $f(x)=\mid x\mid$ $\left(\text{each } y\text{-value is multiplied by } \dfrac{1}{3}\right)$.

Similarly, as shown in Figure 3 – 39, the graph of $h(x)=3\mid x\mid=3f(x)$ can be obtained by vertically stretching the graph of $f(x)=\mid x\mid$ (each y-value is multiplied by 3).

(2) As shown in Figure 3 – 40, the graph of $g(x)=f(2x)=1-(2x)^3=1-8x^3$ can be obtained by horizontally shrinking the graph of $f(x)=1-x^2$.

Similarly, As shown in Figure 3 – 40, the graph of $h(x)=f\left(\dfrac{1}{2}x\right)=1-\left(\dfrac{1}{2}x\right)^3=1-\dfrac{1}{8}x^3$ can be obtained by horizontally stretching the graph of $f(x)=1-x^2$.

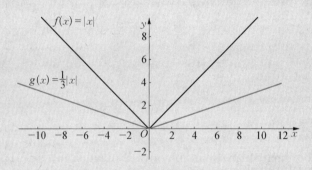

Figure 3 – 38

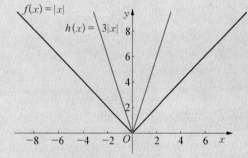

Figure 3 – 39

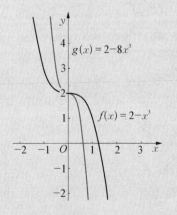

Figure 3 – 40

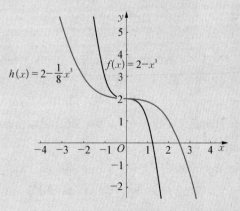

Figure 3 – 41

11 The graph of $y = f(x)$ is shown in Figure 3 - 42. Sketch the graph the following functions：

(1) $y = 2f(x)$.

(2) $y = \dfrac{1}{2}f(x)$.

(3) $y = f(2x)$.

(4) $y = f\left(\dfrac{1}{2}x\right)$.

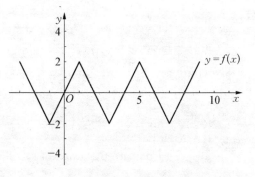

Figure 3 - 42

Solution：

(1)

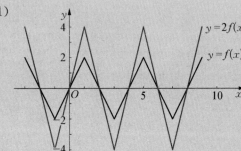

(2)

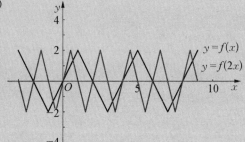

(3)

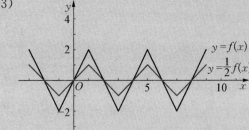

(4)

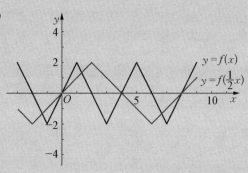

练习 Exercise

1. For each function，sketch (on the same coordinate plane) a graph of each function for $c = -1$, 1, and 2.

　　(1) $f(x) = |x| + c$.　　　　　　　　　　(2) $f(x) = |x - c|$.

　　(3) $f(x) = \sqrt{x} + c$.　　　　　　　　　　(4) $f(x) = \sqrt{x - c}$.

2. In the exercises （1）-（8），write an equation for the function described by the given characteristics.

　　(1) The shape of $f(x) = x^2$, but shifted 3 units to the right and 5 units down.

　　(2) The shape of $f(x) = x^2$, but shifted 4 units to the left，8 units up，and then reflected in the x-axis.

　　(3) The shape of $f(x) = x^3$, but shifted 11 units to the right.

　　(4) The shape of $f(x) = x^3$, but shifted 5 units to the left，6 units down，and then reflected in the y-axis.

　　(5) The shape of $f(x) = |x|$, but shifted 10 units up and then reflected in the x-axis.

(6) The shape of $f(x) = |x|$, but shifted 2 units to the left and 8 units down.

(7) The shape of $f(x) = \sqrt{x}$, but shifted 7 units to the left and then reflected in the origin.

(8) The shape of $f(x) = \sqrt{x}$, but shifted 9 units down and then reflected in the origin.

3. Writing equations from graphs.

(1) Use the graph of $f(x) = x^2$ to write an equation for each function whose graph is shown.

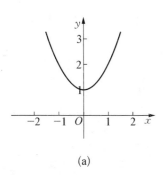
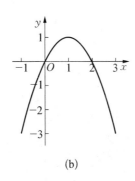
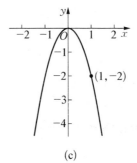
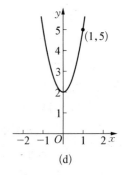

(a)　　　　　　　　(b)　　　　　　　　(c)　　　　　　　　(d)

(2) Use the graph of $f(x) = x^3$ to write an equation for each function whose graph is shown.

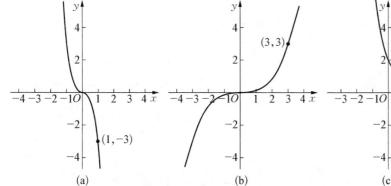
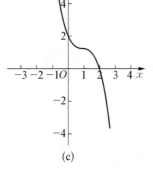
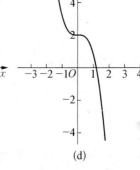

(a)　　　　　　　　(b)　　　　　　　　(c)　　　　　　　　(d)

(3) Use the graph of $f(x) = |x|$ to write an equation for each function whose graph is shown.

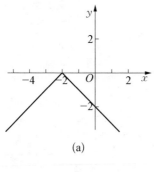
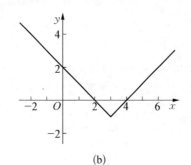

(a)　　　　　　　　　　　　　　(b)

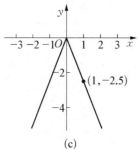
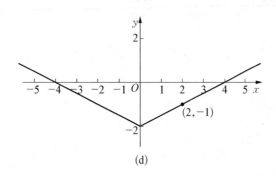

(c)　　　　　　　　　　　　　　(d)

(4) Use the graph of $f(x) = \sqrt{x}$ to write an equation for each function whose graph is shown.

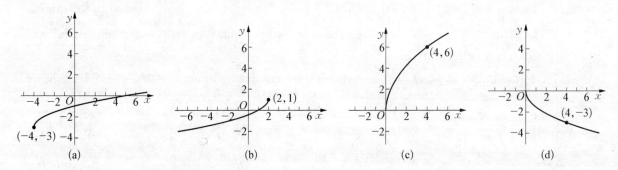

(a)　　　　　(b)　　　　　(c)　　　　　(d)

4. Find the points on a graph.

　(1) The graph of $y = f(x)$ goes through the points $(0, 1)$, $(1, 2)$ and $(2, 3)$. Find the corresponding points on the graph of $y = f(x + 2) - 1$.

　(2) The graph of $y = f(x)$ is obtained from a reflection of the graph of $y = x^2$ with respect to the line $x = 2$. Find the equation of $y = f(x)$.

　(3) Given that $f(x) = x^2 - 4x + 1$, sketch the graph of $y = f(|x|)$, and find the number of points at which the graphs of two functions $y = f(|x|)$ and $y = a$ intersect.

5. Use the graph of $y = f(x)$ (Figure 3 – 43) to find the intervals on which each of the graph in (1)–(5) is increasing or decreasing.

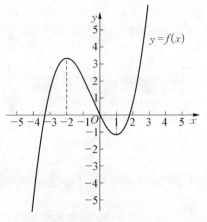

　(1) $y = f(-x)$.

　(2) $y = -f(x)$.

　(3) $y = f(2x)$.

　(4) $y = -f(x - 1)$.

　(5) $y = f(x - 2) + 1$.

Figure 3 – 43

6. The number of horsepower H required to overcome wind drag on an automobile is approximated by $H(x) = 0.004x^2 + 0.006x - 0.033$, $10 \leqslant x \leqslant 160$.

Where x is the speed of the car (in miles per hour).

　(1) Use a graphing utility to graph the function.

　(2) Rewrite the horsepower function so that x represents the speed in kilometers per hour. [Find $H(x/1.6)$.] Identify the type of transformation applied to the graph of the horsepower function.

几类重要的函数　Important Functions

4.1 ◆ 幂函数　The Power Functions

幂函数的定义 Definition of the Power Functions

我们已经初步了解了一般函数的基本性质：图像、单调性、奇偶性等.现在我们来看一类有代表性的函数：**幂函数**(Power Functions).

> **Definition of the Power Function**
>
> The function of the form $y = x^\alpha$, where α is a constant, is called a **power function.**

这里我们只讨论指数 α 是有理数的情形.

初中,我们学习过正比例函数 $y = x$、反比例函数 $y = \dfrac{1}{x}$ 以及二次函数 $y = x^2$.现在我们知道,它们都是幂函数,其指数分别为 1、−1 和 2. Figure 4 - 1 展示了这三个函数的图像.

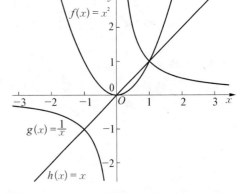

幂函数的图像 Graphing the Power Functions

根据初中学过的分数指数幂的运算规则,我们把幂函数的定义域总结如下：

> **Domains of the Power Functions**
>
> Domain of the power function $y = x^{\frac{n}{m}}$ is:
>
> - $(-\infty, \infty)$ if m is odd and $\dfrac{n}{m} > 0$;
>
> - $(-\infty, 0) \bigcup (0, \infty)$ if m is odd and $\dfrac{n}{m} \leqslant 0$;
>
> - $[0, \infty)$ if m is even and $\dfrac{n}{m} > 0$;
>
> - $(0, \infty)$ if m is even and $\dfrac{n}{m} < 0$.

知道了函数定义域之后,我们就可以像在初中学习过的那样,通过描点来画出幂函数的图像.

1 Draw the graphs of the functions $y = x^3$, $y = x^{-\frac{1}{3}}$ and $y = x^{\frac{2}{3}}$.

Solution: First, Table 4 – 1 gives the values of x and y:

Table 4 – 1

x	−3	−2.8	−2.6	−2.4	−2.2	−2	−1.8	−1.6	−1.4	−1.2	−1	−0.8
x^3	−27	−21.95	−17.58	−13.82	−10.65	−8	−5.832	−4.096	−2.744	−1.728	−1	−0.512
x	−0.6	−0.4	−0.2	0	0.2	0.4	0.6	0.8	1	1.2	1.4	1.6
x^3	−0.216	−0.064	−0.008	0	0.008	0.064	0.216	0.512	1	1.728	2.744	4.096
x	1.8	2	2.2	2.4	2.6	2.8	3	3.2	3.4	3.6	3.8	4
x^3	5.832	8	10.648	13.824	17.576	21.952	27	32.768	39.304	46.656	54.872	64

On the basis of the above table, we can get the approximate image of the power function $y = x^3$ (Figure 4 – 2).

Analogously, we can get the image of the function: $y = x^{-\frac{1}{3}}$ (Figure 4 – 3).

The image of the function $y = x^{\frac{2}{3}}$ (Figure 4 – 4).

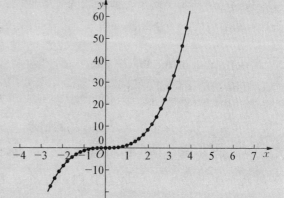

Figure 4 – 2

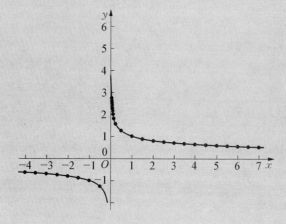

Figure 4 – 3

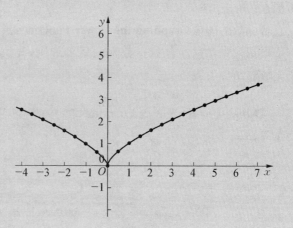

Figure 4 – 4

通过上面的例子我们已经看到,幂函数的图像会随着指数的变化而改变,但是它们的大致形状还是有规律的.事实上,我们可以把指数 α 是有理数的幂函数图像进行归类.

2 Draw the graph of the power functions $y = x^{\frac{n}{m}}$, where m, $n \in \mathbf{Z}$, gcd $(m, n) = 1$, and $m \neq 0$.

Solution: According to the algorithm of power, $x^{\frac{n}{m}} = \sqrt[m]{x^n}$ and $x^{-\frac{n}{m}} = \dfrac{1}{x^{\frac{n}{m}}}$. We will classify the exponents on the basis of the parity of m and the sign of $\dfrac{n}{m}$ (Table 4 - 2).

Table 4 - 2

$\dfrac{n}{m}$		m is odd		m is even
		n is odd	n is even	
>0	>1	(graph)	(graph)	(graph)
	$=1$	(graph)	N/A	N/A
	<1	(graph)	(graph)	(graph)
$=0$		N/A	(graph)	N/A
<0		(graph)	(graph)	(graph)

幂函数的性质 Properties of the Power Functions

3 In the power function $y = x^{\frac{n}{6}}$, $0 \leqslant n \leqslant 6$, which ones are odd functions, even functions or neither of the two?

Solution: The exponents of the seven power functions are: 0, $\frac{1}{6}$, $\frac{1}{3}$, $\frac{1}{2}$, $\frac{2}{3}$, $\frac{5}{6}$ and 1 respectively. According to the Table 4 - 2 of the example 2, we have: the power functions are odd functions when $n = 2$ and 6; the power functions are even functions when $n = 0$ and 4; the others are neither of the two.

4 Find the intervals of monotonicity of the power function $y = x^{\frac{1}{n}}$ ($n \in \mathbf{Z}$ and $n \neq 0$).

Solution: According to the Table 4 - 2 of the example 2, we get: the power functions are increasing on $(-\infty, +\infty)$ when $n > 0$ is odd; the power functions are decreasing on $(0, +\infty)$ when $n < 0$ is even; the power functions are decreasing respectively on $(-\infty, 0)$ when $n < 0$ is odd.

From the above examples, we can get the symmetry and the monotonicity of the power functions:

Properties of the Power Functions

The power function $y = x^{\frac{n}{m}}$ is:

- **odd** if m and n are both odd; **even** if m is odd while n is even; **neither** if m is even.

- **increasing** if n is odd and $\frac{n}{m} > 0$; **decreasing** if n is odd and m is even with $\frac{n}{m} < 0$.

- **increasing** for $x > 0$ and **decreasing** for $x < 0$ if n is even and $\frac{n}{m} > 0$; **decreasing** for $x > 0$ and **increasing** for $x < 0$ if n is even and $\frac{n}{m} < 0$; **decreasing** for either $x > 0$ or $x < 0$ if m, n are both odd and $\frac{n}{m} < 0$.

5 Observing the images of the following power functions (Figure 4 - 5 and Figure 4 - 6), and what are the similarities and differences?

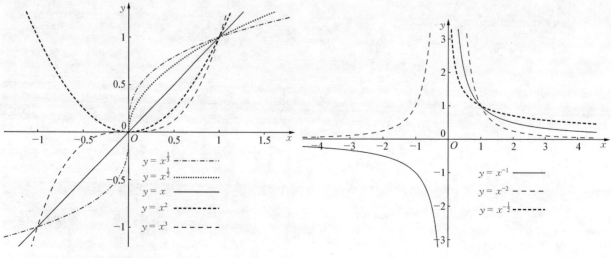

Figure 4 - 5   Figure 4 - 6

Solution: When $\dfrac{n}{m} > 1$, $\dfrac{n}{m} < 0$ and $0 < \dfrac{n}{m} < 1$, the graphs differ from each other by bending towards different directions, which is a property that would be later dubbed as "concavity".

6 The distance a ball falls down from the sky is directly proportional to the square of the time it falls. The ball falls 9 feet in the first second.

(1) Write an equation relating the distance traveled to the time.

(2) How far will the ball fall during the first 5 seconds?

Solution: If d is the distance (in feet) the ball falls and t is the time (in seconds), we have

$$d = kt^2.$$

Now because $d = 9$ when $t = 1$, we can get that $k = 9$. So, the equation to be solved is

$$d = 9t^2.$$

When $t = 5$, the distance is

$$d = 9 \cdot 5^2 = 225 (\text{feet}).$$

So, the ball will fall 225 feet during the first 5 seconds.

7 Arrange the following triples in ascending order without using a calculator:

(1) $1.5^{-\frac{1}{3}}$, $0.9^{-\frac{1}{3}}$, 1.

(2) $\left(-\dfrac{\sqrt{3}}{2}\right)^{-\frac{2}{5}}$, $\left(-\dfrac{5}{4}\right)^{\frac{2}{5}}$, $(-1.2)^{-\frac{4}{5}}$.

Solution: (1) Note that $1 = 1^{-\frac{1}{3}}$, whence the fact that $y = x^{-\frac{1}{3}}$ is decreasing when $x > 0$ implies:

$$1.5^{-\frac{1}{3}} < 1 < 0.9^{-\frac{1}{3}}.$$

(2) Since the function $y = x^{-\frac{2}{5}}$ is even, to arrange the second triple, it suffices to compare $\left(-\dfrac{\sqrt{3}}{2}\right)^{-\frac{2}{5}} = \left(\dfrac{\sqrt{3}}{2}\right)^{-\frac{2}{5}}$, $\left(-\dfrac{5}{4}\right)^{\frac{2}{5}} = \left(\dfrac{4}{5}\right)^{-\frac{2}{5}}$ and $(-1.2)^{-\frac{4}{5}} = (1.44)^{-\frac{2}{5}}$. Because $y = x^{-\frac{2}{5}}$ is decreasing for $x > 0$,

$$(-1.2)^{-\frac{4}{5}} < \left(-\dfrac{5}{4}\right)^{-\frac{2}{5}} < \left(-\dfrac{\sqrt{3}}{2}\right)^{\frac{2}{5}}.$$

练习 Exercise

1. According to the convention of fractional powers, $x^0 = 1$ whenever $x \neq 0$. How about the image of the power function $y = x^0$?

2. Sketch the graphs of the power functions $y = x^{-\frac{1}{4}}$ and $y = x^{\frac{5}{4}}$ in the coordinate plane.

3. Categorize the graphs of $y = x^{\frac{5}{3}}$, $y = x^{\frac{1}{4}}$ and $y = x^{-\frac{1}{6}}$ according to the Table 4 - 2 of Example 2.

4. Determine the symmetry of the power functions $y = x^{-\frac{n}{6}}$ for $1 \leqslant n \leqslant 6$.

5. Find the interval of monotonicity of the power functions $y = x^n (n \in \mathbf{Z})$.

6. The distance s an object falling varies directly with the square of the duration t of the fall neglecting air resistance. An object falls a distance of 144 feet in the first 2 seconds. How far will it fall in the first 5 seconds?

7. Arrange the following triples in ascending order without using a calculator:

   (1) $2^{\frac{2}{3}}$, $(-1.5)^{\frac{2}{3}}$, $(-5)^{\frac{1}{3}}$.

   (2) $0.16^{-\frac{3}{4}}$, $0.5^{-\frac{3}{2}}$, $6.25^{\frac{3}{8}}$.

8. True or False:

   (1) A power function is either even or odd.

   (2) If n is an odd integer and $\dfrac{n}{m} < 0$, then the power function $y = x^{\frac{n}{m}}$ is decreasing.

   (3) The graph of any power function $y = x^{\frac{n}{m}}$ can never go through the fourth quadrant.

9. The function $f(x) = x^{m^2 - 2m - 3} (m \in \mathbf{Z})$ is even. It decreases on $(0, +\infty)$.

   (1) Find $f(x)$.

   (2) Determine the symmetry of $g(x) = a\sqrt{f(x)} - \dfrac{b}{xf(x)}$.

10. The power function $f(x) = (m^2 - 5m + 1)x^{m+1}$ is an odd function.

    (1) Find m.

    (2) Find the range of $g(x) = f(x) + \sqrt{1 - 2x}$, where $x \in \left[0, \dfrac{1}{2}\right]$.

4.2 ◆ 指数函数 Exponential Functions

指数函数的定义 Definition of the Exponential Functions

一般地,函数 $y = a^x$ ($a > 0$,且 $a \neq 1$)叫作**指数函数**,其中 x 是自变量,函数的定义域是 **R**.

Definition of the Exponential Functions

The exponential function f with base a is denoted by $f(x) = a^x$ where $a > 0$, $a \neq 1$, and x is any real number.

我们知道,当 x 是有理数时, a^x ($a > 0$ 且 $a \neq 1$)有完全确定的意义;而当 x 是无理数时,也可以规定 a^x 的意义.例如,对于无理数 $\sqrt{2}$,取它的不足近似值: 1,1.4,1.41,1.414,1.414 2…

于是相应地有: a^1, $a^{1.4}$, $a^{1.41}$, $a^{1.414}$, $a^{1.414\,2}$…

可以观察到它逐渐地趋近于一个常数,这个常数就规定为 $a^{\sqrt{2}}$.

我们将通过下面的例子学习指数函数是单调函数.

❶ A cell divides x times into y cells, please complete the Table 4 - 3:

Solution： According to the law of the cell division，we can get the Table 4 - 4：

Table 4 - 3

x	$y=2^x$
1	
2	
	16
5	
	128
8	
10	

Table 4 - 4

x	$y=2^x$
1	2
2	4
4	16
5	32
7	128
8	256
10	1 024

我们发现 y 随着 x 的增大而增大,这个发现对不对呢? 我们可以通过解析式判断,因为 2^x 是随着 x 的增大而增大,所以我们的发现是正确的.

我们还可以绘制函数 $y=2^x$ 的图像,进行分析.

列表(Table 4 - 5)并描点作图(Figure 4 - 7).

Table 4 - 5

x	$\cdots$	-3	-2	0	1	2	3	$\cdots$
y	$\cdots$	0.125	0.25	1	2	4	8	$\cdots$

观察 Figure 4 - 7,可以看出 y 随 x 的增大而增大.类似地,若函数在定义域上始终递增,我们称之为增函数.若函数在定义域上始终递减,我们称之为减函数.

那么指数函数是增函数,这个判断对吗?

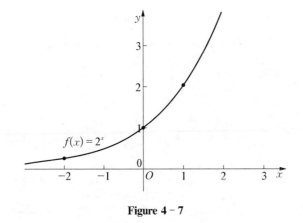

Figure 4 - 7　　　　　　　　**Figure 4 - 8**

通过列举一些指数函数的图像,见 Figure 4 - 8,可以看出有的指数函数是增函数,有的指数函数是减函数.

一般的,指数函数 $y=a^x$($a>0$ 且 $a\neq 1$),当 $a>1$ 时,它是增函数,当 $0<a<1$ 时,它是减函数.

2 Compare the two numbers in the following groups：

(1) $2^{\sqrt{3}}$ and $2^{1.7}$.　　(2) $0.6^{-\frac{2}{3}}$ and $0.6^{-\frac{3}{4}}$.　　(3) $\left(\frac{1}{3}\right)^{-2}$ and 27.

> **Solution：**
>
> (1) Since $2 > 1$, $2^{\sqrt{3}} > 2^{1.7}$.
>
> (2) Since $0 < 0.6 < 1$, $0.6^{-\frac{2}{3}} < 0.6^{-\frac{3}{4}}$.
>
> (3) Since $\left(\frac{1}{3}\right)^{-2} = 3^2$, $27 = 3^3$ and $3 > 1$, $\left(\frac{1}{3}\right)^{-2} < 27$.

3 Use the graph of the function $y = 10^x$ (Figure 4 - 9) to estimate $\sqrt[3]{400}$.

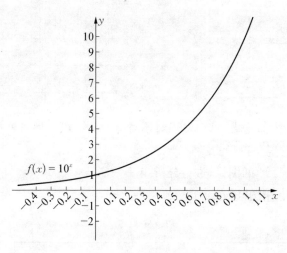

$f(x) = 10^x$

Figure 4 - 9

> **Solution：** Because $\sqrt[3]{400} = (4 \times 10^2)^{\frac{1}{3}}$, we have $4 \approx 10^{0.6}$ from the graph of $y = 10^x$.
> Then, $\sqrt[3]{400} \approx (10^{0.6} \times 10^2)^{\frac{1}{3}} \approx 10^{0.87}$. And $10^{0.87} \approx 7.4$, so $\sqrt[3]{400} \approx 7.4$.

当指数函数是增函数时，若 x 较大，则相应的 y 非常大(如 $2^{100} \approx 1.3 \times 10^{30}$)，增加的速度便十分惊人.我们将通过下面的例子结合指数函数的增长速度分析问题.

4 Let $f(x) = 2^x$ and $g(x) = x^2$, how many times do the graphs of $f(x)$ and $g(x)$ meet?

> **Solution：** Apparently the two graphs intersect only once when $x < 0$ (Figure 4 - 10). Meanwhile, they intersect again at $(2, 4)$ and $(4, 16)$. Since $f(x)$ increases faster than $g(x)$ when $x > 4$, it follows that the aforementioned three points are the only intersections of these two graphs.

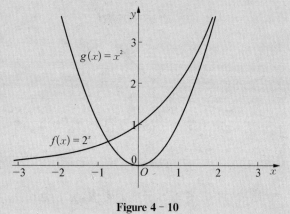

$g(x) = x^2$

$f(x) = 2^x$

Figure 4 - 10

5 Observe the graphs (Figure 4 - 11) and summarize the properties of exponential functions.

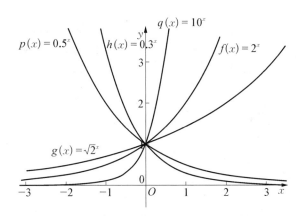

Figure 4 - 11

Solution： The properties of exponential function $y = a^x (a > 0, a \neq 1)$ are shown in the Table 4 - 6.

Table 4 - 6

Property	$0 < a < 1$	$a > 1$
Domain	R	
Range	$\mathbf{R}^+$	
Symmetry	neither odd nor even	
Monotonicity	decreasing	increasing
Graph		
Distribution	above the x-axis	
Fixed point	$(0, 1)$	
Asymptote	$y = 0$	

6 The annual interest rate of one-year fixed deposit of the bank is 2.25%. If the deposit is not withdrawn and kept in the bank, the bank will automatically transfer the principal and 80% of the interest (20% of the interest shall be paid to the bank) to the one-year fixed deposit automatically.

(1) A person deposits $200,000$ yuan in a bank with a one-year fixed deposit. How much is the sum of the principal and interest excluding the interest tax after five years? Round your answer to the closest integer.

(2) If the principal is a yuan, and the annual interest rate is r yuan, the sum of the principal and interest that a client would receive after x years is y yuan. Write the function of y with x.

Solution:

(1) One year later, the sum of the principal and interest is

$$y_1 = 20 + 20 \times 2.25\% \times 80\% = 20(1 + 2.25\% \times 80\%),$$

Two years later, the sum of the principal and interest is

$$y_2 = y_1 + y_1 \times 2.25\% \times 80\% = y_1(1 + 2.25\% \times 80\%) = 20(1 + 2.25\% \times 80\%)^2,$$

......

Five years later, the sum of the principal and interest is

$$y_5 = 20(1 + 2.25\% \times 80\%)^5,$$

We have $y_5 \approx 21.8660$.

So, the answer is 218,660 yuan.

(2) From the solution (1), we can get $y = a(1 + r \cdot 80\%)^x$.

7 A certain radioactive material is constantly changing into other substances, and the remaining material is 84% of the original after each year. Draw the image of the remaining amount of this material with respect to time, and use the image to determine the number of years after which half of the material remains. Round your answer to one significant digit.

Solution: Suppose the initial mass of this substance is 1, after x years, the remaining quantity is y.

After one year, the remaining amount is $y = 1 \times 84\% = 0.84^1$.

After two years, the remaining amount is $y = 0.84 \times 84\% = 0.84^2$.

......

After x years, the remaining amount is $y = 0.84^x$.

From the above formula, we can get the following table (see Table 4 - 7):

Table 4 - 7

x	0	1	2	3	4	6
y	1	0.84	0.71	0.59	0.50	0.35

Draw the graph of the function $y = 0.84^x$ (Figure 4 - 12).

When $y = 0.5$, $x \approx 4$.

It means that the remaining amount of the material is half of the original after four years.

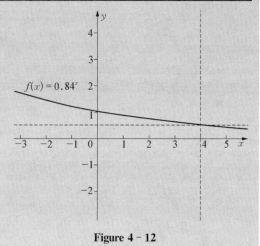

Figure 4 - 12

练习 Exercise

1. Find all pairs of graphs that are symmetric with respect to y-axis.

   $y = 4^x$, $y = 2.5^x$, $y = 0.4^x$, $y = 0.25^x$.

2. Draw the graphs in the same coordinate system.

   (1) $y = \left(\dfrac{3}{2}\right)^x$.　　　　　　　　(2) $y = \left(\dfrac{2}{3}\right)^x$.

3. Calculate a, b, c, d, e with calculator: (round to 0.01)

   $a = 7^2$, $b = 7^{2.25}$, $c = 7^{2.5}$, $d = 7^{2.75}$, $e = 7^3$.

   (1) Evaluate $b - a$, $c - b$, $d - c$, and $e - d$. What can be concluded from these differences?

   (2) Evaluate $\dfrac{b}{a}$, $\dfrac{c}{b}$, $\dfrac{d}{c}$ and $\dfrac{e}{d}$. What can be concluded from these ratios?

4. If the graph of the function $f(x) = 2^{-x+1} + m$ does not go through the first quadrant, find the range of m.

5. Let $f(x) = \dfrac{a^x - 1}{a^x + 1}$ $(a > 0, a \neq 1)$.

   (1) Determine the symmetry of $f(x)$.　　(2) Determine the monotonicity of $f(x)$.

6. Let $f(x) = a^x + \dfrac{x - 2}{x + 1}$ $(a > 1)$.

   (1) Prove that the function $f(x)$ is increasing on $(-1, +\infty)$.

   (2) Use proof by contradiction to show that the equation $f(x) = 0$ does not have negative roots.

7. In a certain forest, there is a cutting quota of 100,000 cubic meters of timber. The annual average growth rate of the timber that can be cut in the forest is 8%, while the timber that can be harvested is y cubic meters after x years.

   (1) Write the function of y in terms of x.

   (2) Find the number of years after which the amount of timber that can be harvested will increase to 400,000 cubic meters.

8. In a discount clothing store, the price is reduced by 10% every day until the clothing is sold out. What is the selling price of the clothing with the original price of 175 yuan by the fifth day?

9. The annual interest rate of a one-year fixed deposit is 2.25% in a bank. One person deposits 10,000 yuan in the bank for 10 years. 20% of interest tax will be paid when the deposit is transferred every year. What is the sum of principal and interest after 10 years?

10. If $f(x) = n^x$ and $g(x) = x^n$, where $n \in \mathbf{N}$ and $n > 1$, how many times do the graphs of $f(x)$ and $g(x)$ intersect?

4.3 ◆ 对数运算　Operations of Logarithms

对数的定义 Definition of Logarithm

　　一般地，如果 a $(a > 0, a \neq 1)$ 的 b 次幂等于 N，即 $a^b = N$，那么数 b 叫作以 a 为底 N 的对数，记作 $\log_a N = b$，其中 a 叫作对数的底数，N 叫作真数。

在对数中,需要注意:

(1) 底数 $a > 0$ 且 $a \neq 1$.

(2) 零和负数没有对数,真数为正数,即 $N > 0$.

Definition of Logarithm

Generally, if $a^b = N$ $(a > 0,\ a \neq 1)$, then b is called the logarithm of N with base a, written as $\log_a N = b$.

The equations $y = \log_a x$ and $x = a^y$ are equivalent. The first equation is in logarithmic form and the second is in exponential form. For example, $2 = \log_3 9$ is equivalent to $9 = 3^2$, and $5^3 = 125$ is equivalent to $\log_5 125 = 3$.

When evaluating logarithms, remember that a logarithm is an exponent. This means that $\log_a x$ is the exponent to which a must be raised to obtain x. For instance, $\log_2 8 = 3$ because 2 raised to the third power is 8.

常用对数函数 The Common Logarithmic Function

通常以 10 为底的对数叫作**常用对数**(common logarithmic). 为了简便,N 的常用对数 $\log_{10} N$ 简记作 $\lg N$.

The logarithmic function with base 10 is called the common logarithmic function. It is denoted by $\log_{10}$ or simply by log. On most calculators, this function is denoted by $\boxed{\text{LOG}}$.

自然对数函数 The Natural Logarithmic Function

在科学技术中,常用到无理数 $e = 2.718\,28\cdots$ 为底的对数,以 e 为底的对数叫作**自然对数**(Natural Logarithmic). 为了简便,N 的自然对数 $\log_e N$ 简记作 $\ln N$.

The logarithmic function with base e is called the natural logarithmic function. It is denoted by the special symbol $\ln x$, read as "the natural log of x" or "el en of x". Note that the natural logarithm is written without a base. The base is understood to be e. On most calculators, this function is denoted by $\boxed{\text{LN}}$.

The following properties follow directly from the definition of the logarithmic function with base a.

Properties of the Logarithms

(1) $\log_a 1 = 0$ because $a^0 = 1$.

(2) $\log_a a = 1$ because $a^1 = a$.

(3) $\log_a a^x = x$ and $a^{\log_a x} = x$.   Inverse Properties

(4) If $\log_a x = \log_a y$, then $x = y$.   One-to-One Property

对于指数的运算,我们有以下三条运算法则.

$a^p \cdot a^q = a^{p+q}$;

$\dfrac{a^p}{a^q} = a^{p-q}$ $\qquad$ $(a > 0,\ a \neq 1,\ p,\ q \in \mathbf{R})$;

$(a^p)^q = a^{pq}$.

那么,对数的运算与指数的运算应该有着相对应的法则.

在研究对数的运算前,先任取两个正数 M、N,用计算器计算并填写完成下表(Table 4 - 8):

Table 4 - 8

M	N	$\lg(MN)$	$\lg\dfrac{M}{N}$	$\lg M + \lg N$	$\lg M - \lg N$
2 001	1 949		0.011 4	6.591 1	
2 008	3.2			3.807 9	
2.36	10.89		−0.664 1		
0.07	68	0.677 6			−2.987 4

从表格(Table 4 – 8)中,你发现了什么规律吗?

对数的运算性质 The Operation Properties of the Logarithms

Let a be a positive number such that $a \neq 1$, and let n be a real number. If M and N are positive real numbers, then the following properties are true.

Product Property: $\log_a(M \cdot N) = \log_a M + \log_a N$;

Quotient Property: $\log_a \dfrac{M}{N} = \log_a M - \log_a N$;

Power Property: $\log_a M^n = n \log_a M$.

Each of the three properties above can be proved by using properties of exponential functions.

下面证明性质(1):

设 $\log_a M = p$,$\log_a N = q$,由对数定义,得:

$$M = a^p,\ N = a^q,$$

$$M \cdot N = a^p \cdot a^q = a^{p+q},$$

$$\log_a(MN) = p + q = \log_a M + \log_a N.$$

所以,$\log_a(MN) = \log_a M + \log_a N$.

下面证明性质(2):

设 $\log_a M = p$,$\log_a N = q$. 由对数定义,得:

$$M = a^p,\ N = a^q,$$

$$\frac{M}{N} = \frac{a^p}{a^q} = a^{p-q},$$

$$\log_a \frac{M}{N} = p - q = \log_a M - \log_a N.$$

所以,$\log_a \dfrac{M}{N} = \log_a M - \log_a N$.

下面证明性质(3):

设 $\log_a M = p$. 由对数定义,得:

$$M = a^p,\ M^n = (a^p)^n = a^{np},$$

$$\log_a M^n = np = n \log_a M.$$

所以，$\log_a M^n = n \log_a M$.

证明思想总结：

运用转化的思想，先通过假设，将对数式转化成指数式，并利用幂的运算性质进行恒等变形；然后再根据对数定义将指数式转化成对数式.

换底公式 Change-of-Base Formula

Let a, b and x be positive real numbers such that $a \neq 1$ and $b \neq 1$. Then $\log_a x$ can be converted to a different base as follow.

$$\log_a x = \frac{\log_b x}{\log_b a}.$$

下面来证明换底公式：

设 $\log_a x = m$，写成指数式 $a^m = x$.

两边取以 b 为底的对数，得：

$$m \log_b a = \log_b x.$$

因为 $a > 0$，$a \neq 1$，$\log_b a \neq 0$，因此上式两边可除以 $\log_b a$，得 $m = \dfrac{\log_b x}{\log_b a}$.

所以，$\log_a x = \dfrac{\log_b x}{\log_b a}$.

推论 Corollary

(1) $\log_a b = \dfrac{1}{\log_b a}$.   (2) $\log_{a^m} b^n = \dfrac{n}{m} \log_a b$.

1 (1) Write the following exponential equations in logarithmic form.

(a) $5^4 = 625$;

(b) $2^{-5} = \dfrac{1}{32}$;

(c) $3^a = 81$;

(d) $\left(\dfrac{1}{3}\right)^m = 5.73$.

(2) Write the following logarithmic equations in exponential form.

(a) $\log_{\frac{1}{2}} 16 = -4$;

(b) $\log_2 \dfrac{1}{128} = -7$;

(c) $\log_a \dfrac{1}{10} = -2$;

(d) $\log_{0.5} 10 = m$.

Solution：

(1) (a) $\log_5 625 = 4$;

(b) $\log_2 \dfrac{1}{32} = -5$;

(c) $\log_3 81 = a$;

(d) $\log_{\frac{1}{3}} 5.73 = m$.

(2) (a) $\left(\dfrac{1}{2}\right)^{-4} = 16$;

(b) $2^{-7} = \dfrac{1}{128}$;

(c) $a^{-2} = \dfrac{1}{10}$;

(d) $0.5^m = 10$.

2 Evaluate each logarithm at the indicated value of x.

(1) $f(x) = \log_2 x$, $x = 32$.

(2) $f(x) = \log_3 x$, $x = 1$.

(3) $f(x) = \log_4 x$, $x = 2$.

(4) $f(x) = \log_{10} x$, $x = \dfrac{1}{100}$.

Solution: (1) $f(32) = \log_2 32 = 5$ because $2^5 = 32$.

(2) $f(1) = \log_3 1 = 0$ because $3^0 = 1$.

(3) $f(2) = \log_4 2 = \dfrac{1}{2}$ because $4^{\frac{1}{2}} = \sqrt{4} = 2$.

(4) $f\left(\dfrac{1}{100}\right) = \log_{10} \dfrac{1}{100} = -2$ because $10^{-2} = \dfrac{1}{10^2} = \dfrac{1}{100}$.

3 Evaluate the following logarithmic values without using calculator.

(1) $\lg 0.01^4$.

(2) $\log_5 \sqrt[3]{5}$.

(3) $\log_2 (4^7 \times 2^5)$.

(4) $\lg 2 + \lg 5$.

(5) $\ln e^6 - \ln e^2$.

(6) $\log_3 \dfrac{27}{5} + \log_3 \dfrac{2}{3} - \log_3 \dfrac{6}{5}$.

(7) $\log_2 \sqrt{\dfrac{7}{48}} + \log_2 12 - \dfrac{1}{2} \log_2 42$.

(8) $\lg 25 + \lg 2 \cdot \lg 50 + (\lg 2)^2$.

Solution:

(1) $\lg 0.01^4 = 4\lg 0.01 = 4 \times (-2) = -8$.

(2) $\log_5 \sqrt[3]{5} = \log_5 5^{\frac{1}{3}} = \dfrac{1}{3}$.

(3) $\log_2 (4^7 \times 2^5) = \log_2 2^{14} + \log_2 2^5 = 14 + 5 = 19$.

(4) $\lg 2 + \lg 5 = \lg (2 \times 5) = \lg 10 = 1$.

(5) $\ln e^6 - \ln e^2 = 6 - 2 = 4$.

(6) $\log_3 \dfrac{27}{5} + \log_3 \dfrac{2}{3} - \log_3 \dfrac{6}{5} = \log_3 \left(\dfrac{27}{5} \times \dfrac{2}{3} \div \dfrac{6}{5}\right) = \log_3 3 = 1$.

(7) $\log_2 \sqrt{\dfrac{7}{48}} + \log_2 12 - \dfrac{1}{2} \log_2 42 = \log_2 \left(\sqrt{\dfrac{7}{48}} \times 12 \div \sqrt{42}\right) = \log_2 \dfrac{\sqrt{2}}{2} = -\dfrac{1}{2}$.

(8) $\lg 25 + \lg 2 \cdot \lg 50 + (\lg 2)^2 = \lg 25 + \lg 2 \cdot (\lg 50 + \lg 2)$

$= \lg 25 + \lg 2 \cdot \lg 100$

$= \lg 25 + 2\lg 2$

$= \lg 25 + \lg 4$

$= \lg 100$

$= 2$

The properties of logarithms are useful for rewriting logarithmic expressions in forms that simplify the operations of algebra. This is true because these properties convert complicated products, quotients, and exponential forms into simpler sums, differences, and products respectively.

4 Expand each logarithmic expression.

(1) $\log_4 5x^3 y$. $(x > 0, y > 0)$

(2) $\ln \dfrac{\sqrt{3x - 5}}{7}$.

Solution：

(1) $\log_4 5x^3 y = \log_4 5 + \log_4 x^3 + \log_4 y$　　　　Product Property

　　　　　　　$= \log_4 5 + 3\log_4 x + \log_4 y.$　　　　Power Property

(2) $\ln \dfrac{\sqrt{3x-5}}{7} = \ln \dfrac{(3x-5)^{\frac{1}{2}}}{7}$　　　　Rewrite using rational exponent

　　　　　　　$= \ln (3x-5)^{\frac{1}{2}} - \ln 7$　　　　Quotient Property

　　　　　　　$= \dfrac{1}{2} \ln (3x-5) - \ln 7.$　　　　Power Property

5 Combine terms of each logarithmic expression.

(1) $\dfrac{1}{2}\lg x + 3\lg (x+1).$　　　　(2) $2\ln (x+2) - \ln x.$　　　　(3) $\dfrac{1}{3}[\log_2 x + \log_2 (x+1)].$

Solution：

(1) $\dfrac{1}{2}\lg x + 3\lg (x+1) = \lg x^{1/2} + \lg (x+1)^3$　　　　Power Property

　　　　　　　　　$= \lg [\sqrt{x}\,(x+1)^3].$　　　　Product Property

(2) $2\ln (x+2) - \ln x = \ln (x+2)^2 - \ln x$　　　　Power Property

　　　　　　　　　$= \ln \dfrac{(x+2)^2}{x}.$　　　　Quotient Property

(3) $\dfrac{1}{3}[\log_2 x + \log_2 (x+1)] = \dfrac{1}{3}\log_2 [x(x+1)]$　　　　Product Property

　　　　　　　　　$= \log_2 [x(x+1)]^{\frac{1}{3}}$　　　　Power Property

　　　　　　　　　$= \log_2 \sqrt[3]{x(x+1)}.$　　　　Rewrite with a Radical

6 If $3^a = 2$, $3^b = 5$, write $\log_3 \sqrt{30}$ in terms of a, b.

Solution：

Since $3^a = 2$, $3^b = 5$, we have $a = \log_3 2$, $b = \log_3 5$. Thus, $\log_3 \sqrt{30} = \dfrac{1}{2}\log_3 30 = \dfrac{1}{2}\log_3 (2 \times 3 \times$

$5) = \dfrac{1}{2}(\log_3 2 + \log_3 3 + \log_3 5) = \dfrac{1}{2}(a + 1 + b).$

7 Scientists use the Richter scale to measure the intensity of an earthquake. If I is the relative energy intensity released by an earthquake, then the Richter magnitude r can be defined as $r = \dfrac{2}{3}\lg I + 2$. Find the ratio of relative energy released by earthquakes with $r = 7.8$ and $r = 6.9$. (Round your answer to the closest integer.)

Solution：

The relative energy intensities of $r = 7.8$ and $r = 6.9$ are I_1 and I_2 respectively.

We can get $\begin{cases} \dfrac{2}{3}\lg I_1 + 2 = 6.9 & ① \\[2mm] \dfrac{2}{3}\lg I_2 + 2 = 7.8 & ② \end{cases}$, From ②－①, $\dfrac{2}{3}(\lg I_2 - \lg I_1) = 0.9.$

It means $\lg \dfrac{I_2}{I_1} = 1.35$.

So, $\dfrac{I_2}{I_1} = 10^{1.35} \approx 22$.

Therefore, the relative energy degree of the earthquake with $r = 7.8$ is 22 times that of $r = 6.9$.

8 Calculate:

(1) $\log_8 9 \cdot \log_{27} 32$.

(2) $\log_2 3 \cdot \log_3 5 \cdot \log_5 8$.

(3) $5^{1-\log_{0.2} 3}$.

(4) $\log_4 3 \cdot \log_9 2 - \log_{\frac{1}{2}} \sqrt[4]{32}$.

Solution:

(1) $\log_8 9 \cdot \log_{27} 32 = \log_{2^3} 3^2 \cdot \log_{3^3} 2^5 = \dfrac{2}{3} \log_2 3 \cdot \dfrac{5}{3} \log_3 2 = \dfrac{10}{9}$.

(2) $\log_2 3 \cdot \log_3 5 \cdot \log_5 8 = \dfrac{1}{\log_3 2} \cdot \log_3 5 \cdot \log_5 8 = \log_2 5 \cdot \log_5 8 = \dfrac{\log_5 8}{\log_5 2} = \log_2 8 = 3$.

(3) $5^{1-\log_{0.2} 3} = 5^{1+\log_5 3} = 5^{\log_5 (5 \times 3)} = 5^{\log_5 15} = 15$.

(4) $\log_4 3 \cdot \log_9 2 - \log_{\frac{1}{2}} \sqrt[4]{32} = \log_{2^2} 3 \cdot \log_{3^2} 2 - \log_{2^{-1}} 2^{\frac{5}{4}}$

$\qquad = \dfrac{1}{2} \log_2 3 \cdot \dfrac{1}{2} \log_3 2 + \dfrac{5}{4} \log_2 2$

$\qquad = \dfrac{1}{4} + \dfrac{5}{4} = \dfrac{3}{2}$.

9 If $\log_{18} 2 = a$, write $\log_3 2$ in terms of a.

Solution:

Since $\log_{18} 2 = \dfrac{\log_3 2}{\log_3 18} = \dfrac{\log_3 2}{2 + \log_3 2} = a$, we can get $\log_3 2 = 2a + a \log_3 2$.

So $\log_3 2 = \dfrac{2a}{1-a}$.

10 (1) If $\log_2 3 = a$, $\log_3 7 = b$, write $\log_{42} 56$ in terms of a, b.

(2) If $\log_{12} 27 = a$, write $\log_6 16$ in terms of a.

Solution: (1) From $\log_3 2 = \dfrac{1}{\log_2 3} = \dfrac{1}{a}$, $\log_3 7 = b$, we can get $\log_{42} 56 = \dfrac{\log_3 56}{\log_3 42} = \dfrac{\log_3 (7 \times 2^3)}{\log_3 (2 \times 3 \times 7)} =$

$\dfrac{\log_3 7 + 3 \log_3 2}{\log_3 2 + \log_3 3 + \log_3 7} = \dfrac{b + 3 \cdot \dfrac{1}{a}}{\dfrac{1}{a} + 1 + b} = \dfrac{ab + 3}{1 + a + ab}$.

(2) Since $\log_{12} 27 = \dfrac{\log_2 27}{\log_2 12} = \dfrac{3 \log_2 3}{2 + \log_2 3} = a$, $\log_2 3 = \dfrac{2a}{3-a}$.

So, $\log_6 16 = \dfrac{\log_2 16}{\log_2 6} = \dfrac{4}{1 + \log_2 3} = \dfrac{4}{1 + \dfrac{2a}{3-a}} = \dfrac{4(3-a)}{3+a}$.

练习 Exercise

1. Evaluate the following logarithmic values without using calculator.

    (1) $\log_9 27$.   (2) $\lg 100^3$.   (3) $\log_2 2\sqrt[3]{2}$.   (4) $\log_3 9 \times \log_3 27$.

    (5) $\lg\sqrt{10} - \lg 0.1^2$.   (6) $\log_{12} 6 + \log_{12} 2$.   (7) $2\log_{18} 3 + \log_{18} 2$.

2. Use the properties of logarithms to expand the expression for the sum, difference, or the constant multiple of logarithms. (Assume all variables are positive.)

    (1) $\ln 4x$.   (2) $\log_3 10z$.   (3) $\log_8 x^4$.   (4) $\lg\dfrac{y}{2}$.

    (5) $\log_5\dfrac{5}{x}$.   (6) $\log_6\dfrac{1}{z^3}$.   (7) $\ln\sqrt{z}$.   (8) $\ln\sqrt[3]{t}$.

    (9) $\ln xyz^2$.   (10) $\ln z(z-1)^2$, $z>1$.   (11) $\lg\dfrac{xy^4}{z^5}$.

    (12) $\log_5\dfrac{x^2}{y^2 z^3}$.   (13) $\ln\dfrac{6}{\sqrt{x^2+1}}$.   (14) $\ln\sqrt{\dfrac{x^2}{y^3}}$.   (15) $\log_2 x^4\sqrt{\dfrac{y}{z^3}}$.

3. Combine terms of each logarithmic expression.

    (1) $\ln 2 + \ln x$.   (2) $\log_5 8 - \log_5 t$.   (3) $2\log_2 x + 4\log_2 y$.

    (4) $\dfrac{2}{3}\log_7(z-2)$.   (5) $\dfrac{1}{4}\log_3 5x$.   (6) $-4\log_6 2x$.

    (7) $\lg x - 2\lg(x+1)$.   (8) $2\ln 8 + 5\ln(z-4)$.   (9) $\lg x - 2\lg y + 3\lg z$.

    (10) $\ln x - [\ln(x+1) + \ln(x-1)]$.   (11) $4[\ln z + \ln(z+5)] - 2\ln(z-5)$.

    (12) $\dfrac{1}{3}[\log_8 y + 2\log_8(y+4)] - \log_8(y-1)$.

4. If $\log_8 3 = a$, $\log_8 5 = b$, write the following formulas in terms of a, b.

    (1) $\log_8 75$.   (2) $\log_8 225$.   (3) $\log_8 0.12$.   (4) $\log_8\dfrac{3}{64}$.

5. Calculate:

    (1) $\log_3 2 \cdot \log_2 27$.   (2) $\log_{25} 8 \cdot \log_8 5$.   (3) $\dfrac{1}{\log_2 6} + \dfrac{1}{\log_3 6}$.   (4) $\dfrac{1}{\log_4 6} + \dfrac{1}{\log_9 6}$.

6. If $\log_9 16 = a$, write $\log_6\sqrt{24}$ in terms of a.

7. Calculate:

    (1) $2\lg\dfrac{5}{3} - \lg\dfrac{7}{4} + 2\lg 3 + \dfrac{1}{2}\lg 49$.   (2) $\dfrac{\lg\sqrt{8} + \lg 27 - \lg\sqrt{1\,000}}{\lg 1.8}$.

    (3) $5^{2+\log_5 3}$.   (4) $\left(\dfrac{1}{3}\right)^{\log_3 4 - 2}$.

8. If x, y, z are positive numbers, and $3^x = 4^y = 6^z$, prove $\dfrac{1}{z} - \dfrac{1}{x} = \dfrac{1}{2y}$.

9. Let $\lg 2 = 0.3010$.

    (1) How many digits does $8^{11}\,25^{17}$ have?

    (2) How many consecutive zeros are there after the decimal point of $\left(\dfrac{1}{4}\right)^{21}\left(\dfrac{1}{5}\right)^{10}$?

10. If $\log_{18} 9 = a\,(a \neq 2)$, $18^b = 5$, find $\log_{36} 45$.

4.4 ◈ 对数函数 Logarithmic Functions

对数函数的定义 Definition of the Logarithmic Functions

一般地,函数 $y=\log_a x$ ($a>0$ 且 $a\neq 1$)就是指数函数 $y=a^x$ ($a>0$ 且 $a\neq 1$)的反函数.因为指数函数 $y=a^x$ 的定义域是 **R**,值域是 $(0,+\infty)$,所以,函数 $y=\log_a x$ 的定义域是 $(0,+\infty)$,值域是 **R**.

函数 $y=\log_a x$ ($a>0$ 且 $a\neq 1$)叫作**对数函数**,其中 x 是自变量,定义域是 $(0,+\infty)$.

Definition of the Logarithmic Function with Base *a*

For $x>0$, $a>0$, and $a\neq 1$, $y=\log_a x$ if and only if $x=a^y$.

The function $f(x)=\log_a x$, read as "log base a of x", is called the logarithmic function with base a.

【试一试】作出函数 $y=\log_2 x$ 的图像.

作图方法 1:描点法作图(Figure 4-13)

作图方法 2:图像变换法作图

因为对数函数和指数函数互为反函数,图像关于直线 $y=x$ 对称,所以只要作出 $y=2^x$ 的图像关于直线 $y=x$ 对称的曲线,就可以得到 $y=\log_2 x$ 的图像(Figure 4-14).

说明:对数函数的图像是通过指数函数的图像得到的,用原函数图像研究其反函数图像是研究函数图像的一种方法.

【想一想】观察图像(Figure 4-15),根据对数函数的意义和指数函数的性质,总结对数函数的性质.

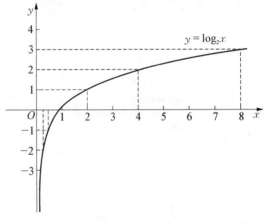

Figure 4-13

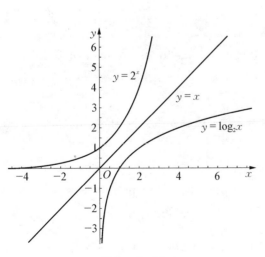

Figure 4-14

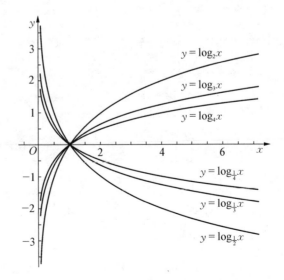

Figure 4-15

对数函数的图像与性质 Graphs and Properties of the Logarithmic Functions

对数函数 $y = \log_a x$（$a > 0$ 且 $a \neq 1$）的性质(see Table 4-9)：

Table 4-9

	$0 < a < 1$	$a > 1$
Domain	$(0, +\infty)$	
Range	**R**	
Symmetry	neither odd nor even	
Monotonicity	decreasing	increasing
Graph		
Intercept	$(1, 0)$	
Asymptote	y-axis	

1 Find the domains of the following functions.

(1) $y = \log_a x^2$.

(2) $y = \log_a \dfrac{x}{4-x}$.

(3) $y = \log_x (5-x)$.

(4) $y = \log_{x+1}(16 - 4^x)$.

Solution:

(1) From $x^2 > 0$, we obtain $x \in (-\infty, 0) \cup (0, +\infty)$. So the domain of function $y = \log_a x^2$ is $(-\infty, 0) \cup (0, +\infty)$.

(2) From $\dfrac{x}{4-x} > 0$, we obtain $x \in (0, 4)$. So the domain of function $y = \log_a \dfrac{x}{4-x}$ is $(0, 4)$.

(3) From $\begin{cases} x > 0, \ x \neq 1 \\ 5 - x > 0 \end{cases}$, we obtain $x \in (0, 1) \cup (1, 5)$. So the domain of function $y = \log_x (5-x)$ is $(0, 1) \cup (1, 5)$.

(4) From $\begin{cases} x + 1 > 0, \ x + 1 \neq 1 \\ 16 - 4^x > 0 \end{cases}$, we obtain $x \in (-1, 0) \cup (0, 2)$. So the domain of function $y = \log_{x+1}(16 - 4^x)$ is $(-1, 0) \cup (0, 2)$.

2 Use the property of the logarithmic function to compare the following numbers.

(1) $\log_3 5$ and $\log_3 7$.

(2) $\log_{0.5} 3$ and $\log_{0.5} \pi$.

(3) $\log_a \dfrac{1}{2}$ and $\log_a \dfrac{1}{3}$, where $a > 0$, $a \neq 1$.

(4) $\log_{0.2} 3$ and $\log_{0.5} 3$.

(5) $\log_2 3$ and $\log_3 2$.

Solution：

(1) We know $y = \log_3 x$ is increasing on $(0, +\infty)$, so $\log_3 5 < \log_3 7$.

(2) We know $y = \log_{0.5} x$ is decreasing on $(0, +\infty)$, so $\log_{0.5} 3 > \log_{0.5} \pi$.

(3) (i) When $a > 1$, the logarithmic function $y = \log_a x$ is increasing on $(0, +\infty)$,

so, $\log_a \frac{1}{2} > \log_a \frac{1}{3}$.

(ii) when $0 < a < 1$, the logarithmic function $y = \log_a x$ is decreasing on $(0, +\infty)$,

so, $\log_a \frac{1}{2} < \log_a \frac{1}{3}$.

(4) Since $\log_{0.2} 3 = \log_{\frac{1}{5}} 3 > \log_{\frac{1}{5}} 5 = -1$, $\log_{0.5} 3 = \log_{\frac{1}{2}} 3 < \log_{\frac{1}{2}} 2 = -1$, then $\log_{0.2} 3 > \log_{0.5} 3$.

(5) Since $\log_2 3 > \log_2 2 = 1$, $\log_3 2 < \log_3 3 = 1$, then $\log_2 3 > \log_3 2$.

3 Solve the following the inequalities.

(1) $\log_{\frac{1}{2}}(2x+1) > -1$.   (2) $\log_2(4x+8) > \log_2 2x$.   (3) $\log_x \frac{1}{4} < 2$.

Solution：

(1) Since $\log_{\frac{1}{2}}(2x+1) > -1 = \log_{\frac{1}{2}} 2$, $0 < 2x+1 < 2$. Solving the inequalities gives $-\frac{1}{2} < x < \frac{1}{2}$. So the solution set is $\left(-\frac{1}{2}, \frac{1}{2}\right)$.

(2) Since $\log_2(4x+8) > \log_2 2x$, $4x+8 > 2x > 0$. Solving the inequalities gives $x > 0$. So the solution set is $(0, +\infty)$.

(3) (i) when $0 < x < 1$, from $\log_x \frac{1}{4} < 2$, we obtain $\frac{1}{4} > x^2$. Hence, we have $0 < x < \frac{1}{2}$.

(ii) when $x > 1$, from $\log_x \frac{1}{4} < 2$, we obtain $\frac{1}{4} < x^2$. Hence, we have $x > 1$.

Overall, the solution set is $\left(0, \frac{1}{2}\right) \cup (1, +\infty)$.

4 Find the intervals of monotonicity of the following functions.

(1) $y = \log_2(x-4)$.   (2) $y = \log_3 x^2$.   (3) $y = \log_{0.5}(-x^2+2x+8)$.

Solution： (1) Since $x-4 > 0 \Rightarrow x > 4$, the domain of the function $y = \log_2(x-4)$ is $(4, +\infty)$.

Let $t = x-4$, then $y = \log_2 t$. When $x > 4$, t increases as x increases, and $y = \log_2 t$ increases as t increases.

Hence, the function $y = \log_2(x-4)$ is increasing on the interval $(4, +\infty)$.

(2) Since $x^2 > 0 \Rightarrow x \neq 0$, the domain of the function $y = \log_3 x^2$ is $(-\infty, 0) \cup (0, +\infty)$.

Let $t = x^2$, then $y = \log_3 t$.

When $x > 0$, t increases as x increases, and y increases as t increases.

Hence, the function $y = \log_3 x^2$ is increasing on the interval $(0, +\infty)$.

When $x < 0$, t decreases as x increases, and y decreases as t decreases.

Hence, the function $y = \log_3 x^2$ is decreasing on the interval $(-\infty, 0)$.

(3) Since $-x^2 + 2x + 8 > 0 \Rightarrow -2 < x < 4$, the domain of the function $y = \log_{0.5}(-x^2 + 2x + 8)$ is $(-2, 4)$.

Let $t = -x^2 + 2x + 8$, then $y = \log_{0.5} t$.

When $-2 < x \leqslant 1$, t increases as x increases, and y decreases as t increases.

Hence, the function $y = \log_{0.5}(-x^2 + 2x + 8)$ is decreasing on the interval $(-2, 1]$.

When $1 \leqslant x < 4$, t decreases as x increases, and y increases as t decreases.

Hence, the function $y = \log_{0.5}(-x^2 + 2x + 8)$ is increasing on the interval $[1, 4)$.

注意：判断函数的单调性必须先求出函数的定义域，单调区间应是定义域的子集.在求符合函数的单调性时，根据"同增异减"的原则进行判断.

5 Solve the following exponential equations.

(1) $2^{3x} = \dfrac{1}{4}$. (2) $9^x - 4 \cdot 3^x - 45 = 0$. (3) $3^x = 10$.

(4) $9^x + 4^x = \dfrac{5}{2} \cdot 6^x$. (5) $9^x + 9^{-x} - 4(3^x + 3^{-x}) + 5 = 0$.

Solution：

(1) $2^{3x} = \dfrac{1}{4} = 2^{-2}$, whence $x = -\dfrac{2}{3}$.

(2) $9^x - 4 \cdot 3^x - 45 = 0 \Rightarrow (3^x)^2 - 4 \cdot 3^x - 45 = 0$, whence $3^x = 9$ (notice that the range of the exponential function is the set of all *positive* real numbers), or equivalently, $x = 2$.

(3) According to the definition of logarithmic functions, $x = \log_3 10$.

(4) $9^x + 4^x = \dfrac{5}{2} \cdot 6^x \Rightarrow \left(\left(\dfrac{3}{2}\right)^x\right)^2 - \dfrac{5}{2} \cdot \left(\dfrac{3}{2}\right)^x + 1 = 0$. Thus, $\left(\dfrac{3}{2}\right)^x = 2$ or $\dfrac{1}{2}$, whence $x = \pm \log_{1.5} 2$.

(5) Let $t = 3^x + 3^{-x}$. The equation is equivalent to $t^2 - 4t + 3 = 0$, then $t = 1$ or $t = 3$. Since $t = 3^x + 3^{-x} \geqslant 2$, it follows that $t = 3$, or equivalently, $x = \log_3 \dfrac{3 \pm \sqrt{5}}{2}$.

6 Solve the following logarithmic equations.

(1) $\log_2(x - 2) = \log_2(x^2 - x - 5)$. (2) $\log_3^2 x + \log_{1/3} x^2 - 3 = 0$.

(3) $\log_4(2^x + 6) = x$. (4) $\log_3(3^x - 1) \log_3\left(3^{x-1} - \dfrac{1}{3}\right) = 2$.

Solution：

(1) The equation is equivalent to the system $\begin{cases} x - 2 > 0 \\ x^2 - x - 5 > 0 \\ x - 2 = x^2 - x - 5 \end{cases}$. Hence, $x = 3$.

(2) The equation is equivalent to $(\log_3 x - 3)(\log_3 x + 1) = 0$. Hence, $\log_3 x = 3$ or $\log_3 x = -1$. Thus, $x = 27$ or $\dfrac{1}{3}$.

(3) The equation is equivalent to $(2^x - 3)(2^x + 2) = 0$. Hence, $2^x = 3$. Thus, $x = \log_2 3$.

(4) Let $t = \log_3(3^x - 1)$. The equation then becomes an equation in t: $t^2 - t - 2 = 0$. Hence, $t = -1$ or $t = 2$. Thus $x = \log_3 10$ or $\log_3 \dfrac{4}{3}$.

练习 Exercise

1. Write the logarithmic equations in exponential forms.

   (1) $\log_4 16 = 2$.　　　(2) $\log_9 \dfrac{1}{81} = -2$.　　(3) $\log_{32} 4 = \dfrac{2}{5}$.　　(4) $\log_{64} 8 = \dfrac{1}{2}$.

2. Write the exponential equations in logarithmic forms.

   (1) $5^3 = 125$.　　　(2) $9^{\frac{3}{2}} = 27$.　　(3) $4^{-3} = \dfrac{1}{64}$.　　(4) $24^0 = 1$.

3. Evaluate the function at the indicated value of x without using a calculator.

   Function　　　　　Value

   (1) $f(x) = \log_2 x$　　　$x = 64$

   (2) $f(x) = \log_{25} x$　　$x = 5$

   (3) $f(x) = \log_8 x$　　　$x = 1$

   (4) $f(x) = \lg x$　　　　$x = 10$

   (5) $g(x) = \log_a x$　　　$x = a^2$

   (6) $g(x) = \log_b x$　　　$x = b^{-3}$

4. Find the domain of the following functions.

   (1) $y = \log_2(x + 1)$.　　　　　　　　(2) $y = \log_{\frac{1}{2}} x^2$.

   (3) $y = \log_a \dfrac{x-1}{x+1} (a > 0$ 且 $a \ne 1)$.

5. If $a > b > c > 1$, compare the following numbers.

   (1) $\log_a b$ and $\log_a c$.　　　　　　　(2) $\log_{\frac{1}{a}} b$ and $\log_{\frac{1}{a}} c$.

6. Solve the following inequalities.

   (1) $\log_3(x - 1) < 2$.

   (2) $\log_{0.5} 3x > \log_{0.5}(2x + 3)$.

   (3) $\log_a(a^2 + 1) < \log_a 2a < 0$.

7. Find the intervals of monotonicity of the following functions.

   (1) $y = \log_3(x + 7)$.　　　　　　　　(2) $y = \log_2(3 - x)$.

   (3) $y = \log_{0.5}(x^2 - 1)$.　　　　　　(4) $y = \log_2(-x^2 + 7x + 18)$.

8. Let the function $f(x) = \log_a(2 + x) - \log_a(2 - x) (a > 0, a \ne 1)$.

   (1) Find the domain of $f(x)$.

   (2) Is the function $f(x)$ odd or even?

   (3) Solve the inequality $f(x) \ge \log_a(3x)$.

9. Let $f(x) = (\log_2 x - 2)\left(\log_4 x - \dfrac{1}{2}\right)$.

   (1) When $x \in [2, 4]$, find the range of $f(x)$.

   (2) If $f(x) \ge m \log_4 x$ holds for all $x \in [4, 6]$, find the range of m.

10. Let $f(x)=\log_{\frac{1}{2}}(x^2-2ax+3)$.

    (1) If the domain of $f(x)$ is $(-\infty,1)\bigcup(3,+\infty)$, find the value of a.

    (2) If the domain and the range of $f(x)$ are $\mathbf{R}$ and $(-\infty,-1]$ respectively, find the value of a.

    (3) If $f(x)$ is increasing on $(-\infty,1]$, find the range of a.

11. Solve the following exponential equations.

    (1) $3^{x^2}=(3^x)^2$.

    (2) $4^x=5^x$.

    (3) $5^{x-1}\cdot10^{3x}=8^x$.

    (4) $3^{x+1}-3^{-x}=2$.

    (5) $3\cdot16^x+36^x=2\cdot81^x$.

    (6) $(\sqrt{5+2\sqrt6})^x+(\sqrt{5-2\sqrt6})^x=10$.

    (7) $\sqrt[x]{9}-\sqrt[x]{6}=\sqrt[x]{4}$.

    (8) $4^{x+\sqrt{x^2-2}}-5\cdot2^{x-1+\sqrt{x^2-2}}=6$.

    (9) $(2x-1)^{x^2}=(2x-1)^{x-2}$.

    (10) $3^x+4^x+5^x=6^x$.

12. Solve the following logarithmic equations.

    (1) $\log_2(x-1)-\log_4(x+5)=0$.

    (2) $\log_4(2-x)=\log_2(x-1)-1$.

    (3) $\log_x(x^2-x)-\log_x2=0$.

    (4) $\lg|2x-3|-\lg|3x-2|=0$.

    (5) $\lg^2|x|+\lg x^2-3=0$.

    (6) $(\sqrt x)^{\log_5x-1}=5$.

    (7) $10^{\lg^2x}+x^{\lg x}=20$.

    (8) $\log_2(2^{-x}-1)\cdot\log_{1/2}(2^{-x+1}-2)=-2$.

13. Find all possible values of a, so that there are:

    i) one solution;

    ii) two solutions;

    iii) or no solution

    to the equation $\lg(x-1)+\lg(3-x)=\lg(1-ax)$.

三角 Trigonometry

5.1 ◆ 弧度制 Radian Measure

物理学中,在研究单摆运动的时候,由角动量守恒可以推导出单摆角的加速度 β 与摆角 θ 的正弦值成正比:

$$\beta = -\frac{g}{\ell}\sin\theta$$

其中 g 是重力加速度, ℓ 是摆长.为了简单起见,我们通常考虑一种特殊的情况:小角度摆.此时,我们可以**近似**地认为摆的角加速度 β 与摆角 θ 自身成正比,从而将单摆作为周期运动来处理.物理课本告诉我们,在此过程中涉及一个**小量近似**:

$$\sin\theta \approx \theta$$

然而,我们在初中所熟悉的锐角的三角值应该是实数,它又是怎样与带单位的角度达成近似的呢?这就需要我们了解角的另一种度量方式:**弧度制**.

角的概念的推广 Generalized Notion of the Angles

一个**角(angle)** 可以看作是一条射线绕着它的端点旋转而成,射线的端点叫作角的**顶点(vertex)**,射线旋转开始的位置叫作角的**始边(initial side)**,终止位置叫作角的**终边(terminal side)**,如图(Figure 5 - 1)所示:

通常我们把角放在一个坐标平面上,使得角的顶点与坐标原点重合,而角的始边与 x 轴的正方向重合.此时,我们说这个角处在**标准位置(standard position)**,如图(Figure 5 - 2)所示:

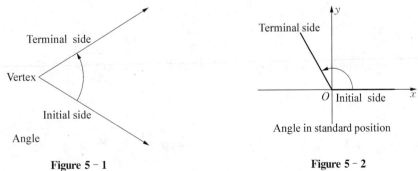

Figure 5 - 1　　　　　　　　　Figure 5 - 2

由于射线有两种相反的旋转方向:逆时针方向和顺时针方向,因此,我们约定逆时针方向旋转所成的角叫作**正角(positive angles)**,顺时针方向旋转所成的叫作**负角(negative angles)**,如图(Figure

5 - 3)所示:

特别地,如果终边相对于始边没有作任何旋转,我们称之为**零角(zero angle)**.我们一般用希腊字母来标记角,如:α、β、θ.

如果两个角的终边相同,我们称它们为**共终边的(coterminal)角**.图(Figure 5 - 4)中的两对角都是共终边的角.

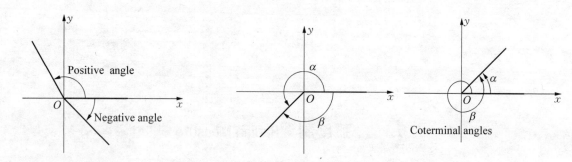

Figure 5 - 3   Figure 5 - 4

显然,共终边的角之间总是相差 $360°$ 的某个倍数.

弧度制 Radian Measure

在初中,我们已经知道角的大小可以用**角度(degree)**来刻画.而在高等数学中,我们有另一种方式来刻画角的大小,即**弧度(radian)**.它将角视为圆心角,从而将角的大小转化为相应的弧的长度.具体地说,把弧长等于半径的弧所对的圆心角叫作 1 **弧度**的角,用符号 rad 表示,读作弧度.

Definition of the Radian

One **radian** is the measure of a central angle θ that intercepts an arc s equal in length to the radius r of the circle. See Figure 5 - 5. Algebraically, it means that $\theta = \dfrac{s}{r}$, where θ is measured in radians. (Note that $\theta = 1$ when $s = r$.)

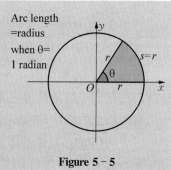

Figure 5 - 5

因为 s 和 r 的单位是一样的,所以与角度不同,弧度没有单位,只是一个实数.由于一个圆周角所对应的弧度是 $\dfrac{s}{r} = \dfrac{2\pi r}{r} = 2\pi$,我们可以得到下列对应关系:

$$\frac{1}{2} \text{ revolution} = \pi \text{ radians}$$

$$\frac{1}{4} \text{ revolution} = \frac{\pi}{2} \text{ radians}$$

$$\frac{1}{6} \text{ revolution} = \frac{\pi}{3} \text{ radians}$$

特别地,共终边的角(在弧度制下)之间总是相差 2π 的某个倍数.

Figure 5 - 6

图(Figure 5 - 6)中列出了一些常用角的弧度.

我们知道坐标平面可以被分为四个象限.因此,对于一个处于标准位置的角,我们可以用它的终边所在的象限来刻画这个角.即：角的终边在第几象限，就称它为**第几象限角(angle lying in the nth -quadrant)**.下图(Figure 5 - 7)展示了当 $0 \leqslant \theta < 2\pi$ 时，它的大小与所在象限的关系.特别注意：锐角是第一象限角，钝角是第二象限角.

终边在坐标轴上的角称为**轴线角(quadrant angles)**，它们不属于任何象限.

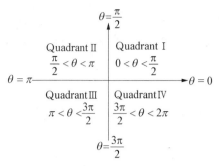

Figure 5 - 7

1 Graph the angles $\frac{\pi}{3}$ and $\frac{5\pi}{2}$.

Solution：As is shown in Figure 5 - 8.

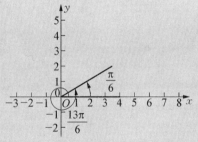

Figure 5 - 8

2 (1) Find the smallest positive angle that is coterminal with $\frac{13\pi}{6}$.

Solution：$\frac{13\pi}{6} - 2\pi = \frac{\pi}{6}$. See Figure 5 - 9.

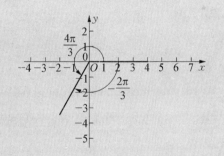

Figure 5 - 9   Figure 5 - 10

(2) Find the largest negative angle that is coterminal with $\frac{4\pi}{3}$.

Solution：$\frac{4\pi}{3} - 2\pi = -\frac{2\pi}{3}$. See Figure 5 - 10.

3 Two positive angles α, β are **complementary** to each other if their sum is $\frac{\pi}{2}$; they are **supplementary** to each other if their sum is π. See Figure 5 - 11.

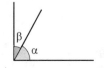
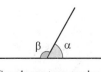

Complementary angles   Supplementary angles

Figure 5 - 11

For example: $\dfrac{2\pi}{5}$ is complementary to $\dfrac{\pi}{2} - \dfrac{2\pi}{5} = \dfrac{\pi}{10}$, while it is supplementary to $\pi - \dfrac{2\pi}{5} = \dfrac{3\pi}{5}$. Meanwhile, since $\dfrac{4\pi}{5}$ is greater than $\dfrac{\pi}{2}$, it cannot be complementary to any angle but only supplementary to $\pi - \dfrac{4\pi}{5} = \dfrac{\pi}{5}$.

4 Let α be an angle lying in the first quadrant. Determine in which quadrants could the angles $\dfrac{\alpha}{2}$ and $\dfrac{\alpha}{3}$ lie.

Solution: Note that α lying in the first quadrant implies that $2k\pi < \alpha < 2k\pi + \dfrac{\pi}{2}$, $k \in \mathbf{Z}$. Hence, $k\pi < \dfrac{\alpha}{2} < k\pi + \dfrac{\pi}{4} < k\pi + \dfrac{\pi}{2}$. Thus when k is even, $\dfrac{\alpha}{2}$ lies in the second quadrant while k is odd, it lies in the third quadrant.

Similarly, $\dfrac{2k\pi}{3} < \dfrac{\alpha}{3} < \dfrac{2k\pi}{3} + \dfrac{\pi}{6}$, $k \in \mathbf{Z}$ implies that $\dfrac{\alpha}{3}$ lies in quadrant I, II or III, respectively as $k = 3l$, $k = 3l + 1$ or $k = 3l + 2$.

弧度与角度的转化 Conversions between Radians and Degrees

出于计算的需要,我们经常在角度制与弧度制之间转化.正如我们在此前已经看到的,角度与弧度之间有一个简单的对应关系:

Conversions between Radians and Degrees:

$$\text{radian} = \text{degree} \times \dfrac{\pi}{180°}$$

$$\text{degree} = \text{radian} \times \dfrac{180°}{\pi}$$

5 Here are some examples of conversions between radians and degrees.

$$135° = 135° \dfrac{\pi}{180°} = \dfrac{3\pi}{4};$$

$$540° = 540° \dfrac{\pi}{180°} = 3\pi;$$

$$-\dfrac{\pi}{2} = \left(-\dfrac{\pi}{2}\right) \dfrac{180°}{\pi} = -90°;$$

$$2 = 2\dfrac{180°}{\pi} \approx 114.59°.$$

6 In which quadrant does the angle of 2008 radians lie? Find the set of its coterminal angles.

Solution: Let α be such that $0 \leqslant \alpha < 2\pi$ while being coterminal with the angle 2008.

Note that $2008 = 638\pi + 3.66\cdots$ whence $\alpha = 3.66\cdots$ which lies in quadrant III. Hence, so does the angle 2008. The desired set of coterminal angles is given by $\{\beta \mid \beta = 2k\pi + 2008, k \in \mathbf{Z}\}$.

应用 Applications

在初中，我们学过弧长公式：

$$\ell = \frac{n^{\circ}\pi}{180^{\circ}}r$$

其中 r 是弧所在圆的半径，n° 是弧所对圆心角的度数. 现在，由弧度制的定义，我们可以方便地得到用弧度表示的弧长公式：

$$s = r\theta$$

其中 θ 是用弧度制表示的圆心角的大小. 特别是，当 $r = 1$ 时，弧长与圆心角的弧度在数值上相等.

7　Find the arc length of an arc with radius 4cm and central angle $\frac{4\pi}{3}$.

Solution： $s = r\theta = r\dfrac{4\pi}{3} \approx 16.76$ cm.

The formula for the length of a circular arc can help you analyze the motion of a particle moving at a *constant speed* along a circular path.

Linear and Angular Speeds

Consider a particle moving at a constant speed along a circular arc of radius r. If s is the length of the arc traveled in time t, then the **linear speed** v of the particle is

$$\text{Linear speed } v = \frac{\text{arc length}}{\text{time}} = \frac{s}{t}.$$

Moreover, if θ is the angle (in radian measure) corresponding to the arc length s, then the **angular speed** ω (the lowercase Greek letter omega) of the particle is

$$\text{Angular speed } \omega = \frac{\text{central angle}}{\text{time}} = \frac{\theta}{t}.$$

8　The second hand of a clock is 9.8 centimeters long. Find the linear speed of the tip of this second hand as it passes around the clock face.

Solution： In one revolution, the arc length traveled is

$$s = 2\pi r = 2\pi \times 9.8 = 19.6\pi \text{ cm.}$$

The time required for the second hand to travel this distance is

$$t = 1 \text{ min} = 60 \text{ sec.}$$

So, the linear speed of the tip of the second hand is

$$\text{Linear speed} = \frac{s}{t} = \frac{19.6\pi \text{ cm}}{60 \text{ sec}} \approx 1.026 \text{ cm/sec.}$$

9　The blades of a wind turbine are 112 feet long. The propeller rotates at 18 revolutions per minute.

（1）Find the angular speed of the propeller in radians per minute.

（2）Find the linear speed of the tips of the blades.

Solution: Because each revolution generates 2π radians, it follows that the propeller turns

$$18 \times 2\pi = 36\pi \text{ rad/min.}$$

In other words, the angular speed is

$$\text{Angular speed} = \frac{\theta}{t} = \frac{36\pi \text{ rad}}{1 \text{ min}} = 36\pi \text{ rad/min.}$$

The linear speed is

$$\text{Linear speed} = \frac{s}{t} = \frac{r\theta}{t} = \frac{112 \times 36\pi \text{ ft}}{1 \text{ min}} \approx 12,667 \text{ ft/min.}$$

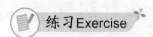 练习 Exercise

1. Answer the following questions concerning generalized angles.

    (1) Find the largest negative and smallest positive angles that are coterminal with each angle below: $45°$, $120°$, $-36°$, $-420°$.

    (2) Graph the following angles in their standard positions: $\dfrac{\pi}{3}$, $\dfrac{5\pi}{2}$.

    (3) Find the largest negative and smallest positive angles that are coterminal with each angle below: $\dfrac{9\pi}{4}$, $-\dfrac{\pi}{3}$.

    (4) Find the complementary and supplementary angles to each angle below, if possible: $\dfrac{\pi}{6}$, $\dfrac{5\pi}{6}$.

    (5) Let α be an angle lying in the second quadrant. Determine in which quadrants could the angle $\dfrac{\alpha}{2}$ lie.

2. Convert between radians and degrees.

    (1) Convert the angles into radians: $60°$, $320°$.

    (2) Convert the angles into degrees: $\dfrac{\pi}{6}$, $\dfrac{5\pi}{3}$.

3. Find the arc length of an arc with radius 27 cm and central angle $\dfrac{8\pi}{9}$.

4. The second hand of the clock is 10 centimeters long. Find the linear speed of the tip of this second hand as it passes around the clock face.

5. The circular blade on a saw rotates at 2,500 revolutions per minute.

    (1) Find the angular speed of the blade in radians per minute.

    (2) The blade has a radius of 5 inches. Find the linear speed of a blade tip.

6. True or False:

    (1) A measurement of 6 radians corresponds to three complete revolutions from the initial side to the terminal side of an angle.

    (2) The difference between the measures of two coterminal angles is always a multiple of $360°$ when expressed in degrees and is always a multiple of 2π radians when expressed in radians.

(3) An angle that measures $-1,260°$ lies in Quadrant III.

7. (1) Assuming that Earth is a sphere of radius $6,378$ kilometers, what is the difference between the latitudes of Beijing and Shanghai, where Beijing is about $1,000$ kilometers north of Shanghai?

(2) As is shown in Figure $5-12$ the radii of the pedal sprocket, the wheel sprocket, and the wheel of a certain model of bicycle are 4 inches, 2 inches, and 14 inches, respectively. A cyclist is pedaling at a rate of 1 revolution per second. Find the speed of the bicycle in feet per second and miles per hour.

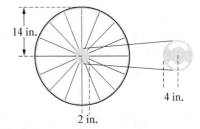

Figure 5 - 12

Use your result from part (1) to write a function for the distance d (in miles) a cyclist travels in terms of the number n of revolutions of the pedal sprocket.

Write a function for the distance d (in miles) a cyclist travels in terms of the time t (in seconds). Compare this function with the function from part (2).

8. (1) Prove that the area of a circular sector of radius r with central angle θ is $A = \frac{1}{2}\theta r^2$.

(2) A sprinkler on a golf green sprays water over a distance of 12 meters and rotates through an angle of $125°$. Draw a diagram that shows the region that the sprinkler can irrigate. Find the area of the region.

(3) A car's rear windshield wiper rotates $140°$. The total length of the wiper mechanism is 20 inches and wipes the windshield over a distance of 12 inches. Find the area covered by the wiper.

9. (1) A fan motor turns at a given angular speed. How does the speed of the tips of the blades change when a fan of greater diameter is on the motor? Explain.

(2) Is a degree or a radian the greater unit of measure? Explain.

(3) When the radius of a circle increases and the magnitude of a central angle is constant, how does the length of the intercepted arc change? Explain your reasoning.

5.2 ◆ 任意角的三角函数
Trigonometric Functions for any Angle

在初中我们已经学习过,锐角的三角值可以将锐角的大小与线段的长度联系起来,从而帮助我们解决一些几何与测量方面的问题.现在,我们已经将角的概念进行了推广.那么可以预见,对于任意的角,应该也存在着与锐角三角值相对应的量,将任意角和一些相关的线段联系起来,提供更多的应用途径.

例如,可以利用图形计算器研究下面的问题:一个在给定圆上的动点,以它为端点的半径和 x 轴正方向的夹角与它的横坐标之间有什么关系?

单位圆 The Unit Circle

在引进弧度制时我们看到,在半径为 r 的圆中,角 α 的弧度数与圆半径的大小无关,因此我们特别关注 $r=1$ 的情形,此时角的弧度数与它所对的弧长在数值上一致.在平面直角坐标系中,称以原点 O 为圆心，1 为半径的圆被称为**单位圆(unit circle)**，如图所示(Figure 5 – 13).

设想将数轴贴合到单位圆上，使得正数对应着逆时针环绕，而负数对应着顺时针环绕，如图所示(Figure 5 – 14).

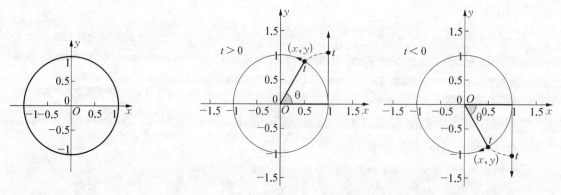

Figure 5 – 13　　　　　　　　　　　　　　　　　**Figure 5 – 14**

在此过程中，每个实数 t 对应于单位圆上的一个点 (x, y). 例如，数 0 对应点 $(1, 0)$. 值得注意的是，因为单位圆的周长是 2π，所以实数 2π 同样对应点 $(1, 0)$. 一般地，通过这样的环绕，每个实数 t 对应着一个圆心角 θ. 它是一个处在标准位置的角，并且大小(用弧度制)恰好是 t.

另一方面，当 $t \in \left(0, \dfrac{\pi}{2}\right)$ 时，在单位圆上的对应点的 x、y 坐标恰好是相应的(锐)角 θ 两个基本的三角函数：正弦和余弦.因此，我们可以把单位圆上与实数 t 对应的点 (x, y) 的两个坐标定义成它的**正弦/余弦**，即：

Definitions of the Trigonometric Functions

Let t be a real number and let (x, y) be the point on the unit circle corresponding to t, then：

$$\sin t = y \qquad \cos t = x$$

下图(Figure 5 – 15)给出了一些特殊角在单位圆上的对应点：

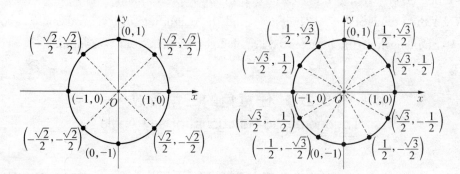

Figure 5 – 15

1 Find the sine and cosine values of the following angles：$\dfrac{\pi}{6}$, $\dfrac{5\pi}{4}$, π, $-\dfrac{\pi}{3}$.

Solution： Start with determining the point on the unit circle corresponding to each angle.

$t = \dfrac{\pi}{6}$: $(x, y) = \left(\dfrac{\sqrt{3}}{2}, \dfrac{1}{2}\right)$. Thus, $\sin \dfrac{\pi}{6} = y = \dfrac{1}{2}$, $\cos \dfrac{\pi}{6} = x = \dfrac{\sqrt{3}}{2}$.

$t = \dfrac{5\pi}{4}$: $(x, y) = \left(-\dfrac{\sqrt{2}}{2}, -\dfrac{\sqrt{2}}{2}\right)$. Thus, $\sin \dfrac{5\pi}{4} = y = -\dfrac{\sqrt{2}}{2}$, $\cos \dfrac{5\pi}{4} = x = -\dfrac{\sqrt{2}}{2}$.

$t = \pi$: $(x, y) = (-1, 0)$. Thus, $\sin \pi = y = 0$, $\cos \pi = x = -1$.

$t = -\dfrac{\pi}{3}$: $(x, y) = \left(\dfrac{1}{2}, -\dfrac{\sqrt{3}}{2}\right)$. Thus, $\sin\left(-\dfrac{\pi}{3}\right) = y = -\dfrac{\sqrt{3}}{2}$, $\cos\left(-\dfrac{\pi}{3}\right) = x = \dfrac{1}{2}$.

任意角的三角函数 Trigonometric Functions for any Angle

初中学习过锐角三角函数的概念,它们可以定量地刻画出直角三角形中边角之间的联系.而现在可以对任意实数定义一组类似的数量,即:正弦/余弦.这两者不仅名称相似,内容也相近.因而可以把初中学习的锐角三角函数的定义拓展到(弧度制下的)任意角,并且将它们与此前对实数定义的三角函数联系在一起.

Definitions of the Trigonometric Functions of any Angle

Let θ be an angle in standard position with (x, y) a point on the terminal side of θ and $r = \sqrt{x^2 + y^2} \neq 0$ (Figure 5-16), then:

$$\sin \theta = \frac{y}{r} \qquad \tan \theta = \frac{y}{x}, x \neq 0$$

$$\cos \theta = \frac{x}{r} \qquad \cot \theta = \frac{x}{y}, y \neq 0$$

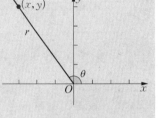

Figure 5-16

由于已经假设 $r = \sqrt{x^2 + y^2}$ 不等于零,因此正弦和余弦对任何 θ 都是有意义的.然而,当 $x = 0$,θ 的正切就没有意义.例如:$\theta = 90°$ 的正切就没有意义.同样地,当 $y = 0$ 时,θ 的余切也是没有意义的.

2 If $(-3, 4)$ lies on the terminal side of θ (Figure 5-17), find the sine and cosine values of θ.

Solution: Since $x = -3$, $y = 4$, $r = 5$.

Thus,

$$\sin \theta = \frac{y}{r} = \frac{4}{5},$$

$$\cos \theta = \frac{x}{r} = -\frac{3}{5},$$

$$\tan \theta = \frac{y}{x} = -\frac{4}{3}.$$

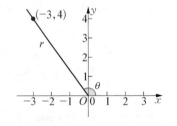

Figure 5-17

我们已经知道象限角的概念,而一个角的各个三角值的**符号**其实可以由它所在的象限确定.例如,因为 $\cos \theta = \dfrac{x}{r}$,所以当 $x > 0$,即 θ 在第一象限和第四象限时 $\cos \theta$ 是正的(注意 r 始终是正的).更多关于象限角的三角值符号的信息可以参考下图(Figure 5-18).

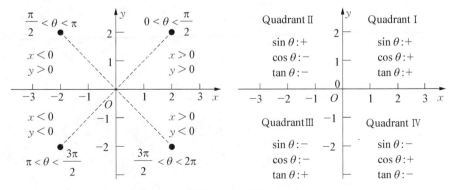

Figure 5-18

3 If $\tan\theta = -\dfrac{5}{4}$, $\cos\theta > 0$, find $\sin\theta$.

Solution: Note that with negative tangent value and positive cosine value, θ must be a fourth quadrant angle. Hence, $\tan\theta = \dfrac{y}{x} = -\dfrac{5}{4}$ implies that $(4, -5)$ must lie on the terminal side of θ. Thus, $r = \sqrt{16 + 25} = \sqrt{41}$, which implies that $\sin\theta = \dfrac{y}{r} = -\dfrac{5}{\sqrt{41}} \approx -0.7809$.

4 Evaluate the cosine and tangent of each angle below: 0, $\dfrac{\pi}{2}$, π, $\dfrac{3\pi}{2}$.

Solution: As is shown in Figure 5 – 19.
One finds that

$$\cos 0 = \frac{x}{r} = \frac{1}{1} = 1 \qquad \tan 0 = \frac{y}{x} = \frac{0}{1} = 0$$

$$\cos\frac{\pi}{2} = \frac{x}{r} = \frac{0}{1} = 0 \qquad \tan\frac{\pi}{2} = \frac{y}{x} = \frac{1}{0} \Rightarrow \text{non-exist}$$

$$\cos\pi = \frac{x}{r} = \frac{-1}{1} = -1 \qquad \tan\pi = \frac{y}{x} = \frac{0}{1} = 0$$

$$\cos\frac{3\pi}{2} = \frac{x}{r} = \frac{0}{1} = 0 \qquad \tan\frac{3\pi}{2} = \frac{y}{x} = \frac{-1}{0} \Rightarrow \text{non-exist}$$

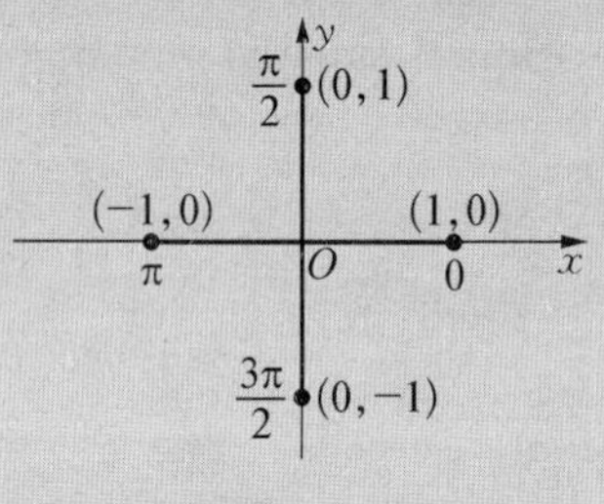

Figure 5 – 19

参照角 Reference Angle

在计算任意角的三角值时,为了方便起见,我们时常把问题转化为求相关的锐角三角值.这个用来帮助计算的锐角被称为**参照角**(reference angle).

Definition of the Reference Angle

Let θ be an angle in standard position. Its **reference angle** is the acute angle θ' formed by the terminal side of θ and the horizontal axis.

部分终边在第二、三、四象限的角的参照角如下图所示(Figure 5 – 20):

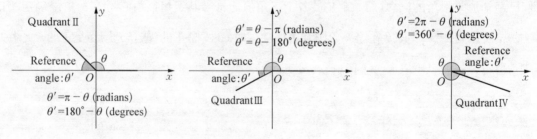

Figure 5 – 20

5 Find the reference angle of each angle below: $300°$, 2.3, $-135°$.

Solution: $300°$ lies in the fourth quadrant, thus, $\theta' = 360° - 300° = 60°$.

2.3 is squeezed between $\dfrac{\pi}{2} \approx 1.5708$ and $\pi \approx 3.1416$, whence lying the second quadrant. Hence, $\theta' = \pi - 2.3 \approx 0.8416$.

— 135° and 225° are coterminal angles, whence both lying in the third quadrant, with the reference angle being $\theta' = 225° - 180° = 45°$.

六个三角函数及其计算 The Six Trigonometric Functions and their Calculations

参照角对于计算三角值是很有帮助的,它能把任意角的三角值转化为熟悉的锐角三角值.见下图 (Figure 5-21),在 θ 的终边上取点 (x, y).

由定义,$\sin\theta = \dfrac{y}{r}$,$\tan\theta = \dfrac{y}{x}$. 而在有一个锐角等于参照角 θ' 的直角三角

形中,它的两条直角边分别长 $|x|$、$|y|$,有:

$$\sin\theta' = \frac{\text{opposite side}}{\text{hypothenuse}} = \frac{|y|}{r}$$

$$\tan\theta' = \frac{\text{opposite side}}{\text{adjacent side}} = \frac{|y|}{|x|}$$

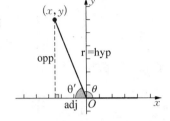

Figure 5 - 21

因此,除了正负号之外,$\sin\theta$ 和 $\sin\theta'$ 是相同的,对于其他三角值也一样.而三角值的符号可以由角所在的象限决定,于是得到以下计算法则.

> **Evaluating the Trigonometric Functions of any Angle**
>
> To find the value of a trigonometric function of any angle θ:
>
> 1. Determine the trigonometric value of the associated reference angle θ'.
>
> 2. Depending on the quadrant in which θ lies, affix the appropriate sign to the trigonometric value.

通过这种方法,可以从一些初中学过的**特殊锐角**的三角值出发,求出许多**特殊角**的三角值,如下表所示(Table 5-1)(空白处由学生完成):

Table 5 - 1

θ (degrees)	θ (radians)	$\sin\theta$	$\cos\theta$	$\tan\theta$
0°	0	0	1	0
30°	$\dfrac{\pi}{6}$	$\dfrac{1}{2}$	$\dfrac{\sqrt{3}}{2}$	$\dfrac{\sqrt{3}}{3}$
45°	$\dfrac{\pi}{4}$	$\dfrac{\sqrt{2}}{2}$	$\dfrac{\sqrt{2}}{2}$	1
60°	$\dfrac{\pi}{3}$	$\dfrac{\sqrt{3}}{2}$	$\dfrac{1}{2}$	$\sqrt{3}$
90°	$\dfrac{\pi}{2}$	1	0	不存在
120°	$\dfrac{2\pi}{3}$			
135°	$\dfrac{3\pi}{4}$			
150°	$\dfrac{5\pi}{6}$			
180°	π	0	−1	0

θ (degrees)	θ (radians)	sin θ	cos θ	tan θ
210°	$\dfrac{7\pi}{6}$			
225°	$\dfrac{5\pi}{4}$			
240°	$\dfrac{4\pi}{3}$			
270°	$\dfrac{3\pi}{2}$	-1	0	不存在
300°	$\dfrac{5\pi}{3}$			
315°	$\dfrac{7\pi}{4}$			
330°	$\dfrac{11\pi}{6}$			

在数学中常用的三角函数,除了初中学过的四个之外,还有两个：**正割**(**secant**)和**余割**(**cosecant**).

Definitions of the Trigonometric Functions of any Angle

Let θ be an angle in standard position with (x, y) a point on the terminal side of θ and $r = \sqrt{x^2 + y^2} \neq 0$ (Figure 5 - 22), then：

$$\sec \theta = \frac{r}{x}, \ x \neq 0$$

$$\csc \theta = \frac{r}{y}, \ y \neq 0$$

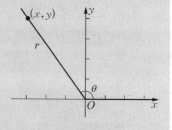

Figure 5 - 22

6 Evaluate the six trigonometric functions of the angles below：$\dfrac{\pi}{6}, \dfrac{5\pi}{4}, -\dfrac{\pi}{3}, \pi$.

Solution： The sine and cosine values were done in Example 1. Here we deal with the rest four.

$\theta = \dfrac{\pi}{6}$ equals its reference angle, thus, $\tan \dfrac{\pi}{6} = \dfrac{\sqrt{3}}{3}$, $\sec \dfrac{\pi}{6} = \dfrac{2\sqrt{3}}{3}$, $\cot \dfrac{\pi}{6} = \sqrt{3}$, $\csc \dfrac{\pi}{6} = 2$.

Reference angle for $\theta = \dfrac{5\pi}{4}$ is $\theta' = \theta - \pi = \dfrac{\pi}{4}$, thus, $\tan \dfrac{5\pi}{4} = 1$, $\sec \dfrac{5\pi}{4} = -\sqrt{2}$, $\cot \dfrac{5\pi}{4} = 1$, $\csc \dfrac{5\pi}{4} = -\sqrt{2}$.

Reference angle for $\theta = -\dfrac{\pi}{3}$ is $\theta' = -\theta = \dfrac{\pi}{3}$, thus, $\tan \left(-\dfrac{\pi}{3}\right) = -\sqrt{3}$, $\sec \left(-\dfrac{\pi}{3}\right) = 2$, $\cot \left(-\dfrac{\pi}{3}\right) = -\dfrac{\sqrt{3}}{3}$, $\csc \left(-\dfrac{\pi}{3}\right) = -\dfrac{2\sqrt{3}}{3}$.

For $\theta = \pi$, note that it is a quadrant angle, whence the method of reference angles is not applicable. Direct computation shows that $\tan \pi = 0$, $\sec \pi = -1$, while $\cot \pi$ and $\csc \pi$ do not exist.

从这六个三角值的定义不难发现，它们之间存在着密切的联系：

Fundamental Trigonometric Identities

Reciprocal Identities

$$\csc\theta = \frac{1}{\sin\theta} \quad \sec\theta = \frac{1}{\cos\theta} \quad \cot\theta = \frac{1}{\tan\theta}$$

Quotient Identities

$$\tan\theta = \frac{\sin\theta}{\cos\theta} \quad \cot\theta = \frac{\cos\theta}{\sin\theta}$$

Pythagorean Identities

$$\sin^2\theta + \cos^2\theta = 1$$

$$1 + \tan^2\theta = \sec^2\theta$$

$$1 + \cot^2\theta = \csc^2\theta$$

A diagram can be deployed to demonstrate the aforementioned complicated net of relationships between trigonometric ratios. As is shown in the hexagon (Figure 5-23):

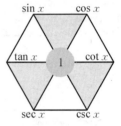

Figure 5-23

- All pairs of ratios that occupy the opposite vertices are reciprocal to each other;
- Each ratio equals to the product of those lying on its two neighboring vertices;
- For each grey triangle, the sum of the squares of the two ratios lying on the top vertices equals that of the ratio on the bottom.

7 Let θ be an angle lying in the second quadrant such that $\sin\theta = \frac{4}{5}$. Find $\cos\theta$ and $\tan\theta$ by trigonometric identities.

Solution: Pythagorean identity $\sin^2\theta + \cos^2\theta = 1$ shows that $\cos^2\theta = 1 - \frac{16}{25} = \frac{9}{25}$. Since cosine takes negative values for angles in quadrant II, it follows that $\cos\theta = -\sqrt{\frac{9}{25}} = -\frac{3}{5}$.

Then, $\tan\theta = \frac{\sin\theta}{\cos\theta}$ implies $\tan\theta = \frac{4/5}{-3/5} = -\frac{4}{3}$.

练习 Exercise

1. If $(-2, 3)$ lies on the terminal side of θ, find its sine, cosine and tangent values.

2. If $\sin\theta = \frac{4}{5}$, $\tan\theta < 0$, find $\cos\theta$.

3. Find the sine and cotangent values of $\frac{3\pi}{2}$.

4. Find the reference angle of each angle below: $213°$, $\frac{14\pi}{9}$, $\frac{4\pi}{5}$.

5. Evaluate the six trigonometric functions of the angles below: $\frac{\pi}{2}$, 0, $-\frac{5\pi}{6}$, $-\frac{3\pi}{4}$.

6. Let θ be an angle lying in the third quadrant such that $\sin\theta = -\dfrac{1}{3}$. Find $\cos\theta$ and $\tan\theta$.

7. True or False:

   (1) Because $\sin(-t) = -\sin t$, the sine of a negative angle is a negative number.

   (2) In each of the four quadrants, the signs of the secant and that of the sine are always the same.

   (3) To find the reference angle of the angle θ (given in degrees), find the integers n such that $0 \leqslant 360°n - \theta \leqslant 360°$. The difference $360°n - \theta$ is the reference angle.

8. (1) The displacement from equilibrium of an oscillating weight suspended by a spring is given by $y(t) = \dfrac{1}{4}\cos 6t$ where y is displacement (in feet) and t is the time (in seconds). Complete Table 5 - 2.

Table 5 - 2

t	0	$\dfrac{1}{4}$	$\dfrac{1}{2}$	$\dfrac{3}{4}$	1
y					

   (2) An airplane, flying at an altitude of 6 miles, is on a flight path that passes directly over an observer (see figure). Let θ be the angle of elevation from the observer to the plane. Find the distance d from the observer to the plane when $\theta = 30°$, $60°$, $90°$, and $120°$.

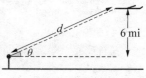

Figure 5 - 24

9. (1) Verify that $\cos 2t \neq 2\cos t$ by approximating $\cos 1.5$ and $2\cos 0.75$.

   (2) Verify that $\sin(t_1 + t_2) \neq \sin t_1 + \sin t_2$ by approximating $\sin 0.25$, $\sin 0.75$, and $\sin 1$.

   (3) Let (x_1, y_1) and (x_2, y_2) be points on the unit circle corresponding to $t = t_1$ and $t = \pi - t_1$, respectively.

   a. Identify the symmetry of the points (x_1, y_1) and (x_2, y_2).

   b. Make a conjecture about any relationship between $\sin t_1$ and $\sin(\pi - t_1)$.

   c. Make a conjecture about any relationship between $\cos t_1$ and $\cos(\pi - t_1)$.

10. (1) Consider an angle in standard position with $r = 12$ centimeters, as shown in Figure 5 - 25. Describe the changes in the values of x, y, $\sin\theta$, $\cos\theta$, and $\tan\theta$ as θ increases continuously from $0°$ to $90°$.

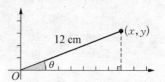

Figure 5 - 25

   (2) The Figure 5 - 26 shows point $P(x, y)$ on a unit circle and right triangle OAP.

   a. Find $\sin t$ and $\cos t$ using the unit circle definitions of sine and cosine.

   b. What is the value of r? Explain.

   c. Use the definitions of sine and cosine given in this section to find $\sin\theta$ and $\cos\theta$. Write your answers in terms of x and y.

   d. Based on your answers to parts a. and c., what can you conclude?

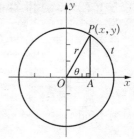

Figure 5 - 26

5.3 ◆ 诱导公式 Symmetry and Shifts

在不同的场合下,需要用到相应的三角函数来描述问题中涉及的(带符号的)比值.由于解决问题时的入手点不同,涉及三角函数的答案在表述上时常会呈现出不同的表达形式.例如:用右图(Figure 5 - 27)来计算 $\dfrac{\theta}{2}$ 的正切值时,可以算 $\tan \alpha$ 或 $\tan \beta = \tan \beta'$. 于是得到

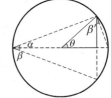

$$\tan \frac{\theta}{2} = \tan \alpha = \frac{\sin \theta}{1 + \cos \theta} \text{ 或者 } \tan \frac{\theta}{2} = \tan \beta' = \frac{1 - \cos \theta}{\sin \theta},$$ 当然,这两个形状相异的答案应该是一样的.

同样的问题在后续的学习中经常出现,为此,需要掌握三角函数的恒等变形.本节与下一节将介绍此类化简过程的基本内容与方法.

Figure 5 - 27

诱导公式 The Fundamental Trigonometric Identities
在上一节中,各个三角函数之间的一些基本等式被归纳为一个六边形关系.下表补充了一些新关系.

The Fundamental Trigonometric Identities (Continued)

Cofunction Identities

$$\sin\left(\frac{\pi}{2} - \theta\right) = \cos \theta \qquad \cos\left(\frac{\pi}{2} - \theta\right) = \sin \theta$$

$$\tan\left(\frac{\pi}{2} - \theta\right) = \cot \theta \qquad \cot\left(\frac{\pi}{2} - \theta\right) = \tan \theta$$

$$\sec\left(\frac{\pi}{2} - \theta\right) = \csc \theta \qquad \csc\left(\frac{\pi}{2} - \theta\right) = \sec \theta$$

Even/Odd Identities

$$\sin(-\theta) = -\sin \theta \qquad \cos(-\theta) = \cos \theta \qquad \tan(-\theta) = -\tan \theta$$

$$\csc(-\theta) = -\csc \theta \qquad \sec(-\theta) = \sec \theta \qquad \cot(-\theta) = -\cot \theta$$

上述三角恒等式的一个重要用途是通过已知的三角函数值来求其他的三角函数值.

应用诱导公式计算 Use the Fundamental Identities to Calculate

❶ If $\sec \theta = -\dfrac{3}{2}$, $\tan \theta > 0$, evaluate the six trigonometric functions of θ.

Solution: Since $\sec \theta < 0$, $\tan \theta > 0$, θ lies in quadrant III. Hence, $\sin \theta < 0$. Thus, $\sin \theta = -\sqrt{1 - \cos^2 \theta} = -\sqrt{1 - \dfrac{1}{\sec^2 \theta}} = -\dfrac{\sqrt{5}}{3}$. The six values are listed below.

$$\sin \theta = -\frac{\sqrt{5}}{3}, \qquad\qquad \csc \theta = \frac{1}{\sin \theta} = -\frac{3\sqrt{5}}{5},$$

$$\cos \theta = \frac{1}{\sec \theta} = -\frac{2}{3}, \qquad\qquad \sec \theta = -\frac{3}{2},$$

$$\tan \theta = \frac{\sin \theta}{\cos \theta} = \frac{\sqrt{5}}{2}, \qquad\qquad \cot \theta = \frac{1}{\tan \theta} = \frac{2\sqrt{5}}{5}.$$

---

❷ Find the six trigonometric values of $\pi \pm \theta$ in terms of those of θ.

Solution： Since $\pi - \theta = \dfrac{\pi}{2} - \left(\theta - \dfrac{\pi}{2}\right) = \dfrac{\pi}{2} - \left(-\left(\dfrac{\pi}{2} - \theta\right)\right)$, it follows that

$$\sin(\pi - \theta) = \sin\left[\dfrac{\pi}{2} - \left(-\left(\dfrac{\pi}{2} - \theta\right)\right)\right]$$

$$= \cos\left[-\left(\dfrac{\pi}{2} - \theta\right)\right]$$

$$= \cos\left(\dfrac{\pi}{2} - \theta\right)$$

$$= \sin\theta$$

Similarly，one obtains that

$$\cos(\pi - \theta) = -\cos\theta, \qquad \csc(\pi - \theta) = \csc\theta,$$
$$\tan(\pi - \theta) = -\tan\theta, \qquad \sec(\pi - \theta) = -\sec\theta,$$
$$\cot(\pi - \theta) = -\cot\theta.$$

For $\pi + \theta$, the same reasoning gives

$$\sin(\pi + \theta) = -\sin\theta, \qquad \csc(\pi + \theta) = -\csc\theta,$$
$$\cos(\pi + \theta) = -\cos\theta, \qquad \sec(\pi + \theta) = -\sec\theta,$$
$$\tan(\pi + \theta) = \tan\theta, \qquad \cot(\pi + \theta) = \cot\theta.$$

3 Simplify：$\dfrac{\sin(-\theta) + \tan(-\theta) + \cot(-\theta) + \csc(-\theta)}{\cos\left(\dfrac{\pi}{2} - \theta\right) + \tan\left(\dfrac{\pi}{2} - \theta\right) + \cot\left(\dfrac{\pi}{2} - \theta\right) + \sec\left(\dfrac{\pi}{2} - \theta\right)}.$

Solution： Note that

$$\sin(-\theta) = -\sin\theta, \qquad \cos\left(\dfrac{\pi}{2} - \theta\right) = \sin\theta,$$
$$\tan(-\theta) = -\tan\theta, \qquad \tan\left(\dfrac{\pi}{2} - \theta\right) = \cot\theta,$$
$$\cot(-\theta) = -\cot\theta, \qquad \cot\left(\dfrac{\pi}{2} - \theta\right) = \tan\theta,$$
$$\csc(-\theta) = -\csc\theta, \qquad \sec\left(\dfrac{\pi}{2} - \theta\right) = \csc\theta.$$

Hence，the answer is -1.

证明简单三角恒等式 Verify the Trigonometric Identities

在推导新的诱导公式时，我们已经看到进行**三角值恒等式**的运算与一般计算题的区别：它要求我们进行**代数**而非**算术**的计算.三角恒等式的变形能帮助我们将一个含有三角值的表达式变得适于使用.为此，我们将证明三角值恒等式的一些基本运算规律总结如下：

Guidelines for Verifying the Trigonometric Identities

1. Work with one side of the equation at a time. It is often better to work with the more complicated side first.

2. Look for opportunities to factor an expression, add fractions, square a binomial, or create a monomial denominator.

3. Look for opportunities to use the fundamental identities. Note which functions are in the final expression you want. Sines and cosines pair up well, as do secants and tangents, and cosecants and cotangents.

4. If the preceding guidelines do not help, then try converting all terms to sines and cosines.

5. Always try something. Even making an attempt that leads to a dead end can provide insight.

When you verify an identity, you cannot assume that the two sides are equal because you are trying to verify that they are equal. As a result, when verifying identities, you cannot use operations such as cross multiplication.

4 Verify the identity $\dfrac{\cot^2\theta}{1+\csc\theta}=\dfrac{1-\sin\theta}{\sin\theta}$.

Solution: Start with the left side.

$$\frac{\cot^2\theta}{1+\csc\theta}=\frac{\csc^2\theta-1}{1+\csc\theta}$$

$$=\frac{(\csc\theta-1)(\csc\theta+1)}{1+\csc\theta}$$

$$=\csc\theta-1.$$

Now simplify the right side.

$$\frac{1-\sin\theta}{\sin\theta}=\frac{1}{\sin\theta}-\frac{\sin\theta}{\sin\theta}=\csc\theta-1.$$

This verifies the identity because both sides are equal to $\csc\theta-1$.

5 Verify the identity $\dfrac{\cos\theta}{1-\sin\theta}=\dfrac{1+\sin\theta}{\cos\theta}$.

Solution: Subtract the right side from the left to obtain that

$$\frac{\cos\theta}{1-\sin\theta}-\frac{1+\sin\theta}{\cos\theta}=\frac{\cos^2\theta-(1-\sin^2\theta)}{(1-\sin\theta)\cos\theta}$$

$$=\frac{(\cos^2\theta+\sin^2\theta)-1}{(1-\sin\theta)\cos\theta}$$

$$=0.$$

6 Verify the identity $\sin^4\theta+\sin^2\theta\cos^2\theta+\cos^2\theta=1$.

Solution: The pythagorean identity $\sin^2\theta+\cos^2\theta=1$ implies that

$$\sin^4\theta+\sin^2\theta\cos^2\theta=\sin^2\theta(\sin^2\theta+\cos^2\theta)=\sin^2\theta.$$

Hence, a second application of the same identity reveals that

$$\sin^4\theta+\sin^2\theta\cos^2\theta+\cos^2\theta=\sin^2\theta+\cos^2\theta=1.$$

7 Verify the identity $\dfrac{\cos^2\alpha-\cos^2\beta}{\cot^2\alpha-\cot^2\beta}=\sin^2\alpha\sin^2\beta$.

Solution： Convert the left side into sines and cosines.

$$\frac{\cos^2 \alpha - \cos^2 \beta}{\cot^2 \alpha - \cot^2 \beta} = \frac{\cos^2 \alpha - \cos^2 \beta}{\cos^2 \alpha / \sin^2 \alpha - \cos^2 \beta / \sin^2 \beta}$$

$$= \frac{\cos^2 \alpha - \cos^2 \beta}{(\cos^2 \alpha \sin^2 \beta - \cos^2 \beta \sin^2 \alpha)/\sin^2 \alpha \sin^2 \beta}$$

$$= \frac{\cos^2 \alpha - \cos^2 \beta}{\cos^2 \alpha \sin^2 \beta - \cos^2 \beta \sin^2 \alpha} \sin^2 \alpha \, \sin^2 \beta$$

$$= \frac{\cos^2 \alpha - \cos^2 \beta}{\cos^2 \alpha (1 - \cos^2 \beta) - \cos^2 \beta (1 - \cos^2 \alpha)} \sin^2 \alpha \sin^2 \beta$$

$$= \frac{\cos^2 \alpha - \cos^2 \beta}{\cos^2 \alpha - \cos^2 \beta} \sin^2 \alpha \sin^2 \beta$$

$$= \sin^2 \alpha \sin^2 \beta.$$

练习 Exercise

1. Answer the following questions.

  (1) If $\sec \theta = -\dfrac{3}{2}$, $\tan \theta > 0$, evaluate the six trigonometric functions of θ.

  (2) Find the six trigonometric values of $\dfrac{\pi}{2} + \theta$ in terms of θ.

  (3) Simplify $\dfrac{1 - 2\sin(180° - \theta)\cos(-\theta)}{\tan(180° + \theta) - 1} - \dfrac{1}{\tan \theta - \cot(-\theta)}$.

2. Verify the identities.

  (1) $\dfrac{\tan^2 \theta}{1 + \sec \theta} = \dfrac{1 - \cos \theta}{\cos \theta}$.

  (2) $\dfrac{\sin \theta}{1 + \cos \theta} = \dfrac{1 - \cos \theta}{\sin \theta}$.

  (3) $\tan^2 \theta - \sin^2 \theta = \tan^2 \theta \sin^2 \theta$.

  (4) $\dfrac{\tan \theta - \cot \theta}{\sec \theta - \csc \theta} = \sin \theta + \cos \theta$.

3. True or False：

  (1) The even and odd trigonometric identities are helpful for determining whether the value of a trigonometric ratio is positive or negative.

  (2) The equation $\sin^2 \theta + \cos^2 \theta = 1 + \tan^2 \theta$ is a trigonometric identity because $\sin^2(0) + \cos^2(0) = 1$ and $1 + \tan^2(0) = 1$.

  (3) $\sin x^2 = \sin^2 x$.

4. The length s of a shadow cast by a vertical gnomon (a device used to tell time) of height h when the angle of the sun above the horizon is θ can be modeled by the equation $s = \dfrac{h \sin(90° - \theta)}{\sin \theta}$.

  (1) Verify that the expression for s is equal to $h \cot \theta$.

  (2) Use a graphing utility to complete Table 5 - 3. Let $h = 5$ feet.

Table 5 - 3

θ	15°	30°	45°	60°	75°	90°
s						

(3) Use your table from part (2) to determine the angles of the sun that result in the maximum and minimum lengths of the shadow.

(4) Based on your results of part (3), what time of day do you think it is when the angle of the sun above the horizon is 90°?

5. (1) Verify the following identities.

a. $2 + \cos^2 \theta - 3\cos^4 \theta = \sin^2 \theta (2 + 3\cos^2 \theta)$;

b. $\dfrac{\cos x - \cos y}{\sin x + \sin y} + \dfrac{\sin x - \sin y}{\cos x + \cos y} = 0$;

c. $\dfrac{\tan x + \tan y}{1 - \tan x \tan y} = \dfrac{\cot x + \cot y}{\cot x \cot y - 1}$.

(2) Use the cofunction identities to evaluate the expression without using a calculator.

a. $\sin^2 25° + \sin^2 65°$;

b. $\tan^2 63° + \cot^2 16° - \sec^2 74° - \csc^2 27°$.

6. (1) Explain how to use Figure 5 - 28 to derive the identity

$$\frac{\sec^2 \theta - 1}{\sec^2 \theta} = \sin^2 \theta.$$

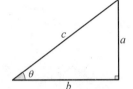

Figure 5 - 28

(2) Which of the following equations are valid whenever both sides make sense? For those which are so, verify them; for those which are not, find one value of the angle θ for which the equation is not true.

a. $\dfrac{\sin (k\theta)}{\cos (k\theta)} = \tan \theta$;

b. $(1 + \cot^2 \theta)\cos^2 \theta = \cot^2 \theta$;

c. $\sin \theta = \sqrt{1 - \cos^2 \theta}$;

d. $1 + \tan \theta = \sec \theta$.

5.4 ◆ 三角恒等式

Advanced Trigonometric Formulas

　　无条件恒等式表明一个数量关系的两种形式,而无条件恒等式的证明,就是把一种数量关系有根据地从一种形式变到另一种需要的形式.三角恒等式是此类恒等式的典型代表.本节将讨论一些最基本、最常用的三角恒等式.它们将为复杂的三角运算、化简提供有力的工具,也将在运算结果的等价变形中起到重要的作用.

和、差角公式 Sum and Difference Formulas of the Angle
　　在数学活动中我们已经发现,$\sin (\alpha + \beta)$ 和 $\cos (\alpha + \beta)$ 与 α、β 的三角值之间的联系比较复杂.实际上,两个角的和与差的三角值还是有规律可循的.以下就是公式列表:

Sum and Difference Formulas of the Angle

$$\sin (\alpha + \beta) = \sin \alpha \cos \beta + \cos \alpha \sin \beta$$

$$\sin (\alpha - \beta) = \sin \alpha \cos \beta - \cos \alpha \sin \beta$$

$$\cos (\alpha + \beta) = \cos \alpha \cos \beta - \sin \alpha \sin \beta$$

$$\cos (\alpha - \beta) = \cos \alpha \cos \beta + \sin \alpha \sin \beta$$

$$\tan(\alpha+\beta)=\frac{\tan\alpha+\tan\beta}{1-\tan\alpha\,\tan\beta}$$

$$\tan(\alpha-\beta)=\frac{\tan\alpha-\tan\beta}{1+\tan\alpha\,\tan\beta}$$

1 Evaluate $\sin\dfrac{\pi}{12}$ without using a calculator.

Solution: Note that $\dfrac{\pi}{12}=\dfrac{\pi}{3}-\dfrac{\pi}{4}$, the difference formula applies.

$$\sin\frac{\pi}{12}=\sin\left(\frac{\pi}{3}-\frac{\pi}{4}\right)$$

$$=\sin\frac{\pi}{3}\cos\frac{\pi}{4}-\cos\frac{\pi}{3}\sin\frac{\pi}{4}$$

$$=\frac{\sqrt{3}}{2}\left(\frac{\sqrt{2}}{2}\right)-\frac{1}{2}\left(\frac{\sqrt{2}}{2}\right)$$

$$=\frac{\sqrt{6}-\sqrt{2}}{4}.$$

2 Let $\sin\theta=\dfrac{4}{5}$, $\cos\varphi=-\dfrac{12}{13}$ $\left(0<\theta<\dfrac{\pi}{2},\dfrac{\pi}{2}<\varphi<\pi\right)$. Find $\sin(\theta+\varphi)$.

Solution: Since $\sin\theta=\dfrac{4}{5}$ and $0<\theta<\dfrac{\pi}{2}$, it follows that $\cos\theta=\dfrac{3}{5}$. Similarly, $\sin\varphi=\dfrac{5}{13}$. Apply the sum formula to obtain that

$$\sin(\theta+\varphi)=\sin\theta\,\cos\varphi+\cos\theta\,\sin\varphi$$

$$=\frac{4}{5}\left(-\frac{12}{13}\right)+\frac{3}{5}\left(\frac{5}{13}\right)$$

$$=-\frac{33}{65}.$$

倍角公式 Multiple-Angle Formulas

在和角公式中取 $\alpha=\beta$，就能得到：

二倍角公式 Double-Angle Formulas

$$\sin2\alpha=2\sin\alpha\,\cos\alpha \qquad \cos2\alpha=\cos^2\alpha-\sin^2\alpha$$

$$\tan2\alpha=\frac{2\tan\alpha}{1-\tan^2\alpha} \qquad =2\cos^2\alpha-1$$

$$=1-2\sin^2\alpha$$

3 If $\cos\theta=\dfrac{5}{13}$, $\dfrac{3\pi}{2}<\theta<2\pi$, find $\sin2\theta$, $\cos2\theta$ and $\tan2\theta$.

Solution: Since θ lies in quadrant IV, $\sin\theta=-\dfrac{12}{13}$, $\tan\theta=-\dfrac{12}{5}$.

Apply the double-angle formulas，we obtain

$$\sin 2\theta = 2\sin\theta\,\cos\theta = 2\left(-\frac{12}{13}\right)\left(\frac{5}{13}\right) = -\frac{120}{169},$$

$$\cos 2\theta = 2\cos^2\theta - 1 = 2\left(\frac{25}{169}\right) - 1 = -\frac{119}{169},$$

$$\tan 2\theta = \frac{2\tan\theta}{1-\tan^2\theta} = \frac{2(-12/5)}{1-(-12/5)^2} = \frac{120}{169}.$$

4 Find $\sin 3x$ in terms of $\sin x$.

Solution: Apply the sum formula and double-angle formulas consecutively to obtain that

$$\begin{aligned}
\sin 3x &= \sin(2x + x) \\
&= \sin 2x\,\cos x + \cos 2x\,\sin x \\
&= 2\sin x\,\cos x\,\cos x + (1 - 2\sin^2 x)\sin x \\
&= 2\sin x\cos^2 x + \sin x - 2\sin^3 x \\
&= 2\sin x(1 - \sin^2 x) + \sin x - 2\sin^3 x \\
&= 2\sin x - 2\sin^3 x + \sin x - 2\sin^3 x \\
&= 3\sin x - 4\sin^3 x.
\end{aligned}$$

5 Find $\sin x$ in terms of $\tan\dfrac{x}{2}$.

Solution: Apply the double-angle formula to find $\sin x = 2\sin\dfrac{x}{2}\cos\dfrac{x}{2}$.

Apply the trigonometric identities $\dfrac{\sin\theta}{\cos\theta} = \tan\theta$ and $\cos^2\theta = \dfrac{1}{1+\tan^2\theta}$ to find that

$$\begin{aligned}
\sin x &= 2\sin\frac{x}{2}\cos\frac{x}{2} \\
&= 2\,\frac{\sin\dfrac{x}{2}}{\cos\dfrac{x}{2}}\cos^2\frac{x}{2} \\
&= 2\tan\frac{x}{2}\cdot\frac{1}{1+\tan^2\dfrac{x}{2}} \\
&= \frac{2\tan\dfrac{x}{2}}{1+\tan^2\dfrac{x}{2}}.
\end{aligned}$$

当然，$\cos x$ 和 $\tan x$ 也可以用 $\tan\dfrac{x}{2}$ 表示，我们把具体的细节留作练习.这组公式能将三角值的分式变成 $\tan\dfrac{x}{2}$ 的分式,这在微积分中很有用,故有"万能公式"之名.

倍角公式的另一个重要作用在于帮助对含有三角值的表达式进行**降次**.

Power-Reducing Formulas

$$\sin^2 \alpha = \frac{1 - \cos 2\alpha}{2}$$

$$\cos^2 \alpha = \frac{1 + \cos 2\alpha}{2}$$

$$\tan^2 \alpha = \frac{1 - \cos 2\alpha}{1 + \cos 2\alpha}$$

6 Find $\sin^4 x$ in terms of the cosine values of some multiple-angles.

Solution:

$$\sin^4 x = (\sin^2 x)^2$$
$$= \left(\frac{1 - \cos 2x}{2}\right)^2$$
$$= \frac{1}{4}(1 - 2\cos 2x + \cos^2 2x)$$
$$= \frac{1}{4}\left(1 - 2\cos 2x + \frac{1 + \cos 4x}{2}\right)$$
$$= \frac{1}{4} - \frac{1}{2}\cos 2x + \frac{1}{8} + \frac{1}{8}\cos 4x$$
$$= \frac{3}{8} - \frac{1}{2}\cos 2x + \frac{1}{8}\cos 4x$$
$$= \frac{1}{8}(3 - 4\cos 2x + \cos 4x).$$

半角公式 Half-Angle Formulas

降次公式也可以用来帮助计算半角的三角值.

Half-Angle Formulas

$$\sin \frac{\alpha}{2} = \pm\sqrt{\frac{1 - \cos \alpha}{2}} \qquad \tan \frac{\alpha}{2} = \frac{1 - \cos \alpha}{\sin \alpha}$$

$$\cos \frac{\alpha}{2} = \pm\sqrt{\frac{1 + \cos \alpha}{2}} \qquad\qquad = \frac{\sin \alpha}{1 + \cos \alpha}$$

The signs of $\sin \frac{\alpha}{2}$ and $\cos \frac{\alpha}{2}$ depend on the quadrant in which $\frac{\alpha}{2}$ lies.

7 Find $\sin \frac{\pi}{12}$ with half-angle formulas.

Solution: Note that $\frac{\pi}{12} = \frac{1}{2}\left(\frac{\pi}{6}\right)$ while $\frac{\pi}{6}$ lies in quadrant I. Hence,

$$\sin \frac{\pi}{12} = \sqrt{\frac{1 - \cos \frac{\pi}{6}}{2}} = \sqrt{\frac{1 - \frac{\sqrt{3}}{2}}{2}} = \frac{\sqrt{2 - \sqrt{3}}}{2} = \frac{\sqrt{6} - \sqrt{2}}{4}.$$

Of course the answer agrees with that obtained in Example 1.

积化和差与和差化积 Product-to-Sum and Sum-to-Product Formulas

有时,出于实际运算的需要,我们会遇到含有三角值表达式的各种问题,有些问题中,两个表达式的和更有利于解决问题,而有些问题中,两个表达式的积则更有效.因此,在同名三角值(即:同为 sin 或 cos 的两个或多个三角值)的和与积之间互相转化是非常必要的.利用和差角公式,我们可以推导出一系列帮助两者之间转化的工具.

Product-to-Sum Formulas

$$\sin\alpha\,\sin\beta=\frac{1}{2}\big[\cos(\alpha-\beta)-\cos(\alpha+\beta)\big]$$

$$\cos\alpha\,\cos\beta=\frac{1}{2}\big[\cos(\alpha-\beta)+\cos(\alpha+\beta)\big]$$

$$\sin\alpha\,\cos\beta=\frac{1}{2}\big[\sin(\alpha+\beta)+\sin(\alpha-\beta)\big]$$

$$\cos\alpha\,\sin\beta=\frac{1}{2}\big[\sin(\alpha+\beta)-\sin(\alpha-\beta)\big]$$

Sum-to-Product Formulas

$$\sin\alpha+\sin\beta=2\sin\frac{\alpha+\beta}{2}\cos\frac{\alpha-\beta}{2}$$

$$\sin\alpha-\sin\beta=2\cos\frac{\alpha+\beta}{2}\sin\frac{\alpha-\beta}{2}$$

$$\cos\alpha+\cos\beta=2\cos\frac{\alpha+\beta}{2}\cos\frac{\alpha-\beta}{2}$$

$$\cos\alpha-\cos\beta=-2\sin\frac{\alpha+\beta}{2}\sin\frac{\alpha-\beta}{2}$$

8 Rewrite the product $\cos 5x\,\sin 4x$ as a sum or difference.

Solution: Using the appropriate product-to-sum formula, you obtain

$$\cos 5x\,\sin 4x=\frac{1}{2}\big[\sin(5x+4x)-\sin(5x-4x)\big]$$

$$=\frac{1}{2}\sin 9x-\frac{1}{2}\sin x.$$

9 Find the exact value of $\cos 195°+\cos 105°$.

Solution: Using the appropriate sum-to-product formula, you obtain

$$\cos 195°+\cos 105°=2\cos\frac{195°+105°}{2}\cos\frac{195°-105°}{2}$$

$$=2\cos 150°\cos 45°$$

$$=2\left(-\frac{\sqrt{3}}{2}\right)\frac{\sqrt{2}}{2}$$

$$=-\frac{\sqrt{6}}{2}.$$

练习Exercise

1. If $\sin\theta = \dfrac{12}{13}$, $\cos\varphi = -\dfrac{3}{5}$ $\left(0 < \theta < \dfrac{\pi}{2}, \dfrac{\pi}{2} < \varphi < \pi\right)$, find $\cos(\theta + \varphi)$.

2. If $\sin\theta = \dfrac{3}{5}$, $\dfrac{\pi}{2} < \theta < \pi$, find $\sin 2\theta$, $\cos 2\theta$ and $\tan 2\theta$.

3. Answer the following questions.

   (1) Find $\cos 3x$ in terms of $\cos x$.

   (2) Find $\cos x$ and $\tan x$ in terms of $\tan\dfrac{x}{2}$.

   (3) Find $\cos^4\theta$ in terms of the cosine values of some multiple-angles.

4. Evaluate $\cos\dfrac{\pi}{12}$ with the indicated formulas.

   (1) Difference formula.   (2) Half-angle formula.

5. Rewrite the product $\sin 5x \cos 3x$ as sum or difference.

6. Find the exact value of $\sin 195° + \sin 105°$.

7. True or False:

   (1) For any pairs of angles θ and φ, $\sin(\theta \pm \varphi) = \sin\theta\cos\varphi \pm \cos\theta\sin\varphi$ and $\cos(\theta \pm \varphi) = \cos\theta\cos\varphi \pm \sin\theta\sin\varphi$.

   (2) $\sin\dfrac{\theta}{2} = -\sqrt{\dfrac{1-\cos\theta}{2}}$ when θ is in the second quadrant.

   (3) If φ and θ are complementary angles, then $\sin(\varphi - \theta) = \cos 2\theta$ and $\cos(\varphi - \theta) = \sin 2\theta$.

8. When two railroad tracks merge, the overlapping portions of the tracks are in the shapes of circular arcs (see Figure 5 - 29). The radius of each arc r (in feet) and the angle θ are related by $\dfrac{x}{2} = 2r\sin^2\dfrac{\theta}{2}$. Write a formula for x in terms of $\cos\theta$.

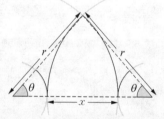

Figure 5 - 29

9. (1) Evaluate the following expressions:

   a. $\dfrac{\sin 120°}{1 + \cos 120°}$;   b. $\cos^2 75° - \sin^2 75°$;

   c. $\dfrac{\tan 45° + \tan 15°}{1 - \tan 15°}$;   d. $\sin 5°\sin 25° - \sin 95°\sin 65°$.

   (2) In what follows, we demonstrate the **formula of auxiliary angle**, which helps to transform $a\sin\theta + b\cos\theta$ $(a^2 + b^2 \neq 0)$ into $A\sin(\theta + \varphi)$.

     a. Verify that the point $\left(\dfrac{a}{\sqrt{a^2+b^2}}, \dfrac{b}{\sqrt{a^2+b^2}}\right)$ lies on the unit circle.

     b. By part a., there is an angle (in radians) corresponding to the above point under the "wrapping" correspondence (see **Trigonometric Functions for any Angle**). Denote this angle by φ. Find $\sin(\theta + \varphi)$.

     c. Show that $a\sin\theta + b\cos\theta = A\sin(\theta + \varphi)$ for angle φ from part b., while $A = \sqrt{a^2 + b^2}$.

10. (1) Observe the following diagrams (Figure 5 – 30) and find a mathematical proof for the Difference Formula.

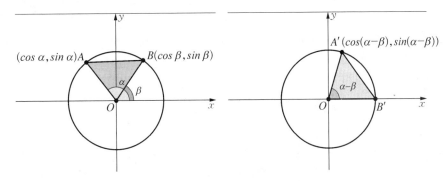

Figure 5 – 30

(2) The *tangent half-angle formula* helps to convert fractions involving a mixture of $\sin x$, $\cos x$ and $\tan x$ into a rational function of the single variable: $t = \tan \dfrac{x}{2}$. This is particularly useful in calculus. Now try this out for the following fractions by converting them into rational functions of t:

a. $\dfrac{\sin x + 1}{\cos x - 1}$;

b. $\dfrac{1}{\sin x + \cos x}$;

c. $\dfrac{1 - r^2}{1 - 2r \cos x + r^2}$, where $0 < r < 1$.

5.5 ◈ 正弦定理和余弦定理 Laws of Sine and Cosine

在过去,人类对于数学的发展往往来自解决实际问题的需要.其中,最为典型的例子之一就是将几何的知识运用于测量.例如,我国南宋数学家秦九韶在他的《数书九章》中借一个土地丈量问题提出了著名的"三斜求积术".为了解释他的公式,秦九韶精心设计了下面的问题:

问沙田一段,有三斜,其小斜一十三里,中斜一十四里,大斜一十五里,里法三百步,欲知为田几何?

由于古人没有书写证明的习惯,因此今天已经无法得知秦九韶当年是如何构思出他的巧妙公式.然而,随着时代的演进,特别是代数方法的发展,今天的每个高中生都有能力解决"三斜求积"的问题.

正弦定理 Law of Sines

在上面的活动中我们已经发现,三角形的边和对角的正弦之间存在着密切的联系:它们是成比例的.这就是**正弦定理**的内容.

Law of Sines

If ABC is a triangle with sides a, b and c, then

$$\frac{a}{\sin A} = \frac{b}{\sin B} = \frac{c}{\sin C}$$

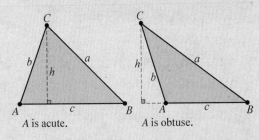

Figure 5 – 31

1 In $\triangle ABC$, let $a=7$, $B=30°$, $C=85°$. Find c (round the answer to two decimal places).

Solution： Since $A=180°-30°-85°=65°$, the Law of Sines implies that $\dfrac{7}{\sin 65°}=\dfrac{c}{\sin 85°}$.

It then follows that $c=7\dfrac{\sin 85°}{\sin 65°}\approx 7.69$.

余弦定理 Law of Cosines

运用勾股定理,我们可以导出三角形边角之间的另一组关系:

Law of Cosines

Standard Form	**Alternative Form**
$a^2=b^2+c^2-2bc\,\cos A$	$\cos A=\dfrac{b^2+c^2-a^2}{2bc}$
$b^2=c^2+a^2-2ca\,\cos B$	$\cos B=\dfrac{c^2+a^2-b^2}{2ca}$
$c^2=a^2+b^2-2ab\,\cos C$	$\cos C=\dfrac{a^2+b^2-c^2}{2ab}$

在已知三角形两边和它们的夹角或者三边的情况下,余弦定理是有用的.

2 In $\triangle ABC$, let $C=45°$, $a=\sqrt{6}$, $b=\sqrt{3}+1$. Find c.

Solution： The Law of Cosines implies that

$$c^2=a^2+b^2-2ab\,\cos C$$
$$=(\sqrt{6})^2+(\sqrt{3}+1)^2-2\sqrt{6}(\sqrt{3}+1)\times\dfrac{\sqrt{2}}{2}$$
$$=4.$$

Hence, $c=2$.

解斜三角形 Solving Oblique Triangles

在初中我们已经学习过解直角三角形的方法.现在,利用三角的工具,我们可以试着解斜三角形.

所谓的解斜三角形,就是在已知三角形的六个要素,即三边 a、b、c 和三角 A、B、C 中的三个时,设法求出另外的三个.在学习全等三角形的判定时我们已经知道,为了确定一个三角形,必须至少知道它的一条边,而另外两个要素可以有各种组合:两条边、两个角,或者一边一角.我们将不同的情况总结成以下四类:

a. 两角和一边(AAS 或 ASA);

b. 两边和其中一边的对角(SSA);

c. 两边和它们的夹角(SAS);

d. 三边(SSS).

我们将通过一系列的例子来展示正弦定理和余弦定理在各种不同条件下对于解三角形的作用.

3 In $\triangle ABC$, let $C=102°$, $B=29°$, and $b=28$ feet. Find the remaining angle and sides.

Solution： The third angle of the triangle is $A=180°-29°-102°=49°$.

By the Law of Sines, $\dfrac{a}{\sin A}=\dfrac{b}{\sin B}=\dfrac{c}{\sin C}$. $b=28$ then, implies that

$$a = \frac{b}{\sin B}(\sin A) = \frac{28}{\sin 29°}(\sin 49°) \approx 43.59 \text{ ft},$$

and $c = \dfrac{b}{\sin B}(\sin C) = \dfrac{28}{\sin 29°}(\sin 102°) \approx 56.49 \text{ ft.}$

4 Find the three angles of the triangle whose sides have lengths $a = 8$ ft, $b = 19$ ft, and $c = 14$ ft.

Solution: It is a good idea first to find the angle opposite to the longest side — side b in this case. Using the alternative form of the Law of Cosines, you find that

$$\cos B = \frac{a^2 + c^2 - b^2}{2ac} = \frac{8^2 + 14^2 - 19^2}{2(8)(14)} \approx -0.45089.$$

Because $\cos B$ is negative, B is an obtuse angle given by $B \approx 116.80°$, using calculator. At this point, it is simpler to use the Law of Sines to determine A.

$$\sin A = a\left(\frac{\sin B}{b}\right) \approx 8\left(\frac{\sin 116.80°}{19}\right) \approx 0.37583.$$

Because B is obtuse and a triangle can have at most one obtuse angle, you know that A must be acute. So, $A \approx 22.08°$ and $C \approx 180° - 22.08° - 116.80° = 41.12°$.

5 Given $A = 25°$, $b = 9$ m and $c = 12$ m, find the remaining angles and side of the triangle.

Solution: Use the Law of Cosines to find the unknown side a in the triangle.

$$a^2 = b^2 + c^2 - 2bc\,\cos A$$

$$a^2 = 9^2 + 12^2 - 2(9)(12)\cos 25°$$

$$a^2 \approx 29.2375$$

So $a \approx 5.4072$ meters. Now given the ratio $\dfrac{\sin A}{a}$, the reciprocal form of the Law of Sines solves for B.

$$\frac{\sin B}{b} = \frac{\sin A}{a}$$

$$\Rightarrow \sin B = b\left(\frac{\sin A}{a}\right)$$

$$\Rightarrow \sin B \approx 9\left(\frac{\sin 25°}{5.4072}\right)$$

$$\Rightarrow \sin B \approx 0.7034.$$

There are two angles between $0°$ and $180°$ whose sine is 0.7034, $B_1 \approx 44.7°$ and $B_2 \approx 180° - 44.7° = 135.3°$.

For $B_1 \approx 44.7°$, $C_1 \approx 180° - 25° - 44.7° = 110.3°$.

For $B_2 \approx 135.3°$, $C_2 \approx 180° - 25° - 135.3° = 19.7°$.

Because side c is the longest side of the triangle, C must be the largest angle of the triangle. So, $B \approx 44.7°$ and $C \approx 110.3°$.

6

   a. In $\triangle ABC$, $a = 22$ inches, $b = 12$ inches, and $A = 42°$. Find the remaining side and angles.

   b. Show that there is no triangle for which $a = 15$, $b = 25$ and $A = 85°$.

   c. Find two triangles for which $a = 12$ meters, $b = 31$ meters and $A = 20.5°$.

Solution:

   a. By the Law of Sines, we have $B \approx 21.41°$. Now, we can determine that $C \approx 116.59°$. Then, the remaining side is $c \approx 29.40$ inches.

   b. Verify this by the Law of Sines. Since $\sin B = 25 \dfrac{\sin 85°}{15} \approx 1.6603 > 1$, which is impossible, it means that there is no such triangle.

   c. By the Law of Sines, we have $\sin B = b \dfrac{\sin A}{a} \approx 0.9047$. There are two angles: $B_1 \approx 64.8°$ and $B_2 \approx 115.2°$. Hence, there are two solutions:

$$B_1 \approx 64.8°, \qquad B_2 \approx 115.2°,$$
$$C_1 \approx 94.7°, \qquad C_2 \approx 44.3°,$$
$$c_1 \approx 34.15 \text{ m}; \qquad c_2 \approx 23.93 \text{ m}.$$

应用：三角形的面积公式 Applications：Area Formulas of Triangles

现在我们可以回答在本节开头提出的面积问题了.为此,我们需要借助余弦定理建立下面这个面积公式：

Heron's Area Formula

Given any triangle with sides of lengths a, b and c, the area of the triangle is

$$\text{Area} = \sqrt{s(s-a)(s-b)(s-c)}$$

where

$$s = \frac{a+b+c}{2}$$

7 问沙田一段,有三斜,其小斜一十三里,中斜一十四里,大斜一十五里,里法三百步,欲知为田几何？〔注：二百四十(平方)步为一顷,百顷为一亩.〕

解：依 Heron 公式,先求出 $s = \dfrac{13+14+15}{2}$（里）,于是

$$面积 = \sqrt{s(s-a)(s-b)(s-c)} = 84 \text{（平方里）}.$$

再利用单位转换,得到: $\dfrac{84 \times 300 \times 300}{240 \times 100} = 315$（顷）.

With the help of the Law of Sines and Cosines, we may establish some other area formulas, as is shown below:

Further Area Formulas

$$Area = \frac{1}{2}ab \sin C$$

$$= 2R^2 \sin A \sin B \sin C$$

$$= \frac{abc}{4R}$$

$$= a^2 \frac{\sin B \sin C}{2\sin A}$$

where R is the radius of the circumscribed circle.

8 In $\triangle ABC$, $a=4$, $b=5$ and $c=6$. Find the radius R of its circumscribed circle.

Solution: Firstly, $s = \dfrac{a+b+c}{2} = \dfrac{15}{2}$. Thus, by Heron's formula, $S_{\triangle ABC} = \sqrt{s(s-a)(s-b)(s-c)} = \dfrac{15\sqrt{7}}{4}$.

Hence, from the alternative area formula $S_{\triangle ABC} = \dfrac{abc}{4R}$, $R = \dfrac{abc}{4S_{\triangle ABC}} = \dfrac{4 \cdot 5 \cdot 6}{4 \dfrac{15\sqrt{7}}{4}} = \dfrac{8\sqrt{7}}{7}$.

练习 Exercise

1. Solve the following problems with suitable theorems(see Figure 5 - 32).

    (1) In $\triangle ABC$, let $a = 11$, $A = 80°$, $C = 50°$. Find b (round the answer to two decimal places).

    (2) In $\triangle ABC$, let $A = 60°$, $b = 5$, $c = 2$. Find a.

    (3) For the triangle in Figure 5 - 32, $A = 30°$, $B = 45°$ and $a = 32$. Find the remaining angle and sides.

    (4) Find the three angles of the triangle whose sides have lengths $a = 6$, $b = 8$ and $c = 12$.

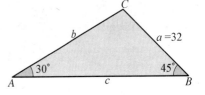

Figure 5 - 32

    (5) Given $A = 80°$, $b = 16$ and $c = 12$, find the remaining angles and side of the triangle.

    (6) Given $A = 31°$, $a = 12$ and $b = 5$, find the remaining side and angles.

    (7) Show that there is no triangle for which $a = 4$, $b = 14$ and $A = 60°$.

    (8) Find two triangles for which $a = 4.5$ feet, $b = 5$ feet and $A = 58°$.

    (9) In $\triangle ABC$, $a = 5$, $b = 9$, $c = 8$. Find its area.

    (10) In $\triangle ABC$, $\angle A = 30°$, $\angle B = 120°$ and $c = 6$. Find the area $S_{\triangle ABC}$.

2. True or False:

    (1) If a triangle contains an obtuse angle, it must be oblique.

    (2) If three sides or three angles of an oblique triangle are known, the triangle can be solved.

    (3) Given triangle with three sides a, b and c, if $a^2 + b^2 > c^2$, it is an acute triangle.

3. (1) The Leaning Tower of Pisa in Italy leans because it was built on unstable soil — a mixture of

clay, sand, and water. The tower is approximately 58.36 meters tall from its foundation (see Figure 5 - 33). The top of the tower leans about 5.45 meters off the center.

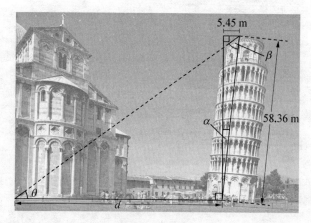

Figure 5 - 33

a. Find the angle of lean α of the tower (in radians).

b. Write β in terms of α and θ, where θ is the angle of elevation to the sun.

c. Use the Law of Sines to write the length d of the shadow cast by the tower as a function of θ.

(2) To approximate the length of a marsh, a surveyor walks 250 meters from point A to point B, then turns $75°$ and walks 220 meters to point C (see Figure 5 - 34). Approximate the length AC of the marsh.

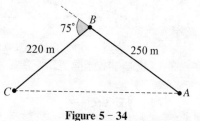

Figure 5 - 34

4. (1) In Figure 5 - 35, D is a point on the side BC. Apply the area formula: $S = \dfrac{1}{2} ab \sin C$ to show that: $\dfrac{\sin \angle BAC}{AD} = \dfrac{\sin \angle CAD}{AB} + \dfrac{\sin \angle BAD}{AC}$.

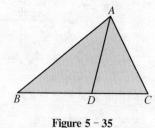

Figure 5 - 35   **Figure 5 - 36**

(2) Here we present an alternative way to obtain the **formula of auxiliary angle** $a \sin \theta + b \cos \theta = A \sin(\theta + \varphi)$ when $0 < \theta < \dfrac{\pi}{2}$, $a > 0$ and $b > 0$.

a. Let $\triangle ABC$ be a right triangle with $\angle ACB = 90°$, $\angle A = \theta$. D is a point on line AC so that $CD = BC$. See Figure 5 - 36.

Apply the Law of Sines in $\triangle ABD$ to show that for any acute angle θ, $\sin \theta + \cos \theta = \sqrt{2} \sin\left(\theta + \dfrac{\pi}{4}\right)$.

b. Establish a similar setup as in part a. to justify the formula of auxiliary angle.

(3) Prove the Law of Sines and the Law of Cosines.

5. (1) Determine whether the Law of Sines or the Law of Cosines is needed to solve the triangle (Figure 5 - 37).

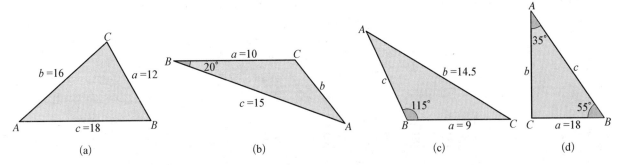

(a) (b) (c) (d)

Figure 5 - 37

(2) In Figure 5 - 38, a triangle is to be formed by drawing a line segment of length a from (4, 3) to the positive x -axis. For what value(s) of a can you form.

a. one triangle;

b. two triangles;

c. no triangle?

Explain.

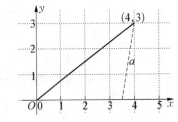

Figure 5 - 38

第 6 章

三角函数　Trigonometric Functions

6.1 ◈ 正弦函数和余弦函数　Sine and Cosine Functions

18 世纪中叶,瑞士大数学家欧拉在他的名著《无穷小分析引论》中建立了三角函数的概念,开创了三角学研究的解析时代.值得一提的是,他使用无穷级数的方法导出了著名的欧拉公式:$e^{ix} = \cos x + i \cdot \sin x$. 当时,欧拉使用的三角函数的符号已经非常接近于今天的记号:sin、cos、tang、cot、sec 和 cosec. 此后,随着对于周期现象的深入研究,三角函数的地位蒸蒸日上,终于成为现代数学的基本工具之一.

实变量的三角函数 Trigonometric Functions as Functions of a Real Variable

根据前一章的讨论,我们不难发现,在(弧度制的)角 x 和它的三角函数值 $\sin x$ 之间存在着一个对应关系,每个(弧度制的)角在此关系下都有唯一确定的值 $\sin x$ 与之相对应.因此,按照函数的观点,我们可以把对应关系:$x \to \sin x$ 看成一个函数,称为自变量 x 的**正弦函数(sine function)**.类似地,我们还有五个三角函数:**余弦函数(cosine function)**、**正切函数(tangent function)**、**余切函数(cotangent function)**、**正割函数(secant function)**和**余割函数(cosecant function)**.它们构成了基本的三角函数:

Basic Trigonometric Functions			
sine	$y = \sin x$	cosine	$y = \cos x$
tangent	$y = \tan x$	cotangent	$y = \cot x$
secant	$y = \sec x$	cosecant	$y = \csc x$

按照三角函数的定义,它们有一个共性:如果两个(弧度制的)角 x_1、x_2 恰好相差 2π 的整数倍,则其对应的角的终边重合,于是,x_1 和 x_2 的同名三角函数或者同时有意义,或者同时无意义.并且,在相应的三角函数都有意义时,取值应当相等.例如,对所有的 $n \in \mathbf{Z}$ 和 $x \in \mathbf{R}$,$\sin(x + 2n\pi) = \sin x$. 像这样,取值关于自变量进行周而复始变化的函数被称为**周期的(periodic)**.

Definition of Periodic Function

A function f is **periodic** if there is a non-zero real number T such that

$$f(x + T) = f(x).$$

for all x in the domain of f. The smallest positive number T for which f is periodic, if exists, is called **the period** of f.

关于周期性概念的需要注意以下几个方面:

a. 周期 T 必须是非零常数;

b. 等式 $f(x + T) = f(x)$ 必须对定义域内的所有 x 成立;

c. 周期函数不一定有最小正周期;周期性与单调性、奇偶性等一样,都是函数的基本性质.

正弦函数和余弦函数的图像 Graphs of Sine and Cosine Functions

函数图像是用来研究函数性质的一个有力工具.本节以正弦、余弦两个函数为例展示如何对函数进行简单的定性分析.

利用图形计算器(如 TI-nSpire CX-C CAS)或者作图软件(如几何画板)容易作出正弦函数 $y = \sin x$ 的图像,称为**正弦曲线(sine curve)**(Figure 6-1).

图中粗线部分表明了 $y = \sin x$ 在一个周期内的图像.

下面通过正弦函数的性质来分析图像呈现出上述形态的原因.

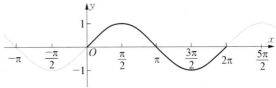

Figure 6-1

1. 定义域

由正弦函数的定义,它的定义域是全体实数 **R**.

2. 值域

根据正弦函数与单位圆的联系,得到它的值域是闭区间 $[-1, 1]$.

3. 奇偶性

依据三角的诱导公式,$\sin(-x) = -\sin x$,于是 $y = \sin x$ 是奇函数.

4. 周期性

$y = \sin x$ 是周期函数,2π 是它的一个周期.以下证明 2π 是它的最小正周期.

假设存在 T,满足 $0 < T < 2\pi$,且是函数 $y = \sin x$ 的周期,即 $\sin(x+T) = \sin x$,令 $x = \dfrac{\pi}{2}$,得 $1 = \sin \dfrac{\pi}{2} = \sin\left(T + \dfrac{\pi}{2}\right) = \cos T$,这与 $0 < T < 2\pi$ 时,$\cos T < 1$ 矛盾.

确定了函数的最小正周期,就可以通过研究 $y = \sin x$ 在一个最小正周期内的性质来推断它在整个定义域中的相应性质.

5. 零点

$y = \sin x$ 在一个周期 $[0, 2\pi]$ 内 $y = \sin x$ 的全部零点是 0、π 和 2π.由周期性,它的所有零点就是 $x = k\pi$,$k \in \mathbf{Z}$.

6. 单调性

$y = \sin x$ 在 $\left[-\dfrac{\pi}{2}, \dfrac{\pi}{2}\right]$ 上单调增,在 $\left[\dfrac{\pi}{2}, \dfrac{3\pi}{2}\right]$ 上单调减.由于周期性函数,$y = \sin x$ 在 $\left[2k\pi - \dfrac{\pi}{2}, 2k\pi + \dfrac{\pi}{2}\right]$ 上是增函数,在 $\left[2k\pi + \dfrac{\pi}{2}, 2k\pi + \dfrac{3\pi}{2}\right]$ 上是减函数,$k \in \mathbf{Z}$.

7. 最值

$y = \sin x$ 在一个周期 $[0, 2\pi]$ 之内满足 $\sin x \leqslant \sin \dfrac{\pi}{2} = 1$,$\sin x \geqslant \sin \dfrac{3\pi}{2} = -1$.由于周期性函数,$y = \sin x$ 在 $x = 2k\pi + \dfrac{\pi}{2}$ 时取得最大值 1,在 $x = 2k\pi - \dfrac{\pi}{2}$ 时取得最小值 -1,$k \in \mathbf{Z}$.

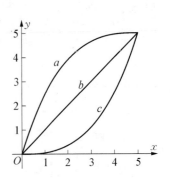

Figure 6-2

8. 凹凸性

除了上述函数基本性质之外,还有一条经常用来刻画函数图像的性质.

见图(Figure 6-2),三条连接原点与点 $(5, 5)$ 的曲线 a、b、c 不仅起点

和终点相同,而且都呈现出上升的态势,但是它们的上升过程各不相同:a 曲线先快后慢,b 曲线匀速上升,而 c 曲线则是先慢后快.这三条曲线上升速度的不同导致了它们弯曲程度的不同.考虑这三段曲线及其正上方的区域,则 a 曲线是向上凹陷的,b 曲线呈现出平直的形状,而 c 曲线则向下凸出.在数学上用一个专门的概念来描述这种区别,即**凹凸性(concavity)**.

> **Definition of Convex/Concave Functions**
>
> Let $f(x)$ be a function defined on an interval I. $f(x)$ is a **concave upward on I**, if the inequality
>
> $$f\left(\frac{x_1+x_2}{2}\right) \leqslant \frac{f(x_1)+f(x_2)}{2}.$$
>
> holds for all pairs of numbers x_1, $x_2 \in I$, with equation holds if and only if $x_1 = x_2$.
>
> Similarly, $f(x)$ is **concave downward on I** if the inequality
>
> $$f\left(\frac{x_1+x_2}{2}\right) \geqslant \frac{f(x_1)+f(x_2)}{2}.$$
>
> holds for all pairs of numbers x_1, $x_2 \in I$, with equation holds if and only if $x_1 = x_2$.

直观地说,凸函数图像上任意两点连线的中点都在图像的上方,而凹函数则正好相反.在微积分的教材中对凸函数会给出更加精准的描述.

$y = \sin x$ 在 $[2k\pi, 2k\pi+\pi]$ 上是凹函数,在 $[2k\pi+\pi, 2k\pi+2\pi]$ 上是凸函数,$k \in \mathbf{Z}$.这个结论可由余弦函数的值域以及和差化积公式得出,留作练习.

综上可知,能够定性地刻画正弦曲线的形状:**在一个周期 $[0, 2\pi]$ 内,曲线从 $(0, 0)$ 出发,先快后慢地"上升"到最高点 $\left(\frac{\pi}{2}, 1\right)$,然后先慢后快地"下降"到 $(\pi, 0)$,接着先快后慢地继续"下降"到最低点 $\left(\frac{3\pi}{2}, -1\right)$,最后先慢后快地重新"上升"到点 $(2\pi, 0)$.完成一个周期之后,向两边"复制"这一个周期的行为,就得到了正弦曲线.** 由此,正弦函数在一个周期 $[0, 2\pi]$ 的图像上有五个关键点:零点 $(0, 0)$、$(\pi, 0)$、$(2\pi, 0)$、最高点 $\left(\frac{\pi}{2}, 1\right)$ 和最低点 $\left(\frac{3\pi}{2}, -1\right)$.实际上,这五个点一旦确定,正弦函数图像的大致形状也就确定了:从最高点与最低点的纵坐标得出正弦函数的**振幅**是 1;两个相邻的与横轴交点之间的距离得出函数**周期**长度的一半;借助微积分可知,每个零点都是函数凹凸性改变的**拐点**.

余弦函数的图像,**余弦曲线(cosine curve)**,也可以类似地进行研究,图像和结论罗列如下(Figure 6-3 和 Table 6-1),具体的推导过程留作练习:

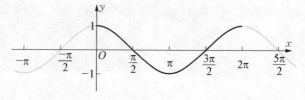

Figure 6-3

Table 6-1

定义域	全体实数 R
值 域	$[-1, 1]$
奇偶性	偶函数

续　表

周期性	最小正周期 2π
零　点	$x = k\pi + \dfrac{\pi}{2}, k \in \mathbf{Z}$
单调性	在 $\left[2k\pi, 2k\pi + \pi\right]$ 上单调递增；在 $\left[2k\pi + \pi, 2k\pi + 2\pi\right]$ 上单调递减，$k \in \mathbf{Z}$
最　值	在 $x = 2k\pi$ 时有最大值 1；在 $x = 2k\pi + \pi$ 时有最小值 -1，$k \in \mathbf{Z}$
凹凸性	在 $\left[2k\pi - \dfrac{\pi}{2}, 2k\pi + \dfrac{\pi}{2}\right]$ 上是凹函数；在 $\left[2k\pi + \dfrac{\pi}{2}, 2k\pi + \dfrac{3\pi}{2}\right]$ 上是凸函数，$k \in \mathbf{Z}$
关键点	$(0, 1)$、$\left(\dfrac{\pi}{2}, 0\right)$、$(\pi, -1)$、$\left(\dfrac{3\pi}{2}, 0\right)$、$(2\pi, 1)$

图像的变换 Transformations of Graphs

除了标准的正弦/余弦曲线之外，在实际应用中会遇到经过各种变换之后的三角曲线．下面通过一系列例子观察平移与伸缩两类变换在应用于三角函数图像时的具体表现．

① Sketch the graphs of $y = \dfrac{1}{2}\cos x$ and $y = -3\cos x$.

Solution： The extremum values of $y = \dfrac{1}{2}\cos x$ are $\pm\dfrac{1}{2}$, while its graph intersects the x-axis in the same points as the cosine curve does. Hence, the corresponding key points are $\left(0, \dfrac{1}{2}\right)$, $\left(\dfrac{\pi}{2}, 0\right)$, $\left(\pi, -\dfrac{1}{2}\right)$, $\left(\dfrac{3\pi}{2}, 0\right)$ and $\left(2\pi, \dfrac{1}{2}\right)$.

Similarly the key points for $y = 3\cos x$ are $(0, -3)$, $\left(\dfrac{\pi}{2}, 0\right)$, $(\pi, 3)$, $\left(\dfrac{3\pi}{2}, 0\right)$ and $(2\pi, -3)$. The graphs are then given in Figure 6 - 4.

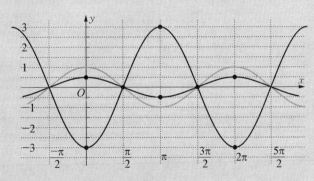

Figure 6 - 4

② Sketch the graph of $y = \sin\dfrac{x}{2}$.

Solution： General facts about horizontal dilations imply that the key points are $(0, 0)$, $(\pi, 1)$, $(2\pi, 0)$, $(3\pi, -1)$ and $(4\pi, 0)$. Hence, the graph is given in Figure 6 - 5.

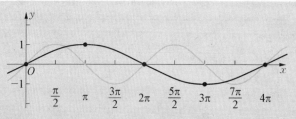

Figure 6 - 5

实际上，用同样的方法可以得到一般的规律：$y = \sin(\omega x)$ 与 $y = \cos(\omega x)(\omega \neq 0)$ 的最小正周期是 $\dfrac{2\pi}{|\omega|}$。

3 Sketch the graph of $y = 2 + \cos x$.

Solution： The amplitude is 1 and the period is 2π. The key points over the interval $[0, 2\pi]$ are $(0, 3)$, $\left(\dfrac{\pi}{2}, 2\right)$, $(\pi, 1)$, $\left(\dfrac{3\pi}{2}, 2\right)$ and $(2\pi, 3)$. Whence the graph reads as Figure 6 - 6.

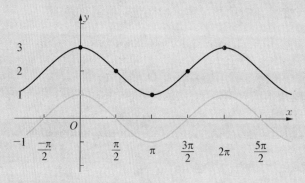

Figure 6 - 6

4 Sketch the graph of $y = \sin\left(x - \dfrac{\pi}{3}\right)$.

Solution： The amplitude is 1 and the period is 2π. Observe that the interval $\left[\dfrac{\pi}{3}, \dfrac{7\pi}{3}\right]$ may serve as one period of the graph. The key points over this interval are $\left(\dfrac{\pi}{3}, 0\right)$, $\left(\dfrac{5\pi}{6}, 1\right)$, $\left(\dfrac{4\pi}{3}, 0\right)$, $\left(\dfrac{11\pi}{6}, -1\right)$ and $\left(\dfrac{7\pi}{3}, 0\right)$. Hence, the graph looks as Figure 6 - 7.

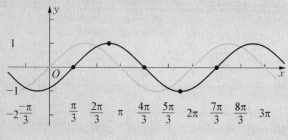

Figure 6 - 7

5 Sketch the graph of $y = -3\cos(2\pi x + 4\pi)$.

Solution: The amplitude is 3 and the period is $\dfrac{2\pi}{2\pi} = 1$. The interval $[-2, -1]$ serves as one period of the graph. The key points over this interval are $(-2, -3)$, $\left(-\dfrac{7}{4}, 0\right)$, $\left(-\dfrac{3}{2}, 3\right)$, $\left(-\dfrac{5}{4}, 0\right)$ and $(-1, -3)$. Hence, the graph looks as Figure 6-8.

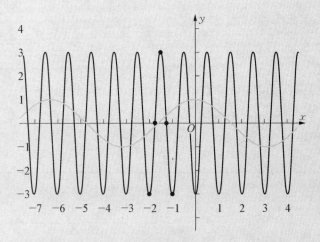

Figure 6-8

一般地,对于 $y = A\sin(\omega x + \varphi) + d$ 的性质也可以做类似研究,具体的细节留作练习.

相关函数的性质 Properties of the Related Functions

6 Determine the period of $y = \sin x + \cos x$ and find the intervals on which it is increasing.

Solution: Since $y = \sin x + \cos x = \sqrt{2}\sin\left(x + \dfrac{\pi}{4}\right)$, it bears the same period as $y = \sin x$ does, namely, 2π. Meanwhile, the intervals on which the function is increasing consist of all values of x such that $2k\pi - \dfrac{\pi}{2} \leqslant x + \dfrac{\pi}{4} \leqslant 2k\pi + \dfrac{\pi}{2}$, i.e., $\left[2k\pi - \dfrac{3\pi}{4}, 2k\pi + \dfrac{\pi}{4}\right]$, $k \in \mathbf{Z}$.

7 Find the extremum values of the following functions.

(1) $y = \sin x - \cos x$.　　　　　　(2) $y = a\sin x + b\cos x$ $(ab \neq 0)$.

(3) $y = \sin 2x + \cos^2 x$.

Solution:

(1) $y = \sqrt{2}\sin\left(x - \dfrac{\pi}{4}\right)$ according to the formula of auxiliary angle, whence the maximum is $\sqrt{2}$, attained when $x = 2k\pi + \dfrac{3\pi}{4}$ $(k \in \mathbf{Z})$, while the minimum is $-\sqrt{2}$, attained when $x = 2k\pi - \dfrac{\pi}{4}$ $(k \in \mathbf{Z})$.

(2) Similarly, $y = \sqrt{a^2 + b^2}\sin(x + \varphi)$, where $\cos\varphi = \dfrac{a}{\sqrt{a^2 + b^2}}$, $\sin\varphi = \dfrac{b}{\sqrt{a^2 + b^2}}$. Hence, the maximum value is $\sqrt{a^2 + b^2}$, attained when $x = 2k\pi + \dfrac{\pi}{2} - \varphi$ $(k \in \mathbf{Z})$, while the minimum is $-\sqrt{a^2 + b^2}$, attained when $x = 2k\pi - \dfrac{\pi}{2} - \varphi$ $(k \in \mathbf{Z})$.

(3) Double-angle formula gives $y = \sin 2x + \dfrac{1}{2}(\cos 2x + 1)$, whence $y = \dfrac{1}{2} + \dfrac{\sqrt{5}}{2}\sin(2x + \varphi)$ follows from the formula of auxiliary angle, with $\cos\varphi = \dfrac{\sqrt{5}}{5}$, $\sin\varphi = \dfrac{2\sqrt{5}}{5}$. Hence, the maximum value is $\dfrac{1+\sqrt{5}}{2}$, attained when $x = k\pi + \dfrac{\pi}{4} - \dfrac{\varphi}{2}$ $(k \in \mathbf{Z})$, while the minimum is $\dfrac{1-\sqrt{5}}{2}$, attained when $x = k\pi - \dfrac{\pi}{4} - \dfrac{\varphi}{2}$ $(k \in \mathbf{Z})$.

应用 Applications

8 The Table 6-2 shows the depths (in meters) of the water at the end of a dock at various times during the morning, where $t = 0$ corresponds to midnight.

Table 6-2

t (Time)	0	3	6	9	12	15	18	21	24
y (Depth)	5.0	7.0	4.9	3.0	5.0	6.9	5.1	3.1	5.0

(1) Use a trigonometric function to model the data.

(2) Find the depths at 1 A.M. and 7 P.M..

(3) A boat needs at least 6 meters of water to moor at the dock. During what times in the afternoon can it safely dock?

Solution:

(1) Plot the data on a coordinate sheet. Apply the cosine model to the form $y = a\cos(bt - c) + d$. The difference between the maximum height and the minimum height of the graph is twice the amplitude of the function. So, the amplitude is $a = \dfrac{1}{2}[(\text{maximum depth}) - (\text{minimum depth})] = \dfrac{1}{2}(7.0 - 3.0) = 2$.

The cosine function completes one half of a cycle between the times at which the maximum and minimum depths occur. So, the period is $p = 2[(\text{time of min. depth}) - (\text{time of max. depth})] = 2(9 - 3) = 12$; which implies that $b = \dfrac{2\pi}{p} \approx 0.524$. Because high tide occurs 3 hours after midnight, consider the left endpoint to be $\dfrac{c}{b} = 3$, so $c \approx 1.571$. Moreover, because the average depth is $\dfrac{1}{2}(7.0 + 3.0) = 5.0$, it follows that $d = 5.0$. Thus, the desired model is $y = 2\cos(0.524t - 1.571) + 5.0$.

(2) The depths at 1 A.M. and 7 P.M. are as follows (unit: meters).

$$y = 2\cos(0.524 \cdot 1 - 1.571) + 5.0 \approx 6.0$$

$$y = 2\cos(0.524 \cdot 19 - 1.571) + 5.0 \approx 4.0$$

(3) Using the graphing utility to graph the model with the line $y = 6.0$. Use the *intersect* feature to determine that the depth is at least 6 meters between 1 P.M. $(t = 13.0)$ and 5 P.M. $(t = 17.0)$.

练习 Exercise

1. Verify the properties of $y = \cos x$ listed in Table 6 – 1 as we did for $y = \sin x$ and apply them to describe the cosine curve.

2. Sketch the graphs of the following functions.

(1) $y = \dfrac{1}{3} \sin x$. (2) $y = \dfrac{1}{3} \cos x$.

(3) $y = 3 \sin x$. (4) $y = 5 \sin x$.

(5) $y = \cos \dfrac{x}{3}$. (6) $y = \sin \dfrac{\pi x}{4}$.

(7) $y = \cos x - 5$. (8) $y = \sin x + 1$.

(9) $y = \cos \left(x + \dfrac{\pi}{4} \right)$. (10) $y = \sin (x - 2\pi)$.

(11) $y = -\dfrac{1}{2} \sin (\pi x + \pi)$. (12) $y = 4\cos \left(x + \dfrac{\pi}{4} \right) + 4$.

3. Determine the period of each function below. Find the intervals on which each of them is monotonic.

(1) $y = \sin x - \cos x$.

(2) $y = a \sin x + b \cos x \, (a^2 + b^2 \neq 0)$.

4. Find the extremum values of the following functions.

(1) $y = \cos 2x + \sin^2 x$.

(2) $y = \sin^2 x + \sin x + 1$.

(3) $y = a \sin x + b \, (a \neq 0)$.

5. Find a sine model for Example 8.

6. True or False:

(1) Since $\sin \left(\dfrac{\pi}{4} + \dfrac{\pi}{2} \right) = \sin \dfrac{\pi}{4}$, $\dfrac{\pi}{2}$ is a period of $y = \sin x$.

(2) The function $y = \sin x \, (x > 0)$ is periodic.

(3) The graph of $y = \sin (x + \pi)$ is obtained from that of $y = \sin x$ by shifting the original graph to the right by π units.

7. (1) When tuning a piano, a technician strikes a tuning fork for the A above middle C and sets up a wave motion that can be approximated by $y = 0.001 \sin 880\pi t$, where t is the time (in seconds).

a. What is the period of the function?

b. The frequency f is given by $f = \dfrac{1}{p}$. What is the frequency of the note?

(2) The percent y (in decimal form) of the moon's face illuminated on day x in the year 2014, where $x = 1$ represents January 1, is shown in Table 6 – 3.

Table 6 - 3

x	1	8	16	24	30	37
y	0.0	0.5	1.0	0.5	0.0	0.5

a. Create a scatter plot of the data.

b. Find a trigonometric model that fits the data.

c. Add the graph of your model for part b to the scatter plot. How well does the model fit the data?

d. What is the period of the model?

e. Estimate the percent of the moon's face illuminated on March 12, 2014.

8. (1) Show that $y = \sin x$ is concave upward on the interval $[2k\pi + \pi, 2k\pi + 2\pi]$, while concave downward on the interval $[2k\pi, 2k\pi + \pi]$, $k \in \mathbf{Z}$.

(2) Explore the properties of $y = A \sin(\omega x + \varphi) + d$, where A, ω, φ and d are positive constants.

9. (1) Some texts define periodic functions as $f(x)$ such that there is a **positive** real number T so that $f(x + T) = f(x)$ for all $x \in D$, the domain of f. Does this alternative definition agree with ours? Namely, do the two classes of "periodic functions" under these two definitions coincide with each other? Explain.

(2) Show that the function $D(x) = \begin{cases} 1, & x \in \mathbf{Q} \\ 0, & x \notin \mathbf{Q} \end{cases}$ is a periodic function without *the period*.

(3) In what follows we will see that the sum of two periodic functions might **not** be periodic.

a. The **floor function** is defined by $\lfloor x \rfloor =$ the largest integer that is less than or equal to x. For example, $\lfloor 4.1 \rfloor = 4$, $\lfloor -1.9 \rfloor = -2$. Show that $y = x - \lfloor x \rfloor$ is a periodic function with period 1.

b. Show that if $\lfloor T \rfloor + \lfloor -T \rfloor = 0$, then $T \in \mathbf{Z}$.

c. Show that the sum $\sin x + x - \lfloor x \rfloor$ of two periodic functions $\sin x$ and $x - \lfloor x \rfloor$ is not periodic.

6.2 ◆ 其他三角函数 Other Trigonometric Functions

除了正弦、余弦之外，三角函数的家族还包含其他四个常见成员：正切、余切、正割、余割.这些三角函数与正弦函数、余弦函数有相似地方，但也有区别.由于后四个三角函数可以通过正弦、余弦函数运算得到，因此研究这些函数的性质可以加深对函数四则运算的理解.同时，这些函数也提供了更加丰富的例子，拓宽了观察一般抽象函数性质时的视野.

其他基本三角函数的图像 Graphs of the Other Basic Trigonometric Functions

依照此前研究正/余弦函数时的方法，我们可以继续研究其他基本三角函数的图像.

1 Sketch the graph of $y = \tan x$.

Solution: To begin with, list the properties of the tangent function in Table 6 - 4.

Table 6 - 4

Domain	$\{x \mid x \in \mathbf{R},\ x \neq k\pi + \dfrac{\pi}{2},\ k \in \mathbf{Z}\}$
Range	$(-\infty, \infty)$
Symmetry	Odd
Period	The period π
Zeroes	$x = k\pi,\ k \in \mathbf{Z}$
Monotonicity	Increase on $\left(k\pi - \dfrac{\pi}{2},\ k\pi + \dfrac{\pi}{2}\right),\ k \in \mathbf{Z}$
Concavity	Concave up in $\left(k\pi,\ k\pi + \dfrac{\pi}{2}\right)$; concave down in $\left(k\pi - \dfrac{\pi}{2},\ k\pi\right),\ k \in \mathbf{Z}$

Hence, the graph of $y = \tan x$ looks like follows (Figure 6 - 9).

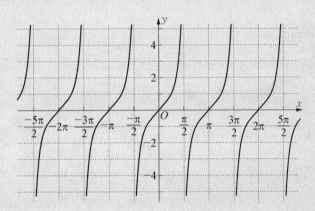

Figure 6 - 9

2 Sketch the graph of $y = \sec x$.

Solution: By taking the reciprocal values of the function $y = \cos x$, we obtain the graph below (Figure 6 - 10).

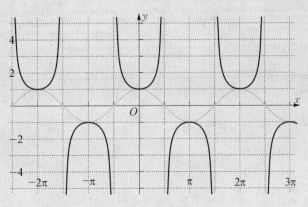

Figure 6 - 10

In particular, we observe the *vertical asymptotes* $x = k\pi + \dfrac{\pi}{2}$ ($k \in \mathbf{Z}$) to the graph.

渐近线* Asymptotes*

在正切和正割函数的图像中，我们看到了一个共同的特征：渐近线.与反比例函数 $y = \dfrac{1}{x}$ 的竖直渐近线 $x = 0$ 类似，直线 $x = k\pi + \dfrac{\pi}{2}$（$k \in \mathbf{Z}$）也被称为 $y = \tan x$ 与 $y = \sec x$ 的**竖直渐近线**.实际上，除了我们通过反比例函数图像的学习并已经熟悉的水平/竖直渐近线之外，某些函数的图像还具有斜渐近线.

3 Recall the function $y = x + \dfrac{1}{x}$, the graph of which was sketched through adding two known graphs in the diagram. It is easy to observe that the function admits a slant asymptote $y = x$. Similarly, any slant line $y = kx + b$ in the coordinate plane can serve as a slant asymptote to some functions (for example: $y = kx + b + \dfrac{1}{x}$).

Moreover, some functions have more than one slant asymptotes. An example is provided by the function $y = \sqrt{x^2 - 1}$, whose graph is shown in Figure 6 – 11.

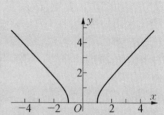

Figure 6 – 11

It is easy to observe that both lines $y = \pm x$ are slant asymptotes to the graph.

In general, the precise definition of asymptotes is closely related to the *limits* of functions, which will play a central role in the subject of calculus.

含三角函数的组合 The Combinations Involving Trigonometric Functions

在通常的应用中，三角函数往往并非单独出现，而是与其他函数以各种方式组合出现的，其中包括三角函数与其他函数的四则运算以及复合运算.

4 Describe the graph of $y = \tan x + \cot x$.

Solution: Since $\tan x + \cot x = \dfrac{2}{\sin 2x}$, consider its reciprocal counterpart $y = \dfrac{\sin 2x}{2}$. It follows that the function is an odd one with domain $\left\{ x \mid x \neq \dfrac{k\pi}{2}, k \in \mathbf{Z} \right\}$. It is periodic with the period being π. The intervals on which the function increases are $\left[k\pi + \dfrac{\pi}{4}, k\pi + \dfrac{\pi}{2} \right)$ and $\left(k\pi + \dfrac{\pi}{2}, k\pi + \dfrac{3\pi}{4} \right]$ ($k \in \mathbf{Z}$) while those on which it decreases are $\left[k\pi - \dfrac{\pi}{4}, k\pi \right)$ and $\left(k\pi, k\pi + \dfrac{\pi}{4} \right]$ ($k \in \mathbf{Z}$). Range of the function is $(-\infty, -2] \cup [2, \infty)$.

5 Sketch the graph of $y = x \sin x$ and observe its behavior as x approaches 0.

Solution: Since $|\sin x| \leqslant 1$, it follows that $0 \leqslant |x| \, |\sin x| \leqslant |x|$, or equivalently $-|x| \leqslant$

$x \sin x \leqslant |x|$. Hence, graph of $f(x) = x \sin x$ is squeezed between those of $y = |x|$ and $y = -|x|$. Visually speaking, the graph lies between lines $y = -x$ and $y = x$.

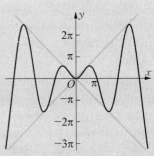

Note that for $n \in \mathbf{Z}$, $f(x) = \pm x$ when $x = \frac{\pi}{2} + n\pi$, while $f(x) = 0$ when $x = n\pi$, whence the graph can be sketched as below (Figure 6-12).

From the graph it is obvious that as x approaches 0, the graph clusters at the origin.

Figure 6-12

6 Determine the symmetry of each function below.

$$f_1(x) = \frac{1 + \sin x - \cos x}{1 + \sin x + \cos x},$$

$$f_2(x) = \sqrt{\cos^2 x - 1},$$

$$f_3(x) = \ln \left(\sin x + \sqrt{\sin^2 x + 1} \right).$$

Solution: For f_1, $1 + \sin x + \cos x \neq 0 \Rightarrow x \neq -\frac{\pi}{2}$ while $\frac{\pi}{2}$ lies in the domain of f_1. Hence, domain of f_1 is not symmetric with respect to 0, which implies that the function is neither odd or even.

For f_2, since $\cos^2 x - 1 = -\sin^2 x \leqslant 0$, domain of f_2 is $\{x \mid x = k\pi, k \in \mathbf{Z}\}$, which is clearly symmetric with respect to 0. Since $f_2(x) = 0$ for all x values in the domain, f_2 is both odd and even.

For f_3, since $\sin x + \sqrt{\sin^2 x + 1} > \sin x + |\sin x| \geqslant 0$, its domain is $\mathbf{R}$. Algebraic manipulations show that $f_3(-x) = \lg \left(-\sin x + \sqrt{\sin^2 x + 1} \right) = \lg \left(\dfrac{1}{\sin x + \sqrt{\sin^2 x + 1}} \right) = -f_3(x)$ while f_3 is clearly non-constant. Hence, f_3 is odd.

7 Sketch the graph of $f(x) = e^{-x} \sin 3x$.

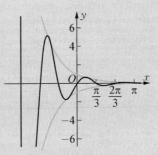

Solution: Clearly, domain of $f(x)$ is $\mathbf{R}$ and $-e^{-x} \leqslant e^{-x} \sin 3x \leqslant e^{-x}$. Furthermore, because $e^{-x} \sin 3x = \pm e^{-x}$ at $x = \frac{\pi}{6} + \frac{n\pi}{3}$ and $e^{-x} \sin 3x = 0$ at $x = \frac{n\pi}{3}$, the graph of f touches the curves $y = \pm e^{-x}$ at $x = \frac{\pi}{6} + \frac{n\pi}{3}$ and has intercepts at $x = \frac{n\pi}{3}$. The sketch is shown in Figure 6-13.

Figure 6-13

8 Explore the properties of the functions below.

$$f_1(x) = \sqrt{1 - |\tan x|},$$

$$f_2(x) = \log_{\cos x} (|\csc x|).$$

Solution: Start with f_1.

Domain $=\left\{x \mid x \neq k\pi+\dfrac{\pi}{2}, \mid \tan x \mid \leqslant 1, k \in \mathbf{Z}\right\}=\left\{x \mid k\pi-\dfrac{\pi}{4} \leqslant x \leqslant k\pi+\dfrac{\pi}{4}, k \in \mathbf{Z}\right\}.$

Symmetry: $f_1(-x)=\sqrt{1-\mid \tan (-x) \mid}=\sqrt{1-\mid \tan x \mid}=f_1(x) \Rightarrow f_1$ is even.

Monotonicity of $y=\tan x$ implies that $y=\mid \tan x \mid$ is decreasing on $\left[k\pi-\dfrac{\pi}{4}, k\pi\right]$ and increasing

on $\left[k\pi, k\pi+\dfrac{\pi}{4}\right]$. Hence, $f_1(x)=\sqrt{1-\mid \tan x \mid}$ is increasing on $\left[k\pi-\dfrac{\pi}{4}, k\pi\right]$ and decreasing on

$\left[k\pi, k\pi+\dfrac{\pi}{4}\right] (k \in \mathbf{Z}).$

Period of $y=\tan x$ implies that both $y=\mid \tan x \mid$ and f_1 admit the same period π.

That the range $=[0, 1]$ follows directly from knowledge of domain and monotonicity.

Similarly, for f_2, one has the following conclusions.

Domain $=\left\{x \mid 2k\pi-\dfrac{\pi}{2}<x<2k\pi, \text{ or } 2k\pi<x<2k\pi+\dfrac{\pi}{2}, k \in \mathbf{Z}\right\}.$

Symmetry: even.

Monotonicity: decreases on $\left(2k\pi-\dfrac{\pi}{2}, 2k\pi\right)$; increases on $\left(2k\pi, 2k\pi+\dfrac{\pi}{2}\right), k \in \mathbf{Z}.$

The period is 2π.

Range is $(-\infty, 0)$.

Details are left to the readers.

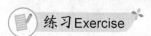 练习Exercise

1. Sketch the graphs of $y=\cot x$ and $y=\csc x$.

2. Sketch the graphs of the functions below.

   (1) $f_1(x)=\tan x-\cot x.$ (2) $f_2(x)=\tan 2x+\sec 2x.$

3. Describe the behavior of the function as x approaches zero.

   (1) $f_1(x)=\dfrac{6}{x}+\cos x, x>0.$ (2) $f_2(x)=\dfrac{4}{x}+\sin 2x, x>0.$

   (3) $f_3(x)=\dfrac{\sin x}{x}.$ (4) $f_4(x)=\dfrac{1-\cos x}{x}.$

   (5) $f_5(x)=\sin\dfrac{1}{x}.$ (6) $f_6(x)=x \sin\dfrac{1}{x}.$

4. Consider the functions given by $f(x)=2\sin x$ and $g(x)=\dfrac{1}{2}\csc x$ on the interval $(0, \pi)$.

   (1) Graph f and g in the same coordinate plane.

   (2) Solve the inequality $f>g$.

   (3) Describe the behavior of each of the functions as x approaches π. How is the behavior of g related to that of f as x approaches π?

5. Describe the behavior of the function as x approaches zero.

   (1) $f_1(x)=e^{-x^2/2}\sin x.$ (2) $f_2(x)=e^{-x}\cos x.$

   (3) $f_3(x)=2^{-x/4}\cos \pi x.$ (4) $f_4(x)=2^{-x^2/4}\sin x.$

6. Explore the desired properties of each function below.

   (1) Find the intervals on which $y = \tan^2 x - 2\tan x + 2$ increases and decreases.

   (2) Find the range of $y = \sqrt{2\cos^2 x + 5\sin x - 1}$.

   (3) Find the extremum values of $y = \dfrac{\sin x \, \cos x}{\sin x + \cos x}$, $x \in \left[0, \dfrac{\pi}{2}\right]$.

   (4) Find the domain and range of $y = \dfrac{1}{2}\cos^2 x + \sin x \, \cos x + \dfrac{3}{2}\sin^2 x$. Determine on which intervals the function is increasing/decreasing. Explore its symmetry and periodicity.

7. Explore the properties of the functions below by specifying the domain, symmetry and periodicity for each of them.

   (1) $f_1(x) = x + \tan x$.   (2) $f_2(x) = x^2 - \sec x$.

   (3) $f_3(x) = x \csc x$.   (4) $f_4(x) = x^2 \cot x$.

8. True or False:

   (1) The function $y = \tan x$ is increasing on its domain.

   (2) Let $f(x)$ be a function with domain $(-\infty, a) \cup (a, \infty)$. Then, the vertical line $x = a$ is a vertical asymptote to the graph of $y = f(x)$.

   (3) A function could have infinitely many asymptotes.

9. (1) An object weighing W pounds is suspended from the ceiling by a steel spring (see Figure 6 - 14). The weight is pulled downward (positive direction) from its equilibrium position and released. The resulting motion of the weight is described by the function $y = \dfrac{1}{2}e^{-t/4}\cos 4t$, $t > 0$, where y is the distance (in feet) and t is the time (in seconds). Describ the behavior of the displacement function for increasing values of time t.

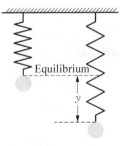

Figure 6 - 14

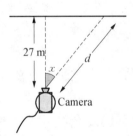

Figure 6 - 15

   (2) A television camera is on a reviewing platform 27 meters from the street on which a parade will be passing from left to right (see Figure 6 - 15). Write the distance d from the camera to a particular unit in the parade as a function of the angle x, and graph the function over the interval $-\dfrac{\pi}{2} < x < \dfrac{\pi}{2}$. (Consider x as negative when a unit in the parade approaches from the left.)

10. (1) Show that the functions $y = \tan\sqrt{x}$ and $y = \tan(x^2)$ are not periodic.

   (2) Consider the function given by $f(x) = x - \cos x$.

   a. Use a graphing utility to graph the function and verify that there exists a zero between

0 and 1. Use the graph to approximate the zero.

b. Starting with $x_0 = 1$, generate a sequence x_1, x_2, x_3, $\cdots$, where $x_n = \cos(x_{n-1})$. What value does the sequence approach?

11. (1) Can you find functions $f(x) = d + a \sin(bx + c)$ and $g(x) = d + a \cos(bx + c)$ $(a \neq 0)$ such that $f(x) + g(x) = 0$ for all x? If so, find all such functions; otherwise, explain.

(2) Pattern recognition:

a. Use the graphing utility to sketch the following two functions: $y_1 = \dfrac{4}{\pi}\left(\sin \pi x + \dfrac{1}{3}\sin 3\pi x\right)$,

$y_2 = \dfrac{4}{\pi}\left(\sin \pi x + \dfrac{1}{3}\sin 3\pi x + \dfrac{1}{5}\sin 5\pi x\right)$.

b. Identify the pattern started in part a. and find a function y_3 that continues the pattern one more term. Use a graphing utility to sketch y_3.

c. The graphs in parts a. and b. approximate the periodic function in Figure 6 – 16. Find a function y_4 that is a better approximation.

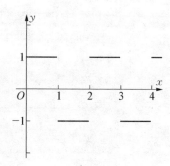

Figure 6 – 16

6.3 ◆ 三角函数的应用
Applications of the Trigonometric Functions

十六世纪,随着文艺复兴时期的到来,欧洲人对于科学的热情摆脱了宗教的压抑,重新被点燃.借着这一契机,三角学得以从天文学里分离出来,成为数学的一个分支.到了十七世纪,函数概念的引入帮助人们把三角学从计算的技术升级为系统的学科.微积分的发明者牛顿(I. Newton)与莱布尼茨(G. Leibniz)用无穷级数来表示各个三角函数;以约翰·伯努利(John Bernoulli)为代表的一批数学家又通过推导和差角公式等一批三角函数的公式,进一步发展了其解析理论;最后,欧拉(L. Euler)于1748年在关于木星和土星运动中的不等式的一篇得奖文章中给出了三角函数的一个十分系统的处理.此后,三角函数在工程技术、理论研究的各个领域开始大显身手.

在物理学中的应用 Applications in Physics

鉴于三角函数的周期性,它们经常被用于描述周期现象,这一用途在物理学中显得尤为突出.下面,我们以简谐振动为例来说明三角函数与周期现象的联系.

Definition of the Simple Harmonic Motion

A point that moves on a coordinate line is said to be in **simple harmonic motion** if its distance d from the origin at time t is given by either $d = a \sin \omega t$ or $d = a \cos \omega t$, where a and ω are real numbers such that $\omega > 0$. The motion has amplitude $|a|$, period $\dfrac{2\pi}{\omega}$, and frequency $\dfrac{\omega}{2\pi}$.

1 Given a simple harmonic motion with amplitude 10 cm and period 4 seconds, find its equation. What is the frequency of this harmonic motion?

Solution: Because the spring is at equilibrium ($d=0$) when $t=0$, use the equation $d=a\sin\omega t$. Moreover, because the maximum displacement from zero is 10 and the period is 4,

$$\begin{cases} \text{Amplitude} = |a| = 10 \\ \text{Period} = \dfrac{2\pi}{\omega} = 4 \Rightarrow \omega = \dfrac{\pi}{2} \cdot \end{cases}$$

Consequently, the equation of the motion is $d=10\sin\dfrac{\pi}{2}t$.

Note that the choice of $a=10$ or $a=-10$ depends on whether the ball initially moves up or down. The frequency is $\dfrac{\omega}{2\pi}=\dfrac{1}{4}$ cycle per second.

2 Given the equation for simple harmonic motion:

$$d=6\cos\dfrac{3\pi}{4}t,$$

find (a) the maximum displacement, (b) the frequency, (c) the value of d when $t=4$, and (d) the least positive value of t for which $d=0$.

Solution: The given equation has the form $d=a\cos\omega t$, with $a=6$ and $\omega=\dfrac{3\pi}{4}$.

(a) The maximum displacement (from the point of equilibrium) is given by the amplitude. So, the maximum displacement is 6.

(b) Frequency $=\dfrac{\omega}{2\pi}=\dfrac{3}{8}$ cycle per unit of time.

(c) $d=6\cos\left[\dfrac{3\pi}{4}(4)\right]=-6$.

(d) To find the least positive value of t for which $d=0$, solve the equation $d=6\cos\dfrac{3\pi}{4}t=0$. This equation is satisfied when $\dfrac{3\pi}{4}t=\dfrac{\pi}{2},\ \dfrac{3\pi}{2},\ \dfrac{5\pi}{2}\cdots$ So the least positive value of t is $\dfrac{2}{3}$.

数学中的三角函数方法 Interactions with the Other Parts of Elementary Math

3 Find the range of $f(x)=2\sqrt{1-x}+\sqrt{4x-3}$.

Solution: Rewrite $f(x)=\sqrt{4-4x}+\sqrt{4x-3}$. Since $4-4x\geqslant 0$, $4x-3\geqslant 0$, while $(4-4x)+(4x-3)=1$, it would be proper to make the following substitutions: $\sqrt{4-4x}=\cos t$, $\sqrt{4x-3}=\sin t$, where $t\in\left[0,\dfrac{\pi}{2}\right]$. Hence, $f(x)=g(t)=\cos t+\sin t=\sqrt{2}\sin\left(t+\dfrac{\pi}{4}\right)$. It follows from the range of sine function that $g(t)\in[1,\sqrt{2}]$, as desired.

4 Let a, b, c, $d\in\mathbf{R}$. Show that $ac+bd\leqslant\sqrt{a^2+b^2}\sqrt{c^2+d^2}$.

Proof: If either $a=b=0$ or $c=d=0$ holds, the inequality becomes an obvious equation. Assume without loss of generality that $(a^2+b^2)(c^2+d^2)\neq 0$. Then, the following substitution becomes available.

$$\begin{cases} \dfrac{a}{\sqrt{a^2+b^2}} = \cos x \\ \dfrac{b}{\sqrt{a^2+b^2}} = \sin x \end{cases}, \quad \begin{cases} \dfrac{c}{\sqrt{c^2+d^2}} = \cos y \\ \dfrac{d}{\sqrt{c^2+d^2}} = \sin y \end{cases}.$$

Hence, $\dfrac{\text{LHS}}{\text{RHS}} = \cos x \cos y + \sin x \sin y = \cos(x-y) \leqslant 1$, as desired.

5 Let a, b, c, d be the lengths of four sides of a convex quadrilateral, arranged in counterclockwise order. Find the largest possible area of this quadrilateral in terms of a, b, c, d.

Solution: Let α be the angle between sides a and b, while the angle between sides c and d is β. Thus, the area is given by $S = \dfrac{1}{2}ab \sin \alpha + \dfrac{1}{2}cd \sin \beta$.

On the other hand, length of the diagonal between angles α and β is computed by the Law of Cosines:

$$a^2 + b^2 - 2ab \cos \alpha = c^2 + d^2 - 2cd \cos \beta,$$

$\Rightarrow$

$$ab \cos \alpha - cd \cos \beta = \frac{1}{2}(a^2 + b^2 - c^2 - d^2).$$

Squaring both sides and substitute the area formula into the equation, one obtains that

$$(ab \cos \alpha - cd \cos \beta)^2 + (ab \sin \alpha + cd \sin \beta)^2 = \frac{1}{4}(a^2 + b^2 - c^2 - d^2)^2 + 4S^2.$$

Expanding both sides to find

$$(ab)^2 + (cd)^2 - 2abcd \cos(\alpha + \beta) = \frac{1}{4}(a^2 + b^2 - c^2 - d^2)^2 + 4S^2.$$

Thus,

$$S^2 = \frac{1}{4}\left[(ab)^2 + (cd)^2 - \frac{1}{4}(a^2 + b^2 - c^2 - d^2)^2 - 2abcd \cos(\alpha + \beta)\right]$$

$$\leqslant \frac{1}{4}\left[(ab)^2 + (cd)^2 - \frac{1}{4}(a^2 + b^2 - c^2 - d^2)^2 + 2abcd\right]$$

$$= \frac{1}{16}(b+c+d-a)(c+d+a-b)(d+a+b-c)(a+b+c-d).$$

Hence, $S \leqslant \dfrac{1}{4}\sqrt{(b+c+d-a)(c+d+a-b)(d+a+b-c)(a+b+c-d)}$ while the maximum value is attained if and only if $\alpha + \beta = \pi$, i.e., the quadrilateral is cyclic.

Remark: A byproduct of the reasoning above is the following area formula for cyclic quadrilaterals: $S = \sqrt{(p-a)(p-b)(p-c)(p-d)}$, where $p = \dfrac{a+b+c+d}{2}$ is the semi circumference of this quadrilateral. Apparently, this reminds us of the Heron's formula for triangles. This maximum value also hints a general principle: that a convex polygon with given side lengths attains the maximum area when it is cyclic.

6 The Chebyshev polynomials of the first kind is a sequence of polynomials $\{T_n(x)\}_{n\ldots 0}$ recursively defined as follows: $\begin{cases} T_0(x)=1,\ T_1(x)=x \\ T_{n+1}(x)=2xT_n(x)-T_{n-1}(x) \end{cases}$. Find $T_n(\cos 1)$.

Solution: It worths noticing that the recurrence relation of T_n's resembles that of $\cos(nt)$:

$$\cos[(n+1)t]=2\cos t\,\cos(nt)-\cos[(n-1)t].$$

Thus, for $x \in [-1, 1]$, we may make the substitution $x=\cos t$ so that $T_n(x)$ can be computed as follows:

$$\begin{cases} T_0(\cos t)=1,\ T_1(\cos t)=\cos t \\ T_{n+1}(\cos t)=2\cos t\,T_n(\cos t)-T_{n-1}(\cos t) \end{cases} \Rightarrow \begin{cases} T_0=1,\ T_1=\cos t \\ T_{n+1}=\cos[(n+1)t] \end{cases}.$$

Hence, $T_n(x)=\cos(n\arccos x)$, which implies that $T_n(\cos 1)=\cos n$.

在其他方面的应用 Other Applications

In surveying and navigation, direction can be given in terms of bearings.

7 A ship leaves port at noon and heads due west at 20 knots, or 20 nautical miles (nm) per hour. At 2 P.M. the ship changes course to N 54° W. Find the ship's bearing and distance from the port of departure at 3 P.M.

Solution: As shown in Figure 6 - 17, for triangle BCD, we have $B=90°-54°=36°$. The two sides of this triangle can be determined to be $b=20\sin 36°$ and $d=20\cos 36°$. For triangle ACD, we can find angle A as follows:

$$\tan A=\frac{b}{d+40}=\frac{20\sin 36°}{20\cos 36°+40}\approx 0.2092494,$$

$$A \approx \arctan 0.2092494 \approx 11.82°.$$

The angle with the north-south line is $90° - 11.82° = 78.18°$. So, the bearing of the ship is N 78.18° W. Finally, from triangle ACD, we have $\sin A=b/c$, which yields

$$c=\frac{b}{\sin A}=\frac{20\sin 36°}{\sin 11.82°}\approx 57.4 \text{ nautical miles.}$$

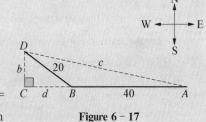

Figure 6 - 17

练习 Exercise

1. Find a model for simple harmonic motion satisfying each specified condition below.

Displacement ($t=0$)	Amplitude	Period
(1) 0	4 centimeters	2 seconds
(2) 0	3 meters	6 seconds
(3) 3 inches	3 inches	1.5 seconds
(4) 2 feet	2 feet	10 seconds
(5) 1 meter	2 meter	1 minute

2. For the simple harmonic motion described by the trigonometric function, find the maximum displacement, the frequency, the value of d when $t=5$, and the least positive value of t for which

$d = 0$.

(1) $d = 9\cos\dfrac{6\pi}{5}t$.

(2) $d = \dfrac{1}{2}\cos 20\pi t$.

(3) $d = \dfrac{1}{4}\sin 6\pi t$.

(4) $d = \dfrac{1}{64}\sin 792\pi t$.

3. Solve the following problems with suitable trigonometric substitutions.

   (1) Find the range of $f(x) = (\sqrt{2 - x^2} - x) \cdot x$.

   (2) Let positive real numbers a, b be such that $a + b = 1$. Show that $\left(a + \dfrac{1}{a}\right)\left(b + \dfrac{1}{b}\right) \geqslant \dfrac{25}{4}$.

   (3) The *Chebyshev polynomials of the second kind* is a sequence of polynomials $\{U_n(x)\}_{n\ldots 0}$
     recursively defined as follows: $\begin{cases} U_0(x) = 1,\ U_1(x) = 2x \\ U_{n+1}(x) = 2xU_n(x) - U_{n-1}(x) \end{cases}$. Find $U_n(\cos 1)$.

4. In $\triangle ABC$, let $BC = a$, while $AB + AC = \ell > a$.

   (1) Find the area S of $\triangle ABC$ in terms of $\alpha = \angle A$.

   (2) Find the maximum value of S and determine the shape of $\triangle ABC$ when it attains this maximum.

   (3) Does this answer echo the principle we mentioned in the remark of example 5? Explain.

5. An airplane is 160 miles north and 85 miles east of an airport. The pilot wants to fly directly to the airport. What bearing should be taken?

6. The Bay of Fundy is an inlet of the Atlantic Ocean bounded by Maine and New Brunswick on the north and Nova Scotia on the south. It is famous for its high tides. At a dock there, the depth of water is 2 ft at low tide and 58 ft at high tide, which occurs 6 h 12 min after low tide. Find a trigonometric function modeling the depth of water at the dock as a function of the time since high tide occurs.

7. True or False:

   (1) The Leaning Tower of Pisa is not vertical, but if you know the angle of elevation θ to the top of the tower when you stand d feet away from it, you can find its height h using the formula $h = d\tan\theta$.

   (2) N $24°$ E means 24 degrees north by east.

8. A reflector is fastened to the front wheel of a bicycle 20 cm from the center of the wheel. The diameter of the wheel and inflated tire is 70 cm. If the bike is traveling at 10 km/h, express the height of the reflector above the ground as a function of time. Assume that at time $t = 0$ seconds, the reflector is at its highest point.

9. (1) Let x, y, $z \in [0, 1]$. Find the maximum of the expression $\sqrt{|x - y|} + \sqrt{|y - z|} + \sqrt{|z - x|}$.

   (2) It is well known that among all triangles inscribed in the same circle, the equilateral one has the largest perimeter. Now we are going to establish this fact through *convexity* of the sine function in terms of inequalities.

     a. If $0 \leqslant x_1 \leqslant x_2 \leqslant x_3 \leqslant x_4 \leqslant \pi$ and $x_1 + x_4 = x_2 + x_3$, then $\sin x_1 + \sin x_4 \leqslant \sin x_2 + \sin x_3$.

     b. Show that $2\sin x + \sin y \leqslant 3\sin\dfrac{2x + y}{3}$ for any x, $y \in (0, \pi)$.

c. Let A, B, C be the three angles of $\triangle ABC$. Show that $\sin A + \sin B + \sin C \leqslant 3\sin\dfrac{\pi}{3}$. Henceforth by the Law of Sines, perimeter of a triangle inscribed in a circle with given radius R reaches its maximum when the triangle is equilateral.

10. (1) Let a, b, A, B be constants and $f(x) = 1 - a\cos x - b\sin x - A\cos 2x - B\sin 2x$. Assume that $f(x) \geqslant 0$ for all real x.

    a. Show that $a^2 + b^2 \leqslant 2$ and $A^2 + B^2 \leqslant 1$;

    b. Determine if it is possible that $a^2 + b^2 = 2$ and $A^2 + B^2 = 1$ hold simultaneously. Give such a quadruple if your answer is "YES", otherwise, explain why not.

  (2) In ancient times, solving algebraic equations is a central problem for mathematicians. After successfully obtained the root formula for quadratic equations $ax^2 + bx + c = 0$, people started to look for similar formulas dealing with cubic equations $ax^3 + bx^2 + cx + d = 0$. Among all the attempts, the one roots in trigonometry might be of special interest to us. The theory is based on the triple angle formula: $\cos 3\theta = 4\cos^3 \theta - 3\cos\theta$. It tackles the class of cubic equations taking the form: $x^3 - px = q$. Can you establish the link between them?

6.4 ◆ 反三角函数 Inverse Trigonometric Functions

    在熟悉三角运算之后,可以通过已知的特殊三角函数值来反推出相应角的大小.然而,更多的时候,给定三角函数值所对应的角并不是特殊角,因此只能借助于计算工具来求得近似值.例如,中学物理经常把一个正切值为 0.75 的锐角近似地认为是 $37°$,而实际上该角的大小约为 $36.87°$.像这样用三角函数值来刻画角的方式,在测量等应用领域是很有用的.因此,为了求得更精确的计算结果,可以保留三角函数值的信息,而将该角的大小用这一三角函数值来加以刻画.

反正弦函数 Inverse Sine Function

    容易发现,作为一个周期函数,$y = \sin x$ 没有反函数.然而,把 $y = \sin x$ 的定义域限制到它的一个单调区间时,就可以根据定义找到一个相应的反函数.出于历史原因和实际计算时的需要,取 $\left[-\dfrac{\pi}{2}, \dfrac{\pi}{2}\right]$ 作为定义反正弦函数的单调区间.

Definition of Inverse Sine Function

The **inverse sine function** is defined by

$$y = \arcsin x \text{ if and only if } \sin y = x.$$

where $-1 \leqslant x \leqslant 1$ and $-\dfrac{\pi}{2} \leqslant y \leqslant \dfrac{\pi}{2}$. The domain of $y = \arcsin x$ is $[-1, 1]$, and the range is $\left[-\dfrac{\pi}{2}, \dfrac{\pi}{2}\right]$.

    按照反正弦函数的定义,容易归纳出下列要点:

    (1) $\arcsin x$ 表示一个角.

    (2) $\arcsin x$ 表示的角落在区间 $\left[-\dfrac{\pi}{2}, \dfrac{\pi}{2}\right]$ 内.

（3）在上述范围内，arcsin x 由它的正弦值唯一确定，该正弦值是 x，即：$\sin(\arcsin x) = x$，$x \in$ $[-1, 1]$.

由于其作为反函数的本质，在引起混淆时，也可以用 $\sin^{-1} x$ 来表示反正弦函数.

1 Find the following inverse trigonometric values if possible:

$$\arcsin\left(-\frac{1}{2}\right) \qquad\qquad \sin^{-1}\frac{\sqrt{3}}{2} \qquad\qquad \sin^{-1}2$$

Solution: Since the only value of y with $-\frac{\pi}{2} \leqslant y \leqslant \frac{\pi}{2}$ such that $\sin y = -\frac{1}{2}$ is $-\frac{\pi}{6}$, it follows that $\arcsin\left(-\frac{1}{2}\right) = -\frac{\pi}{6}$. Similarly, $\sin^{-1}\frac{\sqrt{3}}{2} = \frac{\pi}{3}$.

On the other hand, since the range of sine function is $[-1, 1]$, 2 cannot be a sine value. Hence, $\sin^{-1}2$ does not exist.

2 Graph $y = \arcsin x$.

Solution: Recall that the graphs of a function and its inverse are symmetric with respect to $y = x$. Hence, one obtains the desired graph by plotting that of $y = \sin x \left(-\frac{\pi}{2} \leqslant x \leqslant \frac{\pi}{2}\right)$ followed by a reflection in the line $y = x$, as shown in Figure 6 - 18.

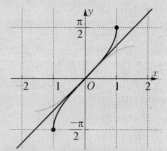

Figure 6 - 18

反正切函数 Inverse Tangent Function

定义反正弦函数时，需要把 $y = \sin x$ 的定义域加以限制.类似地，可以在区间 $\left(-\frac{\pi}{2}, \frac{\pi}{2}\right)$ 上定义正切函数的反函数.

Definition of Inverse Tangent Function

The **inverse tangent function** is defined by

$$y = \arctan x \text{ if and only if } \tan y = x.$$

where $x \in \mathbf{R}$ and $-\frac{\pi}{2} < y < \frac{\pi}{2}$. The domain of $y = \arctan x$ is $\mathbf{R}$, while the range is $\left(-\frac{\pi}{2}, \frac{\pi}{2}\right)$.

3 Explore the possibility to define the inverse cosine function on the interval $[0, \pi]$.

Solution: Note that the cosine function is decreasing when $x \in [0, \pi]$, it is reasonable to define the inverse cosine function on this same interval. Denote by $y = \arccos x$ the resulting inverse. It follows that the function is defined for $-1 \leqslant x \leqslant 1$ with a range of $[0, \pi]$. The graph of the inverse cosine function is shown in Figure 6 - 19.

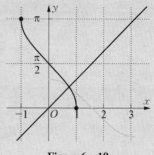

Figure 6 - 19

由于反三角函数表示的是角的大小,因此,结合我们此前已经掌握的三角恒等式,可以得到一些相应的数值等式.这种方法在理论上和实际应用中都是有益的.

4 Find the following values of the functions.

(1) $\sin\left(\arctan\dfrac{4}{3}\right)$.

(2) $\tan\left[\arccos\left(-\dfrac{12}{13}\right)\right]$.

(3) $\cos\left(2\arctan\dfrac{3}{4}\right)$.

(4) $\arcsin(\sin 6)$.

(5) $\arctan\dfrac{1}{7}+2\arctan\dfrac{1}{3}$.

(6) $\arctan\left(\tan\dfrac{4\pi}{5}\right)$.

(7) $\arctan x+\arctan\dfrac{1}{x}$.

(8) $\arcsin(\sin\sqrt{10})-\arccos(\cos\sqrt{10})$.

Solution: Apply trigonometric identities to simplify each expression.

(1) $\sin\left(\arctan\dfrac{4}{3}\right)=\sin\left(\arcsin\dfrac{4}{5}\right)=\dfrac{4}{5}$.

(2) $\tan\left[\arccos\left(-\dfrac{12}{13}\right)\right]=\dfrac{\sin\left[\arccos\left(-\dfrac{12}{13}\right)\right]}{\cos\left[\arccos\left(-\dfrac{12}{13}\right)\right]}=\dfrac{\dfrac{5}{13}}{-\dfrac{12}{13}}=-\dfrac{5}{12}$.

(3) $\cos\left(2\arctan\dfrac{3}{4}\right)=\cos\left(2\arccos\dfrac{4}{5}\right)=2\cos^2\left(\arccos\dfrac{4}{5}\right)-1=\dfrac{7}{25}$.

(4) $\arcsin(\sin 6)=\arcsin[\sin(6-2\pi)]=6-2\pi$.

(5) Let $\alpha=\arctan\dfrac{1}{7}$, $\beta=2\arctan\dfrac{1}{3}$, then $\tan\alpha=\dfrac{1}{7}$. Meanwhile, the double-angle formula for

tangent implies that $\tan\beta=\dfrac{2\times\dfrac{1}{3}}{1-\dfrac{1}{9}}=\dfrac{3}{4}$. Hence, the sum formula for tangent gives $\tan(\alpha+\beta)=$

$\dfrac{\dfrac{1}{7}+\dfrac{3}{4}}{1-\dfrac{1}{7}\times\dfrac{3}{4}}=1$. Now that $\tan\dfrac{\pi}{6}=\dfrac{1}{\sqrt{3}}>\dfrac{1}{3}$, it follows that $\alpha,\beta\in\left(0,\dfrac{\pi}{6}\right)$. Thus, $\alpha+2\beta\in\left(0,\dfrac{\pi}{2}\right)$,

whence the answer is $\dfrac{\pi}{4}$.

(6) $\arctan\left(\tan\dfrac{4\pi}{5}\right)=\arctan\left[\tan\left(\dfrac{4\pi}{5}-\pi\right)\right]=\arctan\left[\tan\left(-\dfrac{\pi}{5}\right)\right]=-\dfrac{\pi}{5}$.

(7) Let $\alpha=\arctan x$, $\beta=\arctan\dfrac{1}{x}$, then $\tan\alpha\tan\beta=1$. Hence, the terminal side of angle $\alpha+\beta$ lies

on the y-axis. If $x>0$, $\alpha,\beta\in\left(0,\dfrac{\pi}{2}\right)\Rightarrow\alpha+\beta=\dfrac{\pi}{2}$, while when $x<0$, $\alpha+\beta\in\left(-\dfrac{\pi}{2},0\right)\Rightarrow\alpha+\beta=$

$-\dfrac{\pi}{2}$. Thus, $\arctan x+\arctan\dfrac{1}{x}=\begin{cases}\dfrac{\pi}{2}, & x>0\\[2mm]-\dfrac{\pi}{2}, & x<0\end{cases}$.

(8) $\arcsin(\sin\sqrt{10}) - \arccos(\cos\sqrt{10})$

$= \arcsin[\sin(\pi - \sqrt{10})] - \arccos[\cos(2\pi - \sqrt{10})]$

$= \pi - \sqrt{10} - (2\pi - \sqrt{10}) = -\pi.$

反三角函数的性质 Properties of the Inverse Trigonometric Functions

By observing the graphs of inverse trigonometric functions, we may study their properties as general abstract functions.

5 For the function $y = \arcsin x$, determine its symmetry, find the intervals on which it is monotonic, as well as its maximum/minimum values, and period (if possible).

Solution: The relationship between functions and their inverses implies that we may establish the properties of $y = \arcsin x$ from their counterpart of $y = \sin x (-1 \leqslant x \leqslant 1)$. Thus, the function is odd, increasing all over its domain, with the maximum value of $\dfrac{\pi}{2}$, attained at $x = 1$ and the minimum value of $-\dfrac{\pi}{2}$, attained at $x = -1$. Due to the restriction of the domain, it cannot be periodic.

6 For the function $y = \arctan x$, determine its symmetry, find the intervals on which it is monotonic, as well as its maximum/minimum values, and the period (if possible).

Solution: We work on a similar pattern as above. The function is odd, increasing all over its domain, with no maximum value or minimum value $\left(\text{due to the presence of horizontal asymptotes } y = \pm\dfrac{\pi}{2}\right)$. The increasing nature implies that the function cannot be periodic.

含有反三角函数的复合函数 Composed Functions with Inverse Trigs

As we all know, in case a function $y = f(x)$ is "invertible", then $f(x)$ and its inverse $f^{-1}(x)$ satisfy the *cancellation equations*: $f(f^{-1}(x)) = f^{-1}(f(x)) = x$. However, the nature of trigonometric functions provides the inverse trigs with some interesting special features when being involved with composition of the functions. Here we list some of such properties.

Inverse Properties of Trigonometric Functions

If $-1 \leqslant x \leqslant 1$ and $-\dfrac{\pi}{2} \leqslant y \leqslant \dfrac{\pi}{2}$, then

$\sin(\arcsin x) = x$ and $\arcsin(\sin y) = y$,

If $-1 \leqslant x \leqslant 1$ and $0 \leqslant y \leqslant \pi$, then

$\cos(\arccos x) = x$ and $\arccos(\cos y) = y$.

If x is a real number and $-\dfrac{\pi}{2} < y < \dfrac{\pi}{2}$, then

$\tan(\arctan x) = x$ and $\arctan(\tan y) = y$.

7 (1) Evaluate $\arcsin\left(\sin\dfrac{\pi}{4}\right)$ and $\arcsin\left(\sin\dfrac{3\pi}{4}\right)$.

(2) Which one is larger, $\arcsin(\sin\sqrt{2})$ or $\arcsin(\sin\sqrt{3})$?

(3) Show that the function $y = \arcsin(\sin x)$ is periodic and determine its period.

Solution: $\arcsin\left(\sin\dfrac{\pi}{4}\right)=\dfrac{\pi}{4}$, $\arcsin\left(\sin\dfrac{3\pi}{4}\right)=\arcsin\left(\sin\left(\pi-\dfrac{3\pi}{4}\right)\right)=\dfrac{\pi}{4}$.

Since $0<\sqrt{2}<\dfrac{\pi}{2}$, we have $\arcsin(\sin\sqrt{2})=\sqrt{2}$. On the other hand, $\dfrac{\pi}{2}<\sqrt{3}<\pi$ implies that $\arcsin(\sin\sqrt{3})=\arcsin(\sin(\pi-\sqrt{3}))=\pi-\sqrt{3}$. Now that $\sqrt{2}-(\pi-\sqrt{3})=\sqrt{2}+\sqrt{3}-\pi>0$, henceforth $\arcsin(\sin\sqrt{2})>\arcsin(\sin\sqrt{3})$.

By cancellation equations, when $2k\pi-\dfrac{\pi}{2}\leqslant x\leqslant 2k\pi+\dfrac{\pi}{2}$ ($k\in\mathbf{Z}$), $\arcsin(\sin x)=x-2k\pi$, while as $2k\pi+\dfrac{\pi}{2}\leqslant x\leqslant 2k\pi+\dfrac{3\pi}{2}$ ($k\in\mathbf{Z}$), $\arcsin(\sin x)=\arcsin(\sin(\pi-x))=2k\pi+\pi-x$. Hence, the graph of $y=\arcsin(\sin x)$ appears as a zigzag, of which the period is 2π. See Figure 6-20:

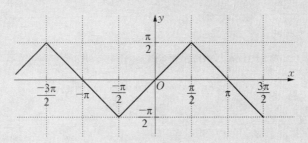

Figure 6 - 20

8 (1) Simplify the following composed expressions: $\cos(\arcsin x)$, $\tan(\arcsin x)$, $\sin(\arccos x)$, $\tan(\arccos x)$, $\sin(\arctan x)$, $\cos(\arctan x)$.

(2) Explore the properties of the function $y=\arcsin(\sin x)$.

Solution: When simplifying the composed trigonometric functions, we have to take the domains into consideration.

For $\arcsin x$, $-1\leqslant x\leqslant 1$ and $-\dfrac{\pi}{2}\leqslant y\leqslant\dfrac{\pi}{2}$, thus, the cosine value is non-negative, which implies that $\cos(\arcsin x)=\sqrt{1-(\sin(\arcsin x))^2}=\sqrt{1-x^2}$.

Similarly, $\tan(\arcsin x)=\dfrac{\sin(\arcsin x)}{\cos(\arcsin x)}=\dfrac{x}{\sqrt{1-x^2}}(x\neq\pm1)$.

As for $\arccos x$, $-1\leqslant x\leqslant 1$ and $0\leqslant y\leqslant\pi$, thus, the sine value is non-negative, which implies that $\sin(\arccos(x))=\sqrt{1-(\cos(\arccos x))^2}=\sqrt{1-x^2}$.

It then follows that $\tan(\arccos x)=\dfrac{\sin(\arccos x)}{\cos(\arccos x)}=\dfrac{\sqrt{1-x^2}}{x}(x\neq0)$.

The same reasoning works for $\arctan x$, whose range is $\left(-\dfrac{\pi}{2},\dfrac{\pi}{2}\right)$. Applying the trigonometric identity $\sec x=\sqrt{1+\tan^2 x}$ (noticing that the secant function takes positive value within this domain), we obtain that $\sin(\arctan x)=\dfrac{x}{\sqrt{1+x^2}}$.

Finally, $\cos(\arctan x) = \dfrac{\sin(\arctan x)}{\tan(\arctan x)} = \dfrac{\frac{x}{\sqrt{1+x^2}}}{x} = \dfrac{1}{\sqrt{1+x^2}}.$

According to the previous example, $y = \arcsin(\sin x)$ is an odd function, with the period of 2π. The function attains the maximum of $\dfrac{\pi}{2}$ at $x = 2k\pi + \dfrac{\pi}{2}$ $(k \in \mathbf{Z})$. It attains the minimum of $-\dfrac{\pi}{2}$ at $x = 2k\pi - \dfrac{\pi}{2}$ $(k \in \mathbf{Z})$. The function increases on the intervals $\left[2k\pi - \dfrac{\pi}{2}, 2k\pi + \dfrac{\pi}{2}\right]$ $(k \in \mathbf{Z})$, while decreases on the intervals $\left[2k\pi + \dfrac{\pi}{2}, 2k\pi + \dfrac{3\pi}{2}\right]$ $(k \in \mathbf{Z})$.

Remark: Similarly, we may establish properties of $y = \arccos(\cos x)$, $y = \arctan(\tan x)$, etc. Noticing that the domains might vary.

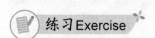 练习 Exercise

1. Find the following inverse trigonometric values if possible.

   (1) $\arcsin \dfrac{1}{2}$.   (2) $\arctan(-\sqrt{3})$.   (3) $\arctan \sqrt{3}$.   (4) $\arcsin 0$.

   (5) $\arccos \dfrac{1}{2}$.   (6) $\arccos\left(-\dfrac{1}{2}\right)$.   (7) $\arcsin \dfrac{\sqrt{2}}{2}$.   (8) $\arccos 0$.

   (9) $\arctan \dfrac{\sqrt{3}}{3}$.   (10) $\sin^{-1}\left(-\dfrac{\sqrt{3}}{2}\right)$.   (11) $\tan^{-1}\left(-\dfrac{\sqrt{3}}{3}\right)$.   (12) $\arctan(1)$.

   (13) $\cos^{-1}\left(-\dfrac{\sqrt{3}}{2}\right)$.   (14) $\tan^{-1} 0$.   (15) $\cos^{-1} 1$.   (16) $\sin^{-1}\left(-\dfrac{\sqrt{2}}{2}\right)$.

2. Observe the graph of $y = \arccos x$ and explore its properties: determine whether it is even or odd; find its intervals of increasing and decreasing; determine its maximum/minimum values; and find its period if any.

3. Find the following values of functions.

   (1) $\sin[\arctan(-1)]$.   (2) $\cos\left(\arctan \dfrac{\sqrt{2}}{2}\right)$.

   (3) $\tan\left[\arctan\left(-\dfrac{\sqrt{3}}{3}\right) + \arctan \sqrt{3}\right]$.   (4) $\arctan 1 + \arctan 2 + \arctan 3$.

4. Verify the following identities of (inverse) trigonometric functions.

   (1) $\arcsin x + \arccos x = \dfrac{\pi}{2}$.   (2) $\arcsin x = \arctan \dfrac{x}{\sqrt{1-x^2}}$.

   Can you find more of such examples?

5. True or False:

   (1) Let $f(x) = \sin x$, $g(x) = \arcsin x$. Then, $(f \circ g)(x) = (g \circ f)(x) = x$.

   (2) $\arccos x = \arctan \dfrac{\sqrt{1-x^2}}{x}$.

6. A security car with its spotlight on is parked 20 meters from a warehouse. Consider θ and x as shown in Figure 6-21.

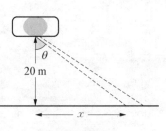

Figure 6 - 21

(1) Write θ in terms of x.

(2) Find θ when $x = 5$ meters and $x = 12$ meters.

7. (1) Find all possible values of c so that the function $f(x) = \arctan \dfrac{2-2x}{1+4x} + c\left(-\dfrac{1}{4} < x < \dfrac{1}{4}\right)$ is odd.

(2) A **trigonometric map** is any one of sin, cos, tan, arcsin, arccos and arctan. For any pair of real numbers a, b, a can be **carried to** b, denoted by $a \rightarrow b$, if there is a sequence of trigonometric maps t_i so that: $x_1 = t_0(a)$, $x_2 = t_1(x_1)$, $\cdots$, $x_n = t_{n-1}(x_{n-1})$, $b = t_n(x_n)$.

a. Show that any positive real number x can be carried to $\dfrac{1}{x}$.

b. Find sequences of trigonometric maps that carry 0 to $\sqrt{\dfrac{7}{2}}$ and $\dfrac{3}{4}$, respectively.

c. Show that for any positive rational number x, 0 can be carried to $\sqrt{x}$.

8. According to Rhind papyrus, one of the earliest mathematical documents, antique Egyptians deal with the arithmetic of fractions in a special manner. They always broke a single fraction $\dfrac{m}{n}$ into a sum of reciprocals of the natural numbers, namely, before working on the arithmetic of fractions, they rewrite the numbers as follows:

$$\frac{m}{n} = \frac{1}{n_1} + \frac{1}{n_2} + \cdots + \frac{1}{n_k}.$$

where n_i's are distinctive integers. Thus, people today still dub such an expansion of fractions as the *Egyptian fractions*. In what follows, we will seek for a trigonometric version of Egyptian fractions.

(1) Verify the identities: $\arctan 1 = \arctan \dfrac{1}{2} + \arctan \dfrac{1}{3}$; $\arctan \dfrac{1}{3} = \arctan \dfrac{1}{5} + \arctan \dfrac{1}{8}$.

(2) Show that $\arctan \dfrac{1}{n} = \arctan \dfrac{1}{n+1} + \arctan \dfrac{1}{n^2+n+1}$ for any positive integer n.

(3) For any fraction $\dfrac{m}{n} \in (0, 1)$ such that $\gcd(m, n) = 1$, put $d = \lfloor \dfrac{n}{m} \rfloor + 1$. Show that there are some integers r and N with $0 < r < m$ such that $\arctan \dfrac{m}{n} = \arctan \dfrac{1}{d} + \arctan \dfrac{r}{N}$.

(4) Explain how the result in part c. could help us to break any $\arctan \dfrac{m}{n}\left(0 < \dfrac{m}{n} < 1\right)$ into the sum of several $\arctan \dfrac{1}{n_i}$'s.

6.5 ◈ 解简单三角方程 Solving the Basic Trigonometric Equations

在实际应用三角函数解决问题时,通常需要通过解读问题背景来建立一些方程,然后求解这些方程,从而得到所求角的大小.在研究这些问题的过程当中,产生了解三角方程的迫切需要.

另一方面,从数学本身的角度来说,解方程也是自古以来数学研究的一个核心问题.而在求解的过程中,往往需要运用三角函数的各种性质:利用定义域来确定解的存在性;利用单调性来确定解的唯一性;利用值域来排除增根;利用三角恒等式来转化复杂的方程……这些都强烈地依赖于对三角函数的认识.因此,通过解三角方程,可以提升对三角函数性质的认识.

基本三角方程 Basic Trigonometric Equations

含有未知数的三角运算或反三角运算的方程,称为**三角方程**(trigonometric equation).使三角方程成立的所有数值的集合,称为该三角方程的**解集**(solution set of a trigonometric equation).

其中,最为简单的一类三角方程,即形如:$\sin x = a$,$\cos x = a$ 或 $\tan x = a$ 的方程,称为**最简三角方程**,或**基本三角方程**(basic trigonometric equations).

1 Solve the following basic trigonometric equations.

(1) $\sin x = a$. (2) $\cos x = a$. (3) $\tan x = a$.

Solution: For $\sin x = a$, distinguish between several cases concerning the range of a.

$|a| > 1$: No solution.

$a = 1$: The only solution to equation $\sin x = 1$ within the interval $\left[-\dfrac{\pi}{2}, \dfrac{3\pi}{2}\right)$ is $x = \dfrac{\pi}{2}$. Thus, general solutions to $\sin x = 1$ are $x = 2k\pi + \dfrac{\pi}{2}$, $k \in \mathbf{Z}$.

$a = -1$: The only solution to equation $\sin x = -1$ within the interval $\left[-\dfrac{\pi}{2}, \dfrac{3\pi}{2}\right)$ is $x = -\dfrac{\pi}{2}$. Thus, general solutions to $\sin x = -1$ are $x = 2k\pi - \dfrac{\pi}{2}$, $k \in \mathbf{Z}$.

$|a| < 1$: The only solution to equation $\sin x = a$ within the interval $\left[-\dfrac{\pi}{2}, \dfrac{\pi}{2}\right)$ is $x = \arcsin a$, while the only solution within the interval $\left[\dfrac{\pi}{2}, \dfrac{3\pi}{2}\right)$ is $x = \pi - \arcsin a$. Thus, general solutions to $\sin x = a$ are $x = k\pi + (-1)^k \arcsin a$, $k \in \mathbf{Z}$.

2 Solve the following trigonometric equations.

(1) $\sin x + \sqrt{2} = -\sin x$. (2) $3\tan^2 x - 1 = 0$. (3) $\cot x \cos^2 x = 2\cot x$.

Solution: Convert each equation above into the basic ones.

(1) $\sin x + \sqrt{2} = -\sin x \Rightarrow \sin x = -\dfrac{\sqrt{2}}{2}$. Thus, $x = 2k\pi - \dfrac{\pi}{4}$ or $2k\pi - \dfrac{3\pi}{4}$ ($k \in \mathbf{Z}$).

(2) $3\tan^2 x - 1 = 0 \Rightarrow \tan x = \pm\dfrac{\sqrt{3}}{3}$. Thus, $x = \dfrac{\pi}{6} + k\pi$ or $\dfrac{5\pi}{6} + k\pi$ ($k \in \mathbf{Z}$).

(3) $\cot x \cos^2 x = 2\cot x \Rightarrow \cot x (\cos^2 x - 2) = 0$. Since $\cos^2 x \leqslant 1$, the new equation amounts to say that $\cot x = 0$. Thus, $x = \dfrac{\pi}{2} + k\pi$ ($k \in \mathbf{Z}$).

含二次项的三角方程 Equations of Quadratic Type

Many trigonometric equations take the form of a quadratic function $au^2 + bu + c = 0$. Here are a couple of examples:

Quadratic in $\sin x$	Quadratic in $\sec x$
$2\sin^2 x - \sin x - 1 = 0$	$\sec^2 x - 3\sec x - 2 = 0$

$$2(\sin x)^2 - \sin x - 1 = 0 \qquad\qquad (\sec x)^2 - 3(\sec x) - 2 = 0$$

To solve equations of this type, factor the quadratic or, if this is not possible, use the **Quadratic Formula**: $x_{1,2} = \dfrac{-b \pm \sqrt{b^2 - 4ac}}{2a}$.

3 Solve the following trigonometric equations.

(1) $\tan^2 x - 3\tan x + 2 = 0$. 　　　　　(2) $2\sin^2 x + 3\cos x - 3 = 0$.

Solution:

(1) Apply the quadratic formula (or factorize the equation), we obtain that: $\tan x = 1$ or 2. Thus, according to the definition of inverse trigonometric functions, when $\tan x = 1$, $x = \arctan 1 + k\pi = \dfrac{\pi}{4} + k\pi$, while when $\tan x = 2$, $x = \arctan 2 + k\pi$, $k \in \mathbf{Z}$.

(2) This equation contains both sine and cosine functions. Apply the identity $\sin^2 x = 1 - \cos^2 x$ to re-write the equation as $2\cos^2 x - 3\cos x + 1 = 0$, which factors as $(2\cos x - 1)(\cos x - 1) = 0$.

Set each factor equal to zero to find the solutions in the interval $[0, 2\pi)$.

$$2\cos x - 1 = 0 \Rightarrow \cos x = \frac{1}{2} \Rightarrow x = \frac{\pi}{3}, \frac{5\pi}{3},$$

$$\cos x - 1 = 0 \Rightarrow \cos x = 1 \Rightarrow x = 0.$$

Because $\cos x$ has a period of 2π, the general form of the solution is obtained by adding multiples of 2π to get

$$x = 2k\pi, \ x = \frac{\pi}{3} + 2k\pi, \ x = \frac{5\pi}{3} + 2k\pi, \ k \in \mathbf{Z}.$$

4 Solve the following trigonometric equations in the interval $[0, 2\pi)$.

(1) $\cos x + 1 = \sin x$. 　　　　　(2) $3\sin x + 4\cos x = 5$.

Solution:

These equations can be converted into the quadratic type, yet one need to verify if the process of squaring both sides brings extra solutions.

(1) Square both sides of the equation and factorize it to find that $2\cos x(\cos x + 1) = 0$. Thus, $\cos x = 0$ or -1, whence $x = \dfrac{\pi}{2}$, π, or $\dfrac{3\pi}{2}$. One verifies that $x = \dfrac{3\pi}{2}$ is NOT a solution.

(2) Similarly, the equation is re-written as $(5\cos x - 4)^2 = 0$. Thus, $\cos x = \dfrac{4}{5}$, whence $x = \arccos \dfrac{4}{5}$, or $2\pi - \arccos \dfrac{4}{5}$. One verifies that $x = 2\pi - \arccos \dfrac{4}{5}$ is NOT a solution.

倍角的方程 Equations Involving Multiple Angles

Other equations may involve trigonometric functions of multiple angles of the forms $\sin kx$, $\cos kx$, etc. To solve equations of this type, first solve the equation for kx, then divide your result by k, of course, in the correct way.

5 Solve the following trigonometric equations.

(1) $2\cos 3t - 1 = 0$; 　　　　　(2) $3\tan \dfrac{x}{2} + 3 = 0$.

Solution：

(1) $2\cos 3t - 1 = 0 \Rightarrow \cos 3t = \dfrac{1}{2}$.

Within the interval $[0, 2\pi)$, $3t = \dfrac{\pi}{3}$ or $\dfrac{5\pi}{3}$. In general, $t = \dfrac{\pi}{9} + \dfrac{2k\pi}{3}$ or $\dfrac{5\pi}{9} + \dfrac{2k\pi}{3}$, $k \in \mathbf{Z}$.

(2) Similarly, we obtain that $\tan \dfrac{x}{2} = -1$, whence $\dfrac{x}{2} = \dfrac{3\pi}{4} + k\pi$, $k \in \mathbf{Z}$. Thus, $x = \dfrac{3\pi}{2} + 2k\pi$, $k \in \mathbf{Z}$.

6 Solve the following trigonometric equations.

(1) $\cos 7x = \cos x$；　　　(2) $\tan 4x = \tan 2x$；　　　(3) $\sin 2x \cos 5x = \sin x \cos 6x$.

Solution：

(1) $\cos 7x = \cos x \Rightarrow 7x = 2k\pi \pm x$, thus, $x = \dfrac{k\pi}{3}$ or $\dfrac{k\pi}{4}$, $k \in \mathbf{Z}$.

(2) $\tan 4x = \tan 2x \Rightarrow 4x = k\pi + 2x$, thus, $x = \dfrac{k\pi}{2}$, $k \in \mathbf{Z}$.

(3) Apply the product-to-sum formula, we obtain that $\sin 7x - \sin 3x = \sin 7x - \sin 5x$, whence $\sin 3x = \sin 5x \Rightarrow 5x = 3x + 2k\pi$ or $5x = 2k\pi + \pi - 3x$. Thus, $x = k\pi$ or $\dfrac{2k+1}{8}\pi$, $k \in \mathbf{Z}$.

其他三角方程 Other Trigonometric Equations

一般来说，解三角方程需要综合运用关于三角函数的知识，特别是各种三角恒等式.有时，也需要结合其他函数的性质进行运算.

7 Solve the following trigonometric equations.

(1) $\sin x + \cos x = 1$.

(2) $\cot x = \dfrac{3\cos x}{1 + \sin x}$.

(3) $\sin x - \cos x + \sin 2x = 1$.

(4) $2\cos^2 x - \sin x \cos x = \dfrac{1}{2}$.

Solution：

(1) $\sin x + \cos x = 1 \Rightarrow \sin x \cos x = 0$, thus, $x = 2k\pi + \dfrac{\pi}{2}$ or $2k\pi$, $k \in \mathbf{Z}$.

(2) $\cot x = \dfrac{3\cos x}{1 + \sin x} \Rightarrow \cos x \dfrac{1 - 2\sin x}{(1 + \sin x)\sin x} = 0$. Thus, $\cos x = 0$, or $\sin x = \dfrac{1}{2}$ while the denominator implies that $\sin x \neq 0, -1$. Hence, $x = \dfrac{\pi}{2} + 2k\pi$, $\dfrac{\pi}{6} + 2k\pi$ or $\dfrac{5\pi}{6} + 2k\pi$, $k \in \mathbf{Z}$.

(3) $\sin x - \cos x + \sin 2x = 1 \Rightarrow \sin x - \cos x = (\sin x - \cos x)^2$, whence $\sin x - \cos x = 0$ or 1. Thus, $x = \dfrac{\pi}{4} + k\pi$, $2k\pi + \pi$ or $2k\pi + \dfrac{\pi}{2}$, $k \in \mathbf{Z}$.

(4) Apparently, $\cos x \neq 0$. Hence, we can divide both sides of the equation by $\cos^2 x$ to obtain that $2 - \tan x = \dfrac{1}{2}(\tan^2 x + 1)$, which gives $x = k\pi + \dfrac{\pi}{4}$ or $k\pi - \arctan 3$, $k \in \mathbf{Z}$.

8 Solve the following trigonometric equations.

(1) $81^{\sin^2 x} + 81^{\cos^2 x} = 30$.

(2) $\sin(\pi \cos x) = \cos(\pi \sin x)$.

Solution：

(1) For $81^{\sin^2 x} + 81^{\cos^2 x} = 30$, make the substitution by taking $u = 81^{\sin^2 x}$, thus, $u + \dfrac{81}{u} = 30$. Solve the equation of u to find $\sin x = \pm \dfrac{1}{2}$ or $\pm \dfrac{\sqrt{3}}{2}$. Hence, the solution is $x = k\pi \pm \dfrac{\pi}{6}$ or $k\pi \pm \dfrac{\pi}{3}$, $k \in \mathbf{Z}$.

(2) Since $\sin(\pi \cos x) = \cos(\pi \sin x) = \sin\left(\dfrac{\pi}{2} - \pi \sin x\right)$, it follows that we have either $\pi \cos x = 2k\pi + \dfrac{\pi}{2} - \pi \sin x$ or $\pi \cos x = 2k\pi + \dfrac{\pi}{2} + \pi \sin x$. Thus, $\cos x \pm \sin x = 2k + \dfrac{1}{2}$, which is possible only if $k = 0$. Hence, $x = 2k\pi \pm \dfrac{\pi}{4} \pm \arccos \dfrac{\sqrt{2}}{4}$, $k \in \mathbf{Z}$.

练习 Exercise

1. Solve the following trigonometric equations.

   (1) $2\cos x + 1 = 0$.   (2) $2\sin x + 1 = 0$.

   (3) $\sqrt{3} \csc x - 2 = 0$.   (4) $\tan x + \sqrt{3} = 0$.

   (5) $3\sec^2 x - 4 = 0$.   (6) $3\cot^2 x - 1 = 0$.

   (7) $\sin x(\sin x + 1) = 0$.   (8) $(3\tan^2 x - 1)(\tan^2 x - 3) = 0$.

   (9) $4\cos^2 x - 1 = 0$.   (10) $\sin^2 x = 3\cos^2 x$.

   (11) $2\sin^2 2x = 1$.   (12) $\tan^2 3x = 3$.

   (13) $\tan 3x(\tan x - 1) = 0$.   (14) $\cos 2x(2\cos x + 1) = 0$.

2. Solve the following trigonometric equations.

   (1) $2\sin 2x - 2(\sqrt{3}\sin x - \sqrt{2}\cos x) - \sqrt{6} = 0$.   (2) $\sin x \cos x + \sin x + \cos x = 1$.

   (3) $|\sin x| + |\cos x| = \sqrt{2}$.   (4) $m \sin x = (m-1)\cos \dfrac{1}{2}x \ (m > 1)$.

   (5) $\tan\left(\dfrac{3\pi}{2} - x\right) = 3\tan x$.   (6) $\tan\left(x + \dfrac{\pi}{4}\right) + \tan\left(x - \dfrac{\pi}{4}\right) = 2\cot x$.

   (7) $\sin(\pi \arctan x) = \cos(\pi \arctan x)$.

3. True or False：

   (1) The equation $2\sin 4t - 1 = 0$ has four times the number of the solutions in the interval $[0, 2\pi)$ as the equation $2\sin t - 1 = 0$.

   (2) To solve the equation $\cot x \cos^2 x = 2\cot x$, we eliminate the common factor $\cot x$ from both side to find $\cos^2 x = 2$, which is absurd. Hence, the equation has no real solution.

4. (1) A batted baseball leaves the bat at an angle of θ with the horizontal and an initial velocity of $v_0 = 100$ feet per second. The ball is caught by an outfielder 300 feet from home plate (see Figure 6 - 22). Find θ if the range r of a projectile is given by $r = \dfrac{1}{32}v_0^2 \sin 2\theta$.

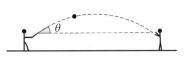

Figure 6 - 22

(2) A Ferris wheel is built such that the height h (in feet) above ground of a seat on the wheel at time t (in minutes) can be modeled by

$$h(t) = 53 + 50\sin\left(\frac{\pi}{16}t - \frac{\pi}{2}\right).$$

The wheel makes one revolution every 32 seconds. The ride begins when $t = 0$.

a. During the first 32 seconds of the ride, when will a person on the Ferris wheel be 53 feet above ground?

b. When will a person be at the top of the Ferris wheel for the first time during the ride? If the ride lasts 160 seconds, how many times will a person be at the top of the ride, and at what times?

5. (1) In the following exercises, use a graphing utility to graph the function and approximate the maximum and minimum points on the graph, and solve the trigonometric equation and demonstrate that its solutions are the x-coordinates of the maximum and minimum points of f. (Calculus is required to find the trigonometric equations.)

Function	Trigonometric Equation
a. $f(x) = \sin x + \cos x$	$\cos x - \sin x = 0$
b. $f(x) = \sin x \cos x$	$-\sin^2 x + \cos^2 x = 0$

(2) Find the smallest positive fixed point of the function f. [A *fixed point* of a function f is a real number c such that $f(c) = c$.]

a. $f(x) = \tan\dfrac{\pi x}{4}$　　　　　　b. $f(x) = 2\cos\dfrac{\pi x}{3}$

6. (1) Find all solutions to the equation $\tan\lfloor x \rfloor \cdot \tan(x - \lfloor x \rfloor) = 1$, where $\lfloor x \rfloor$ is the floor function.

(2) In what follows, we explore the *iterations* of trigonometric functions.

a. Which is larger, $\cos(\cos x)$ or $\sin(\sin x)$?

b. Solve the trigonometric equation $\cos(\cos(\cos(\cos x))) = \sin(\sin(\sin(\sin x)))$.

c. Use a graphical calculator (or computational software) to determine all solutions to the trigonometric equation $\cos(\cos(\cos x)) = \sin(\sin(\sin x))$ in the interval $[-\pi, \pi]$. Explain your answer by checking the monotonicity of the two functions.

第7章

数列与数学归纳法
Sequences and Mathematical Induction

7.1 ◆ 数列 Sequences

中国古代庄周所著的《庄子·天下篇》中引用过一句话:"一尺之锤,日取其半,万事不竭."其含义是:一根一尺长的木棒,每天截下其一半,这样的过程可以无限地进行下去. 如果把木棒每天的长度记录下来,可得到一列数:

$$1, \frac{1}{2}, \frac{1}{4}, \frac{1}{8}, \cdots, \frac{1}{2^n}, \cdots$$

这样按一定次序排列起来的一列数叫作数列.

数列 Sequences

按一定顺序排列起来的一列数叫作**数列**(sequence of number).数列中的每一个数叫作这个**数列的项**,数列的各项按先后顺序依次称为这个数列的第 1 项(或首项),第 2 项,…,第 n 项,…

数列的一般形式可以写成 $a_1, a_2, a_3, \cdots, a_n, \cdots$,简记为 $\{a_n\}$,其中 a_n 是数列的第 n 项.

项数有限的数列叫作**有穷数列**(finite sequence);项数无限的数列叫作**无穷数列**(infinite sequence).从第 2 项起,每一项都大于它的前一项的数列叫作**递增数列**;从第 2 项起,每一项都小于它的前一项的数列叫作**递减数列**;各项相等的数列叫作**常数列**.

在数列中,当数列的项的序号 n 确定时,相应的项 a_n 也就唯一确定了.于是数列的项 a_n 与项的序号 n 之间存在着对应关系,这种对应关系可描述如下:

项的序号   1,   2,   3,   4,   …, n,   …
          ↓   ↓   ↓   ↓   ↓
项 $a_1,$ $a_2,$ $a_3,$ $a_4,$ …, $a_n,$ …

因此,从函数的观点看,数列可以看成以正整数集 $\mathbf{N}^*$[或它的有限子集$\{1, 2, 3, \cdots, n\}$]为定义域的函数 $a_n = f(n)$,当自变量按从小到大的顺序依次取值时,$f(n)$ 所对应的一列数. 若将数列中的序号 n 与对应的项 a_n 用坐标 (n, a_n) 表示,则在平面直角坐标系中所得的数列的图像是一列离散的点.

当数列 $\{a_n\}$ 的第 n 项 a_n 与项的序号 n 之间的关系:$a_n = f(n)$ 可以用一个公式来表示时,这个公式就叫作这个数列的**通项公式**(the formula of general term). 例如,数列 $1, \frac{1}{2}, \frac{1}{3}, \frac{1}{4}, \cdots$ 的通项公式可以是 $a_n = \frac{1}{n}$ ($n \in \mathbf{N}^*$);数列 $1, 1, 1, 1, 1$ 的通项公式可以为 $a_n = 1$ ($1 \leqslant n \leqslant 5, n \in \mathbf{N}^*$).

如果已知数列 $\{a_n\}$ 的第 1 项(或前 n 项),且任一项 a_n 与它的前一项 a_{n-1} (或前 n 项)间的关系可以用一个公式来表示,那么这个公式就称作这个数列的**递推公式(recurrence formula)**.递推公式也是定义数列的一种方式.

例如,数列 $a_n = n + 3 \ (1 \leqslant n \leqslant 7)$ 可以用递推公式表示:$\begin{cases} a_1 = 4 \\ a_n = a_{n-1} + 1 (2 \leqslant n \leqslant 7) \end{cases}$.

In mathematics, the word sequence is used in much the same way as in ordinary English. A sequence is a collection of numbers with given order.

Mathematically, you can think of a sequence as a **function** whose domain is the set of positive integers. Rather than using function notation, however, sequences are usually written using subscript notation, as indicated in the following definition.

> **Definition of the Sequence**
>
> An **infinite sequence** is a function whose domain is (part of) the set of positive integers.
> The function values
>
> $$a_1, a_2, a_3, \cdots, a_n, \cdots$$
>
> are the **terms** of the sequence. When the domain of the function consists of the first n positive integers only, the sequence is a **finite sequence**.

Some sequences are defined **recursively**. To define a sequence recursively, you need to be given one or more of the first few terms. All the other terms of the sequence are then defined using previous terms.

1 Find the first four terms of the following sequences.

(1) $a_n = 3n - 1$. (2) $a_n = 5 + (-1)^n$.

Solution: (1) The first four terms of the sequence given by $a_n = 3n - 1$ are as follows:

$$a_1 = 3 \times 1 - 1 = 2,$$
$$a_2 = 3 \times 2 - 1 = 5,$$
$$a_3 = 3 \times 3 - 1 = 8,$$
$$a_4 = 3 \times 4 - 1 = 11.$$

(2) The first four terms of the sequence given by $a_n = 5 + (-1)^n$ are as follows:

$$a_1 = 5 + (-1)^1 = 5 - 1 = 4,$$
$$a_2 = 5 + (-1)^2 = 5 + 1 = 6,$$
$$a_3 = 5 + (-1)^3 = 5 - 1 = 4,$$
$$a_4 = 5 + (-1)^4 = 5 + 1 = 6.$$

2 Find the first four terms of the sequence given by $a_n = \dfrac{(-1)^n}{2n + 3}$.

Solution: The first four terms of the sequence are as follows:

$$a_1 = \frac{(-1)^1}{2 \times 1 + 3} = \frac{-1}{2 + 3} = -\frac{1}{5},$$
$$a_2 = \frac{(-1)^2}{2 \times 2 + 3} = \frac{1}{4 + 3} = \frac{1}{7},$$

$$a_3 = \frac{(-1)^3}{2 \times 3 + 3} = \frac{-1}{6+3} = -\frac{1}{9},$$

$$a_4 = \frac{(-1)^4}{2 \times 4 + 3} = \frac{1}{8+3} = \frac{1}{11}.$$

Remark: Find the first four terms of the sequence whose term is $a_n = \dfrac{(-1)^{n+1}}{2n+3}$. Are they the same as the first four terms of the sequence in Example 2? Tell the difference, if any.

3 Find a general formula of each sequence with given first five terms.

(1) $\dfrac{2^2 - 1}{3}, \dfrac{4^2 - 2}{5}, \dfrac{6^2 - 3}{7}, \dfrac{8^2 - 4}{9}, \dfrac{10^2 - 5}{11}.$

(2) $\dfrac{1}{2}, -\dfrac{1}{6}, \dfrac{1}{12}, -\dfrac{1}{20}, \dfrac{1}{30}.$

(3) $-\dfrac{1}{2}, \dfrac{2}{5}, -\dfrac{2}{5}, \dfrac{8}{17}, -\dfrac{8}{13}.$

(4) $1, 0, 1, 0, 1.$

Solution: (1) The pattern of the first five items in this sequence is as follows:

$$\frac{(2 \times 1)^2 - 1}{2 \times 1 + 1}, \frac{(2 \times 2)^2 - 2}{2 \times 2 + 1}, \frac{(2 \times 3)^2 - 3}{2 \times 3 + 1}, \frac{(2 \times 4)^2 - 4}{2 \times 4 + 1}, \frac{(2 \times 5)^2 - 5}{2 \times 5 + 1}.$$

So the general formula of the sequence is $a_n = \dfrac{(2n)^2 - n}{2n + 1}$.

(2) The pattern of the first five items in this sequence is as follows:

$$\frac{1}{1 \times 2}, -\frac{1}{2 \times 3}, \frac{1}{3 \times 4}, -\frac{1}{4 \times 5}, \frac{1}{5 \times 6},$$

and the signs of the items change according to the law of $(-1)^{n+1}$.

So a general formula of the sequence is $a_n = (-1)^{n+1} \dfrac{1}{n(n+1)}$.

(3) The pattern of the first five items in this sequence is as follows:

$$-\frac{2^0}{1^2 + 1}, \frac{2^1}{2^2 + 1}, -\frac{2}{5} = -\frac{4}{10} = -\frac{2^2}{3^2 + 1}, \frac{2^3}{4^2 + 1}, -\frac{8}{13} = -\frac{16}{26} = -\frac{2^4}{5^2 + 1}.$$

So a general formula of the sequence is $a_n = (-1)^n \cdot \dfrac{2^{n-1}}{n^2 + 1}$.

(4) The pattern of the first five items in this sequence is as follows:

$$\frac{1+1}{2}, \frac{1-1}{2}, \frac{1+1}{2}, \frac{1-1}{2}, \frac{1+1}{2}.$$

So a general formula of the sequence is $a_n = \dfrac{1 + (-1)^{n+1}}{2}$.

Remark: According to the periodicity of the terms of the sequence in example (4), the general term formula of the sequence can also be $a_n = \sin^2 \dfrac{n\pi}{2}$. Simply listing the first few terms is not sufficient to define a unique sequence. To see this, consider the following sequences, both of which have the same first three terms:

$$\frac{1}{2}, \frac{1}{4}, \frac{1}{8}, \frac{1}{16}, \cdots, \frac{1}{2^n}, \cdots$$

$$\frac{1}{2}, \frac{1}{4}, \frac{1}{8}, \frac{1}{15}, \cdots, \frac{6}{(n+1)(n^2-n+6)}, \cdots$$

4 Find the first five terms of the sequence defined recursively as

$$a_1 = 3, \; a_k = 2a_{k-1} - 1, \text{ where } k \geqslant 2.$$

Solution: The first five terms of the sequence are as follows:

$$a_1 = 3,$$
$$a_2 = 2a_{2-1} - 1 = 2a_1 - 1 = 2 \times 3 - 1 = 5,$$
$$a_3 = 2a_{3-1} - 1 = 2a_2 - 1 = 2 \times 5 - 1 = 9,$$
$$a_4 = 2a_{4-1} - 1 = 2a_3 - 1 = 2 \times 9 - 1 = 17,$$
$$a_5 = 2a_{5-1} - 1 = 2a_4 - 1 = 2 \times 17 - 1 = 33.$$

5 Find the first five terms of each recurrence sequence and find a general formula.

(1) $a_1 = 0, \; a_{n+1} = a_n + (2n - 1) \; (n \in \mathbf{N}^*)$.

(2) $a_1 = 1, \; a_{n+1} = \dfrac{2a_n}{a_n + 2} \; (n \in \mathbf{N}^*)$.

Solution: (1) $a_1 = 0, \; a_2 = a_1 + 1 = 1, \; a_3 = a_2 + 3 = 4, \; a_4 = a_3 + 5 = 9, \; a_5 = a_4 + 7 = 16$.

The first five items of the sequence are 0, 1, 4, 9, 16.

A general formula of the sequence is $a_n = (n - 1)^2$.

(2) $a_1 = 1, \; a_2 = \dfrac{2a_1}{a_1 + 2} = \dfrac{2}{3}, \; a_3 = \dfrac{2a_2}{a_2 + 2} = \dfrac{2}{4}, \; a_4 = \dfrac{2a_3}{a_3 + 2} = \dfrac{2}{5}, \; a_5 = \dfrac{2a_4}{a_4 + 2} = \dfrac{2}{6}$.

The first five items of the sequence are $1, \dfrac{2}{3}, \dfrac{1}{2}, \dfrac{2}{5}, \dfrac{1}{3}$.

A general formula of the sequence is $a_n = \dfrac{2}{n+1}$.

6 As shown in Figure 7 - 1, the numbers A output from the block diagram form a sequence $\{x_n\}$ in order.

Answer the following questions:

(1) If you input $A = \dfrac{49}{65}$, write all the terms in the sequence $\{x_n\}$.

(2) If the output sequence $\{x_n\}$ is an infinite constant sequence, find the value of the input initial value A.

(3) If a number A is input, the infinite sequence $\{x_n\}$ generated is an increasing sequence, find the range of A.

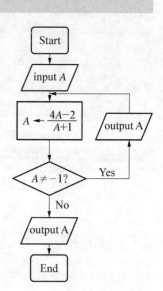

Figure 7 - 1

Solution: Let $x_0 = A$, then the recurrence relation of the sequence output by the block diagram is

$$\begin{cases} x_0 = A & (A \neq -1) \\ x_n = \dfrac{4x_{n-1} - 2}{x_{n-1} + 1} & (n \in \mathbf{N}^*) \end{cases}.$$

(1) Since $x_0 = A = \dfrac{49}{65}$, we get that

$$x_1 = \frac{4x_0 - 2}{x_0 + 1} = \frac{11}{19}, \ x_2 = \frac{4x_1 - 2}{x_1 + 1} = \frac{1}{5}, \ x_3 = \frac{4x_2 - 2}{x_2 + 1} = -1.$$

That is, all the terms in the sequence $\{x_n\}$ are $\dfrac{11}{19}, \dfrac{1}{5}, -1$.

(2) If the output sequence $\{x_n\}$ is constant, $A = \dfrac{4A - 2}{A + 1}$.

Solving the equation gives $A = 1$ or $A = 2$.

(3) If the infinite sequence $\{x_n\}$ generated is increasing, then for any $n \in \mathbf{N}^*$, $x_n < x_{n+1}$.

Therefore, we have that $x_0 < x_1$, i.e. $A < \dfrac{4A - 2}{A + 1}$.

Solving the inequality gives $A < -1$ or $1 < A < 2$.

When $A < -1$, since $x_1 = \dfrac{4A - 2}{A + 1} = 4 - \dfrac{6}{A + 1} > 4$, we get that $x_1 > x_2$, which does not satisfy the conditions.

When $1 < A < 2$, since $x_1 = \dfrac{4A - 2}{A + 1} = 4 - \dfrac{6}{A + 1} \in (1, 2)$, we get that

$$x_1 < x_2 \text{ and } x_2 = \frac{4x_1 - 2}{x_1 + 1} = 4 - \frac{6}{x_1 + 1} \in (1, 2).$$

Then $x_2 < x_3$ and $x_3 \in (1, 2)$, and so on.

Hence we can see that when $1 < A < 2$, $x_1 < x_2 < x_3 < \cdots < x_n < \cdots$.

In summary, when $1 < A < 2$, the infinite sequence $\{x_n\}$ generated is increasing.

7 For a sequence $\{a_n\}$, one often uses S_n to represent the sum of the first nth terms of the sequence, which is, $S_n = a_1 + a_2 + a_3 + \cdots + a_n$. Obviously, $a_n = \begin{cases} S_1 & (n = 1) \\ S_n - S_{n-1} & (n \geq 2) \end{cases}$.

If the sum of the first nth terms of a sequence satisfies the following conditions respectively, find a general formula of the corresponding sequence.

(1) $S_n = 2^n + 1$.   (2) $S_n = n^2 + 4n$.   (3) $a_1 = 1, S_n = n^2 a_n \ (n \in \mathbf{N}^*)$.

Solution: (1) When $n = 1$, $a_1 = S_1 = 3$.

When $n \geq 2$, $a_n = S_n - S_{n-1} = 2^n + 1 - (2^{n-1} + 1) = 2^n - 2^{n-1} = 2^{n-1}$.

Hence, $a_n = \begin{cases} 3 & (n = 1) \\ 2^{n-1} & (n \geq 2) \end{cases}$.

(2) When $n = 1$, $a_1 = S_1 = 5$.   ①

When $n \geq 2$, $a_n = S_n - S_{n-1} = (n^2 + 4n) - [(n-1)^2 + 4(n-1)] = 2n + 3$.   ②

In formula ②, when $n=1$, $2n+3=5$.

Hence, it can be seen from ① and ② that a general formula of the sequence is $a_n = 2n+3 (n \in \mathbf{N}^*)$.

(4) When $n \geqslant 2$, $a_n = S_n - S_{n-1} = n^2 a_n - (n-1)^2 a_{n-1}$, then we get that

$$(n^2 - 1)a_n = (n-1)^2 a_{n-1},$$

that is, $\dfrac{a_n}{a_{n-1}} = \dfrac{n-1}{n+1} (n \geqslant 2)$.

Therefore, $a_n = \dfrac{a_n}{a_{n-1}} \cdot \dfrac{a_{n-1}}{a_{n-2}} \cdot \dfrac{a_{n-2}}{a_{n-3}} \cdots \dfrac{a_2}{a_1} \cdot a_1 = \dfrac{n-1}{n+1} \cdot \dfrac{n-2}{n} \cdot \dfrac{n-3}{n-1} \cdots \dfrac{1}{3} \cdot 1 = \dfrac{2}{n(n+1)}$.

When $n=1$, the value of the above formula is also 1.

Hence, a general formula of the sequence is $a_n = \dfrac{2}{n(n+1)}$.

练习 Exercise

1. Find the first five terms of the sequence.

(1) $a_n = 3n - 7$.   (2) $a_n = 3 - \dfrac{1}{2^n}$.   (3) $a_n = (-2)^n$.   (4) $a_n = \left(\dfrac{1}{3}\right)^n$.

(5) $a_n = \dfrac{n}{n+5}$.   (6) $a_n = \dfrac{5n}{3n^2 - 1}$.   (7) $a_n = \dfrac{1 + (-1)^n}{n}$.   (8) $a_n = \dfrac{(-1)^n}{n^2}$.

(9) $a_n = \dfrac{2^n}{3^2}$.   (10) $a_n = \dfrac{4}{7}$.   (11) $a_n = (-1)^n \left(\dfrac{n}{n+1}\right)$ (12) $a_n = \dfrac{(-1)^{n+1}}{n^2 + 1}$.

2. Find an expression for the nth term of the sequence.

(1) $3, 7, 11, 15, 19, \cdots$.   (2) $0, 3, 8, 15, 24, \cdots$.

(3) $1, -7, 13, -19, 25, -31, \cdots$.   (4) $3, 5, 9, 17, 33, \cdots$.

(5) $1, \dfrac{1}{4}, \dfrac{1}{9}, \dfrac{1}{16}, \dfrac{1}{25}, \cdots$.   (6) $\dfrac{1}{2}, \dfrac{1}{6}, \dfrac{1}{12}, \dfrac{1}{20}, \dfrac{1}{30} \cdots$.

(7) $\dfrac{2}{3}, \dfrac{4}{15}, \dfrac{6}{35}, \dfrac{8}{63}, \dfrac{10}{99}, \cdots$.   (8) $-\dfrac{2}{3}, \dfrac{3}{4}, -\dfrac{4}{5}, \dfrac{5}{6}, -\dfrac{6}{7}, \cdots$.

(9) $1, -1, 1, -1, 1, -1, \cdots$.   (10) $1, 3, 1, 3, 1, 3, \cdots$.

3. Find the first five terms of the sequence defined recursively.

(1) $a_1 = 28$, $a_{k+1} = a_k - 4 (k \in \mathbf{N}^*)$.

(2) $a_1 = 3$, $a_{k+1} = 2(a_k - 1) (k \in \mathbf{N}^*)$.

(3) $a_1 = 1$, $a_{k+1} = a_k^2 + 1 (k \in \mathbf{N}^*)$.

(4) $a_1 = 1$, $a_2 = 2$, $a_k = a_{k-2} + \dfrac{1}{2} a_{k-1} (k \in \mathbf{N}^*, k \geqslant 3)$.

(5) $a_1 = -1$, $a_2 = 1$, $a_k = a_{k-2} + a_{k-1} (k \in \mathbf{N}^*, k \geqslant 3)$.

4. Find the first five terms of each recurrence sequence and find a general formula.

(1) $a_1 = 6$, $a_{n+1} = a_n + 2 (n \in \mathbf{N}^*)$.

(2) $a_1 = 14$, $a_{n+1} = (-2)a_n (n \in \mathbf{N}^*)$.

(3) $a_1 = 1$, $a_{n+1} = a_n + n (n \in \mathbf{N}^*)$.

(4) $a_1 = 3$, $a_{n+1} = -a_n + 8 (n \in \mathbf{N}^*)$.

5. According to the block diagram (as shown in Figure 7 – 2), the output numbers x, y form sequences $\{x_n\}$, $\{y_n\}$ respectively in the order of output. Try to establish the recurrence formula of these two sequences and find the first five terms of the sequences.

6. If the sum of the first nth terms of a sequence satisfies the following conditions respectively, find the general term formula of the corresponding sequences.

(1) $S_n = 2n^2 + 3n + 1$.　　　　　　　(2) $S_n = 2 \cdot 3^n - 1$.

7. A $3 \times 3 \times 3$ cube is composed of 27 unit cubes (the length, width and height of a unit cube are 1 unit). Only the visible faces of each cube are painted yellow, as shown in Figure 7 – 3.

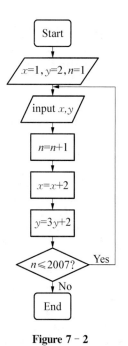

Figure 7 – 2

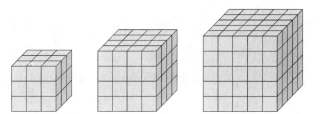

Figure 7 – 3

(1) Complete the table to determine how many unit cubes of the $3 \times 3 \times 3$ cube have 0 yellow faces, 1 yellow face, 2 yellow faces, and 3 yellow faces.

Number of Yellow Cube Faces	0	1	2	3
$3 \times 3 \times 3$				

(2) Repeat part (1) for a $4 \times 4 \times 4$ cube and a $5 \times 5 \times 5$ cube.

(3) Write formulas you could use to repeat part (1) for an $n \times n \times n$ cube.

7.2 ◈ 等差数列　Arithmetic Sequences

等差数列 Arithmetic Sequences

一般地,如果一个数列从第 2 项起,每一项与它的前一项的差等于同一个常数: $a_n - a_{n-1} = d \ (n \geqslant 2)$,那么这个数列叫作**等差数列**(arithmetic sequence),这个常数叫作等差数列的**公差**(common difference). 公差通常用小写字母 d 表示.

最简单的等差数列有 3 项: 若 a, A, b 是等差数列,则 A 叫作 a 与 b 的**等差中项**(arithmetic mean). 由等差数列的定义可知: a, A, b 成等差数列的充要条件是 $A = \dfrac{a+b}{2}$. 也就是,如果三个数成等差数列,那么等差中项等于另两个项的算术平均数.

Definition of the Arithmetic Sequence

A sequence is **arithmetic** when the differences between consecutive terms are the same. So, the sequence

$$a_1, a_2, a_3, \cdots, a_n, \cdots$$

is arithmetic when there is a number d such that

$$a_2 - a_1 = a_3 - a_2 = a_4 - a_3 = \cdots = d.$$

The number d is called the **common difference** of the arithmetic sequence.

等差数列 $\{a_n\}$ 的通项公式 The nth Term of an Arithmetic Sequence

设等差数列 $\{a_n\}$ 的首项是 a_1，公差是 d，根据等差数列的定义有

$$a_n - a_{n-1} = d (n \geqslant 2).$$

所以

$$a_2 - a_1 = d,$$
$$a_3 - a_2 = d,$$
$$a_4 - a_3 = d,$$
$$\cdots$$
$$a_n - a_{n-1} = d (n \geqslant 2).$$

以上 $n-1$ 个等式两边分别相加得：

$$a_n - a_1 = (n-1)d, \text{ 即 } a_n = a_1 + (n-1)d.$$

当 $n=1$ 时，上面等式也成立，这说明当 $n \in \mathbf{N}^*$ 时等式 $a_n = a_1 + (n-1)d$ 都成立，因此它就是等差数列 $\{a_n\}$ 的**通项公式**.

而 $a_n - a_{n-1} = d (n \geqslant 2)$ 或 $a_n = a_{n-1} + d (n \geqslant 2)$ 则是以 a_1 为首项，以 d 为公差的等差数列 $\{a_n\}$ 的**递推公式**.

The nth Term of an Arithmetic Sequence

The nth term of an arithmetic sequence has the form

$$a_n = a_1 + (n-1)d.$$

where d is the common difference and a_1 is the first term.

When you know the nth term of an arithmetic sequence and you know the common difference of the sequence, you can find the $(n+1)$ th term by using the **recursion formula** $a_{n+1} = a_n + d$.

1 Given an arithmetic sequence whose first term is $a_1 = 3$ and whose common difference is $d = 2$.

(1) Find the first five terms of the arithmetic sequence, and graph the terms on a set of coordinate axes.

(2) Find a formula for the nth term of the arithmetic sequence.

Solution：

(1) Since $a_1 = 3$ and $d = 2$, we obtain the first five terms as follows：

$$a_1 = 3,$$
$$a_2 = 3 + 2 = 5,$$
$$a_3 = 3 + 2 \times 2 = 7,$$
$$a_4 = 3 + 2 \times 3 = 9,$$
$$a_5 = 3 + 2 \times 4 = 11.$$

Figure 7 – 4 shows the first five terms of this arithmetic sequence.

(2) We know that the formula for the nth term is of the form $a_n = a_1 + (n-1)d$.

Moreover, because the common difference is $d = 2$ and the first term is $a_1 = 3$, the formula must have the form

$$a_n = 3 + 2(n-1).$$

So, the formula for the nth term is $a_n = 2n + 1$.

Remark: The equation $a_n = 2n + 1$ is a linear function of n, which describes a line, but a_n is defined only when n is a positive integer. The graph of the sequence consists of discrete points on the line $a_n = 2n + 1$, as shown in Figure 7 – 4. In other words, the terms "arithmetic" and "linear" are closely connected.

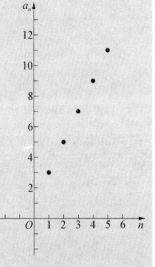

Figure 7 – 4

2 Given that c is the arithmetic mean of a and b.

(1) If $a = 2$ and $b = 32$, find the value of c.

(2) If $a = 13$ and $c = 6$, find the value of b.

Solution: Since c is the arithmetic mean of a and b, we have that $c = \dfrac{a+b}{2}$.

(1) Substituting $a = 2$ and $b = 32$ in the formula $c = \dfrac{a+b}{2}$ gives $c = \dfrac{2+32}{2} = 17$.

(2) Substituting $a = 13$ and $c = 6$ in the formula $c = \dfrac{a+b}{2}$ gives $6 = \dfrac{13+b}{2}$.

Solving the equation gives $b = -1$.

3 In an arithmetic sequence, the 4th term is 20, and the 13th term is 65. Find a formula for the nth term of this sequence.

Solution: We know that $a_4 = 20$ and $a_{13} = 65$. So, we must add the common difference d nine times to the 4th term to obtain the 13th term. Therefore, the 4th and 13th terms of the sequence are related by the equation

$$a_{13} = a_4 + 9d.$$

Because $a_4 = 20$ and $a_{13} = 65$, we can solve for d as follows.

$$65 = 20 + 9d,$$

$$45 = 9d,$$

$$5 = d.$$

Hence, the formula for the nth term of this sequence is

$$a_n = a_4 + (n-4)d = 20 + 5(n-4) = 5n.$$

Remark: If the first term of an arithmetic sequence is a_1 and the common difference is d, according to the formula of general term of the arithmetic sequence, we can know that $a_n = a_1 + (n-$

$1)d$ and $a_m = a_1 + (m-1)d$ (where m、$n \in \mathbf{N}^*$ and $n > m$). Subtracting these two formulas, we get that $a_n - a_m = (n-m)d$, that is, $a_n = a_m + (n-m)d$, which is a generalization of the general formula of arithmetic sequence.

4 Given that the sequence $\{a_n\}$ is a decreasing arithmetic sequence, and $a_1 + a_5 = 10$, $a_2 a_4 = 21$. Find a formula for the nth term of this sequence.

Solution 1: Let the first term of the arithmetic sequence be a_1 and the common difference be d, where $d < 0$.

Since $a_1 + a_5 = 10$ and $a_2 a_4 = 21$, we get that $\begin{cases} a_1 + a_1 + 4d = 10 \\ (a_1 + d)(a_1 + 3d) = 21 \end{cases}$.

Solving the system of equations gives $\begin{cases} a_1 = 9 \\ d = -2 \end{cases}$ or $\begin{cases} a_1 = 1 \\ d = 2 \end{cases}$.

Because $d < 0$, we discard $\begin{cases} a_1 = 1 \\ d = 2 \end{cases}$. Therefore, we know that $\begin{cases} a_1 = 9 \\ d = -2 \end{cases}$.

Hence, the formula for the nth term of this sequence is

$$a_n = a_1 + (n-1)d = 9 - 2(n-1) = -2n + 11.$$

Solution 2: Since $a_2 + a_4 = a_1 + a_5 = 10$, we get that $\begin{cases} a_2 + a_4 = 10 \\ a_2 a_4 = 21 \end{cases}$. Solving the system of equations gives $\begin{cases} a_2 = 7 \\ a_4 = 3 \end{cases}$ or $\begin{cases} a_2 = 3 \\ a_4 = 7 \end{cases}$.

Because the sequence $\{a_n\}$ is a decreasing arithmetic sequence, we discard $\begin{cases} a_2 = 3 \\ a_4 = 7 \end{cases}$. Therefore, we know that $\begin{cases} a_2 = 7 \\ a_4 = 3 \end{cases}$.

Hence, the common difference of the sequence $\{a_n\}$ is $d = \dfrac{a_4 - a_2}{4-2} = \dfrac{3-7}{2} = -2$, and the formula for the nth term of this sequence is $a_n = a_2 + (n-2)d = 7 - 2(n-2) = -2n + 11$.

Remark: If sequence $\{a_n\}$ is an arithmetic sequence, m, n, p, $q \in \mathbf{N}^*$, and $m+n = p+q$, then $a_m + a_n = a_p + a_q$. In particular, $a_1 + a_n = a_2 + a_{n-1} = a_3 + a_{n-2} = \cdots$.

等差数列的前 n 项和 The Sum of a Finite Arithmetic Sequence

等差数列 $\{a_n\}$ 的首项是 a_1，公差是 d，它的前 n 项和

$$S_n = a_1 + a_2 + a_3 + \cdots + a_{n-2} + a_{n-1} + a_n$$
$$= a_1 + (a_1 + d) + (a_1 + 2d) + \cdots + [a_1 + (n-1)d].$$

用另一种方式表示 S_n 为

$$S_n = a_n + a_{n-1} + a_{n-2} + \cdots + a_3 + a_2 + a_1$$
$$= a_n + (a_n - d) + (a_n - 2d) + \cdots + [a_n - (n-1)d].$$

两式相加可得

$$2S_n = \underbrace{(a_1 + a_n) + (a_1 + a_n) + (a_1 + a_n) + \cdots + (a_1 + a_n)}_{n \text{个} (a_1+a_n)} = n(a_1 + a_n)$$

由此得到等差数列 $\{a_n\}$ 的前 n 项和的公式

$$S_n = \frac{n}{2}(a_1 + a_n).$$

因为 $a_n = a_1 + (n-1)d$，所以上面的公式又可以写成

$$S_n = na_1 + \frac{n(n-1)}{2}d.$$

The Sum of a Finite Arithmetic Sequence

The sum of a finite arithmetic sequence with n terms is $S_n = \frac{n}{2}(a_1 + a_n)$.

5 Find the partial sums of the following arithmetic sequences.

(1) Find the 150th partial sum of the arithmetic sequence 5, 18, 31, 44, 57, $\cdots$.

(2) Find the sum of the arithmetic sequence 100, 95, 90, 85, $\cdots$, 25.

Solution:

(1) For this arithmetic sequence, $a_1 = 5$ and $d = 18 - 5 = 13$.

So, $a_n = 5 + 13(n-1)$ and the nth term is $a_n = 13n - 8$.

Therefore, $a_{150} = 13 \times 150 - 8 = 1\,942$, and the sum of the first 150 terms is

$$S_{150} = \frac{n}{2}(a_1 + a_{150}) = \frac{150}{2} \times (5 + 1\,942) = 75 \times 1\,947 = 146\,025.$$

(2) For this arithmetic sequence, $a_1 = 100$ and $d = 95 - 100 = -5$.

So, $a_n = 100 + (-5)(n-1)$ and the nth term is $a_n = -5n + 105$.

Since the nth term is $a_n = -5n + 105 = 25$, we get that $n = 16$.

Hence, the sum of the arithmetic sequence is

$$S_{16} = \frac{n}{2}(a_1 + a_{16}) = \frac{16}{2} \times (100 + 25) = 8 \times 125 = 1\,000.$$

6 Given that the sum of the first 10 terms of an arithmetic sequence is 30 and the sum of the first 20 terms of the arithmetic sequence is 100. Find the 30th partial sum of this arithmetic sequence.

Solution 1: From the given conditions, $S_{10} = 30$, $S_{20} = 100$.

Substituting them into the formula $S_n = na_1 + \frac{n(n-1)}{2}d$, we get that $\begin{cases} 10a_1 + \frac{10 \times 9}{2}d = 30 \\ 20a_1 + \frac{20 \times 19}{2}d = 100 \end{cases}$.

Solving the system of equations gives $d = \frac{2}{5}$, $a_1 = \frac{16}{5}$.

Hence, the sum of the first 30 terms is $S_{30} = 30a_1 + \frac{30 \times 29}{2}d = 210$.

Solution 2: As we know,

$$S_{10}=a_1+a_2+\cdots+a_{10},$$

$$S_{20}-S_{10}=a_{11}+a_{12}+\cdots+a_{20},$$

$$S_{30}-S_{20}=a_{21}+a_{22}+\cdots+a_{30}.$$

Then we get that $(S_{20}-S_{10})-S_{10}=(S_{30}-S_{20})-(S_{20}-S_{10})=10^2d$, that is, the sequence S_{10}, $S_{20}-S_{10}$, $S_{30}-S_{20}$ is arithmetic.

Since $(S_{20}-S_{10})-S_{10}=(S_{30}-S_{20})-(S_{20}-S_{10})$, we obtain that

$$S_{30}=3(S_{20}-S_{10})=3\times(100-30)=210.$$

7 Let the sum of the first n terms of the arithmetic sequence $\{a_n\}$ be S_n. Given that $a_3=12$, $S_{12}>0, S_{13}<0$.

(1) Find the value range of the common difference d.

(2) Point out which of $S_1, S_2, \cdots, S_{12}$ is the largest one and explain.

Solution: (1) From the given conditions, $\begin{cases} S_{12}=12a_1+\dfrac{12\times11}{2}d>0 \\ S_{13}=13a_1+\dfrac{13\times12}{2}d<0 \end{cases}$, so $\begin{cases} 2a_1+11d>0 & \text{①} \\ a_1+6d<0 & \text{②} \end{cases}$.

Since $a_3=a_1+2d=12$, we get that $a_1=12-2d$ ③.

Substituting ③ into ① and ② gives $\begin{cases} 24+7d>0 \\ 12+4d<0 \end{cases}$, therefore, $-\dfrac{24}{7}<d<-3$.

(2) **Solution 1**: It's know from $d<0$ that $\{a_n\}$ is a decreasing sequence, so when $a_n\geqslant0$ and $a_{n+1}<0$ where $1\leqslant n\leqslant12$, $n\in\mathbf{N}$, S_n is largest.

Since $S_{12}=6(a_6+a_7)>0$, $S_{13}=13a_7<0$, we get that $a_7<0$, $a_6>-a_7>0$.

Hence, among $S_1, S_2, \cdots, S_{12}$, S_6 has the largest value.

Solution 2: $S_n=na_1+\dfrac{n(n-1)}{2}d=\dfrac{d}{2}n^2+\left(a_1-\dfrac{d}{2}\right)n$.

Since $a_1=12-2d$, we know that $S_n=\dfrac{d}{2}n^2+\left(12-\dfrac{5}{2}d\right)n$.

Consider the function $f(x)=\dfrac{d}{2}x^2+\left(12-\dfrac{5}{2}d\right)x$, we can know from $\dfrac{d}{2}<0$ that $f(x)$ reaches maximum when $x=-\dfrac{12}{d}+\dfrac{5}{2}$.

For the arithmetic sequence $\{a_n\}$, $-\dfrac{24}{7}<d<-3$, so we get that $6<-\dfrac{12}{d}+\dfrac{5}{2}<\dfrac{13}{2}$.

According to the graph of the quadratic function $f(x)=\dfrac{d}{2}x^2+\left(12-\dfrac{5}{2}d\right)x$, we obtain that S_6 is maximum among $S_1, S_2, \cdots, S_{12}$.

8 A small company sells \$10,000 worth of toys during its first year. The company wants to increase annual sales by \$3,500 each year for the next four years. Assuming that this goal is achieved, find the total sales of the company in the first five years.

Solution: The annual sales form an arithmetic sequence in which

$$a_1 = 10\,000 \text{ and } d = 3\,500.$$

So,

$$a_n = 10\,000 + 3\,500(n-1).$$

and the nth term of the sequence is

$$a_n = 3\,500n + 6\,500.$$

Therefore, the 5th term of the sequence is

$$a_5 = 3\,500 \times 5 + 6\,500 = 24\,000.$$

The sum of the first 5 terms of the sequence is

$$S_5 = \frac{n}{2}(a_1 + a_5) = \frac{5}{2} \times (10\,000 + 24\,000) = 2.5 \times 34\,000 = 85\,000.$$

So, the total sales for the first 5 years will be \$85,000.

练习 Exercise

1. Determine whether the sequence is arithmetic. If so, then find the common difference.

   (1) $10, 8, 6, 4, 2, \cdots$.　　　　　　　　(2) $4, 9, 14, 19, 24, \cdots$.

   (3) $1, 2, 4, 8, 16, \cdots$.　　　　　　　　(4) $80, 40, 20, 10, 5, \cdots$.

   (5) $\dfrac{9}{4}, 2, \dfrac{7}{4}, \dfrac{3}{2}, \dfrac{5}{4}, \cdots$.　　　　　　(6) $5.3, 5.7, 6.1, 6.5, 6.9, \cdots$.

   (7) $\ln 1, \ln 2, \ln 3, \ln 4, \ln 5, \cdots$.　　(8) $1^2, 2^2, 3^2, 4^2, 5^2, \cdots$.

2. Find a formula for a_n for the arithmetic sequence.

   (1) $a_1 = 1$, $d = 3$.　　　　　　　　　(2) $a_1 = 15$, $d = 4$.

   (3) $a_1 = 100$, $d = -8$.　　　　　　　(4) $a_1 = 0$, $d = -\dfrac{2}{3}$.

   (5) $4, \dfrac{3}{2}, -1, -\dfrac{7}{2}, \cdots$.　　　　　　(6) $10, 5, 0, -5, -10, \cdots$.

   (7) $a_1 = 5$, $a_4 = 15$.　　　　　　　(8) $a_1 = -4$, $a_5 = 16$.

   (9) $a_3 = 94$, $a_6 = 85$.　　　　　　(10) $a_5 = 190$, $a_{10} = 115$.

3. Given that c is the arithmetic mean of a and b.

   (1) If $a = 15$ and $b = -1$, find the value of c.

   (2) If $b = -3$ and $c = 5$, find the value of a.

4. Given an arithmetic sequence $\{a_n\}$, with $a_4 + a_5 + a_6 + a_7 = 56$ and $a_4 \cdot a_7 = 187$. Find a formula for the nth term of this sequence.

5. Given that the sum of the first three terms of an arithmetic sequence is 12, and the product of them is 48. Find a formula for the nth term of this sequence.

6. In arithmetic sequences $\{a_n\}$ and $\{b_n\}$, $a_1 = 34$, $b_1 = 66$, $a_{96} + b_{96} = 100$.

   (1) Find the value of $a_{2\,020} + b_{2\,020}$.

(2) Find the 100th partial sum of the sequence $\{a_n + b_n\}$.

7. Find the indicated nth partial sum of the arithmetic sequence.

(1) 8, 20, 32, 44, $\cdots$, $n = 10$.

(2) 75, 70, 65, 60, $\cdots$, $n = 25$.

(3) $a_1 = 100$, $a_{15} = 170$, $n = 20$.

(4) $a_1 = -7$, $a_8 = -35$, $n = 16$.

(5) $a_1 = 39$, $d = -3$, $a_n = 3$.

8. Given an arithmetic sequence $\{a_n\}$.

(1) If the sum of the first 10 terms is $S_{10} = 100$, the sum of the first 100 terms is $S_{100} = 10$, find the sum of the first 110 terms.

(2) If the sum of the first n terms is $S_n = 8$, the sum of the first $2n$ terms is $S_{2n} = 14$, find the sum of the first $3n$ terms.

9. In an arithmetic sequence $\{a_n\}$, $a_1 = 25$, $S_9 = S_{17}$. If the sum of the first n terms S_n reaches the maximum, find the values of n and S_n.

10. In an arithmetic sequence $\{a_n\}$, the sum of the first three terms is 6, and the sum of the last three terms is 60. If $S_n = 231$, find the value of n.

11. Let the sum of the first n terms of the arithmetic sequences $\{a_n\}$ and $\{b_n\}$ be A_n and B_n respectively. If $\dfrac{A_n}{B_n} = \dfrac{7n+1}{4n+27}$ ($n \in \mathbf{N}^*$), find the value of $\dfrac{a_{11}}{b_{11}}$.

12. A company is holding a sales competition in which the top eight sellers receive cash prizes. First place receives a cash prize of \$500, second place receives \$450, third place receives \$400, and so on.

(a) Write a sequence a_n that represents the cash prize awarded in terms of the place n in which the seller places.

(b) Find the total amount of prize money awarded at the competition.

13. A certain brand of printers with the original sales price of \$800 per set are sold in shopping malls A and B. Shopping mall A uses the following method to promote sales: the unit price of one set is \$780, the unit price of two sets is \$760, and so on. For each additional one, the unit price of each set will be reduced by \$20, but the lowest price of each set cannot be lower than \$440. Shopping mall B will sell at 75% of the original price. If a company needs to buy some of these printers, which shopping mall should it go in order to save money?

7.3 ◆ 等比数列 Geometric Sequences

等比数列 Geometric Sequences

一般地，如果一个数列 a_1, a_2, a_3, $\cdots$, a_n, $\cdots$ 从第 2 项起，每一项与它的前一项的比等于同一个非

零常数：$\dfrac{a_n}{a_{n-1}} = r$ ($n \geqslant 2$)，那么这个数列叫作**等比数列**（geometric sequence），这个常数叫作等比数列的

公比（common ratio）. 公比通常用小写字母 r 表示（$r \neq 0$）.

最简单的等比数列有 3 项：若 a, G, b 成等比数列，则 G 叫作 a 与 b 的**等比中项**（geometric mean). 由等比数列的定义可知：a，G，b 成等比数列，则 $G^2 = ab$. 也就是，如果三个数成等比数列，那么等比中项的平方等于另两项的积.

Definition of the Geometric Sequence

A sequence is **geometric** when the ratios of consecutive terms are the same. So, the sequence

$$a_1, a_2, a_3, \cdots, a_n, \cdots$$

is geometric when there is a number r such that

$$\frac{a_2}{a_1} = \frac{a_3}{a_2} = \frac{a_4}{a_3} = \cdots = r, \ r \neq 0.$$

The number r is called the **common ratio** of the geometric sequence.

等比数列 $\{a_n\}$ 的通项公式 The nth Term of an Geometric Sequence

设等比数列 $\{a_n\}$ 的首项是 a_1，公比是 r，根据等比数列的定义有 $\dfrac{a_n}{a_{n-1}} = r (n \geqslant 2)$.

所以

$$\frac{a_2}{a_1} = r$$

$$\frac{a_3}{a_2} = r$$

$$\frac{a_4}{a_3} = r$$

$$\cdots$$

$$\frac{a_n}{a_{n-1}} = r (n \geqslant 2)$$

以上 $n-1$ 个等式两边分别相乘得：

$$\frac{a_n}{a_1} = r^{n-1}, \ 即 \ a_n = a_1 r^{n-1}.$$

当 $n=1$ 时，上面等式也成立，这说明当 $n \in \mathbf{N}^*$ 时等式 $a_n = a_1 r^{n-1}$ 都成立，因此它就是等比数列 $\{a_n\}$ 的**通项公式**.

而 $\dfrac{a_n}{a_{n-1}} = r (n \geqslant 2)$ 或 $a_n = a_{n-1} r (n \geqslant 2)$ 则是以 a_1 为首项，以 r 为公比的等比数列 $\{a_n\}$ 的**递推公式**.

The nth Term of a Geometric Sequence

The nth term of a geometric sequence has the form

$$a_n = a_1 r^{n-1},$$

where r is the common ratio of consecutive terms of the sequence.

When you know the nth term of a geometric sequence and you know the common ratio of the sequence, you can find the $(n+1)$th term by multiplying by r. That is, $a_{n+1} = a_n r$.

1 Given a geometric sequence whose first term is $a_1 = 3$ and whose common ratio is $r = 2$.

(1) Find the first five terms of the geometric sequence, and graph the terms on a set of coordinate axes.

(2) Find a formula for the nth term of the geometric sequence.

Solution:

(1) Since $a_1 = 3$ and $r = 2$, we obtain the first five terms as follows:

$$a_1 = 3$$
$$a_2 = 3 \times 2^1 = 6$$
$$a_3 = 3 \times 2^2 = 12$$
$$a_4 = 3 \times 2^3 = 24$$
$$a_5 = 3 \times 2^4 = 48$$

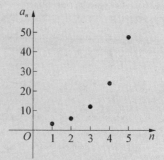

Figure 7-5 shows the first five terms of this geometric sequence.

(2) We know that the formula for the nth term is of the form $a_n = a_1 r^{n-1}$.

Figure 7-5

Moreover, because the common ratio is $r = 2$ and the first term is $a_1 = 3$, the formula must have the form

$$a_n = 3 \cdot 2^{n-1}.$$

Remark: The equation $a_n = 3 \cdot 2^{n-1} = \dfrac{3}{2} \cdot 2^n$ is an exponential function of n, which describes an exponential curve, but a_n is defined only when n is a positive integer. The graph of the sequence consists of discrete points on the exponential curve $a_n = \dfrac{3}{2} \cdot 2^n$, as shown in figure 7-5. In other words, the terms "geometric" and "exponential" are closely connected.

2 Given that c is the geometric mean of a and b,

(1) If $a = 2$ and $b = 32$, find the value of c.

(2) If $a = 4$ and $c = 6$, find the value of b.

Solution: Since c is the geometric mean of a and b, we have that $c^2 = ab$.

(1) Substituting $a = 2$ and $b = 32$ in the formula $c^2 = ab$ gives $c^2 = 2 \times 32 = 64$.
Hence, $c = \pm 8$.

(2) Substituting $a = 4$ and $c = 6$ in the formula $c^2 = ab$ gives $6^2 = 4b$.
Solving the equation gives $b = 9$.

3 In a geometric sequence, the fourth term is 24, and the ninth term is -768. Find a formula for the nth term of this sequence.

Solution: We know that $a_4 = 24$ and $a_9 = -768$. So, we must multiply by the common ratio r five times to the 4th term to obtain the 9th term. Therefore, the 4th and 9th terms of the sequence are related by the equation

$$a_9 = a_4 r^5.$$

Because $a_9 = -768$ and $a_4 = 24$, we can solve for r as follows.

$$-768 = 24r^5,$$
$$-32 = r^5,$$
$$-2 = r.$$

Since $a_4 = a_1 r^3$, we get that $24 = a_1 \cdot (-2)^3$. Solving the equation gives $a_1 = -3$.

Hence, the formula for the nth term of this sequence is

$$a_n = a_1 r^{n-1} = -3 \cdot (-2)^{n-1}.$$

Remark: If the first term of a geometric sequence is a_1 and the common ratio is r, according to the formula of general term of the geometric sequence, we can know that $a_n = a_1 r^{n-1}$ and $a_m = a_1 r^{m-1}$ (where m、$n \in \mathbf{N}^*$ and $n > m$). From these two formulas, we get that $\dfrac{a_n}{a_m} = r^{n-m}$, that is, $a_n = a_m r^{n-m}$, which is a generalization of the general formula of geometric sequence.

4　In a geometric sequence $\{a_n\}$,

(1) if $a_1 a_9 = 64$, $a_3 + a_7 = 20$, find a_{11};

(2) if $a_n > 0$, $a_1 a_{100} = 100$, find the value of $\lg a_1 + \lg a_2 + \lg a_3 + \cdots + \lg a_{100}$.

Solution: (1) In the geometric sequence $\{a_n\}$, $a_3 a_7 = a_1 a_9 = 64$.

Then we have that $\begin{cases} a_3 a_7 = 64 \\ a_3 + a_7 = 20 \end{cases}$, which gives $\begin{cases} a_3 = 16 \\ a_7 = 4 \end{cases}$ or $\begin{cases} a_3 = 4 \\ a_7 = 16 \end{cases}$.

When $a_3 = 16$, $a_7 = 4$, $r^4 = \dfrac{a_7}{a_3} = \dfrac{4}{16} = \dfrac{1}{4}$, so $a_{11} = a_7 r^{11-7} = a_7 r^4 = 4 \times \dfrac{1}{4} = 1$.

When $a_3 = 4$, $a_7 = 16$, $r^4 = \dfrac{a_7}{a_3} = \dfrac{16}{4} = 4$, so $a_{11} = a_7 r^{11-7} = a_7 r^4 = 16 \times 4 = 64$.

In summary, $a_{11} = 1$ or $a_{11} = 64$.

(2) In the geometric sequence $\{a_n\}$, $a_1 a_{100} = a_2 a_{98} = a_3 a_{97} = \cdots = a_{50} a_{51} = 100$.

$$
\begin{aligned}
\lg a_1 + \lg a_2 + \lg a_3 + \cdots + \lg a_{100} &= \lg(a_1 a_2 a_3 \cdots a_{100}) \\
&= \lg[(a_1 a_{100})(a_2 a_{99}) \cdots (a_{50} a_{51})] \\
&= \lg(100)^{50} \\
&= 50 \times \lg 100 \\
&= 50 \times 2 \\
&= 100.
\end{aligned}
$$

Remark: If sequence $\{a_n\}$ is a geometric sequence, m, n, p, $q \in \mathbf{N}^*$, and $m + n = p + q$, then $a_m \cdot a_n = a_p \cdot a_q$. In particular, $a_1 \cdot a_n = a_2 \cdot a_{n-1} = a_3 \cdot a_{n-2} = \cdots$.

等比数列的前 n 项和 The Sum of a Finite Geometric Sequence

设等比数列$\{a_n\}$的首项是a_1，公比是r，它的前n项和

$$S_n = a_1 + a_1 r + a_1 r^2 + \cdots + a_1 r^{n-2} + a_1 r^{n-1}.$$

将等比数列的每一项乘以公比r，得到

$$rS_n = a_1r + a_1r^2 + a_1r^3 + \cdots + a_1r^{n-1} + a_1r^n.$$

两式相减可得 $S_n - rS_n = a_1 - a_1r^n$，即 $(1-r)S_n = a_1(1-r^n)$.

当 $r \neq 1$ 时，$S_n = \dfrac{a_1(1-r^n)}{1-r}$.

因为 $a_n = a_1r^{n-1}$，所以 $S_n = \dfrac{a_1 - a_nr}{1-r}$.

当 $r = 1$ 时，$a_1 = a_2 = \cdots = a_n$，显然 $S_n = na_1$.

综上所述，可以得到以 a_1 为首项，以 r 为公比的等比数列 $\{a_n\}$ 的前 n 项和公式是

$$S_n = \begin{cases} na_1 & (r=1) \\ \dfrac{a_1(1-r^n)}{1-r} = \dfrac{a_1 - a_nr}{1-r} & (r \neq 1) \end{cases}.$$

The Sum of a Finite Geometric Sequence

The sum of a finite geometric sequence

$$a_1, \ a_1r, \ a_1r^2, \ a_1r^3, \ a_1r^4, \ \cdots, \ a_1r^{n-1}.$$

with common ratio $r \neq 1$ is given by $S_n = \displaystyle\sum_{i=1}^{n} a_1r^{i-1} = a_1\left(\dfrac{1-r^n}{1-r}\right)$.

5 Find the partial sum of the following geometric sequences.

(1) Find the 10th partial sum of the geometric sequence $2, \ -6, \ 18, \ -54, \cdots$.

(2) Find the partial sum of the geometric sequence $27, \ 9, \ 3, \cdots, \dfrac{1}{243}$.

Solution:

(1) For this geometric sequence, $a_1 = 2$ and $r = \dfrac{-6}{2} = -3$.

So the sum of the first 10 terms is

$$S_{10} = \frac{a_1(1-r^{10})}{1-r} = \frac{2[1-(-3)^{10}]}{1-(-3)} = -29\ 524.$$

(2) For this geometric sequence, $a_1 = 27$, $r = \dfrac{9}{27} = \dfrac{1}{3}$ and $a_n = \dfrac{1}{243}$.

So we get that $27 \cdot \left(\dfrac{1}{3}\right)^{n-1} = \dfrac{1}{243}$.

Solving the equation gives $n = 9$.

Hence, the partial sum of the geometric sequence is

$$S_9 = \frac{a_1(1-q^9)}{1-q} = \frac{27\left[1-\left(\dfrac{1}{3}\right)^9\right]}{1-\left(\dfrac{1}{3}\right)} = \frac{9\ 841}{243}.$$

6 Given that the sum of the first n terms of the sequence $\{a_n\}$ is $S_n = 3^n + a$. If the sequence $\{a_n\}$ is a geometric sequence, find the condition which constant a satisfies.

Solution: When $n=1$,

$$a_1 = S_1 = 3 + a.$$

When $n \geqslant 2$,

$$a_n = S_n - S_{n-1} = (3^n + a) - (3^{n-1} + a) = 2 \cdot 3^{n-1}.$$

The sequence $\{a_n\}$ is a geometric sequence only when $3 + a = 2$. That is, $a = -1$.

7　Given that all the terms of the geometric sequence $\{a_n\}$ are positive, and the first term is $a_1 = \dfrac{1}{2}$. Let the sum of the first n terms of this sequence be S_n, and $2^{10} S_{30} - (2^{10} + 1) S_{20} + S_{10} = 0$.

(1) Find a formula for the nth term of this sequence.

(2) Find the sum of the first n terms of the sequence $\{n S_n\}$.

Solution: (1) From the given condition, $2^{10} (S_{30} - S_{20}) = S_{20} - S_{10}$, that is,

$$2^{10} (a_{21} + a_{22} + \cdots + a_{30}) = a_{11} + a_{12} + \cdots + a_{20},$$

$$2^{10} \cdot r^{10} (a_{11} + a_{12} + \cdots + a_{20}) = a_{11} + a_{12} + \cdots + a_{20}.$$

Since $a_n > 0$, we have that $2^{10} r^{10} = 1$. Solving the equation gives $r = \dfrac{1}{2}$.

Hence, $a_n = a_1 r^{n-1} = \dfrac{1}{2^n}, n = 1, 2, 3, \cdots$.

(2) Because the sequence $\{a_n\}$ is a geometric sequence whose first term is $a_1 = \dfrac{1}{2}$ and whose

common ratio is $r = \dfrac{1}{2}$, we get that $S_n = \dfrac{\dfrac{1}{2}\left(1 - \dfrac{1}{2^n}\right)}{1 - \dfrac{1}{2}} = 1 - \dfrac{1}{2^n}$.

Therefore, $n S_n = n - \dfrac{n}{2^n}$.

Let T_n be the sum of the first n terms of the sequence $\{n S_n\}$, then

$$T_n = (1 + 2 + \cdots + n) - \left(\dfrac{1}{2} + \dfrac{2}{2^2} + \cdots + \dfrac{n}{2^n}\right).$$

Multiplying the series for T_n by $\dfrac{1}{2}$ gives

$$\dfrac{T_n}{2} = \dfrac{1}{2}(1 + 2 + \cdots + n) - \left(\dfrac{1}{2^2} + \dfrac{2}{2^3} + \cdots + \dfrac{n-1}{2^n} + \dfrac{n}{2^{n+1}}\right).$$

Subtracting the above two equations, we get that

$$\dfrac{T_n}{2} = \dfrac{1}{2}(1 + 2 + \cdots + n) - \left(\dfrac{1}{2} + \dfrac{1}{2^2} + \cdots + \dfrac{1}{2^n}\right) + \dfrac{n}{2^{n+1}} = \dfrac{n(n+1)}{4} - \dfrac{\dfrac{1}{2}\left(1 - \dfrac{1}{2^n}\right)}{1 - \dfrac{1}{2}} + \dfrac{n}{2^{n+1}}.$$

That is, $T_n = \dfrac{n(n+1)}{2} + \dfrac{1}{2^{n-1}} + \dfrac{n}{2^n} - 2$.

8 An investor deposits \$100 on the first day of each month in an account that pays 3% interest compounded monthly. What is the balance by the end of 3 years?

Solution: To find the balance in the account after 36 months, consider each of the 36 deposits separately. The first deposit will gain interest for 36 months, and its balance will be

$$a_{36} = 100 \times \left(1 + \frac{0.03}{12}\right)^{36} = 100 \times (1.002\ 5)^{36}.$$

The second deposit will gain interest for 35 months, and its balance will be

$$a_{35} = 100 \times \left(1 + \frac{0.03}{12}\right)^{35} = 100 \times (1.002\ 5)^{35}.$$

The last deposit will gain interest for only 1 month, and its balance will be

$$a_1 = 100 \times \left(1 + \frac{0.03}{12}\right)^{1} = 100 \times 1.002\ 5 = 100.25.$$

The total balance in the annuity will be the sum of the balances of the 36 deposits. Using the formula for the sum of a finite geometric sequence, with $a_1 = 100.25$, $r = 1.002\ 5$, and $n = 36$, we have

$$S_{36} = \frac{a_1(1 - r^{36})}{1 - r} = \frac{100.25 \times [1 - (1.002\ 5)^{36}]}{1 - 1.002\ 5} \approx 3\ 771.46.$$

So, the balance by the end of 3 years will be approximately \$3 771.46.

练习 Exercise

1. Determine whether the sequence is geometric. If so, find the common ratio.

(1) 2, 10, 50, 250, ⋯.　　　　　　　(2) 3, 12, 21, 30, ⋯.

(3) $\frac{1}{8}, \frac{1}{4}, \frac{1}{2}, 1, \cdots$.　　　　　　　(4) $9, -6, 4, -\frac{8}{3}, \cdots$.

(5) $1, \frac{1}{2}, \frac{1}{3}, \frac{1}{4}, \cdots$.　　　　　　　(6) 5, 1, 0.2, 0.04, ⋯.

(7) $1, -\sqrt{7}, 7, -7\sqrt{7}, \cdots$.　　　　　　(8) $2, \frac{4}{\sqrt{3}}, \frac{8}{3}, \frac{16}{3\sqrt{3}}, \cdots$.

2. Find a formula for the nth term of the geometric sequence.

(1) $a_1 = 4$, $q = \frac{1}{2}$.　　　　　　　(2) $a_1 = 5$, $q = \frac{7}{2}$.

(3) $a_1 = 6$, $q = -\frac{1}{3}$.　　　　　　(4) $a_1 = 64$, $q = -\frac{1}{4}$.

(5) $12, 6, 3, \frac{3}{2}, \cdots$.　　　　　　　(6) $-2, 6, -18, 54, \cdots$.

(7) $a_1 = 2$, $a_4 = 16$.　　　　　　　(8) $a_1 = 512$, $a_5 = 32$.

(9) $a_3 = 36$, $a_6 = -972$.　　　　　　(10) $a_3 = 120$, $a_5 = 240$.

3. Given that c is the geometric mean of a and b.

(1) If $a = 3$ and $b = 8$, find the value of c.

(2) If $b = -4$ and $c = 12$, find the value of a.

4. Given that the sequence $\{a_n\}$ is a geometric sequence, and $a_3 + a_6 = 36$, $a_4 + a_7 = 18$. If $a_n = \dfrac{1}{2}$, find the value of n.

5. Let $\{a_n\}$ be a geometric sequence whose terms are all positive.

   (1) If $a_2 a_4 + 2a_3 a_5 + a_4 a_6 = 25$, find the value of $a_3 + a_5$.

   (2) If $a_5 \cdot a_6 = 81$, find the value of $\log_3 a_1 + \log_3 a_2 + \log_3 a_3 + \cdots + \log_3 a_{10}$.

6. Find the indicated nth partial sums of the geometric sequence.

   (1) $10, 20, 40, 80, \cdots, n = 10$.   (2) $3, -6, 12, -24, \cdots, n = 9$.

   (3) $45, 15, 5, \dfrac{5}{3}, \cdots, n = 6$.   (4) $a_1 = -2.7$, $r = -\dfrac{1}{3}$, $n = 5$.

   (5) $a_1 = 6$, $a_4 = \dfrac{3}{4}$, $n = 7$.

7. Use summation notation to write the sum.

   (1) $10 + 30 + 90 + \cdots + 7\,290$.   (2) $15 - 3 + \dfrac{3}{5} - \cdots - \dfrac{3}{625}$.

   (3) $0.1 + 0.4 + 1.6 + \cdots + 102.4$.   (4) $32 + 24 + 18 + \cdots + 10.125$.

8. In a sequence $\{a_n\}$, the first term is $a_1 = \dfrac{2}{3}$, and $a_{n+1} = \dfrac{2a_n}{a_n + 1}$, $n = 1, 2, 3, \cdots$.

   (1) Prove that the sequence $\left\{\dfrac{1}{a_n} - 1\right\}$ is a geometric sequence.

   (2) Find the sum of the first n terms of the sequence $\left\{\dfrac{n}{a_n}\right\}$.

9. In a sequence $\{a_n\}$, let S_n be the sum of its first n terms, and $S_{n+1} = 4a_n + 2$ $(n = 1, 2, 3 \cdots)$, $a_1 = 1$.

   (1) If $b_n = a_{n+1} - 2a_n$ $(n = 1, 2, 3 \cdots)$, prove that the sequence $\{b_n\}$ is a geometric sequence, and find a formula for the nth term of this sequence.

   (2) If $c_n = \dfrac{a_n}{2^n}$ $(n = 1, 2, 3 \cdots)$, prove that the sequence $\{c_n\}$ is an arithmetic sequence, and find a formula for the nth term of this sequence.

   (3) Find a formula for the nth term of the sequence $\{a_n\}$ and the sum of its first n terms.

10. If someone sends the good news to 2 people within one hour after hearing the good news, this 2 people will send the good news to the other 2 people who have not heard the good news at the same speed, and each person only send the news to 2 people, and so on. What is the time required to spread the good news to a small town with 2 047 people (including the first person) ?

11. Considering the social and economic benefits, a village invests money in ecological environment construction and develops tourism industry. According to the plan, 8 million yuan will be invested in this year, and the annual investment will be reduced by $\dfrac{1}{5}$ compared with the previous year. The income of local tourism industry is estimated to be 4 million yuan this year. Due to the promotion effect of the construction on tourism, it is expected that the tourism revenue in the future will increase by $\dfrac{1}{4}$ per year compared with that of the previous year.

    (1) Let the total investment in n years (this year as the first year) be a_n million yuan, and the

total income of tourism be b_n million yuan. Find the expressions of a_n and b_n in terms of n.

(2) How many years at least will it take so that the total revenue of tourism exceeds the total investment?

7.4 ◇ 数学归纳法 Mathematical Induction

多米诺骨牌(domino)是一种用木制、骨制或塑料制成的长方体骨牌. 玩时将骨牌按一定间距的尺寸排成单行,或分行排成一片,轻轻碰倒第一枚骨牌,其余的骨牌就会产生连锁反应,依次倒下,或形成一条长龙,或形成一幅图案,骨牌撞击之声,清脆悦耳;骨牌倒下之时,变化万千.

多米诺是一种游戏,多米诺是一种运动,多米诺还是一种文化.它的尺寸、重量标准依据多米诺运动规则制成,适用于专业比赛,与蝴蝶效应相似.

数学归纳法Mathematical Induction:

与正整数 n 有关的数学命题是数学研究中常见的一类问题,对于这类问题,我们可以通过举反例来说明命题是错误的,但不可能用穷举法来验证其正确性,而往往采用**数学归纳法**进行证明,它的证明步骤如下:

(1) 证明当 n 取第一个值 n_0($n_0 \in \mathbf{N}^*$,例如 $n_0 = 1$ 或 $n_0 = 2$)时,命题成立.

(2) 假设当 $n = k$ ($k \in \mathbf{N}^*$, $k \geqslant n_0$)时命题成立,再证明当 $n = k + 1$ 时命题也成立.

根据(1)、(2)两个步骤,我们可以断定这个命题对于从 n_0 开始的所有正整数 n 都成立.

Proof by Mathematical Induction

Let P be a statement involving the positive integer n.

Step 1. Show that P is true for $n = n_0$.

Step 2. Assume that P is true for $n = k$, where k is a positive integer, $k \geqslant n_0$, and then prove that P must be true for $n = k + 1$.

Then the statement P must be true for all positive integers $n \geqslant n_0$.

用数学归纳法证明命题的这两个步骤,是缺一不可的.如果只完成第(1)步而缺少第(2)步,不能说明命题对于从 n_0 开始的所有正整数 n 都成立. 例如,法国数学家费马的猜想:对于任意自然数, $2^{2^n} + 1$ 都是质数.这是一个不幸的猜想,瑞士数学家欧拉发现当 $n = 5$ 时, $2^{2^5} + 1 = 641 \times 6\,700\,417$ 不是质数.

同样,若只有第(2)步而缺少第(1)步,也可能得出不正确的结论. 例如,若用数学归纳法证明命题: 5^n , $n \in \mathbf{N}^*$ 都是偶数. 在缺少第(1)步的情况下,我们假设当 $n = k$, $k \in \mathbf{N}^*$ 时, 5^k 是偶数,那么当 $n = k + 1$ 时,因为 5^k 是偶数,所以 $5^{k+1} = 5^k \cdot 5$ 也是偶数.而事实上,当 $n = 1$ 时,命题就不成立.这说明缺少第(1)步这个基础,第(2)步的归纳假设就没有根据,第(2)步就成了空中楼阁,证明也就没有意义了.

1 Use mathematical induction to prove the formula

$S_n = 1 + 3 + 5 + 7 + \cdots + (2n - 1) = n^2$ for all integers $n \geqslant 1$.

Solution :

Step 1 When $n = 1$, the formula is valid, because $S_1 = 1 = 1^2$.

Step 2 Assuming that the formula

$$S_k = 1 + 3 + 5 + 7 + \cdots + (2k - 1) = k^2$$

---

is true, we must show that the formula $S_{k+1} = (k+1)^2$ is true.

$$S_{k+1} = 1 + 3 + 5 + 7 + \cdots + (2k-1) + [2(k+1)-1]$$
$$= [1 + 3 + 5 + 7 + \cdots + (2k-1)] + (2k+2-1)$$
$$= S_k + (2k+1)$$
$$= k^2 + 2k + 1$$
$$= (k+1)^2.$$

Combining the results of step 1 and step 2, you can conclude by mathematical induction that the formula is valid for all integers $n \geqslant 1$.

Remark: When using mathematical induction to prove a summation formula (such as the one in Example 1), it is helpful to think of S_{k+1} as $S_{k+1} = S_k + a_{k+1}$, where a_{k+1} is the $(k+1)$ th term of the original sum.

2 Use mathematical induction to prove the formula

$$S_n = 1^2 + 2^2 + 3^2 + 4^2 + \cdots + n^2 = \frac{n(n+1)(n+2)}{6} \text{ for all integers } n \geqslant 1.$$

Solution:

Step 1　When $n = 1$, the formula is valid, because $S_1 = 1 = \dfrac{1(2)(3)}{6}$.

Step 2　Assuming that

$$S_k = 1^2 + 2^2 + 3^2 + 4^2 + \cdots + k^2 = \frac{k(k+1)(2k+1)}{6},$$

we must show that

$$S_{k+1} = \frac{(k+1)(k+1+1)[2(k+1)+1]}{6}$$
$$= \frac{(k+1)(k+2)(2k+3)}{6}.$$

To do this, we can write the following.

$$S_{k+1} = S_k + a_{k+1}$$
$$= (1^2 + 2^2 + 3^2 + 4^2 + \cdots + k^2) + (k+1)^2$$
$$= \frac{k(k+1)(2k+1)}{6} + (k+1)^2$$
$$= \frac{k(k+1)(2k+1) + 6(k+1)^2}{6}$$
$$= \frac{(k+1)[k(2k+1) + 6(k+1)]}{6}$$
$$= \frac{(k+1)(2k^2 + 7k + 6)}{6}$$
$$= \frac{(k+1)(k+2)(2k+3)}{6}.$$

Combining the results of step 1 and step 2, we can conclude by mathematical induction that the formula is valid for all positive integers n.

The formula in Example 2 is one of the collection of useful summation formulas. These formulas dealing with the sums of various powers of the first n positive integers are as follows.

Sums of the Powers of Integers

1. $1+2+3+4+\cdots+n=\dfrac{n(n+1)}{2}$.

2. $1^2+2^2+3^2+4^2+\cdots+n^2=\dfrac{n(n+1)(2n+1)}{6}$.

3. $1^3+2^3+3^3+4^3+\cdots+n^3=\dfrac{n^2(n+1)^2}{4}$.

4. $1^4+2^4+3^4+4^4+\cdots+n^4=\dfrac{n(n+1)(2n+1)(3n^2+3n-1)}{30}$.

3 Use mathematical induction to prove the inequality

$$1+\frac{1}{2}+\frac{1}{3}+\cdots+\frac{1}{2^n-1}>\frac{n}{2} \text{ for all integers } n\geqslant 1.$$

Solution:

Step 1 When $n=1$, the inequality holds, because $1>\dfrac{1}{2}$.

Step 2 Assuming that the inequality holds for $n=k$,

$$1+\frac{1}{2}+\frac{1}{3}+\cdots+\frac{1}{2^k-1}>\frac{k}{2},$$

we must show that the inequality holds for $n=k+1$.

$$\left(1+\frac{1}{2}+\frac{1}{3}+\cdots+\frac{1}{2^k-1}\right)+\left(\frac{1}{2^k}+\frac{1}{2^k+1}+\cdots\frac{1}{2^{k+1}-1}\right)$$

$$>\frac{k}{2}+\left(\frac{1}{2^k}+\frac{1}{2^k+1}+\cdots\frac{1}{2^{k+1}-1}\right)$$

$$>\frac{k}{2}+\frac{2^k}{2^{k+1}-1}$$

$$>\frac{k}{2}+\frac{2^k}{2^{k+1}}$$

$$=\frac{k}{2}+\frac{1}{2}$$

$$=\frac{k+1}{2}.$$

Combining the results of step 1 and step 2, we can conclude by mathematical induction that the inequality holds for all positive integers n.

4 Prove that 3 is a factor of 4^n-1 for all positive integers n.

Solution:

Step 1 For $n=1$, the statement is true because

$$4^1-1=3.$$

So, 3 is a factor.

Step 2 Assuming that 3 is a factor of $4^k - 1$, we must show that 3 is a factor of $4^{k+1} - 1$.

To do this, write the following.

$$4^{k+1} - 1 = 4^{k+1} - 4^k + 4^k - 1$$
$$= 4^k(4-1) + (4^k - 1)$$
$$= 4^k \cdot 3 + (4^k - 1).$$

Because 3 is a factor of $4^k \cdot 3$ and 3 is also a factor of $4^k - 1$, it follows that 3 is a factor of $4^{k+1} - 1$.

Combining the results of step 1 and step 2, we can conclude by mathematical induction that 3 is a factor of $4^n - 1$ for all positive integers n.

5 Let there be n straight lines in a plane, with no parallel pairs or concurrent triples. Prove the following claims.

(1) There are altogether $f(n) = \frac{1}{2}n(n-1)$ points of intersections.

(2) They can form $g(n) = n^2$ pieces of lines, including segments, rays and entire lines.

(3) The plane is divided into $h(n) = \frac{1}{2}n(n+1) + 1$ regions.

Solution:

Step 1 For $n = 1$, the statement is true because $f(1) = 0$, $g(1) = 1$, $h(1) = 2$.

Step 2 Assuming that the statement is true for $n = k$,

$$f(k) = \frac{1}{2}k(k-1), \ g(k) = k^2, \ h(k) = \frac{1}{2}k(k+1) + 1,$$

we must show that the statement is true for $n = k+1$.

As the $(k+1)$ th line intersects all of the other k lines at distinct points, we have

$$f(k+1) = f(k) + k = \frac{1}{2}k(k-1) + k = \frac{1}{2}k(k+1).$$

As the $(k+1)$ th line is divided by the other k lines into $k+1$ pieces, and each of the other k lines is divided by the points of intersections with the $(k+1)$ th line, we have

$$g(k+1) = g(k) + (k+1) + k = g(k) + 2k + 1 = k^2 + 2k + 1 = (k+1)^2.$$

As the $(k+1)$ th line is divided into $k+1$ pieces, and each piece divides the portion of the plane containing it, we have

$$h(k+1) = h(k) + (k+1) = \frac{1}{2}k(k+1) + 1 + (k+1) = \frac{1}{2}(k+1)(k+2) + 1.$$

Combining the results of step 1 and step 2, you can conclude by mathematical induction that the statement is true for all positive integers n.

6 Find a formula for the finite sum and prove its validity.

$$\frac{1}{1 \cdot 2} + \frac{1}{2 \cdot 3} + \frac{1}{3 \cdot 4} + \frac{1}{4 \cdot 5} + \cdots + \frac{1}{n(n+1)}.$$

Solution：

Begin by finding the first few sums.

$$S_1 = \frac{1}{1 \cdot 2} = \frac{1}{2} = \frac{1}{1+1},$$

$$S_2 = \frac{1}{1 \cdot 2} + \frac{1}{2 \cdot 3} = \frac{4}{6} = \frac{2}{3} = \frac{2}{2+1},$$

$$S_3 = \frac{1}{1 \cdot 2} + \frac{1}{2 \cdot 3} + \frac{1}{3 \cdot 4} = \frac{9}{12} = \frac{3}{4} = \frac{3}{3+1}.$$

For this sequence, it appears that the formula for the kth sum is

$$S_k = \frac{1}{1 \cdot 2} + \frac{1}{2 \cdot 3} + \frac{1}{3 \cdot 4} + \frac{1}{4 \cdot 5} + \cdots + \frac{1}{k(k+1)} = \frac{k}{k+1}.$$

To prove the validity of this hypothesis, use mathematical induction. Note that we have already verified the formula for $n=1$, so begin by assuming that the formula is valid for $n=k$ and trying to show that it is valid for $n=k+1$.

$$S_{k+1} = \left[\frac{1}{1 \cdot 2} + \frac{1}{2 \cdot 3} + \frac{1}{3 \cdot 4} + \frac{1}{4 \cdot 5} + \cdots + \frac{1}{k(k+1)} \right] + \frac{1}{(k+1)(k+2)}$$

$$= \frac{k}{k+1} + \frac{1}{(k+1)(k+2)}$$

$$= \frac{k(k+2)+1}{(k+1)(k+2)} = \frac{k^2+2k+1}{(k+1)(k+2)} = \frac{(k+1)^2}{(k+1)(k+2)} = \frac{k+1}{k+2}.$$

So, by mathematical induction the hypothesis is valid.

7　The first four terms of a sequence are 1, $1+2+1$, $1+2+3+2+1$, $1+2+3+4+3+2+1$. Find a formula for $a_n = 1+2+3+\cdots+(n-1)+n+(n-1)+\cdots+3+2+1$, and use mathematical induction to prove it.

Solution：

Begin by finding the first four terms as follows：

$$1 = 1^2,$$
$$1+2+1 = 4 = 2^2,$$
$$1+2+3+2+1 = 9 = 3^2,$$
$$1+2+3+4+3+2+1 = 16 = 4^2.$$

For this sequence, it appears that the formula for the nth term is

$$a_n = 1+2+3+\cdots+(n-1)+n+(n-1)+\cdots+3+2+1 = n^2.$$

To prove the validity of this hypothesis, use mathematical induction. Note that we have already verified the formula for $n=1$.

Now assuming that the formula is valid for $n=k$, that is,

$$a_k = 1+2+3+\cdots+(k-1)+k+(k-1)+\cdots+3+2+1 = k^2,$$

we must show that the formula $a_{k+1} = (k+1)^2$ is true.

$$a_{k+1} = 1 + 2 + 3 + \cdots + k + (k+1) + k + \cdots + 3 + 2 + 1$$
$$= a_k + (k+1) + k$$
$$= k^2 + 2k + 1$$
$$= (k+1)^2.$$

So, by mathematical induction the hypothesis is valid.

8 If m is a factor of $f(n) = (2n+7) \cdot 3^n + 9$ for all positive integers n, find the largest positive integer m and prove it.

Solution:

As $f(1) = (2+7) \cdot 3^1 + 9 = 36$,

$f(2) = (4+7) \cdot 3^2 + 9 = 108 = 36 \times 3$,

$f(3) = (6+7) \cdot 3^2 + 9 = 360 = 36 \times 10$,

$f(4) = (8+7) \cdot 3^4 + 9 = 1\ 224 = 36 \times 24$,

it appears that $m = 36$.

To prove that 36 is a factor of $f(n) = (2n+7) \cdot 3^n + 9$ for all positive integers n, use mathematical induction.

Note that we have already verified that for $n = 1$, 36 is a factor of $f(1) = 36$.

Now assuming that 36 is a factor of $f(k) = (2k+7) \cdot 3^k + 9$, we must show that 36 is a factor of $f(k+1)$.

$$f(k+1) = [2(k+1)+7] \cdot 3^{k+1} + 9 = 3[(2k+7) \cdot 3^k + 9] + 18(3^{k-1} - 1)$$
$$= 3f(k) + 18(3^{k-1} - 1).$$

As $3^{k-1} - 1$ is an even number for all positive integer k, we can see that 36 is a factor of $18(3^{k-1} - 1)$. So 36 is a factor of $f(k+1)$.

Therefore, 36 is a factor of $f(n) = (2n+7) \cdot 3^n + 9$ for all positive integers n.

For the integers m that larger than 36, m is not a factor of $f(1) = 36$. Hence, we can conclude that the largest positive integer m is 36.

练习 Exercise

1. Use mathematical induction to prove the formula for every positive integer n.

(1) $1^3 + 2^3 + 3^3 + \cdots + n^3 = \dfrac{n^2 (n+1)^2}{4}$.

(2) $1^2 + 3^2 + 5^2 + \cdots + (2n-1)^2 = \dfrac{n(2n-1)(2n+1)}{3}$.

(3) $(n+1)(n+2)(n+3)\cdots(n+n) = 2^n \cdot 1 \cdot 3 \cdot \cdots \cdot (2n-1)$.

(4) $\displaystyle\sum_{i=1}^{n} i(i+1) = \dfrac{n(n+1)(n+2)}{3}$.

2. Use mathematical induction to prove the inequality for the indicated integer values of n.

(1) $\dfrac{1}{\sqrt{1}} + \dfrac{1}{\sqrt{2}} + \dfrac{1}{\sqrt{3}} + \cdots + \dfrac{1}{\sqrt{n}} > \sqrt{n}$, $(n \geqslant 2, n \in \mathbf{N}^*)$.

(2) $\dfrac{1}{n+1}+\dfrac{1}{n+2}+\dfrac{1}{n+3}+\cdots+\dfrac{1}{2n}>\dfrac{13}{24}$ $(n\geqslant 2,\ n\in \mathbf{N}^{*})$.

(3) $1+\dfrac{1}{2}+\dfrac{1}{3}+\cdots+\dfrac{1}{2^{n}}\leqslant\dfrac{1}{2}+n$ $(n\in\mathbf{N}^{*})$.

(4) $|\sin nx|\leqslant n|\sin x|$ $(n\in\mathbf{N}^{*})$.

3. Use mathematical induction to prove the following statements for all positive integers n.

(1) 3 is a factor of $n^{3}+3n^{2}+2n$.

(2) 5 is a factor of $2^{2n+1}+3^{2n-1}$.

(3) 9 is a factor of $(3n+1)\cdot 7^{n}-1$.

(4) $x^{2}+x+1$ is a factor of $x^{n+2}+(x+1)^{2n+1}$.

4. Use mathematical induction to prove the formula:

$$\tan\alpha\cdot\tan 2\alpha+\tan 2\alpha\cdot\tan 3\alpha+\cdots+\tan(n-1)\alpha\cdot\tan n\alpha=\dfrac{\tan n\alpha}{\tan\alpha}-n\quad(n\geqslant 2,\ n\in\mathbf{N}^{*}).$$

5. Let there be n circles in a plane, where every two circles intersect at two points and every three circles do not intersect at the same point. Prove that the plane is divided into $n^{2}-n+2$ regions.

6. In a sequence $\{a_{n}\}$, the first term is $a_{1}=\dfrac{1}{2}$, and $a_{n+1}=\dfrac{a_{n}}{2a_{n}+3}$ $(n\in\mathbf{N}^{*})$.

(1) Find a_{1}, a_{2}, a_{3} and a_{4}.

(2) Find a general formula for $\{a_{n}\}$ and prove it.

7. In a sequence $\{a_{n}\}$ whose terms are all positive, let S_{n} be the sum of its first n terms, with $S_{n}=\dfrac{1}{2}\left(a_{n}+\dfrac{1}{a_{n}}\right)$ $(n=1,\ 2,\ 3\cdots)$.

(1) Find a_{1}, a_{2}, a_{3} and a_{4}.

(2) Find a general formula for $\{a_{n}\}$ and prove it.

8. If the formula $1\cdot 2^{2}+2\cdot 3^{2}+3\cdot 4^{2}+\cdots+n(n+1)^{2}=\dfrac{n(n+1)}{12}(an^{2}+bn+c)$ holds for all positive integers n, find the constants a, b, c.

9. Let $\{a_{n}\}$ be a sequence defined by the general formula $a_{n}=n^{2}+n$. If the formula $\dfrac{1}{1+a_{1}}+\dfrac{1}{2+a_{2}}+\cdots+\dfrac{1}{n+a_{n}}=\dfrac{pn^{2}+qn+r}{4(n+1)(n+2)}$ holds for all positive integers n, find the constants p, q, r.

10. In the sequences $\{a_{n}\}$ and $\{b_{n}\}$, $a_{n}=1+3+5+\cdots+(2n+1)$, $b_{n}=1+2+2^{2}+\cdots+2^{n-1}$, $n=1$, 2, $3\cdots$. Determine whether a_{n} or b_{n} is the larger one of two and prove it.

7.5 ◆ 数列的极限 Limits of the Infinite Sequences

数列的极限 Limits of the Infinite Sequences

　　一般地,在项数 n 无限增大的变化过程中,如果无穷数列 $\{a_{n}\}$ 中的项 a_{n} 无限趋近于某个常数 A,那么 A 叫作**数列** $\{a_{n}\}$ **的极限**,或叫作**数列** $\{a_{n}\}$ **收敛于** A.记作 $\lim\limits_{n\to\infty}a_{n}=A$.读作:$n$ 趋向无穷大时,a_{n} 的极限等于 A.

常用数列的极限

(1) $\lim\limits_{n\to\infty}\dfrac{1}{n}=0$;

(2) $\lim\limits_{n\to\infty}C=C$ (C 是常数);

(3) $|a|<1$ 时,$\lim\limits_{n\to\infty}a^n=0$;

(4) $\lim\limits_{n\to\infty}\left(1+\dfrac{1}{n}\right)^n=e$.

In everyday usage, the word "limit" sometimes suggests a barrier, but in mathematical usage it is better to think of a limit as a target. If a_n becomes arbitrarily close to a single number A as n goes to infinity, the limit of a_n as n goes to infinity is A. This limit is written as

$$\lim_{n\to\infty} a_n = A.$$

Consider the infinite geometric sequence

$$\frac{1}{2},\ \frac{1}{4},\ \frac{1}{8},\ \cdots,\ \left(\frac{1}{2}\right)^n,\ \cdots$$

When we substitute larger and larger values of n, $a_n=\left(\dfrac{1}{2}\right)^n$ becomes a smaller and smaller positive number. It never becomes zero, but we can make a_n come as close to zero as we like just by finding a large enough value for n. The preceding discussion can be summarized by the following equation:

$$\lim_{n\to\infty}\left(\frac{1}{2}\right)^n=0.$$

Limit Laws

If $\lim\limits_{n\to\infty} a_n=A$ and $\lim\limits_{n\to\infty} b_n=B$, then

(1) $\lim\limits_{n\to\infty}(a_n\pm b_n)=\lim\limits_{n\to\infty} a_n\pm\lim\limits_{n\to\infty} b_n=A\pm B$.

(2) if C is a constant, then $\lim\limits_{n\to\infty}(C\cdot b_n)=\lim\limits_{n\to\infty} C\cdot\lim\limits_{n\to\infty} b_n=C\cdot B$.

(3) $\lim\limits_{n\to\infty}(a_n\cdot b_n)=\lim\limits_{n\to\infty} a_n\cdot\lim\limits_{n\to\infty} b_n=A\cdot B$.

(4) $\lim\limits_{n\to\infty}\dfrac{a_n}{b_n}=\dfrac{\lim\limits_{n\to\infty} a_n}{\lim\limits_{n\to\infty} b_n}=\dfrac{A}{B}\ (B\neq 0)$.

数列极限的运算性质表明:如果两个数列都有极限,那么这两个数列对应各项的和、差、积、商所组成的数列也都有极限,其极限分别等于这两个数列的极限的和、差、积、商(其中作为除数的数列,它的极限不能为零).

两个数列的极限的运算法则还可以推广到有限个数列的情况.例如:如果 $\lim\limits_{n\to\infty} a_n=A$,$\lim\limits_{n\to\infty} b_n=B$,$\lim\limits_{n\to\infty} c_n=C$,那么 $\lim\limits_{n\to\infty}(a_n+b_n-c_n)=A+B-C$,$\lim\limits_{n\to\infty}\left(\dfrac{a_n\cdot b_n}{c_n}\right)=\dfrac{A\cdot B}{C}\ (C\neq 0)$ 等.

1 True or False

(1) The limit of $\dfrac{1+(-1)^n}{2}$ as n goes to infinity is 0 and 1.

(2) The limit of $(-1)^{n+1}\cdot\dfrac{1}{2^{n-1}}$ as n goes to infinity is 0.

(3) The sequence $\sin 1,\ \sin\dfrac{1}{2},\ \sin\dfrac{1}{3},\ \cdots,\ \sin\dfrac{1}{n},\ \cdots$ has no limit.

(4) The sequence $\dfrac{1}{3}$, $\dfrac{1}{3^2}$, $\dfrac{1}{3^3}$, $\cdots$, $\dfrac{1}{3^{10\,000}}$ has limit 0.

(5) If the nth term of the sequence is $a_n = \begin{cases} \dfrac{1}{n^2}, & 1 \leqslant n \leqslant 1\,000 \\[2mm] \dfrac{n^2}{n^2-2n}, & n \geqslant 1\,001 \end{cases}$, we get that $\lim\limits_{n \to \infty} a_n = 0$ when

$n \leqslant 1\,000$ and $\lim\limits_{n \to \infty} a_n = 1$ when $n \geqslant 1\,001$.

Solution：

(1) False. If the limit of a sequence exists, its limit is unique.

(2) True. The terms of the sequence approaches 0 as n gets larger and larger, so the limit of

$(-1)^{n+1} \cdot \dfrac{1}{2^{n-1}}$ as n goes to infinity is 0.

(3) False. As n goes to infinity, the limit of $\dfrac{1}{n}$ is 0, so the limit of $\sin \dfrac{1}{n}$ is 0.

(4) False. A finite sequence has no limit.

(5) False. The limit of a sequence is constant if the terms of the sequence become arbitrarily close to a single number as n goes to infinity. So the limit of the sequence has nothing to do with the previous finite terms of the sequence.

2 Find the following limits.

(1) $\lim\limits_{n \to \infty} \dfrac{3n+4}{n}$.

(2) $\lim\limits_{n \to \infty} \dfrac{(n-1)(2n-1)}{6n^2}$.

(3) $\lim\limits_{n \to \infty} \dfrac{5n^2+\sqrt{n}}{3n^3+7}$.

(4) $\lim\limits_{n \to \infty} \dfrac{7n^3}{4n^2-5}$.

Solution： (1) $\lim\limits_{n \to \infty} \dfrac{3n+4}{n} = \lim\limits_{n \to \infty}\left(\dfrac{3n}{n} + \dfrac{4}{n}\right) = \lim\limits_{n \to \infty} 3 + 4\lim\limits_{n \to \infty}\dfrac{1}{n} = 3 + 4 \times 0 = 3$.

(2) $\lim\limits_{n \to \infty} \dfrac{(n-1)(2n-1)}{6n^2} = \lim\limits_{n \to \infty} \dfrac{2n^2-3n+1}{6n^2}$

$= \lim\limits_{n \to \infty}\left(\dfrac{1}{3} - \dfrac{1}{2n} + \dfrac{1}{6n^2}\right)$

$= \lim\limits_{n \to \infty}\dfrac{1}{3} - \dfrac{1}{2}\lim\limits_{n \to \infty}\dfrac{1}{n} + \dfrac{1}{6}\lim\limits_{n \to \infty}\dfrac{1}{n} \cdot \lim\limits_{n \to \infty}\dfrac{1}{n}$

$= \dfrac{1}{3} - \dfrac{1}{2} \times 0 + \dfrac{1}{6} \times 0 \times 0 = \dfrac{1}{3}$.

(3) $\lim\limits_{n \to \infty}\dfrac{5n^2+\sqrt{n}}{3n^3+7} = \lim\limits_{n \to \infty}\dfrac{\dfrac{5}{n}+\dfrac{1}{n^{5/2}}}{3+\dfrac{7}{n^3}} = \dfrac{\lim\limits_{n \to \infty}\left(\dfrac{5}{n}+\dfrac{1}{n^{5/2}}\right)}{\lim\limits_{n \to \infty}\left(3+\dfrac{7}{n^3}\right)} = \dfrac{5\lim\limits_{n \to \infty}\dfrac{1}{n}+\left(\lim\limits_{n \to \infty}\dfrac{1}{n}\right)^{5/2}}{\lim\limits_{n \to \infty}3+7\left(\lim\limits_{n \to \infty}\dfrac{1}{n}\right)^3} = \dfrac{5 \times 0 + 0^{5/2}}{3 + 7 \times 0^3} = 0$.

(4) Dividing both the numerator and the denominator by n^2, we get

$$\dfrac{7n^3}{4n^2-5} = \dfrac{7n}{4-\dfrac{5}{n^2}}.$$

When n is very large, $\dfrac{5}{n^2}$ is very close to 0. Therefore, $\dfrac{7n}{4-\dfrac{5}{n^2}} \approx \dfrac{7n}{4}$ when n is very large. Thus,

since $\dfrac{7n}{4}$ increases without bound as n does, $\lim\limits_{n\to\infty}\dfrac{7n}{4}=\infty$ and $\lim\limits_{n\to\infty}\dfrac{7n^3}{4n^2-5}=\infty$.

Remark: If the numerator and denominator of a fraction are polynomials, we have the following conclusions.

(1) When the highest degree of numerator is equal to that of the denominator, the limit is the ratio of the coefficients of leading terms.

(2) When the highest degree of the numerator is less than that of the denominator, the limit is 0.

(3) When the highest degree of the numerator is greater than that of the denominator, the limit does not exist.

3 Find the following limits.

(1) $\lim\limits_{n\to\infty}\left(\dfrac{1}{n^2}+\dfrac{4}{n^2}+\dfrac{7}{n^2}+\cdots+\dfrac{3n-2}{n^2}\right)$.

(2) $\lim\limits_{n\to\infty}\left[\dfrac{1}{2\times 5}+\dfrac{1}{5\times 8}+\dfrac{1}{8\times 11}+\cdots+\dfrac{1}{(3n-1)(3n+2)}\right]$.

Solution:

(1) $\lim\limits_{n\to\infty}\left(\dfrac{1}{n^2}+\dfrac{4}{n^2}+\dfrac{7}{n^2}+\cdots+\dfrac{3n-2}{n^2}\right)$

$=\lim\limits_{n\to\infty}\dfrac{1+4+7+\cdots+(3n-2)}{n^2}$

$=\lim\limits_{n\to\infty}\dfrac{\dfrac{n(1+3n-2)}{2}}{n^2}$

$=\lim\limits_{n\to\infty}\dfrac{3n-1}{2n}$

$=\dfrac{3}{2}$.

(2) $\lim\limits_{n\to\infty}\left[\dfrac{1}{2\times 5}+\dfrac{1}{5\times 8}+\dfrac{1}{8\times 11}+\cdots+\dfrac{1}{(3n-1)(3n+2)}\right]$

$=\lim\limits_{n\to\infty}\dfrac{1}{3}\left(\dfrac{1}{2}-\dfrac{1}{5}+\dfrac{1}{5}-\dfrac{1}{8}+\dfrac{1}{8}-\dfrac{1}{11}+\cdots+\dfrac{1}{3n-1}-\dfrac{1}{3n+2}\right)$

$=\dfrac{1}{3}\lim\limits_{n\to\infty}\left(\dfrac{1}{2}-\dfrac{1}{3n+2}\right)$

$=\lim\limits_{n\to\infty}\dfrac{n}{6n+4}$

$=\dfrac{1}{6}$.

4 Find the following limits.

(1) $\lim\limits_{n\to\infty}\dfrac{3^{n+2}-4^{n+3}}{4^n+3^{n+1}}$.

(2) $\lim\limits_{n\to\infty}\dfrac{a^n+2^{n-1}}{2^n+a^{n+1}}$ ($a\in\mathbf{R}$, $a\neq-2$).

Solution：

(1) $\lim\limits_{n\to\infty}\dfrac{3^{n+2}-4^{n+3}}{4^n+3^{n+1}}=\lim\limits_{n\to\infty}\dfrac{\dfrac{3^{n+2}}{4^n}-\dfrac{4^{n+3}}{4^n}}{\dfrac{4^n}{4^n}+\dfrac{3^{n+1}}{4^n}}=\lim\limits_{n\to\infty}\dfrac{9\cdot\left(\dfrac{3}{4}\right)^n-64}{1+3\cdot\left(\dfrac{3}{4}\right)^n}=\dfrac{\lim\limits_{n\to\infty}\left[9\cdot\left(\dfrac{3}{4}\right)^n-64\right]}{\lim\limits_{n\to\infty}\left[1+3\cdot\left(\dfrac{3}{4}\right)^n\right]}$

$=\dfrac{9\cdot\lim\limits_{n\to\infty}\left(\dfrac{3}{4}\right)^n-64}{1+3\cdot\lim\limits_{n\to\infty}\left(\dfrac{3}{4}\right)^n}=\dfrac{9\times0-64}{1+3\times0}=-64.$

(2) If $|a|>2$, $\left|\dfrac{2}{a}\right|<1$, then $\lim\limits_{n\to\infty}\dfrac{a^n+2^{n-1}}{2^n+a^{n+1}}=\lim\limits_{n\to\infty}\dfrac{1+\dfrac{1}{2}\left(\dfrac{2}{a}\right)^n}{\left(\dfrac{2}{a}\right)^n+a}=\dfrac{1}{a}.$

If $|a|<2$, $\left|\dfrac{a}{2}\right|<1$, then $\lim\limits_{n\to\infty}\dfrac{a^n+2^{n-1}}{2^n+a^{n+1}}=\lim\limits_{n\to\infty}\dfrac{\left(\dfrac{a}{2}\right)^n+\dfrac{1}{2}}{1+a\left(\dfrac{a}{2}\right)^n}=\dfrac{1}{2}.$

If $a=2$, then $\lim\limits_{n\to\infty}\dfrac{a^n+2^{n-1}}{2^n+a^{n+1}}=\lim\limits_{n\to\infty}\dfrac{2^n+2^{n-1}}{2^n+2^{n+1}}=\dfrac{2+1}{2+4}=\dfrac{1}{2}.$

In summary, $\lim\limits_{n\to\infty}\dfrac{a^n+2^{n-1}}{2^n+a^{n+1}}=\begin{cases}\dfrac{1}{a} & |a|>2 \\ \dfrac{1}{2} & -2<a\leqslant 2\end{cases}.$

5 Find the following limits.

(1) $\lim\limits_{n\to\infty}\left(\dfrac{n+3}{n+1}\right)^n.$ (2) $\lim\limits_{n\to\infty}\left(\dfrac{n}{n+2}\right)^n.$

Solution：

(1) $\lim\limits_{n\to\infty}\left(\dfrac{n+3}{n+1}\right)^n=\lim\limits_{n\to\infty}\left[\left(1+\dfrac{2}{n+1}\right)^{\frac{n+1}{2}}\right]^{\frac{2n}{n+1}}=e^2.$

(2) $\lim\limits_{n\to\infty}\left(\dfrac{n}{n+2}\right)^n=\lim\limits_{n\to\infty}\left(1-\dfrac{2}{n+2}\right)^n=\lim\limits_{n\to\infty}\left\{\left[1+\left(-\dfrac{2}{n+2}\right)\right]^{-\frac{n+2}{2}}\right\}^{\frac{-2n}{n+2}}=e^{-2}.$

无穷等比数列的各项和 Sum of the Infinite Geometric Sequences

我们把 $|r|<1$ 的无穷等比数列的前 n 项和 S_n 当 $n\to\infty$ 时的极限叫作**无穷等比数列的各项和**，并用符号 S 表示，即 $S=\dfrac{a_1}{1-r}$ ($|r|<1$).

The sum of the terms of an infinite geometric sequence is called an infinite geometric series or simply a geometric series.

Sum of the Infinite Geometric Series

If $|r|<1$, the infinite geometric series

$$a_1+a_1r+a_1r^2+\cdots+a_1r^n+\cdots$$

converges to the sum $S=\dfrac{a_1}{1-r}$.

If $|r|\geqslant 1$ and $a_1\neq 0$, then the series diverges.

Proof: The nth partial sum of the geometric series is

$$S = \frac{a_1(1-r^n)}{1-r}.$$

a. Therefore, if $|r| < 1$,

$$\lim_{n \to \infty} S = \lim_{n \to \infty} \frac{a_1(1-r^n)}{1-r} = \frac{a_1(1-0)}{1-r} = \frac{a_1}{1-r}.$$

b. However, if $|r| > 1$, r^n increases or decreases without bound as n approaches infinity. Thus, S_n becomes infinite and the series diverges.

c. If $r = 1$, the series becomes the divergent series

$$a_1 + a_1 + a_1 + \cdots$$

d. If $r = -1$, the series becomes the divergent series

$$a_1 - a_1 + a_1 - a_1 + \cdots$$

6 Express the following repeating decimals as rational numbers.

(1) $0.\dot{7}$.   (2) $2.\dot{1}\dot{3}$.   (3) $1.1\dot{3}2\dot{1}$.

Solution: (1) $0.\dot{7} = \frac{7}{10} + \frac{7}{100} + \cdots + \frac{7}{10^n} + \cdots = \frac{\frac{7}{10}}{1 - \frac{1}{10}} = \frac{7}{9}$.

(2) $2.\dot{1}\dot{3} = 2 + \frac{13}{100} + \frac{13}{10\,000} + \cdots + \frac{13}{10^{2n}} + \cdots = 2 + \frac{\frac{13}{100}}{1 - \frac{1}{100}} = 2 + \frac{13}{99} = 2\frac{13}{99}$.

(3) $1.1\dot{3}2\dot{1} = 1.1 + \frac{321}{10^4} + \frac{321}{10^7} + \frac{321}{10^{10}} + \cdots + \frac{321}{10^{3n+1}} + \cdots = 1.1 + \frac{\frac{13}{10\,000}}{1 - \frac{1}{10^3}} = 1\frac{1\,320}{9\,990} = 1\frac{44}{333}$.

7 For what values of x does the following infinite series converge?

$$1 + (x-2) + (x-2)^2 + (x-2)^3 + \cdots$$

Solution: This is an infinite geometric series with $r = x - 2$. By the theorem of the sum of an infinite geometric series, the series converges when $|r| < 1$, that is, $|x - 2| < 1$ or $1 < x < 3$.

This interval $1 < x < 3$ for which the series converges is called **the interval of convergence** for the series.

8 As shown in Figure 7 - 6, there is a square $ABCD$ with the side length of 1. Join the midpoints of the sides of the square to get a small square $A_1B_1C_1D_1$, then join the midpoints of the sides of the small square to get a smaller square $A_2B_2C_2D_2$, and this process continues infinitely. Find the sum of the perimeters and the areas of all these squares.

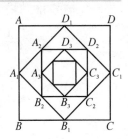

Figure 7 - 6

Solution: From the given conditions, we get that

the side length of the first square is $a_1 = 1$,

the side length of the second square is $a_2 = \dfrac{\sqrt{2}}{2}$,

...

the side length of the nth square is $a_n = \sqrt{\left(\dfrac{a_{n-1}}{2}\right)^2 + \left(\dfrac{a_{n-1}}{2}\right)^2} = \dfrac{\sqrt{2}}{2} a_{n-1}$, $n \geqslant 2$.

The side lengths of all squares form a sequence as follows:

$$1, \frac{\sqrt{2}}{2}, \frac{1}{2}, \frac{\sqrt{2}}{4}, \cdots, \left(\frac{\sqrt{2}}{2}\right)^{n-1}, \cdots.$$

Then the sequence formed by the perimeters of all squares is

$$4, 2\sqrt{2}, 2, \sqrt{2}, \cdots, 4 \cdot \left(\frac{\sqrt{2}}{2}\right)^{n-1}, \cdots.$$

This is a geometric series with $a_1 = 4$ and $r = \dfrac{\sqrt{2}}{2}$. Therefore, the sum of the perimeters of all these squares is

$$l = \frac{4}{1 - \dfrac{\sqrt{2}}{2}} = 8 + 4\sqrt{2}.$$

The sequence formed by the areas of all squares is

$$1, \frac{1}{2}, \frac{1}{4}, \frac{1}{8}, \cdots, \frac{1}{2^{n-1}}, \cdots.$$

This is a geometric series with $a_1 = 1$ and $r = \dfrac{1}{2}$. So the sum of the perimeters of all these squares is

$$S = \frac{1}{1 - \dfrac{1}{2}} = 2.$$

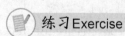 练习 Exercise

1. Determine whether the following sequence has a limit. If there is a limit, find the limit of the sequence.

    (1) $a_n = \dfrac{1}{n+1}$.

    (2) $a_n = \dfrac{3n-1}{n}$.

    (3) $a_n = \left(-\dfrac{1}{2}\right)^n$.

    (4) $a_n = (-1)^n$.

2. Find the following limits.

    (1) $\lim\limits_{n \to \infty} \dfrac{4n-3}{2n+1}$.

    (2) $\lim\limits_{n \to \infty} \dfrac{n^2+1}{2n^2}$.

(3) $\lim\limits_{n\to\infty}\dfrac{2n^4}{6n^5+7}$.

(4) $\lim\limits_{n\to\infty}\dfrac{\sqrt{n}}{n+1}$.

3. Find the following limits.

(1) $\lim\limits_{n\to\infty}\dfrac{(2n+1)(3n^2-2)}{4n^3-5n^2+6n-7}$.

(2) $\lim\limits_{n\to\infty}\left(\dfrac{1}{n^2+1}+\dfrac{2}{n^2+1}+\dfrac{3}{n^2+1}+\cdots+\dfrac{2n}{n^2+1}\right)$.

(3) $\lim\limits_{n\to\infty}\left(1+\dfrac{1}{1+2}+\dfrac{1}{1+2+3}+\cdots+\dfrac{1}{1+2+3+\cdots+n}\right)$.

(4) $\lim\limits_{n\to\infty}\left(1-\dfrac{1}{2^2}\right)\left(1-\dfrac{1}{3^2}\right)\left(1-\dfrac{1}{4^2}\right)\cdots\left(1-\dfrac{1}{n^2}\right)$.

(5) $\lim\limits_{n\to\infty}n^2\left[\dfrac{100}{n}-\left(\dfrac{1}{n+1}+\dfrac{1}{n+2}+\cdots+\dfrac{1}{n+100}\right)\right]$.

4. Find the following limits.

(1) $\lim\limits_{n\to\infty}\dfrac{2^{n+2}+3^{n+3}}{3^n-2^{n+1}}$.

(2) $\lim\limits_{n\to\infty}\dfrac{(-2)^{n+1}+(-3)^{n-1}}{(-2)^{n+4}+(-3)^{n+1}}$.

(3) $\lim\limits_{n\to\infty}\dfrac{(\sqrt{3}+\sqrt{2})^{n+1}+(\sqrt{3}-\sqrt{2})^{n+2}}{(\sqrt{3}+\sqrt{2})^{n}-(\sqrt{3}-\sqrt{2})^{n+1}}$.

(4) $\lim\limits_{n\to\infty}\dfrac{1+3+3^2+\cdots+3^n}{3^n+a^{n+1}}$.

5. Find the following limits.

(1) $\lim\limits_{n\to\infty}\left(1+\dfrac{1}{n}\right)^{n+2}$.

(2) $\lim\limits_{n\to\infty}\left(1-\dfrac{1}{n}\right)^{n}$.

(3) $\lim\limits_{n\to\infty}\left(\dfrac{2n-1}{2n-4}\right)^{n+1}$.

(4) $\lim\limits_{n\to\infty}\left(\dfrac{2n+3}{2n+1}\right)^{4n-1}$.

6. (1) If $\lim\limits_{n\to\infty}\dfrac{4^n}{4^{n+2}+(m+2)^n}=\dfrac{1}{16}$, find the range of m.

(2) If $\lim\limits_{n\to\infty}(2n-\sqrt{4n^2+kn+3})=1$, find the range of k.

7. Express the following repeating decimals as rational numbers.

(1) $0.\dot{4}$. (2) $2.\dot{3}\dot{8}$. (3) $2.2\dot{3}\dot{4}$. (4) $3.7\dot{2}1\dot{5}$.

8. Find the following limits.

(1) $\lim\limits_{n\to\infty}\dfrac{1+\dfrac{1}{2}+\dfrac{1}{2^2}+\cdots+\dfrac{1}{2^n}}{1-\dfrac{1}{2}+\dfrac{1}{2^2}+\cdots+(-1)^n\dfrac{1}{2^n}}$.

(2) $\lim\limits_{n\to\infty}\left(\dfrac{2+3}{6}+\dfrac{2^2+3^2}{6^2}+\cdots+\dfrac{2^n+3^n}{6^n}\right)$.

9. If the sum of the terms of the infinite geometric sequence $\{a_n\}$ is 4, find the range of the first term a_1.

10. As shown in Figure 7−7, there is an equilateral $\triangle A_1B_1C_1$ with the side length of a. Draw three equal circles that are inscribed in $\triangle A_1B_1C_1$ and tangent to each other, and then join the centers of these three equal circles to obtain an equilateral $\triangle A_2B_2C_2$. In the regular $\triangle A_2B_2C_2$, draw three equal circles that are inscribed in $\triangle A_2B_2C_2$ and tangent to each other, and then join the centers of these three equal circles to obtain a new equilateral $\triangle A_3B_3C_3$. This process continues indefinitely to get a sequence of equilateral triangles. Find the sum of areas of all

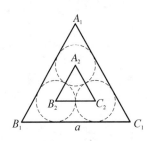

Figure 7−7

these equilateral triangles.

11. A ball is dropped from a height of 6 feet and begins bouncing as shown in the Figure 7 – 8. The height of each bounce is three-fourths the height of the previous bounce. Find the total vertical distance the ball travels before coming to rest.

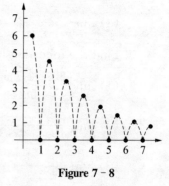

Figure 7 – 8

12. As shown in Figure 7 – 9, the Koch's snowflake curve is defined as follows. The sides of an equilateral triangle are tri-sected. A new equilateral triangle is placed on the middle third of each trisection. The sides common to the previous figure and the new triangles are then removed. This process continues indefinitely using the sides of the last figure obtained.

(1) Find the area enclose by the snowflake curve if each side of the initial equilateral triangle is one unit in length.

(2) Show that the limit of the sequence of perimeters of the snowflake curve is infinite.

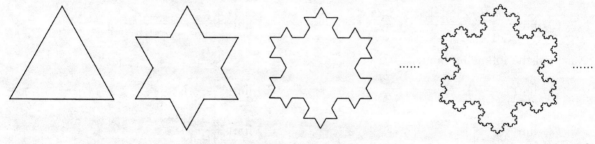

Figure 7 – 9

习 题 答 案

第 1 章 集 合 与 命 题

1.1 集合

1. (1) Set $A = \{1, 4, 7, 10, 13\} = \{x \mid x = 3n - 2, 1 \leqslant n \leqslant 5\}$.

(2) Set $B = \{-2, -4, -6, -8, -10\} = \{x \mid x = -2n, 1 \leqslant n \leqslant 5\}$.

(3) Set $C = \{1, 5, 25, 125, 625\} = \{x \mid x = 5^{n-1}, 1 \leqslant n \leqslant 5\}$.

(4) Set $D = \{0, \pm\dfrac{1}{2}, \pm\dfrac{2}{5}, \pm\dfrac{3}{10}, \pm\dfrac{4}{17}\cdots\} = \{x \mid x = \dfrac{n}{n^2 + 1}, n \in \mathbf{Z}\}$.

2. $a = 2$ or $a = 4$.

3. For the quadratic equation in the variable x such as $x^2 + (a - 1)x + b = 0$ has two repeated real roots, we must have that $\Delta = (a - 1)^2 - 4b = 0$.

Since $a \in A$, then $a^2 - 2a + 1 = 4b$.

Solve the system of equations $\begin{cases} (a - 1)^2 - 4b = 0 \\ a^2 - 2a + 1 = 4b \end{cases}$, then $\begin{cases} a = \dfrac{1}{3} \\ b = \dfrac{1}{9} \end{cases}$.

Therefore $a = \dfrac{1}{3}$ and $b = \dfrac{1}{9}$.

4. Since $5 \in A$, $a^2 + 2a - 3 = 5$, then $a = 2$ or $a = -4$.

If $a = 2$, we get set $B = \{5, 2\}$, obviously $5 \in B$, so $a = 2$ is not the solution.

If $a = -4$, we get set $A = \{2, 3, 5\}$, set $B = \{-1, 2\}$.

Therefore $a = -4$.

5. C.

6. D.

7. $a = -1$.

8. (1) As $\{x \mid a - 2 < x < a + 2\} \subseteq \{x \mid -2 < x < 3\}$, we get $\begin{cases} a + 2 \leqslant 3 \\ a - 2 \geqslant -2 \end{cases}$.

Solve the system of equations, we get $0 \leqslant a \leqslant 1$.

Therefore $0 \leqslant a \leqslant 1$.

(2) As $\{x \mid -2 < x < 3\} \subseteq \{x \mid a - 2 < x < a + 2\}$, we get $\begin{cases} a + 2 \geqslant 3 \\ a - 2 \leqslant -2 \end{cases}$.

Thus $\begin{cases} a \geqslant 1 \\ a \leqslant 0 \end{cases}$.

Therefore there is no real number a that satisfies $B \subseteq A$.

9. $A \bigcap B = \{(1, 0), (-2, 3)\}$.

10. (1) $p = -8$, $q = 6$.　　(2) $A \bigcup B = \{2, 3, 5\}$.

11. $a = 2$ or -4, $b = 3$.

12. (1) $A \cap \overline{B} = \{(2, 3)\}$.   (2) $\overline{A \cup B} = \{(2, 3)\}$.

1.2 命题的形式及等价关系

1. (1) False.   (2) True.   (3) False.   (4) False.

2. $A \Leftrightarrow C$.

3. $m \geqslant 4$.

4. Converse proposition: If $a < b$, then $c < 0$ and $ac > bc$.

   Inverse proposition: If $c \geqslant 0$ or $ac \leqslant bc$, then $a \geqslant b$.

   Contrapositive proposition: If $a \geqslant b$, then $c \geqslant 0$ or $ac \leqslant bc$.

5. Contrapositive proposition: If the quadratic equation in the variable x such as $mx^2 - x + n = 0$ has a real repeated root or no existed real root, then $mn \geqslant 0$. The contrapositive proposition is false.

   As the quadratic equation in the variable x such as $mx^2 - x + n = 0$ has a real repeated root or no existed real root, then

   $\Delta = 1 - 4mn \leqslant 0$. Therefore, $mn \geqslant \dfrac{1}{4}$.

6. (1) Prove: $11 = 6^2 - 5^2$, $12 = 4^2 - 2^2$, $2k + 1 = (k+1)^2 - k^2 (k \in \mathbf{Z})$.

   (2) Prove: Assume $10 \in A$, then $10 = m^2 - n^2 = (m+n)(m+n)(m \in \mathbf{Z}, n \in \mathbf{Z})$.

   So $\begin{cases} m - n = 1 \\ m + n = 10 \end{cases}$, $\begin{cases} m - n = 2 \\ m + n = 5 \end{cases}$, $\begin{cases} m - n = 10 \\ m + n = 1 \end{cases}$ and $\begin{cases} m - n = 5 \\ m + n = 2 \end{cases}$ have no integer solution.

   Therefore, the assumption is wrong, $10 \notin A$.

7. (1) As $p \Rightarrow q$ and $q \nRightarrow p$, p is sufficient for q.

   (2) As $p \nRightarrow q$ and $q \Rightarrow p$, p is necessary for q.

   (3) As $p \Leftrightarrow q$, p is sufficient and necessary for q.

8. (1) Sufficient condition: $x = y$ (The answer is not unique).

   (2) Necessary condition: $a + b < 3$ (The answer is not unique).

9. (1) As $p \Rightarrow q$ and $q \nRightarrow p$, proposition p is sufficient but not necessary for q.

   (2) Given $\overline{\gamma} \Rightarrow \beta$, then $\overline{\beta} \Rightarrow \gamma$.

   Since $\alpha \Rightarrow \overline{\beta}$, $\overline{\beta} \Rightarrow \gamma$, we have $\alpha \Rightarrow \gamma$.

   Therefore, γ is necessary for α.

10. As α is a sufficient condition of β, $\alpha \Rightarrow \beta$.

    Thus $m + 1 < -1$ or $m - 1 > 3$.

    Therefore $m < -2$ or $m > 4$.

第 2 章　不　等　式

2.1 不等式的性质

1. (1) $x > \dfrac{5}{4}$.   (2) $x > 1$.   (3) $x < \dfrac{1}{6}$.

2. (1) As we know $a > b$, $ab > 0 \Rightarrow \dfrac{1}{a} < \dfrac{1}{b}$. If $a < b$, but $ab > 0$ is not mentioned, then we can get $\dfrac{1}{a} < \dfrac{1}{b}$ or $\dfrac{1}{a} > \dfrac{1}{b}$. So it is false.

   (2) If $c < 0$, then $c^{-3} < 0$. Since $ac^{-3} > bc^{-3}$, divide both sides by c^{-3}, then $a < b$. So it is false.

   (3) Let $a = 3$, $b = 0$, $c = -3$, which satisfies $a > b$, $b > c$, but $a - b = 3 = b - c = 3$. So it is false.

3. Simplify $(n^3 + 1) - (n^2 + n) = n^2(n - 1) - (n - 1) = (n + 1)(n - 1)^2$.

   Since $n > -1$ and $n \neq 1$, $(n + 1)(n - 1)^2 > 0$. So $n^3 + 1 > n^2 + n$.

4. (1) $\left. \begin{array}{c} a > b \\ a > c \end{array} \right\} \Rightarrow 2a > b + c \Rightarrow 3a > a + b + c = 0 \Rightarrow a > 0$. Similarly, $c < 0$. So $ac < 0$.

(2) Since $b = -a - c$, $a > b$, $b > c$, $\begin{cases} a > -a - c \\ -a - c > c \end{cases} \Rightarrow \begin{cases} 2a > -c \\ -a > 2c \end{cases} \Rightarrow \begin{cases} \dfrac{c}{a} > -2 \\ \dfrac{c}{a} < -\dfrac{1}{2} \end{cases}$. So $-2 < \dfrac{c}{a} < -\dfrac{1}{2}$.

5. Rationalize A and B, then we get $A = \sqrt{m+1} - \sqrt{m} = \dfrac{1}{\sqrt{m+1} + \sqrt{m}}$ and $B = \sqrt{m} - \sqrt{m-1} = \dfrac{1}{\sqrt{m} + \sqrt{m-1}}$.

As $m > 1$, $\sqrt{m+1} + \sqrt{m} > \sqrt{m} + \sqrt{m-1}$, we get the conclusion $A < B$.

6. $(x^6 + 1) - (x^4 + x^2) = x^4(x^2 - 1) - (x^2 - 1) = (x^2 + 1)(x^2 - 1)^2$.

If $x = \pm 1$, $x^6 + 1 = x^4 + x^2$; If $x \neq \pm 1$, $x^6 + 1 > x^4 + x^2$.

7. $(5x^2 + y^2 + z^2) - (2xy + 4x + 2z - 2) = (x - y)^2 + (2x - 1)^2 + (z - 1)^2 \geqslant 0$,

So $5x^2 + y^2 + z^2 \geqslant 2xy + 4x + 2z - 2$. $\left(5x^2 + y^2 + z^2 = 2xy + 4x + 2z - 2, \text{ if and only if } x = y = \dfrac{1}{2}, z = 1.\right)$

8. $(a^2 - b^2 + c^2) - (a - b + c)^2 = -2b^2 + 2ab - 2ac + 2bc = 2ab - 4b^2 + 2bc$

$$= 2b(a - 2b + c) = 2b(a - 2\sqrt{ac} + c) = 2b(\sqrt{a} - \sqrt{c})^2 \geqslant 0,$$

So $a^2 - b^2 + c^2 \geqslant (a - b + c)^2$.

9. $\left(1 + \dfrac{\sqrt{2}}{a}\right)^3 - \left[2 - \left(1 - \dfrac{\sqrt{2}}{a}\right)^3\right]$

$= \left(1 + \dfrac{\sqrt{2}}{a}\right)^3 + \left(1 - \dfrac{\sqrt{2}}{a}\right)^3 - 2$

$= \left[\left(1 + \dfrac{\sqrt{2}}{a}\right) + \left(1 - \dfrac{\sqrt{2}}{a}\right)\right]\left[\left(1 + \dfrac{\sqrt{2}}{a}\right)^2 - \left(1 + \dfrac{\sqrt{2}}{a}\right)\left(1 - \dfrac{\sqrt{2}}{a}\right) + \left(1 - \dfrac{\sqrt{2}}{a}\right)^2\right] - 2$

$= 2\left(2 + \dfrac{4}{a^2} - 1 + \dfrac{2}{a^2}\right) - 2 = \dfrac{12}{a^2} > 0$, so $\left(1 + \dfrac{\sqrt{2}}{a}\right)^3 > 2 - \left(1 - \dfrac{\sqrt{2}}{a}\right)^3$.

10. Let $f(x) = ax^2 + bx (a \neq 0)$.

We have $\begin{cases} f(-1) = a - b \\ f(1) = a + b \end{cases}$, which gives $\begin{cases} a = \dfrac{1}{2}[f(1) + f(-1)] \\ b = \dfrac{1}{2}[f(1) - f(-1)] \end{cases}$.

$f(-2) = 4a - 2b = 3f(-1) + f(1)$, $1 \leqslant f(-1) \leqslant 2$, $3 \leqslant f(1) \leqslant 4$,

So $6 \leqslant f(-2) \leqslant 10$.

11. $a^2 + b^2 \geqslant 2ab$, $b^2 + c^2 \geqslant 2bc$, $c^2 + a^2 \geqslant 2ca$,

$a^2 + b^2 + b^2 + c^2 + c^2 + a^2 \geqslant 2ab + 2bc + 2ca$.

$2(a^2 + b^2 + c^2) \geqslant 2ab + 2bc + 2ca$.

$a^2 + b^2 + c^2 \geqslant ab + bc + ca$.

$a^2 + b^2 + c^2 = ab + bc + ca$, if and only if $a = b = c$.

12. (1) If $ab > 0$, then $\dfrac{a}{b} > 0$, $\dfrac{b}{a} > 0$, we have $\dfrac{b}{a} + \dfrac{a}{b} \geqslant 2\sqrt{\dfrac{b}{a} \cdot \dfrac{a}{b}} = 2$.

$\dfrac{b}{a} + \dfrac{a}{b} = 2$, if and only if $\dfrac{b}{a} = \dfrac{a}{b}(a = b \neq 0)$.

(2) If $ab < 0$, then $\dfrac{a}{b} < 0$, $\dfrac{b}{a} < 0$. Hence, $-\dfrac{a}{b} > 0$, $-\dfrac{b}{a} > 0$.

We have $\left(-\dfrac{b}{a}\right) + \left(-\dfrac{a}{b}\right) \geqslant 2\sqrt{\left(-\dfrac{b}{a}\right) \cdot \left(-\dfrac{a}{b}\right)} = 2$. So $\dfrac{b}{a} + \dfrac{a}{b} \leqslant -2$.

$\dfrac{b}{a} + \dfrac{a}{b} = -2$, if and only if $-\dfrac{b}{a} = -\dfrac{a}{b}(a = -b \neq 0)$.

So $\dfrac{b}{a} + \dfrac{a}{b} \geqslant 2$ or $\dfrac{b}{a} + \dfrac{a}{b} \leqslant -2$.

2.2 一元二次不等式的解法

1. (1) **R**.　(2) $\varnothing$.　(3) $\left(-\infty, \dfrac{2\sqrt{3}}{3}\right) \bigcup \left(\dfrac{2\sqrt{3}}{3}, +\infty\right)$.　(4) $\left\{-\dfrac{15}{17}\right\}$.

2. (1) $(-2, 0] \bigcup [2, 4)$.　(2) $[-5, -4) \bigcup (3, 6]$.　(3) $\varnothing$.

3. According to the question, we can get the inequality $\dfrac{1}{20}x + \dfrac{1}{180}x^2 > 39.5$,

   Then $x^2 + 9x - 7\,110 > 0$, the root of $x^2 + 9x - 7\,110 = 0$ is $x_1 \approx -88.94$, $x_2 \approx 79.94$,

   So the set of $x^2 + 9x - 7\,110 > 0$ is $(-\infty, -88.94) \bigcup (79.94, +\infty)$ and the speed is at least 79.94 km/h.

4. According to the question, we can get $\Delta < 0$, then $(a-1)^2 - 16 < 0$. Thus, $-3 < a < 5$.

5. According to the question, we can get $\begin{cases} m < 0 \\ \Delta < 0 \end{cases}$, then $\begin{cases} m < 0 \\ (m-1)^2 - 4m \cdot (m-1) < 0 \end{cases}$. So $m < -\dfrac{1}{3}$.

6. $a = 0$, the solution set is $(-\infty, 1)$;

   $a < 0$, the solution set is $\left(\dfrac{1}{a}, 1\right)$;

   $0 < a < 1$, the solution set is $(-\infty, 1) \bigcup \left(\dfrac{1}{a}, +\infty\right)$;

   $a = 1$, the solution set is $(-\infty, 1) \bigcup (1, +\infty)$;

   $1 < a$, the solution set is $\left(-\infty, \dfrac{1}{a}\right) \bigcup (1, +\infty)$.

2.3 多项式除法、余式定理和因式定理

1. (1) $4x^3 - 7x^2 - 11x + 5 = (4x+2)\left(x^2 - \dfrac{9}{4}x - \dfrac{13}{8}\right) + \dfrac{33}{4}$.

   (2) $x^3 - 9x + 1 = (x^2 + 1) \cdot x - 10x + 1$.

2. (1) $3x^3 - 17x^2 + 15x - 23 = (x-4)(3x^2 - 5x - 5) - 43$.

   (2) $5x^3 + 6x + 7 = (x+2)(5x^2 - 10x + 26) - 45$.

3. (1) $f(1) = 0$, $f(-2) = -3$, $f\left(\dfrac{1}{2}\right) = \dfrac{3}{4}$.

   (2) $f(-1) = 37$, $f(2) = -26$, $f(3) = -35$.

4. (1) $f(x) = 2x^3 + 3x^2 - 3x - 2 = (x-1)(x+2)(2x+1)$.

   (2) $f(x) = x^4 - 2x^3 - 11x^2 + 6x + 24 = (x+2)(x-4)(x+\sqrt{3})(x-\sqrt{3})$.

   (3) $f(x) = 6x^3 + 17x^2 - 5x - 6 = (2x+1)(3x-2)(x+3)$.

5. $V(x) = (x+1)(x+2)(x+3)$, the dimensions of the boxes are $x+1$, $x+2$ and $x+3$.

6. $\dfrac{x^{3n} + 9x^{2n} + 27x^n + 27}{x^n + 2} = (x^{2n} + 7x^n + 13) + \dfrac{1}{x^n + 2}$.

7. $k = 2$.

8. (1) According to the rational root theorem, the possible rational zeros could be $\pm 1, \pm 2, \pm 4, \pm\dfrac{1}{2}$.

   (2) According to the rational root theorem, the possible rational zeros could be $\pm 1, \pm 5, \pm\dfrac{1}{2}, \pm\dfrac{5}{2}, \pm\dfrac{1}{3}, \pm\dfrac{5}{3}$,

   $\pm\dfrac{1}{6}, \pm\dfrac{5}{6}$.

9. (1) the zeros of $f(x)$ are $x = -1$, $x = 1$ and $x = \dfrac{5}{2}$.

   (2) the zeros of $f(x)$ are $x = -\dfrac{1}{3}$, $x = \dfrac{3}{2}$ and $x = \pm\sqrt{2}$.

10. (1) $x \approx 2.1$.　(2) $x \approx -1.6$ and $x \approx 2.8$.

11. (1) $x \approx 1.6$.　(2) $x \approx 0.7$.

12. You can get the equation $(a-3)a(a+6) = 2(a-3-2)(a-2)(a+6-2)$. Solving the equation, we get the integer root $a = 10$.

13. If $a_n x^n + a_{n-1} x^{n-1} + a_{n-2} x^{n-2} + \cdots + a_0 = 0$ $(a_n \neq 0)$ has roots r_1, r_2, r_3, $\cdots$, r_n, then $r_1 + r_2 + r_3 + \cdots + r_n = -\dfrac{a_{n-1}}{a_n}$,

$r_1 r_2 r_3 \cdots r_n = (-1)^n \dfrac{a_0}{a_n}$.

2.4 多项式函数和多项式不等式

1. (1) (c)   (2) (f)   (3) (a)   (4) (e)   (5) (d)   (6) (b)

2. (1) False   (2) True   (3) False   (4) True

3. (1)   (2)

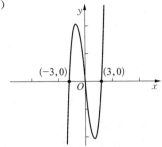   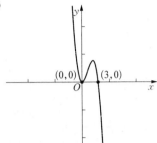

   (3)   (4)

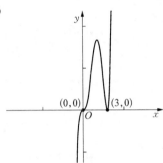   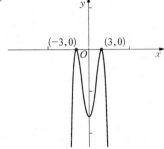

4. $f(x) = -\dfrac{1}{2} x^2 (x+2)^3 (x-1)$.

5. (1) $f(x) = (x-4)(x+1)$.

   (2) $f(x) = x(x-1)(x-2)$.

   (3) $f(x) = -\dfrac{1}{2}(x+1)^2(x-2)$.

   (4) $f(x) = -(x-1)^3(x+2)$.

6. $f(x) = -\dfrac{1}{6}(x+3)^2(x-2)^2$.

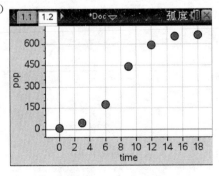

7. $f(x) = \dfrac{2}{9} x^2 (x-5)$.

8. (1) $(-3, -\sqrt{2}) \cup (\sqrt{2}, +\infty)$.   (2) $(-2, 1) \cup (1, 5)$.   (3) $(-\infty, -2) \cup (-2, -1) \cup (1, 2)$.

   (4) $\left[-\dfrac{13}{2}, -2 \right] \cup [2, +\infty)$.

9. (1)

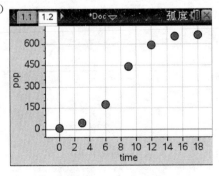

   (2) $f(t) = at^3 + bt^2 + ct + d$, where $a = -0.382\,6$, $b = 9.384\,5$, $c = -9.168\,0$, $d = 3.933\,3$.

(3) $7.48 < t < 21.8$.

2.5 分式不等式 & 绝对值不等式的解法

1. (1) $(-\infty, 3) \cup (4, 5)$.　(2) $\left(-4, \dfrac{5}{2}\right] \cup (7, +\infty)$.　(3) $(-1, 0) \cup (1, +\infty)$.　(4) $(-1, 2) \cup (2, +\infty)$.

(5) $\left(-\infty, -\dfrac{1}{2}\right) \cup \left(\dfrac{1}{3}, \dfrac{2}{5}\right) \cup (2, +\infty)$.　(6) $(-1, 1) \cup (2, 3)$.

2. $\left[\dfrac{n}{m}, 1\right) \cup [2, +\infty)$.

3. $1 < k < 3$.

4. (1) $(-2, 6)$.　(2) $(-\infty, 0] \cup [6, +\infty)$.

5. (1) $[1, 4) \cup (8, 11]$.　(2) $(2, 3) \cup (3, 4)$.

6. (1) $\left(-\infty, -\dfrac{3}{2}\right) \cup \left(\dfrac{7}{2}, +\infty\right)$.　(2) $\left(-\dfrac{1}{2}, \dfrac{13}{2}\right)$.

7. (1) $\left(\dfrac{5}{2}, +\infty\right)$.　(2) $\mathbf{R}$.　(3) $\left(-\infty, \dfrac{5}{4}\right) \cup \left[\dfrac{7}{4}, +\infty\right)$.　(4) $\left[-\dfrac{1}{5}, \dfrac{2}{3}\right) \cup \left(\dfrac{2}{3}, 5\right]$.

8. $m \leqslant 1$.

9. (1) a. $a = 2$, $b = -1$, so $|2+(-1)| < |2|+|-1|$;

b. $a = 2$, $b = 1$, so $|2+1| = |2|+|1|$;

c. $a = -2$, $b = -1$, so $|-2+(-1)| = |-2|+|-1|$.

(2) Proof: Since $|a-b| = |a+(-b)|$, and $|a+(-b)| \leqslant |a|+|-b|$,

then $|a-b| \leqslant |a|+|-b|$. So $|a-b| \leqslant |a|+|b|$.

$|a| = |a+b-b| \leqslant |a+b|+|b|$,

so $|a|-|b| \leqslant |a+b|$.

第 3 章　函　　数

3.1 函数的概念与函数关系的建立

1. (1) yes.　(2) no.　(3) yes.　(4) no.　(5) yes.　(6) no.　(7) yes.　(8) no.

2. The relation mapping numbers to letters is not a function, and the other mapping letters to numbers is a function.

3. (1)

x	-2	-1	0	1	2
$f(x)$	-2	1	2	1	-2

(2)

t	-3	0	3	6	9
$g(t)$	2	1	0	1	2

(3)

s	-2	-1	0	1	2
$h(s)$	1	4	5	4	5

4. (1) $(-\infty, +\infty)$.　(2) $(-\infty, 0) \cup (0, +\infty)$.　(3) $\left[\dfrac{5}{2}, +\infty\right)$.　(4) $(-\infty, -2) \cup (-2, 2) \cup (2, +\infty)$.

(5) $\left[1, \dfrac{4}{3}\right) \cup \left(\dfrac{4}{3}, +\infty\right)$.　(6) $(6, +\infty)$.

5. $S = 2|x|\sqrt{4-x^2}$, $x \in (-2, 2)$.

6. (I) $y = [60(1+0.5x) - 40(1+x)] \times [1\,000(1+0.8x)] = -8\,000x^2 + 6\,000x + 20\,000 = -2\,000(4x^2 - 3x - 10)$,

$(0 < x < 1)$.

(II) In order to increase the daily profit, then $y > (60-40) \times 1\,000$ and $0 < x < 1$, that is $-4x^2 + 3x > 0$, and $0 < x < 1$. Solving the inequality, we have $0 < x < \dfrac{3}{4}$.

7. $y = \begin{cases} \dfrac{1}{2}x^2, & 0 < x \leqslant 2 \\ 2x - 2, & 2 < x \leqslant 5 \\ 10 - \dfrac{1}{2}(x-7)^2, & 5 < x \leqslant 7 \end{cases}$.

8. (1) If two functions have the same domain, same range, and the same law.

(2) $f(x)$ and $g(x)$ are equal.

(3) $f(x)$ and $g(x)$ are not equal, since they have different domains.

3.2 函数的运算与反函数

1. (1) $f(x) + g(x) = x^2 + 4x - 5$, $x \in \mathbf{R}$; $f(x) - g(x) = x^2 - 4x + 5$, $x \in \mathbf{R}$; $f(x) \cdot g(x) = 4x^3 - 5x^2$, $x \in \mathbf{R}$;

$\dfrac{f(x)}{g(x)} = \dfrac{x^2}{4x - 5}$, $\left\{ x \mid x \neq \dfrac{5}{4} \right\}$.

(2) $f(x) + g(x) = \sqrt{x^2 + 6} - \dfrac{x^2}{x^2 + 1}$, $x \in \mathbf{R}$; $f(x) - g(x) = \sqrt{x^2 + 6} - \dfrac{x^2}{x^2 + 1}$, $x \in \mathbf{R}$; $f(x) \cdot g(x) = $

$\dfrac{x^2 \sqrt{x^2 + 6}}{x^2 + 1}$, $x \in \mathbf{R}$; $\dfrac{f(x)}{g(x)} = \dfrac{(x^2 + 1) \sqrt{x^2 + 6}}{x^2}$, $\{ x \mid x \neq 0 \}$.

(3) $f(x) + g(x) = 3\sqrt{x} + 2$, $\{ x \mid 0 \leqslant x \leqslant 1 \}$; $f(x) - g(x) = \sqrt{x} + 2\sqrt{1-x} - 2$, $\{ x \mid 0 \leqslant x \leqslant 1 \}$; $f(x) \cdot$

$g(x) = 3x - 1 + 4\sqrt{x} + 2\sqrt{1-x} - \sqrt{x(1-x)}$, $\{ x \mid 0 \leqslant x \leqslant 1 \}$; $\dfrac{f(x)}{g(x)} = \dfrac{2\sqrt{x} + \sqrt{1-x}}{\sqrt{x} - \sqrt{1-x} + 2}$, $\{ x \mid 0 \leqslant$

$x \leqslant 1 \}$.

(4) $f(x) + g(x) = \dfrac{1 + x(x+4)^2}{x^3 + 4x^2}$, $\{ x \mid x \neq -4, 0 \}$; $f(x) - g(x) = \dfrac{1 - x(x+4)^2}{x^3 + 4x^2}$, $\{ x \mid x \neq -4, 0 \}$; $f(x) \cdot$

$g(x) = \dfrac{1}{x^3}$, $\{ x \mid x \neq -4, 0 \}$; $\dfrac{f(x)}{g(x)} = \dfrac{1}{x(x+4)^2}$, $\{ x \mid x \neq -4, 0 \}$.

2. (1)

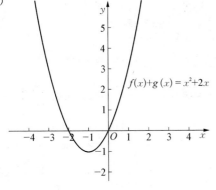 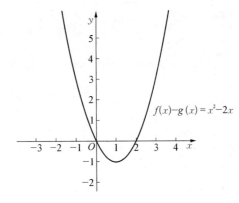

(2)

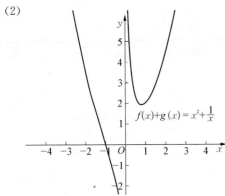 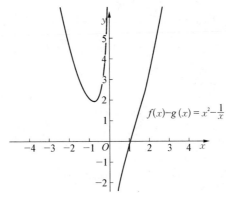

3. (1) $\sqrt{5}$.　(2) 1.　(3) $\dfrac{11}{3}$.　(4) $\dfrac{5}{3}$.

4. $(f \circ g)(x) = \sqrt{3x^2 - 8x + 4} = \sqrt{(3x - 2)(x - 2)}$, then $(3x - 2)(x - 2) \geqslant 0$, the domain of $(f \circ g)(x)$ is $\left(-\infty, \dfrac{2}{3}\right] \bigcup [2, +\infty)$.

5. (1) Since $(f \circ g)(x) = 1 - 2x^2 = 1 - \dfrac{1}{2}(2x)^2$, then $f(x) = 1 - \dfrac{1}{2}x^2$.

   (2) Since $(f \circ g)(x) = (\sqrt{x})^2 + 2\sqrt{x} = (\sqrt{x} + 1)^2 - 1$, then $f(x) = x^2 - 1$.

   (3) Since $(f \circ g)(x) = \dfrac{x}{1 - x^2} = \dfrac{\frac{1}{x}}{\frac{1}{x^2} - 1}$, then $f(x) = \dfrac{x}{x^2 - 1}$.

6. Let $x + 1 = t$, then $x = t - 1$, so $f(t) = 2(t - 1)^2 + 1$.

   Let $t = x - 1$, then $f(x - 1) = 2(x - 2)^2 + 1 = 2x^2 - 8x + 9$.

7. (1) $y = \dfrac{x - 2}{3}$.　(2) $y = -\dfrac{3}{x}$.　(3) $y = -\sqrt{x}$, $(x \geqslant 0)$.　(4) $y = (x - 1)^2$, $(x \geqslant 1)$.

8. By $\dfrac{x - 1}{x} = \sqrt{2}$, we get $x = -\sqrt{2} - 1$. So $f^{-1}(\sqrt{2}) = -\sqrt{2} - 1$.

9. (1) By $y = \left(\dfrac{x - 1}{x + 1}\right)^2 (x > 1)$ we get, $x = \dfrac{1 + \sqrt{y}}{1 - \sqrt{y}}$. By $x > 1$ we have, $0 < y < 1$.

   So, $f^{-1}(x) = \dfrac{1 + \sqrt{x}}{1 - \sqrt{x}} (0 < x < 1)$.

   (2) Since $(1 - \sqrt{x})f^{-1}(x) > a(a - \sqrt{x})$, $1 + \sqrt{x} > a^2 - a\sqrt{x}$, that is $(a + 1)\sqrt{x} > (a - 1)(a + 1)$.

   Obviously $a \neq -1$.

   When $a < -1$, $a + 1 < 0$, $a - 1 < -2$, then $\sqrt{x} < a - 1$ is true for $x \in \left[\dfrac{1}{16}, \dfrac{1}{4}\right]$, it is not consistent with $\sqrt{x} \geqslant 0$.

   When $a > -1$, $a + 1 > 0$, then $\sqrt{x} > a - 1$ is true for $x \in \left[\dfrac{1}{16}, \dfrac{1}{4}\right]$. With $\sqrt{x} \in \left[\dfrac{1}{4}, \dfrac{1}{2}\right]$, then $a - 1 < \dfrac{1}{4}$, $a < \dfrac{5}{4}$.

   Therefore $-1 < a < \dfrac{5}{4}$.

10. (1) From $y = 2\left(\dfrac{1}{2} - \dfrac{1}{a^x + 1}\right)$ we have, $x = \log_a \dfrac{1 + y}{1 - y}$, then the inverse function is $f^{-1}(x) = \log_a \dfrac{1 + x}{1 - x}$, $(-1 < x < 1)$.

    (2) $\log_a \dfrac{1 + x}{1 - x} > 1$,

    When $a > 1$, $\dfrac{1 + x}{1 - x} > a$, then $\dfrac{a - 1}{a + 1} < x < 1$.

    When $0 < a < 1$, $0 < \dfrac{1 + x}{1 - x} < a$, then $-1 < x < \dfrac{a - 1}{a + 1}$.

11. No. By $y = f(x + 1)$ we have, $x + 1 = f^{-1}(y)$, $x = f^{-1}(y) - 1$. So the inverse function of $y = f(x + 1)$ is $y = f^{-1}(x) - 1$, not $y = f^{-1}(x + 1)$.

3.3 函数的性质

1. Since $-2 < m - 1 < 1 - 2m < 2$, we have $-\dfrac{1}{2} < m < \dfrac{2}{3}$.

2. The decreasing interval is $(-\infty, -1]$, and the increasing interval is $[5, +\infty)$.

3. If $a = 0$, $f(x) = \begin{cases} -x + 1, & x \leqslant 1 \\ -x + \dfrac{3}{4}, & x > 1 \end{cases}$ is decreasing;

If $a \neq 0$, $\begin{cases} a > 0, \dfrac{1}{2a} \geqslant 1 \\ 2a - 1 < 0 \\ a - 1 + 1 \geqslant 2a - 1 + \dfrac{3}{4} \end{cases}$, $\Rightarrow 0 < a \leqslant \dfrac{1}{4}$.

Therefore $0 \leqslant a \leqslant \dfrac{1}{4}$.

4. $f(x) = \dfrac{x^2 + a}{x} = x + \dfrac{a}{x}$,

For any x_1, $x_2 \in (2, +\infty)$, if $x_1 < x_2$, then

$f(x_1) - f(x_2) = (x_1 - x_2) + \left(\dfrac{a}{x_1} - \dfrac{a}{x_2} \right) = \dfrac{(x_1 x_2 - a)(x_1 - x_2)}{x_1 x_2}$.

Since $f(x) = \dfrac{x^2 + a}{x}$ is increasing for $(2, +\infty)$, then $f(x_1) - f(x_2) < 0$.

As $x_1 - x_2 < 0$, $x_1 x_2 > 4$, then $x_1 x_2 - a > 0$. So, $a \leqslant 4$.

Given $a > 0$, we can have the range of a is $(0, 4]$.

5. (1) Proof:

For any $x_1 < x_2$, then $x_1 - x_2 < 0$, $f(x_1 - x_2) < 1$.

Since $f(x_1) = f(x_2 + (x_1 - x_2)) = f(x_2) \cdot f(x_1 - x_2)$,

then $\dfrac{f(x_1)}{f(x_2)} = f(x_1 - x_2) < 1$.

As $f(x_2) > 0$, we have $f(x_1) > f(x_2)$,

Therefore $f(x)$ is increasing for $x \in \mathbf{R}$.

(2) Solution:

Since $f(x^2) \cdot f(x) = f(x^2 + x)$, and $4 = 2 \times 2 = f(1) \cdot f(1) = f(1 + 1) = f(2)$,

$f(x^2) \cdot f(x) < 4$ can be written as $f(x^2 + x) < f(2)$.

As $f(x)$ is increasing for $x \in \mathbf{R}$,

we can have $x^2 + x < 2$.

Solving the inequality gives $-2 < x < 1$.

Therefore, the solution set is $\{x \mid -2 < x < 1\}$.

6. (1) neither odd nor even.　(2) odd.　(3) both odd and even.　(4) even.　(5) even.

7. (1) $(-1, 0) \cup (0, 1)$.　(2) $[-3, -1) \cup (0, 1)$.

8. (1) When $x < 0$, $f(x) = 2x^2 + 3x - 1$.

(2) $f(x) = \begin{cases} -2x^2 + 3x + 1, & x > 0 \\ 0, & x = 0 \\ 2x^2 + 3x - 1, & x < 0 \end{cases}$.

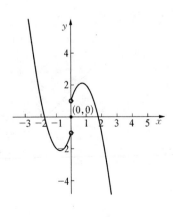

9. -26.

10. $(-\infty, -2] \cup [2, +\infty)$.

11. (1) The function $f(x)$ is increasing for $x \in [-1, 1]$.

For any x_1, $x_2 \in [-1, 1]$, $x_1 < x_2$, then $-x_2 \in [-1, 1]$, $x_1 + (-x_2) \neq 0$,

$x_1 - x_2 < 0$,

Since $f(x)$ is an odd function, $\dfrac{f(x_1) - f(x_2)}{x_1 - x_2} = \dfrac{f(x_1) + f(-x_2)}{x_1 + (-x_2)} > 0$.

So, $f(x_1) - f(x_2) < 0$.

Therefore, the function $f(x)$ is increasing for $x \in [-1, 1]$.

(2) $-1 \leqslant x + \dfrac{1}{2} < \dfrac{1}{x - 1} \leqslant 1 \Rightarrow x \in \left[-\dfrac{3}{2}, -1 \right)$.

(3) As the function $f(x)$ is increasing, $f(x) \leqslant f(1) = 1$.

Then for any $p \in [-1, 1]$, $-2mp + m^2 + 1 \geqslant 1$.

So $\begin{cases} -2m + m^2 + 1 \geqslant 1 \\ 2m + m^2 + 1 \geqslant 1 \end{cases}$.

Solving the system of inequalities gives $m \in (-\infty, -2] \cup [2, +\infty)$.

12. (1) maximum is $\frac{73}{8}$, no minimum.　(2) minimum is $\frac{3}{4}$, maximum is 13.　(3) no minimum, maximum is 31.

(4) minimum is 1, maximum is 21.

13. (1) minimum is -2, no maximum.　(2) minimum is $\frac{1}{2}$, no maximum.　(3) maximum is 2, minimum is 0.

(4) minimum is 0, maximum is $\frac{4}{3}$.　(5) no minimum, maximum is 1.

14. (1) $(-\infty, -2] \cup [2, +\infty)$.　(2) $[2, +\infty)$.　(3) $\left[\frac{5}{2}, +\infty\right)$.　(4) $\left[0, \frac{1}{2}\right]$.

(5) $[1, 5]$.　(6) $[3, +\infty)$.

15. Let R be the radius of the bottom and h be the height. The surface area is $S = 2\pi Rh + 2\pi R^2$.

As the volume $V = \pi R^2 h$ is constant, replacing h with V we have $S(R) = \frac{2V}{R} + 2\pi R^2$,

Using AM-GM inequality $S(R) = \frac{V}{R} + \frac{V}{R} + 2\pi R^2 \geqslant 3\sqrt[3]{\frac{V}{R} \cdot \frac{V}{R} \cdot 2\pi R^2}$.

$S(R) = 3\sqrt[3]{\frac{V}{R} \cdot \frac{V}{R} \cdot 2\pi R^2}$ If and only if $\frac{V}{R} = 2\pi R^2$, then $R = \sqrt[3]{\frac{V}{2\pi}}$.

As $V = \pi R^2 h$, $h = 2R$.

Therefore, the minimum area of material is obtained when $R = \sqrt[3]{\frac{V}{2\pi}}$, and $h = 2R$.

16. (1) When $a = 0$, $f(x)$ is even function; when $a \neq 0$, $f(x)$ is neither even nor odd;

(2) $f(x) = \begin{cases} x^2 + x - a + 1, & x \geqslant a \\ x^2 - x + a + 1, & x < a \end{cases}$,

If $a \leqslant -\frac{1}{2}$, the minimum of $f(x)$ is $f\left(-\frac{1}{2}\right) = \frac{3}{4} - a$;

If $-\frac{1}{2} < a \leqslant \frac{1}{2}$, the minimum of $f(x)$ is $f(a) = a^2 + 1$;

If $a > \frac{1}{2}$, the minimum of $f(x)$ is $f(a) = \frac{3}{4} + a$.

3.4 函数图像的变换

1. (1)

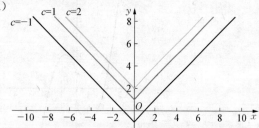

(2)

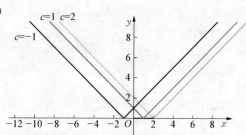

(3)

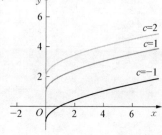

(4)

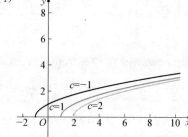

2. (1) $y = (x-3)^2 - 5$.　(2) $y = -(x+4)^2 - 8$.　(3) $y = (x-11)^3$.　(4) $y = -(x-5)^3 - 6$.

(5) $y = -|x| - 10$.　(6) $y = |x+2| - 8$.　(7) $y = -\sqrt{-x+7}$.　(8) $y = -\sqrt{-x} + 9$.

3. (1) (a) $y = x^2 + 1$;　(b) $y = -(x-1)^2 + 1$;　(c) $y = -2x^2$;　(d) $y = 3x^2 + 2$.

(2) (a) $y = -3x^3$;　(b) $y = \dfrac{1}{9}x^3$;　(c) $y = -(x-1)^3 + 1$; (d) $y = -x^3 + 2$.

(3) (a) $y = -|x+2|$;　(b) $y = |x-3| - 1$;　(c) $y = -2.5|x|$;　(d) $y = \dfrac{1}{2}|x| - 2$.

(4) (a) $y = \sqrt{x+4} - 3$;　(b) $y = -\sqrt{2-x} + 1$;　(c) $y = 3\sqrt{x}$;　(d) $y = -\dfrac{3}{2}\sqrt{x}$.

4. (1) $(-2, 0)$, $(-1, 1)$, $(0, 2)$.　(2) $f(x) = (4-x)^2$.

(3) As shown in the graph：

When $a < -3$, there is no intersection，

When $-3 < a < 1$, there are 4 intersections of $y = f(x)$ and $y = a$,

When $a = 1$, there are 3 intersections of $y = f(x)$ and $y = a$,

When $a = -3$ or $a > 1$, there are 2 intersections of $y = f(x)$ and $y = a$.

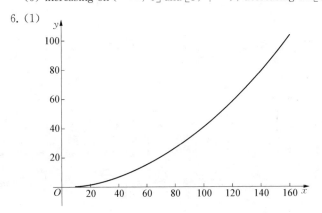

5. (1) increasing on $[-1, 2]$, decreasing on $(-\infty, -1]$ and $[2, +\infty)$.

(2) increasing on $[-2, 1]$, decreasing on $(-\infty, -2]$ and $[1, +\infty)$.

(3) increasing on $(-\infty, -1]$ and $\left[\dfrac{1}{2}, +\infty\right)$, decreasing on $\left[-1, \dfrac{1}{2}\right]$.

(4) increasing on $[-1, 2]$, decreasing on $(-\infty, -1]$ and $[2, +\infty)$.

(5) increasing on $(-\infty, 0]$ and $[3, +\infty)$, decreasing on $[0, 3]$.

6. (1)

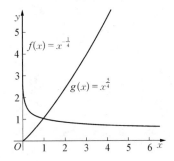

(2) $y = 0.001\,562\,5x^2 + 0.003\,75x - 0.033$, $16 \leqslant x \leqslant 256$.

第 4 章　几类重要的函数

4.1　幂函数

1. A line $y = 0$ with a point $(0, 1)$ removed.

2. See the right graph below.

3. (1) $y = x^{\frac{5}{3}}$ (2) $y = x^{\frac{1}{4}}$ (3) $y = x^{-\frac{1}{6}}$

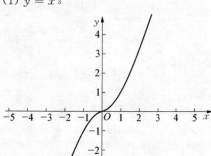
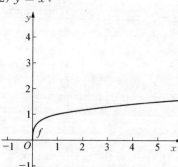
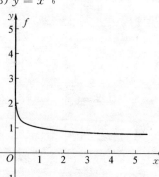

4. When $n = 1$, 3, 5, the functions are neither odd or even;

When $n = 2$, 6, the functions are odd;

When $n = 4$, the function is even.

5. When n is an even number and $n > 0$, $y = x^n$ increases on $[0, +\infty)$, and decreases on $(-\infty, 0]$;

When n is an even number and $n < 0$, $y = x^n$ increases on $(-\infty, 0)$, and decreases on $(0, +\infty)$;

When n is an odd number and $n > 0$, $y = x^n$ increases on $\mathbf{R}$;

When n is an odd number and $n < 0$, $y = x^n$ decreases on $(-\infty, 0)$ and $(0, +\infty)$.

6. 900 feet.

7. (1) $(-5)^{\frac{1}{3}} < (-1.5)^{\frac{2}{3}} < 2^{\frac{2}{3}}$. (2) $6.25^{\frac{3}{8}} < 0.5^{-\frac{3}{2}} < 0.16^{-\frac{3}{4}}$.

8. (1) False. (2) False. (3) True.

9. (1) $m = 1$, $f(x) = x^{-4}$.

(2) When $a \neq 0$ and $b \neq 0$, $g(x)$ is neither odd nor even;

When $a = 0$ and $b \neq 0$, $g(x)$ is an odd function;

When $a \neq 0$ and $b = 0$, $g(x)$ is an even function;

When $a = 0$ and $b = 0$, $g(x)$ is both an even and odd function.

10. (1) $m = 0$. (2) Let $\sqrt{1-2x} = t$, $t \in [0, 1]$, $g(x) = -\frac{1}{2}t^2 + t + \frac{1}{2} \in \left[\frac{1}{2}, 1\right]$.

4.2 指数函数

1. $y = 4^x$ and $y = 0.25^x$; $y = 2.5^x$ and $y = 0.4^x$.

2.

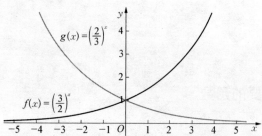

3. $a = 49$, $b = 79.70$, $c = 129.64$, $d = 210.87$, $e = 343$.

(1) The difference increases. (2) The quotient remains constant.

4. $m \leqslant -2$.

5. (1) odd function. (2) When $0 < a < 1$, $f(x)$ is decreasing; When $a > 1$, $f(x)$ is increasing.

6. (1) $f(x) = a^x + 1 - \frac{3}{x+1}$.

(2) Hint: When $x \in (-\infty, -1) \cup (-1, 0)$, $a^x + 1 \in \left(1, 1+\frac{1}{a}\right) \cup \left(1+\frac{1}{a}, 2\right)$, $-\frac{3}{x+1} \in (-\infty, -3) \cup (0, +\infty)$.

7. (1) $y = 100\,000\,(1+8\%)^x$. (2) From $100\,000\,(1+8\%)^x = 400\,000$, we can get $x \approx 18$.

8. $175\,(1-10\%)^5 \approx 103.3$.

9. $10\,000\,(1+2.25\%\times80\%)^9(1+2.25\%)\approx12\,005.86.$

10. When n is an even number, there are three intersection points;

When n is an odd number, there are two intersection points.

4.3 对数运算

1. (1) $\dfrac{3}{2}$.　(2) 6.　(3) $\dfrac{4}{3}$.　(4) 6.　(5) $\dfrac{5}{2}$.　(6) 1.　(7) 1.

2. (1) $2\ln 2+\ln x$.　(2) $\log_3 10+\log_3 z$.　(3) $\dfrac{4}{3}\log_2 x$.　(4) $\lg y-\lg 2$.　(5) $1-\log_5 x$.　(6) $-3\log_6 z$.

(7) $\dfrac{1}{2}\ln z$.　(8) $\dfrac{1}{3}\ln t$.　(9) $\ln x+\ln y+2\ln z$.　(10) $\ln z+2\ln(z-1)$.　(11) $\lg x+4\lg y-5\lg z$.

(12) $2\log_5 x-2\log_5 y-3\log_5 z$.　(13) $\ln 6-\dfrac{1}{2}\ln(x^2+1)$.　(14) $\ln x-\dfrac{3}{2}\ln y$.

(15) $4\log_2 x+\dfrac{1}{2}\log_2 y-\dfrac{3}{2}\log_2 z$.

3. (1) $\ln 2x$.　(2) $\log_5\dfrac{8}{t}$.　(3) $\log_2 x^2 y^4$.　(4) $\log_7\sqrt[3]{(z-2)^2}$.　(5) $\log_3\sqrt[4]{5x}$.　(6) $\log_6\dfrac{1}{16x^4}$.　(7) $\lg\dfrac{x}{(x+1)^2}$.

(8) $\ln\dfrac{64}{(z-4)^5}$.　(9) $\lg\dfrac{xz^3}{y^2}$.　(10) $\ln\dfrac{x}{x^2-1}$.　(11) $\ln\dfrac{z^4(z+5)^4}{(z-5)^2}$.　(12) $\log_8\dfrac{\sqrt[3]{y}(y+4)^2}{y-1}$.

4. (1) $a+2b$.　(2) $2(a+b)$.　(3) $a-2b$.　(4) $a-2$.

5. (1) 3.　(2) $\dfrac{1}{2}$.　(3) 1.　(4) 2.

6. $\dfrac{3a+2}{2(a+2)}$.

7. (1) 2.　(2) $\dfrac{3}{2}$.　(3) 75.　(4) $\dfrac{9}{4}$.

8. Hint: Let $3^x=4^y=6^z=t(t>1)$, then $\dfrac{1}{x}=\log_t 3$, $\dfrac{1}{y}=\log_t 4$, $\dfrac{1}{z}=\log_t 6$.

9. (1) 34.　(2) 19.

10. $\dfrac{a+b}{2-a}$.

4.4 对数函数

1. (1) $4^2=16$.　(2) $9^{-2}=\dfrac{1}{81}$.　(3) $32^{\frac{2}{5}}=4$.　(4) $64^{\frac{1}{2}}=8$.

2. (1) $\log_5 125=3$.　(2) $\log_9 27=\dfrac{3}{2}$.　(3) $\log_4\dfrac{1}{64}=-3$.　(4) $\log_{24}1=0$.

3. (1) 6.　(2) $\dfrac{1}{2}$.　(3) 0.　(4) 1.　(5) 2.　(6) -3.

4. (1) $(-1,+\infty)$.　(2) $(-\infty,0)\cup(0,+\infty)$.　(3) $(-\infty,-1)\cup(1,+\infty)$.

5. (1) $\log_a b>\log_a c$.　(2) $\log_{\frac{1}{a}}b<\log_{\frac{1}{a}}c$.

6. (1) $(1,10)$.　(2) $(0,3)$.　(3) $\left(\dfrac{1}{2},1\right)$.

7. (1) Increasing interval: $(-7,+\infty)$.　(2) Decreasing interval: $(-\infty,3)$.

(3) Increasing interval: $(-\infty,-1)$; Decreasing interval: $(1,+\infty)$.

(4) Increasing interval: $\left(-2,\dfrac{7}{2}\right]$; Decreasing interval: $\left[\dfrac{7}{2},9\right)$.

8. (1) $(-2,2)$.　(2) odd function.　(3) When $0<a<1$, the solution set is $\left[\dfrac{2}{3},1\right]$. When $a>1$, the solution set is

$[1,2)\cup\left(0,\dfrac{2}{3}\right]$.

9. (1) $\left[-\dfrac{1}{8},0\right]$.　(2) $(-\infty,0]$ $\left(\text{hint: } m\leqslant 2t+\dfrac{1}{t}-3\right)$.

10. (1) $a=2$.　(2) $a=\pm1$.　(3) $[1,2)$.

11. (1) $x = 0, 2$. (2) $x = 0$. (3) $x = \dfrac{1}{4}$. (4) $x = 0$. (5) $x = \dfrac{1}{2}$. (6) $x = \pm 2$. (7) $x = \log_{\frac{1+\sqrt{5}}{2}} \dfrac{3}{2}$.

(8) $x = \dfrac{3}{2}$. (9) $x = 0, 1$. (10) $x = 3$.

12. (1) $x = 4$. (2) $x = 2\sqrt{2} - 1$. (3) $x = 2$. (4) $x = \pm 1$. (5) $x = \pm 10, \pm \dfrac{1}{1\,000}$. (6) $x = \dfrac{1}{5}$, 25.

(7) $x = 10, \dfrac{1}{10}$. (8) $x = -\log_2 3, -\log_2 \dfrac{5}{4}$.

13. i) $a = 0$ or $\dfrac{1}{3} \leqslant a < 1$; ii) $0 < a < \dfrac{1}{3}$; iii) $a < 0$ or $a \geqslant 1$.

第 5 章 三 角

5.1 弧度制

1. (1)

Angle	45°	120°	−36°	−420°
Largest Negative	−315°	−240°	−36°	−60°
Smallest Positive	45°	120°	324°	300°

(2) $\dfrac{\pi}{3}$: ; $\dfrac{5\pi}{2}$:

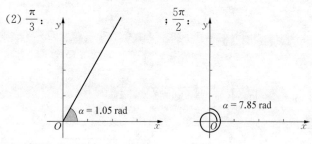

(3)

Angle	$\dfrac{9\pi}{4}$	$-\dfrac{\pi}{3}$
Largest Negative	$-\dfrac{7\pi}{4}$	$-\dfrac{\pi}{3}$
Smallest Positive	$\dfrac{\pi}{4}$	$\dfrac{5\pi}{3}$

(4) $\dfrac{\pi}{6}$: complementary $= \dfrac{\pi}{3}$, supplementary $= \dfrac{5\pi}{6}$; $\dfrac{5\pi}{6}$: complementary $=$ N/A, supplementary $= \dfrac{\pi}{6}$.

(5) I or III

2.

Degrees	60°	320°	30°	300°
Radians	$\dfrac{\pi}{3}$	$\dfrac{16\pi}{9}$	$\dfrac{\pi}{6}$	$\dfrac{5\pi}{3}$

3. 24π cm.

4. $\dfrac{\pi}{3}$ cm/sec.

5. (1) $5\,000\pi$ rad/min. (2) $25\,000\pi$ in/min.

6. (1) F. (2) T. (3) F.

7. (1) 8.98°. (2) (a) 14.66 ft/sec, 10.00 mile/hour; (b) $d = \dfrac{7\pi}{7\,920} n$; (c) $d = \dfrac{7\pi}{7\,920} t$.

8. (1) $\theta = \dfrac{n\pi}{180} \Rightarrow A = \dfrac{n\pi}{360}r^2 = \dfrac{1}{2} \cdot \dfrac{n\pi}{180} \cdot r^2 = \dfrac{1}{2}\theta r^2$. (2) 157.08 m². (3) 312.76 in².

9. (1) increase according to the ratio between the radii of new and old blades. (2) one radian is greater.

(3) increase according to the speed of increase in radius.

5.2 任意角的三角函数

1. $\sin\theta = \dfrac{3\sqrt{13}}{13}$, $\cos\theta = -\dfrac{2\sqrt{13}}{13}$, $\tan\theta = -\dfrac{3}{2}$.

2. $\cos\theta = -\dfrac{3}{5}$.

3. $\sin\dfrac{3\pi}{2} = -1$, $\cot\dfrac{3\pi}{2} = 0$.

4. $213° \to 33°$, $\dfrac{14\pi}{9} \to \dfrac{4\pi}{9}$, $\dfrac{4\pi}{5} \to \dfrac{\pi}{5}$.

5.

Angle	$\dfrac{\pi}{2}$	0	$-\dfrac{5\pi}{6}$	$-\dfrac{3\pi}{4}$
Sine	1	0	$-\dfrac{1}{2}$	$-\dfrac{\sqrt{2}}{2}$
Cosine	0	1	$-\dfrac{\sqrt{3}}{2}$	$-\dfrac{\sqrt{2}}{2}$
Tangent	N/A	0	$\dfrac{\sqrt{3}}{3}$	1
Cotangent	0	N/A	$\sqrt{3}$	1
Secant	N/A	1	$-\dfrac{2\sqrt{3}}{3}$	$-\sqrt{2}$
Cosecant	1	N/A	-2	$-\sqrt{2}$

6. $\cos\theta = -\dfrac{2\sqrt{2}}{3}$, $\tan\theta = \dfrac{\sqrt{2}}{4}$.

7. (1) F. (2) F. (3) F.

8. (1)

t	0	$\dfrac{1}{4}$	$\dfrac{1}{2}$	$\dfrac{3}{4}$	1
y	$\dfrac{1}{4}$	$\dfrac{1}{4}\cos\dfrac{3}{2}$	$\dfrac{1}{4}\cos 3$	$\dfrac{1}{4}\cos\dfrac{9}{2}$	$\dfrac{1}{4}\cos 6$

(2)

θ	30°	60°	90°	120°
d	12	$4\sqrt{3}$	6	$4\sqrt{3}$

9. (1) $\cos 1.5 \approx 0.070\,7$, $2\cos 0.75 \approx 1.463\,4$.

(2) $\sin 0.25 \approx 0.247\,4$, $\sin 0.75 \approx 0.681\,6$, $\sin 1 \approx 0.841\,5$.

(3) a. The two points are symmetric with respect to the $y-$axis; b. $\sin t_1 = \sin(\pi - t_1)$; c. $\cos t_1 = -\cos(\pi - t_1)$.

10. (1) x decreases from 12 to 0; y increases from 0 to 12; $\sin\theta$ increases from 0 to 1, proportional to y; $\cos\theta$ decreases

from 1 to 0, proportional to x; $\tan\theta$ increases from 0 to positive infinity, proportional to $\dfrac{y}{x}$.

(2) a. $\sin t = y$, $\cos t = x$; b. $r = 1$; c. $\sin\theta = y$, $\cos\theta = x$; d. $\sin t = \sin\theta$.

5.3 诱导公式

1. (1) $\sin\theta = -\dfrac{\sqrt{5}}{3}$, $\cos\theta = -\dfrac{2}{3}$, $\tan\theta = \dfrac{\sqrt{5}}{2}$, $\cot\theta = \dfrac{2\sqrt{5}}{5}$, $\sec\theta = -\dfrac{3}{2}$, $\csc\theta = -\dfrac{3\sqrt{5}}{5}$.

(2)

Angle	Sine	Cosine	Tangent	Cotangent	Secant	Cosecant
$\dfrac{\pi}{2}+\theta$	$\cos\theta$	$-\sin\theta$	$-\cot\theta$	$-\tan\theta$	$-\csc\theta$	$\sec\theta$

(3) $-\cos^2\theta$.

2. (1) $\dfrac{\tan^2\theta}{1+\sec\theta}=\dfrac{\sin^2\theta}{\cos^2\theta+\cos\theta}=\dfrac{1-\cos^2\theta}{\cos\theta(\cos\theta+1)}=\dfrac{1-\cos\theta}{\cos\theta}$.

(2) $\dfrac{\sin\theta}{1+\cos\theta}=\dfrac{\sin\theta(1-\cos\theta)}{1-\cos^2\theta}=\dfrac{\sin\theta(1-\cos\theta)}{\sin^2\theta}=\dfrac{1-\cos\theta}{\sin\theta}$.

(3) $\tan^2\theta-\sin^2\theta=\sin^2\theta(\sec^2\theta-1)=\sin^2\theta\tan^2\theta$.

(4) $\dfrac{\tan\theta-\cot\theta}{\sec\theta-\csc\theta}=\dfrac{\sin^2\theta-\cos^2\theta}{\sin\theta-\cos\theta}=\sin\theta+\cos\theta$.

3. (1) F. (2) F. (3) F.

4. (1) $\dfrac{h\sin(90°-\theta)}{\sin\theta}=h\dfrac{\cos\theta}{\sin\theta}=h\cot\theta$.

(2)

θ	15°	30°	45°	60°	75°	90°
s	$10+5\sqrt{3}$	$5\sqrt{3}$	5	$\dfrac{5\sqrt{3}}{3}$	$10-5\sqrt{3}$	0

(3) Maximum：N/A；minimum：90°.

(4) About 12 P.M.

5. (1) a. $2+\cos^2\theta-3\cos^4\theta=(1-\cos^2\theta)(2+3\cos^2\theta)=\sin^2\theta(2+3\cos^2\theta)$；

b. LHS

$$=\dfrac{\cos x-\cos y}{\sin x+\sin y}+\dfrac{\sin^2 x-\sin^2 y}{(\sin x+\sin y)(\cos x+\cos y)}$$

$$=\dfrac{\cos x-\cos y}{\sin x+\sin y}+\dfrac{\cos^2 y-\cos^2 x}{(\sin x+\sin y)(\cos x+\cos y)}$$

$$=\dfrac{\cos x-\cos y}{\sin x+\sin y}+\dfrac{\cos y-\cos x}{\sin x+\sin y}$$

$$=0.$$

c. $\dfrac{\tan x+\tan y}{1-\tan x\tan y}=\dfrac{\dfrac{1}{\tan y}+\dfrac{1}{\tan x}}{\dfrac{1}{\tan x\tan y}-1}=\dfrac{\cot x+\cot y}{\cot x\cot y-1}$.

(2) a. 1；b. -2.

6. (1) Take $b=1$, then $c^2=\sec^2\theta$, $a^2=c^2-b^2=\sec^2\theta-1$, while $\dfrac{a^2}{c^2}=\sin^2\theta$.

(2) a. When $k=1$, YES by definition; when $k=0$, take $\theta=\dfrac{\pi}{4}$; otherwise, take $\theta=\dfrac{1}{k}$；

b. $(1+\cot^2\theta)\cos^2\theta=\csc^2\theta\cdot\cos^2\theta=\cot^2\theta$；c. Take $\theta=\dfrac{3\pi}{2}$；d. Take $\theta=\dfrac{\pi}{4}$.

5.4 三角恒等式

1. $-\dfrac{63}{65}$.

2. $\sin 2\theta=-\dfrac{24}{25}$, $\cos 2\theta=\dfrac{7}{25}$, $\tan 2\theta=-\dfrac{24}{7}$.

3. (1) $\cos 3x=4\cos^3 x-3\cos x$. (2) $\cos x=\dfrac{1-\tan^2\dfrac{x}{2}}{1+\tan^2\dfrac{x}{2}}$, $\tan x=\dfrac{2\tan\dfrac{x}{2}}{1-\tan^2\dfrac{x}{2}}$.

(3) $\cos^4 \theta = \dfrac{3}{8} + \dfrac{1}{2}\cos 2\theta + \dfrac{1}{8}\cos 4\theta$.

4. (1) $\cos \dfrac{\pi}{12} = \cos\left(\dfrac{\pi}{3} - \dfrac{\pi}{4}\right) = \dfrac{\sqrt{6} + \sqrt{2}}{4}$.   (2) $\cos \dfrac{\pi}{12} = \sqrt{\dfrac{1 + \cos \dfrac{\pi}{6}}{2}} = \dfrac{\sqrt{6} + \sqrt{2}}{4}$.

5. $\sin 5x \cos 3x = \dfrac{1}{2}(\sin 8x + \sin 2x) = \dfrac{1}{2}\left[\sin 8x - \sin(-2x)\right]$.

6. $\dfrac{\sqrt{2}}{2}$.

7. (1) F.   (2) F.   (3) T.

8. $x = 2r - 2r\cos\theta$.

9. (1) a. $\sqrt{3}$; b. $-\dfrac{\sqrt{3}}{2}$; c. $\sqrt{3}$; d. $-\dfrac{\sqrt{3}}{2}$.

    (2) a. $\left(\dfrac{a}{\sqrt{a^2 + b^2}}\right)^2 + \left(\dfrac{b}{\sqrt{a^2 + b^2}}\right)^2 = 1$; b. $\sin(\theta + \varphi) = \dfrac{1}{\sqrt{a^2 + b^2}}(a\sin\theta + b\cos\theta)$; c. see part b.

10. (1) $|AB| = \sqrt{(\cos\alpha - \cos\beta)^2 + (\sin\alpha - \sin\beta)^2} = \sqrt{2 - 2(\cos\alpha\cos\beta + \sin\alpha\sin\beta)}$,

    $|A'B'| = \sqrt{(\cos(\alpha - \beta) - 1)^2 + \sin^2(\alpha - \beta)} = \sqrt{2 - 2\cos(\alpha - \beta)}$,

    we have $\cos(\alpha - \beta) = \cos\alpha\cos\beta + \sin\alpha\sin\beta$.

    (2) a. $\dfrac{t^2 + 2t + 1}{-2t^2}$; b. $\dfrac{1 + t^2}{1 + 2t - t^2}$; c. $\dfrac{(1 - r^2)(1 + t^2)}{(1 + r)^2 t^2 + (1 - r)^2}$.

5.5 正弦定理和余弦定理

1. (1) 8.56.   (2) $\sqrt{19}$.   (3) $b = 32\sqrt{2}$, $c = 16(\sqrt{6} + \sqrt{2})$, $C = 105°$.   (4) $A \approx 26.38°$, $B \approx 36.34°$, $C \approx$
117.28°.   (5) $a \approx 18.26$, $B \approx 59.66°$, $C \approx 40.34°$.   (6) $B \approx 12.39°$, $C \approx 136.61°$, $c \approx 16.01$.   (7) $b\sin A > a \Rightarrow$
$\sin B > 1$.   (8) $B_1 \approx 70.44°$, $C_1 \approx 51.56°$, $c_1 \approx 4.16$, $B_2 \approx 109.56°$, $C_2 \approx 12.44°$, $c_1 \approx 1.14$.   (9) $6\sqrt{11}$.
(10) $9\sqrt{3}$.

2. (1) T.   (2) F.   (3) F.

3. (1) a. 0.094; b. $\beta = \left(\dfrac{\pi}{2} - \alpha\right) - \theta$; c. $d = 58.36\dfrac{\cos(\alpha + \theta)}{\sin\theta}$.   (2) 373 m.

4. (1) $S_{\triangle ABC} = S_{\triangle ABD} + S_{\triangle ACD}$, $S_{\triangle ABC} = \dfrac{1}{2}AB \cdot AC \cdot \sin\angle BAC$, $S_{\triangle ABD} = \dfrac{1}{2}AB \cdot AD \cdot \sin\angle BAD$, $S_{\triangle ACD} = \dfrac{1}{2}AC \cdot$

    $AD \cdot \sin\angle CAD$. Thus, $\dfrac{\sin\angle BAC}{AD} = \dfrac{\sin\angle CAD}{AB} + \dfrac{\sin\angle BAD}{AC}$.

    (2) a. Let $AB = 1$. $AD = \sin\theta + \cos\theta = \dfrac{AB}{\sin\angle D} \cdot \sin\angle ABD = \dfrac{\sin\left(\theta + \dfrac{\pi}{4}\right)}{\sin\dfrac{\pi}{4}} = \sqrt{2}\sin\left(\theta + \dfrac{\pi}{4}\right)$, where $\theta = \angle A$.

    b. Let $AB = b$, $\angle A = \theta$, $\dfrac{CD}{BC} = \dfrac{a}{b}$. Then, $AD = b\cos\theta + a\sin\theta$, while $\dfrac{AD}{\sin(\theta + \varphi)} = \dfrac{b}{\sin\varphi}$, where $\varphi = \angle D$. Hence,

    $a\sin\theta + b\cos\theta = b\sin\theta\cot\varphi + b\cos\theta$. Since $\cot\varphi = \dfrac{CD}{BC} = \dfrac{a}{b}$, the claim follows.

    (3) $a\sin B = b\sin A = h \Rightarrow \dfrac{a}{\sin A} = \dfrac{b}{\sin B}$. The Law of Sines follows.

    $a^2 = (b\sin A)^2 + (c - b\cos A)^2 = c^2 + b^2 - 2bc\cos A$. Other facts of the Law of Cosines follow similarly.

5. (1) See the table below.

a	b	c	A	B	C
12	16	18	40.81°	60.61°	78.58°
10	6.56	15	31.40°	20°	128.60°
9	14.5	8.18	34.23°	115°	30.77°
18	25.71	31.38	35°	55°	90°

(2) a. $a = 3$ or $a \geqslant 5$; b. $3 < a < 5$; c. $a < 3$.

第6章 三 角 函 数

6.1 正弦函数和余弦函数

1. Within one period $[0, 2\pi]$, curve $y = \cos x$ starts from $(0, 1)$ and descends to $\left(\dfrac{\pi}{2}, 0\right)$ with increasing speed, followed by a further descend to $(\pi, -1)$ with decreasing speed. The curve then rises to $\left(\dfrac{3\pi}{2}, 0\right)$ with increasing speed, followed by a further rise to $(2\pi, 1)$ with decreasing speed. Repeating this on both sides to obtain the cosine curve.

2. (1) $y = \dfrac{1}{3}\sin x$.　　　　　　　　　　　(2) $y = \dfrac{1}{3}\cos x$.

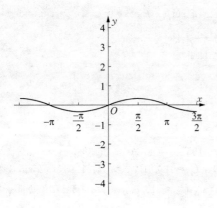 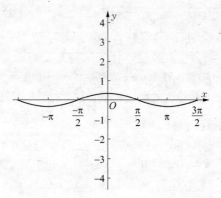

(3) $y = 3\sin x$.　　　　　　　　　　　(4) $y = 5\sin x$.

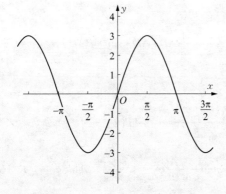 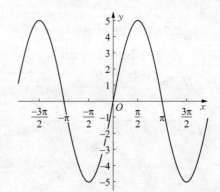

(5) $y = \cos \dfrac{x}{3}$.　　　　　　　　　　　(6) $y = \sin \dfrac{\pi x}{4}$.

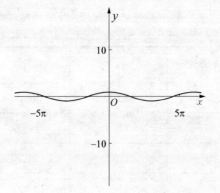 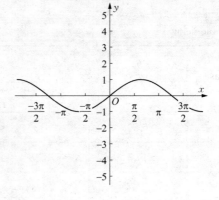

(7) $y = \cos x - 5$.

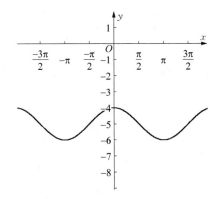

(8) $y = \sin x + 1$.

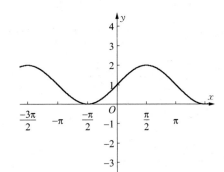

(9) $y = \cos\left(x + \dfrac{\pi}{4}\right)$.

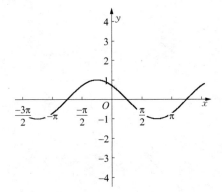

(10) $y = \sin(x - 2\pi)$.

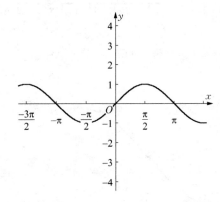

(11) $y = -\dfrac{1}{2}\sin(\pi x + \pi)$.

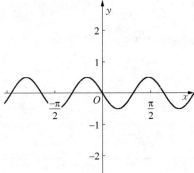

(12) $y = 4\cos\left(x + \dfrac{\pi}{4}\right) + 4$.

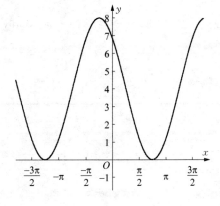

3. (1) 2π, increases on $\left[2k\pi - \dfrac{\pi}{4},\ 2k\pi + \dfrac{3\pi}{4}\right]$, decreases on $\left[2k\pi + \dfrac{3\pi}{4},\ 2k\pi + \dfrac{7\pi}{4}\right]$, $k \in \mathbf{Z}$.

(2) 2π, increases on $\left[2k\pi - \dfrac{\pi}{2} - \varphi,\ 2k\pi + \dfrac{\pi}{2} - \varphi\right]$, decreases on $\left[2k\pi + \dfrac{\pi}{2} - \varphi,\ 2k\pi + \dfrac{3\pi}{2} - \varphi\right]$,

$$k \in \mathbf{Z},\ \begin{cases} \cos\varphi = \dfrac{a}{\sqrt{a^2 + b^2}} \\ \sin\varphi = \dfrac{b}{\sqrt{a^2 + b^2}} \end{cases}.$$

4. (1) minimum $= 0$ when $x = k\pi + \dfrac{\pi}{2}$, maximum $= 1$ when $x = k\pi$, $k \in \mathbf{Z}$.

(2) minimum $= \dfrac{3}{4}$ when $x = k\pi - (-1)^k \dfrac{\pi}{6}$, maximum $= 3$ when $x = 2k\pi + \dfrac{\pi}{2}$, $k \in \mathbf{Z}$.

(3) minimum $= b - |a|$ when $x = 2k\pi - \mathrm{sgn}(a)\dfrac{\pi}{2}$, maximum $= b + |a|$ when $x = 2k\pi + \mathrm{sgn}(a)\dfrac{\pi}{2}$, $k \in \mathbf{Z}$.

5. $y = 2\sin(0.524t) + 5.0$.

6. (1) F.　(2) T.　(3) T.

7. (1) a. $\dfrac{1}{440}$; b. 440.

(2) a.

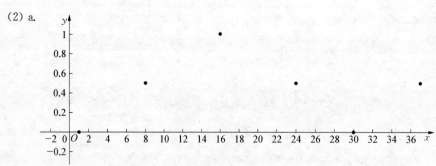

b. $y = \dfrac{1}{2} - \dfrac{1}{2}\cos\dfrac{2(x-1)\pi}{29}$.

c.

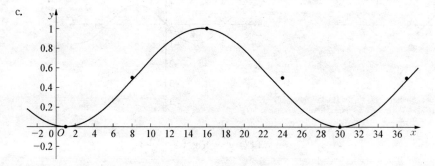

d. 29; e. 0.928.

8. (1) Let x_1, $x_2 \in [2k\pi + \pi, 2k\pi + 2\pi]$ (not necessarily distinct). Since $\sin x \leqslant 0$ for all $x \in [2k\pi + \pi, 2k\pi + 2\pi]$, $\dfrac{\sin x_1 + \sin x_2}{2} = \sin\dfrac{x_1 + x_2}{2}\cos\dfrac{x_1 - x_2}{2} \geqslant \sin\dfrac{x_1 + x_2}{2}$. The other claim follows similarly.

(2) $y = A\sin(\omega x + \varphi) + d$, A, ω, φ, $d > 0$.

Domain	**R**
Range	$[d - A, d + A]$
Symmetry	Even when $\varphi = k\pi + \dfrac{\pi}{2}$, $k \in \mathbf{Z}$. Odd when $\varphi = k\pi$, $k \in \mathbf{Z}$ and $d = 0$
Period	$\dfrac{2\pi}{\omega}$
Zeroes	$x = \dfrac{k\pi - \varphi}{\omega}$, $k \in \mathbf{Z}$
Monotonicity	Increasing on $\left[\dfrac{4k\pi - \pi - 2\varphi}{2\omega}, \dfrac{4k\pi + \pi - 2\varphi}{2\omega}\right]$ Decreasing on $\left[\dfrac{4k\pi + \pi - 2\varphi}{2\omega}, \dfrac{4k\pi + 3\pi - 2\varphi}{2\omega}\right]$, $k \in \mathbf{Z}$

续 表

Domain	**R**
Extremum	Maximum value $d + A$ when $x = \dfrac{4k\pi + \pi - 2\varphi}{2\omega}$ Minimum value $d - A$ when $x = \dfrac{4k\pi - \pi - 2\varphi}{2\omega}$, $k \in \mathbf{Z}$
Concavity	Concave upward on $\left[\dfrac{2k\pi + \pi - \varphi}{\omega}, \dfrac{2k\pi + 2\pi - \varphi}{\omega} \right]$ Concave downward on $\left[\dfrac{2k\pi - \varphi}{\omega}, \dfrac{2k\pi + \pi - \varphi}{\omega} \right]$, $k \in \mathbf{Z}$
Key Points	$\left(-\dfrac{\varphi}{\omega}, d \right)$, $\left(\dfrac{\pi - 2\varphi}{2\omega}, d + A \right)$, $\left(\dfrac{\pi - \varphi}{\omega}, d \right)$, $\left(\dfrac{3\pi - \varphi}{2\omega}, d - A \right)$, $\left(\dfrac{2\pi - \varphi}{\omega}, d \right)$

9. (1) No. The alternative definition does not include functions with domains taking the shape of $(-\infty, a]$.

(2) Assume that the function admits the period T. Then, $D(T) = D(0) \Rightarrow T \in \mathbf{Q}$. Hence, $D\left(x + \dfrac{T}{2}\right) = D(x)$ for all x, whence $\dfrac{T}{2}$ is a smaller positive period of $D(x)$, contradiction.

(3) a. $\lfloor x + 1 \rfloor = \lfloor x \rfloor + 1 \Rightarrow [(x + 1) - \lfloor x + 1 \rfloor] - [x - \lfloor x \rfloor] = 0$.

b. Let $T = n + \alpha$, $\alpha \in [0, 1)$. Then, $-T = -n - 1 + (1 - \alpha)$. Hence, $\lfloor T \rfloor = n$, while
$$\lfloor -T \rfloor = \begin{cases} -n - 1, & \alpha > 0 \\ -n, & \alpha = 0 \end{cases}.$$
The claim follows.

c. Assume the contrast and let T be a period of $f(x) = \sin x + x - \lfloor x \rfloor$. Then, $f(\pm T) = f(0) = 0$. Hence, $0 = f(T) + f(-T) = -(\lfloor T \rfloor + \lfloor -T \rfloor) \Rightarrow T \in \mathbf{Z}$, which is absurd.

6.2 其他三角函数

1.

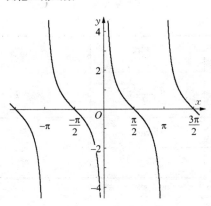

$y = \cot x$

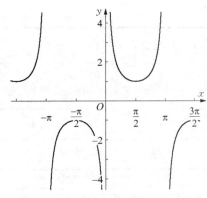

$y = \csc x$

2.

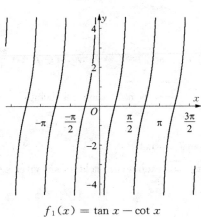

$f_1(x) = \tan x - \cot x$

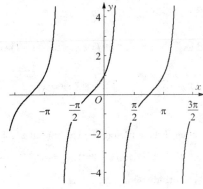

$f_2(x) = \tan 2x + \sec 2x$

3. (1) $f_1 \to +\infty$ as $x \to 0$ from the right while $f_1 \to -\infty$ as $x \to 0$ from the left.

(2) $f_2(x) \to +\infty$ as $x \to 0$ from the right while $f_2(x) \to -\infty$ as $x \to 0$ from the left.

(3) $f_3(x) \to 1$ as $x \to 0$.   (4) $f_4(x) \to 0$ as $x \to 0$.

(5) $f_5(x)$ oscillates between ± 1 as $x \to 0$.   (6) $f_6(x) \to 0$ as $x \to 0$.

4. (1)

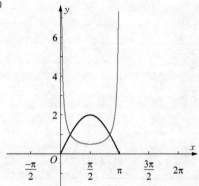

(2) $\left(\dfrac{\pi}{6}, \dfrac{5\pi}{6}\right)$.   (3) $f(x) \to 0$ from the right as $x \to \pi$ from the left. Hence, $g(x) \to +\infty$.

5. (1) $f_1(x) \to 0$.   (2) $f_2(x) \to 1$.   (3) $f_3(x) \to 1$.   (4) $f_4(x) \to 0$.

6. (1) Increases on $\left[k\pi + \dfrac{\pi}{4}, k\pi + \dfrac{\pi}{2}\right)$, decreases on $\left(k\pi - \dfrac{\pi}{2}, k\pi + \dfrac{\pi}{4}\right]$, $k \in \mathbf{Z}$.

(2) $[0, 2]$.

(3) Maximum $= \dfrac{\sqrt{2}}{4}$ when $x = \dfrac{\pi}{4}$; minimum $= 0$ when $x = 0$ or $\dfrac{\pi}{2}$.

(4) Domain: $\mathbf{R}$; range: $\left[1 - \dfrac{\sqrt{2}}{2}, 1 + \dfrac{\sqrt{2}}{2}\right]$. Increases on $\left[k\pi - \dfrac{\pi}{8}, k\pi + \dfrac{3\pi}{8}\right]$, decreases on $\left[k\pi + \dfrac{3\pi}{8}, k\pi + \dfrac{7\pi}{8}\right]$, $k \in \mathbf{Z}$. It is neither even nor odd, with period $= \pi$.

7. (In what follows, $k \in \mathbf{Z}$.)

	$f_1(x)$	$f_2(x)$	$f_3(x)$	$f_4(x)$
Domain	$\left\{x \mid x \neq k\pi + \dfrac{\pi}{2}\right\}$	$\left\{x \mid x \neq k\pi + \dfrac{\pi}{2}\right\}$	$\{x \mid x \neq k\pi\}$	$\{x \mid x \neq k\pi\}$
Symmetry	Odd	Even	Even	Odd
Period	N/A	N/A	N/A	N/A

8. (1) F.   (2) F.   (3) T.

9. (1) As time elapses, the displacement decays.

(2) $d = 27\sec x$ $\left(-\dfrac{\pi}{2} < x < \dfrac{\pi}{2}\right)$

10. (1) Assume the contrast and let T be a period of $f(x) = \tan\sqrt{x}$. Then, $\tan\sqrt{T} = \tan\sqrt{0} \Rightarrow T = (n\pi)^2$, $n \in \mathbf{Z}$. Yet $\dfrac{\pi^2}{4}$ does not lie the domain of $f(x)$ while $\dfrac{\pi^2}{4} + T$ does $\left(\text{since } \sqrt{\dfrac{\pi^2}{4} + T} = \dfrac{\sqrt{n^2 + 1}}{2}\pi \text{ is not an integral multiple of } \dfrac{\pi}{2}\right)$, contradiction.

Assume the contrast and let T be a period of $f(x) = \tan x^2$. Then, $\tan T^2 = \tan 0^2 \Rightarrow T = \sqrt{n\pi}$, $n \in \mathbf{N}^*$. Yet $\tan(\sqrt{\pi})^2 = \tan(\sqrt{\pi} + \sqrt{n\pi})^2 = 0$ and $\tan(\sqrt{2\pi})^2 = \tan(\sqrt{2\pi} + \sqrt{n\pi})^2 = 0$ cannot both hold for any given $n \in \mathbf{N}^*$ (since $\sqrt{2}$ is irrational), contradiction.

(2) a. $\approx 0.739\,1$; b. the same root.

11. (1) $b = 0$, $2d + a(\sin c + \cos c) = 0$.

(2) a.

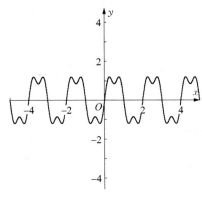
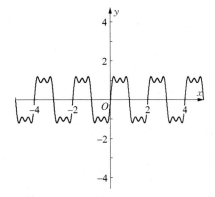

$$y_1 = \frac{4}{\pi}\left(\sin \pi x + \frac{1}{3}\sin 3\pi x\right) \qquad y_2 = \frac{4}{\pi}\left(\sin \pi x + \frac{1}{3}\sin 3\pi x + \frac{1}{5}\sin 5\pi x\right)$$

b. $y_3 = \frac{4}{\pi}\left(\sin \pi x + \frac{1}{3}\sin 3\pi x + \frac{1}{5}\sin 5\pi x + \frac{1}{7}\sin 7\pi x\right)$.

c. $y_4 = \frac{4}{\pi}\left(\sin \pi x + \frac{1}{3}\sin 3\pi x + \frac{1}{5}\sin 5\pi x + \frac{1}{7}\sin 7\pi x + \frac{1}{9}\sin 9\pi x\right)$.

6.3 三角函数的应用

1. (1) $y = 4\sin \pi t$.　(2) $y = 3\sin \frac{\pi}{3}t$.　(3) $y = 3\cos \frac{4\pi}{3}t$.　(4) $y = 2\cos \frac{\pi}{5}t$.　(5) $y = 2\sin\left(2\pi t + \frac{\pi}{6}\right)$.

2.

No.	Displacement	Frequency	$d(5)$	Zero
(1)	9	$\frac{3}{5}$	9	$\frac{5}{12}$
(2)	$\frac{1}{2}$	10	$\frac{1}{2}$	$\frac{1}{40}$
(3)	$\frac{1}{4}$	3	0	$\frac{1}{6}$
(4)	$\frac{1}{64}$	396	0	$\frac{1}{792}$

3. (1) Maximum $= \sqrt{2} - 1$ when $x = \sqrt{2}\sin \frac{\pi}{8}$, minimum $= -\sqrt{2} - 1$ when $x = -\sqrt{2}\sin \frac{3\pi}{8}$.

(2) $a = \sin^2 \theta$, $b = \cos^2 \theta \Rightarrow$ LHS $= \sin^2 \theta \cos^2 \theta + \dfrac{2}{\sin^2 \theta \cos^2 \theta} - 2$. The claim follows from the monotonicity of function

$y = t + \dfrac{2}{t}$ and the fact that $\sin^2 \theta \cos^2 \theta \in \left[0, \dfrac{1}{4}\right]$.

(3) $\dfrac{\sin(n+1)}{\sin 1}$.

4. (1) $S = \dfrac{\ell^2 - a^2}{4} \cdot \dfrac{\sin \alpha}{1 + \cos \alpha}$.

(2) $\cos \alpha \geqslant 1 - \dfrac{2a^2}{\ell^2} \Rightarrow \dfrac{\sin \alpha}{1 + \cos \alpha} = \sqrt{\dfrac{1 - \cos \alpha}{1 + \cos \alpha}} \leqslant \dfrac{a}{\sqrt{\ell^2 - a^2}}$. Hence, maximum $= \dfrac{a\sqrt{\ell^2 - a^2}}{4}$, attained when the

triangle is isosceles.

(3) Yes. Since isosceles triangle is the shape that is "closest" to a circle under the given constraint.

5. W $62.02°$ S

6. $y = 30 + 28\cos \dfrac{5\pi}{31}t$ $(t \geqslant 0)$.

7. (1) F.　(2) T.

8. $h = 35 + 20\cos\dfrac{500t}{63}$ $(t \geqslant 0)$.

9. (1) $1 + \sqrt{2}$ when (for example) $x = 0$, $y = \dfrac{1}{2}$, $z = 1$.

(2) a. $\sin x_1 + \sin x_4 = 2\sin\dfrac{x_1 + x_4}{2}\cos\dfrac{x_1 - x_4}{2}$, $\sin x_2 + \sin x_3 = 2\sin\dfrac{x_2 + x_3}{2}\cos\dfrac{x_2 - x_3}{2}$, with $\sin\dfrac{x_1 + x_4}{2} = $

$\sin\dfrac{x_2 + x_3}{2} > 0$, while $\cos\dfrac{x_1 - x_4}{2} \leqslant \cos\dfrac{x_2 - x_3}{2}$.

b. According to a., $\text{LHS} + \sin\dfrac{2x + y}{3} = (\sin x + \sin y) + \left(\sin x + \sin\dfrac{2x + y}{3}\right)$

$\leqslant \left(\sin\dfrac{2x + y}{3} + \sin\dfrac{2y + x}{3}\right) + \left(\sin x + \sin\dfrac{2x + y}{3}\right) = 2\sin\dfrac{2x + y}{3} + \left(\sin\dfrac{2y + x}{3} + \sin x\right)$

$\leqslant 2\sin\dfrac{2x + y}{3} + 2\sin\dfrac{2x + y}{3}$. The claim follows.

c. $\sin A + \sin B + \sin C \leqslant 2\sin\dfrac{A + B}{2} + \sin C \leqslant 3\sin\dfrac{A + B + C}{3} = 3\sin\dfrac{\pi}{3}$ by b.

10. (1) a. Substitute $x + \pi$ for x in $A\cos 2x + B\sin 2x \leqslant 1 - a\cos x - b\sin x$, which follows from $f(x) \geqslant 0$, one obtains that $A\cos 2x + B\sin 2x \leqslant 1 + a\cos x + b\sin x$. Adding them together to find $A\cos 2x + B\sin 2x \leqslant 1$ for all real x, which implies that $A^2 + B^2 \leqslant 1$.

Similarly, substitute $x + \dfrac{\pi}{2}$ for x in $a\cos x + b\sin x \leqslant 1 - A\cos 2x - B\sin 2x$ to find that $-a\sin x + b\cos x \leqslant$

$1 + A\cos 2x + B\sin 2x$, whence $\sqrt{2}\left[a\sin\left(\dfrac{\pi}{4} - x\right) + b\sin\left(\dfrac{\pi}{4} + x\right)\right] \leqslant 2$. Now that $\dfrac{\pi}{4} + x = \dfrac{\pi}{2} - $

$\left(\dfrac{\pi}{4} - x\right)$, it follows that $\sqrt{a^2 + b^2}\sin\left(\dfrac{\pi}{4} - x + \varphi\right) \leqslant \sqrt{2}$ for all x and the auxiliary angle φ associated with the pair (a, b). Hence, $a^2 + b^2 \leqslant 2$.

b. Not possible. Assume the contrast and let (a, b, A, B) be such a quadruple. Let β be an auxiliary angle such that $A\cos 2x + B\sin 2x = \sqrt{A^2 + B^2}\cos(2x + 2\beta)$. Set $t = x + \beta$. The function $f(x) = g(t) = 1 - a\cos(t - \beta) - b\sin(t - \beta) - \cos 2t$.

It follows that $a\cos(t - \beta) + b\sin(t - \beta) = \sqrt{2}\sin(t + \alpha)$ for some α.

Then, $2\sin^2 t - \sqrt{2}\sin(t + \alpha) \geqslant 0$ for all $t \in \mathbf{R}$. Hence, $\sin \alpha \leqslant 0$, $\sin(\pi + \alpha) \leqslant 0 \Rightarrow \sin \alpha \geqslant 0$. Thus, $\alpha = k\pi$, $k \in \mathbf{Z}$. Yet $2\sin^2 t \pm \sqrt{2}\sin t \geqslant 0$ cannot be true for all $t \in \mathbf{R}$, contradiction.

(2) Let $x = k\cos\theta$ be such that $k^3 : pk = 4 : 3$, i.e., $k = 2\sqrt{\dfrac{p}{3}}$. Hence, the equation becomes $\cos 3\theta = \dfrac{3\sqrt{3}q}{2p\sqrt{p}}$. In case $\left|\dfrac{3\sqrt{3}q}{2p\sqrt{p}}\right| \leqslant 1$, the equation is solved. Otherwise, one would turn to *complex numbers* for a solution.

6.4 反三角函数

1. (1) $\dfrac{\pi}{6}$. (2) $-\dfrac{\pi}{3}$. (3) $\dfrac{\pi}{3}$. (4) 0. (5) $\dfrac{\pi}{3}$. (6) $\dfrac{2\pi}{3}$. (7) $\dfrac{\pi}{4}$. (8) $\dfrac{\pi}{2}$. (9) $\dfrac{\pi}{6}$. (10) $-\dfrac{\pi}{3}$. (11) $-\dfrac{\pi}{6}$.

(12) $\dfrac{\pi}{4}$. (13) $\dfrac{5\pi}{6}$. (14) 0. (15) 0. (16) $-\dfrac{\pi}{4}$.

2. Neither even nor odd; decreasing on $[-1, 1]$; maximum value $= \pi$ when $x = -1$, minimum value $= 0$ when $x = 1$; no period.

3. (1) $-\dfrac{\sqrt{2}}{2}$. (2) $\dfrac{\sqrt{6}}{3}$. (3) $\dfrac{\sqrt{3}}{3}$. (4) π.

4. (1) $\arcsin x \in \left[-\dfrac{\pi}{2}, \dfrac{\pi}{2}\right] \Rightarrow \dfrac{\pi}{2} - \arcsin x \in [0, \pi]$.

Thus, $\cos\left(\dfrac{\pi}{2} - \arcsin x\right) = x \Rightarrow \dfrac{\pi}{2} - \arcsin x = \arccos x$.

(2) $\tan(\arcsin x) = \dfrac{x}{\cos(\arcsin x)}$, $\arcsin x \in \left[-\dfrac{\pi}{2}, \dfrac{\pi}{2}\right] \Rightarrow \cos(\arcsin x) = \sqrt{1-x^2}$. Thus, $\tan(\arcsin x) =$

$\dfrac{x}{\sqrt{1-x^2}}$. Again, $\arcsin x \in \left[-\dfrac{\pi}{2}, \dfrac{\pi}{2}\right] \Rightarrow \arctan \dfrac{x}{\sqrt{1-x^2}} = \arcsin x$.

5. (1) F.　(2) F.

6. (1) $\theta = \arctan \dfrac{x}{20}$.　(2) $\theta = \arctan \dfrac{1}{4} \approx 14.04°$, $\theta = \arctan \dfrac{3}{5} \approx 30.96°$.

7. (1) $c = \arctan \dfrac{1}{2} - \dfrac{\pi}{2}$.

(2) a. $\dfrac{1}{x} = \tan(\arcsin(\cos(\arctan x)))$.

b. $\dfrac{1}{\sqrt{2}} = \cos(\arctan(\cos 0))$, hence $0 \to \dfrac{1}{\sqrt{2}}$.

For any positive x, $\dfrac{1}{\sqrt{x^2+1}} = \cos(\arctan x)$, whence $x \to \sqrt{x^2+1}$ by a. In particular, for $n \in \mathbf{N}^*$, $n \to$

$\sqrt{n^2+1} \to \cdots \to \sqrt{n^2+2n+1} = n+1$.

Apply this procedure to $\dfrac{1}{\sqrt{2}}$ to obtain $\sqrt{\dfrac{3}{2}}$, $\sqrt{\dfrac{5}{2}}$ and $\sqrt{\dfrac{7}{2}}$.

Similarly, $0 \to \sqrt{\dfrac{7}{2}} \to \sqrt{\dfrac{2}{7}} \to \sqrt{\dfrac{2}{7}+1} = \sqrt{\dfrac{9}{7}} \to \sqrt{\dfrac{7}{9}} \to \sqrt{\dfrac{7}{9}+1} = \dfrac{4}{3} \to \dfrac{3}{4}$.

c. Let $x = \dfrac{m}{n}$, $m, n \in \mathbf{N}^*$, $\gcd(m, n) = 1$. Then, $\gcd(m^2, n^2) = 1$. Hence, Euclidean algorithm shows that $0 =$

$\sqrt{\dfrac{0}{1}} \to \dfrac{m}{n} = \sqrt{\dfrac{m^2}{n^2}}$ by reversing the procedure of finding the greatest common divisor.

8. (1) Take $n = 1, 3$, resp. in (2).

(2) $\arctan \dfrac{1}{n+1} + \arctan \dfrac{1}{n^2+n+1} \in \left(0, \dfrac{\pi}{2}\right)$ while $\tan\left(\arctan \dfrac{1}{n+1} + \arctan \dfrac{1}{n^2+n+1}\right)$

$= \dfrac{\dfrac{1}{n+1} + \dfrac{1}{n^2+n+1}}{1 - \dfrac{1}{n+1} \cdot \dfrac{1}{n^2+n+1}} = \dfrac{n^2+2n+2}{n^3+2n^2+2n}$. The claim follows.

(3) $r = md - n$, $N = nd + m$.

(4) After extracting $\arctan \dfrac{1}{d}$, the remaining $\arctan \dfrac{r}{N}$ can be reduced to $\arctan \dfrac{r_1}{N_1}$ so that $\gcd(r_1, N_1) = 1$. An inductive construction follows.

6.5　解简单三角方程

1. (In what follows, $k \in \mathbf{Z}$.)

(1) $x = 2k\pi \pm \dfrac{2\pi}{3}$.　(2) $x = k\pi - (-1)^k \dfrac{\pi}{6}$.　(3) $x = k\pi + (-1)^k \dfrac{\pi}{3}$.　(4) $x = k\pi - \dfrac{\pi}{3}$.　(5) $x = k\pi \pm \dfrac{\pi}{3}$.

(6) $x = k\pi \pm \dfrac{\pi}{3}$.　(7) $x = k\pi$, $2k\pi - \dfrac{\pi}{2}$.　(8) $x = k\pi \pm \dfrac{\pi}{3}$, $k\pi \pm \dfrac{\pi}{6}$.　(9) $x = k\pi \pm \dfrac{\pi}{3}$.　(10) $x = k\pi \pm \dfrac{\pi}{3}$.

(11) $x = \dfrac{k\pi}{2} \pm \dfrac{\pi}{8}$.　(12) $x = \dfrac{k\pi}{3} \pm \dfrac{\pi}{9}$.　(13) $x = \dfrac{k\pi}{3}$, $k\pi + \dfrac{\pi}{4}$.　(14) $x = \dfrac{k\pi}{2} + \dfrac{\pi}{4}$, $2k\pi \pm \dfrac{2\pi}{3}$.

2. (In what follows, $k \in \mathbf{Z}$.)

(1) $x = k\pi - (-1)^k \dfrac{\pi}{4}$, $2k\pi \pm \dfrac{\pi}{6}$.　(2) $x = 2k\pi$, $2k\pi + \dfrac{\pi}{2}$.　(3) $x = \dfrac{k\pi}{2} + \dfrac{\pi}{4}$.

(4) $x = 2k\pi + \pi$, $2k\pi + 2 \cdot (-1)^k \arcsin \dfrac{m-1}{2m}$.　(5) $x = k\pi \pm \dfrac{\pi}{6}$.　(6) $x = k\pi \pm \dfrac{\pi}{6}$.

(7) $x = \tan\left(k + \dfrac{1}{4}\right)$.

3. (1) T.　(2) F.

4. (1) $\arcsin \dfrac{3}{5} \approx 36.87°$ or $\dfrac{\pi}{2} - \arcsin \dfrac{3}{5} \approx 53.13°$.　(2) a. $t = 8$, 24; b. $t = 16$, 5 times when $t = 16$, 48, 80, 112, 144.

5. (1) (In what follows, $k \in \mathbf{Z}$.)

　　a. $x = k\pi + \dfrac{\pi}{4}$, $f\left(k\pi + \dfrac{\pi}{4}\right) = (-1)^k \sqrt{2}$; b. $x = \dfrac{k\pi}{2} + \dfrac{\pi}{4}$, $f\left(\dfrac{k\pi}{2} + \dfrac{\pi}{4}\right) = \dfrac{(-1)^k}{2}$.

　　(2) a. $x = 1$; b. $x = 1$.

6. (1) $x = k\pi + \dfrac{\pi}{2}$, $k \in \mathbf{Z}$.

　　(2) a. $\cos(\cos x) > \sin(\sin x)$; b. No solution; c. $x = 0.960\,2$, $2.181\,3$.

第 7 章　数列与数学归纳法

7.1　数列

1. (1) -4, -1, 2, 5, 8.　(2) $\dfrac{5}{2}$, $\dfrac{11}{4}$, $\dfrac{23}{8}$, $\dfrac{47}{16}$, $\dfrac{95}{32}$.　(3) -2, 4, -8, 16, -32.

　(4) $\dfrac{1}{3}$, $\dfrac{1}{9}$, $\dfrac{1}{27}$, $\dfrac{1}{81}$, $\dfrac{1}{243}$.　(5) $\dfrac{1}{6}$, $\dfrac{2}{7}$, $\dfrac{3}{8}$, $\dfrac{4}{9}$, $\dfrac{1}{2}$.　(6) $\dfrac{5}{2}$, $\dfrac{10}{11}$, $\dfrac{15}{26}$, $\dfrac{20}{47}$, $\dfrac{25}{74}$.

　(7) 0, 1, 0, $\dfrac{1}{2}$, 0.　(8) -1, $\dfrac{1}{4}$, $-\dfrac{1}{9}$, $\dfrac{1}{16}$, $-\dfrac{1}{25}$.　(9) $\dfrac{2}{9}$, $\dfrac{4}{9}$, $\dfrac{8}{9}$, $\dfrac{16}{9}$, $\dfrac{32}{9}$.

　(10) $\dfrac{4}{7}$, $\dfrac{4}{7}$, $\dfrac{4}{7}$, $\dfrac{4}{7}$, $\dfrac{4}{7}$.　(11) $-\dfrac{1}{2}$, $\dfrac{2}{3}$, $-\dfrac{3}{4}$, $\dfrac{4}{5}$, $-\dfrac{5}{6}$.　(12) $\dfrac{1}{2}$, $-\dfrac{1}{5}$, $\dfrac{1}{10}$, $-\dfrac{1}{17}$, $\dfrac{1}{26}$.

2. (1) $a_n = 4n - 1$.　(2) $a_n = n^2 - 1$.　(3) $a_n = (-1)^{n+1}(6n - 5)$.　(4) $a_n = 2^n + 1$.

　(5) $a_n = \dfrac{1}{n^2}$.　(6) $a_n = \dfrac{1}{n(n+1)}$.　(7) $a_n = \dfrac{2n}{4n^2 - 1}$.　(8) $a_n = (-1)^n \dfrac{n+1}{n+2}$.

　(9) $a_n = (-1)^{n-1}$.　(10) $a_n = 2 + (-1)^n$.

3. (1) 28, 24, 20, 16, 12.　(2) 3, 4, 6, 10, 18.　(3) 1, 2, 5, 26, 677.　(4) 1, 2, 2, 3, $\dfrac{7}{2}$.

　(5) -1, 1, 0, 1, 1.

4. (1) 6, 8, 10, 12, 14, $a_n = 2n + 4$.　(2) 14, -28, 56, -112, 224, $a_n = 14 \cdot (-2)^{n-1}$.

　(3) 1, 2, 4, 7, 11, $a_n = 1 + \dfrac{n(n-1)}{2}$.　(4) 3, 5, 3, 5, 3, $a_n = 4 + (-1)^n$.

5. $x_1 = 1$, $x_{n+1} = x_n + 2$, $n \in \mathbf{N}^*$, $n \leqslant 2\,007$. The first five terms are as follows: 1, 3, 5, 7, 9.

　$y_1 = 2$, $y_{n+1} = 3y_n + 2$, $n \in \mathbf{N}^*$, $n \leqslant 2\,007$. The first five terms are as follows: 2, 8, 26, 80, 242.

6. (1) $a_n = \begin{cases} 6, & n = 1 \\ 4n + 1, & n \geqslant 2 \end{cases}$.　(2) $a_n = \begin{cases} 5, & n = 1 \\ 4 \cdot 3^{n-1}, & n \geqslant 2 \end{cases}$.

7. (1)

Number of Yellow Cube Faces	0	1	2	3
$3 \times 3 \times 3$	1	6	12	8

(2)

Number of Yellow Cube Faces	0	1	2	3
$4 \times 4 \times 4$	8	24	24	8

Number of Yellow Cube Faces	0	1	2	3
$5 \times 5 \times 5$	27	54	36	8

(3)

Number of Yellow Cube Faces	0	1	2	3
$n \times n \times n$, $n \geqslant 3$, $n \in \mathbf{N}^*$	$(n-2)^3$	$6(n-2)^2$	$12(n-2)$	8

7.2 等差数列

1. (1) Yes, $d = -2$.   (2) Yes, $d = 5$.   (3) No.   (4) No.   (5) Yes, $d = -\dfrac{1}{4}$.   (6) Yes, $d = 0.4$.   (7) No.

(8) No.

2. (1) $a_n = 3n - 2$.   (2) $a_n = 4n + 11$.   (3) $a_n = -8n + 108$.   (4) $a_n = -\dfrac{2}{3}n + \dfrac{2}{3}$.   (5) $a_n = -\dfrac{5}{2}n + \dfrac{13}{2}$.

(6) $a_n = -5n + 15$.   (7) $a_n = \dfrac{10}{3}n + \dfrac{5}{3}$.   (8) $a_n = 5n - 9$.   (9) $a_n = -3n + 103$.   (10) $a_n = -15n + 265$.

3. (1) $c = 7$.   (2) $a = 13$.

4. From the given condition, $\begin{cases} a_4 + a_7 = 28 \\ a_4 \cdot a_7 = 187 \end{cases}$.

Solving the system of equations gives $\begin{cases} a_4 = 11 \\ a_7 = 17 \end{cases}$ or $\begin{cases} a_4 = 17 \\ a_7 = 11 \end{cases}$.

So a formula for the n th term of this sequence is $a_n = 2n + 3$ or $a_n = -2n + 25$.

5. From the given condition, $\begin{cases} a_1 + a_2 + a_3 = 12 \\ a_1 a_2 a_3 = 48 \\ a_1 + a_3 = 2a_2 \end{cases}$.

Solving the system of equations gives $\begin{cases} a_1 = 2 \\ a_2 = 4 \\ a_3 = 6 \end{cases}$ or $\begin{cases} a_1 = 6 \\ a_2 = 4 \\ a_3 = 2 \end{cases}$.

So a formula for the n th term of this sequence is $a_n = 2n$ or $a_n = -2n + 8$.

6. Let $c_n = a_n + b_n$. Since sequences $\{a_n\}$ and $\{b_n\}$ are arithmetic sequences, we know that $a_n - a_{n-1} = d_1$, $b_n - b_{n-1} = d_2$.

So $c_n - c_{n-1} = a_n + b_n - (a_{n-1} + b_{n-1}) = d_1 + d_2$, that is, $\{c_n\}$ is an arithmetic sequence.

Since $c_1 = a_1 + b_1 = 34 + 66 = 100$ and $c_{96} = a_{96} + b_{96} = 100$, we get that $c_n = 100$ for all positive integers n.

(1) $a_{2\,020} + b_{2\,020} = c_{2\,020} = 100$.

(2) The 100th partial sum of the sequence $\{a_n + b_n\}$ is $100 \times 100 = 10\,000$.

7. (1) Since $a_1 = 8$, $d = 20 - 8 = 12$, $n = 10$, we get that $S_{10} = 10 \times 8 + \dfrac{10 \times 9}{2} \times 12 = 620$.

(2) Since $a_1 = 75$, $d = 70 - 75 = -5$, $n = 25$, we get that $S_{25} = 25 \times 75 + \dfrac{25 \times 24}{2} \times (-5) = 375$.

(3) Since $a_1 = 100$, $d = \dfrac{a_{15} - a_1}{15 - 1} = \dfrac{170 - 100}{14} = 5$, $n = 20$, we get that $S_{20} = 20 \times 100 + \dfrac{20 \times 19}{2} \times 5 = 2\,950$.

(4) Since $a_1 = -7$, $d = \dfrac{a_8 - a_1}{8 - 1} = \dfrac{-35 - (-7)}{7} = -4$, $n = 16$,

we get that $S_{16} = 16 \times (-7) + \dfrac{16 \times 15}{2} \times (-4) = -592$.

(5) Since $a_1 = 39$, $d = -3$, $a_n = 3$, we get that $n = \dfrac{a_n - a_1}{d} + 1 = \dfrac{3 - 39}{-3} + 1 = 13$.

Hence, $S_{13} = \dfrac{13(a_1 + a_{13})}{2} = \dfrac{13 \times (39 + 3)}{2} = 273$.

8. (1) Let $S_n = An^2 + Bn$. Then we have that $\begin{cases} S_{10} = 10^2 A + 10B = 100 \quad \text{①} \\ S_{100} = 100^2 A + 100B = 10 \quad \text{②} \end{cases}$.

From ① $-$ ②, we get that $(110 \times 90)A + 90B = -90$, that is, $110A + B = -1$.

Hence, $S_{110} = 110^2 A + 110B = 110 \cdot (110A + B) = 110 \times (-1) = -110$.

(2) Since $S_n = a_1 + a_2 + \cdots + a_n$, $S_{2n} - S_n = a_{n+1} + a_{n+2} + \cdots + a_{2n}$, $S_{3n} - S_{2n} = a_{2n+1} + a_{2n+2} + \cdots + a_{3n}$, we get that

$(S_{2n} - S_n) - S_n = (S_{3n} - S_{2n}) - (S_{2n} - S_n) = n^2 d$.

Hence, $S_{3n} = 3S_{2n} - 3S_n = 3 \times (14 - 8) = 18$.

9. Since $S_9 = S_{17}$, we have that $a_{10} + a_{11} + \cdots + a_{17} = 0$.

Then we get that $a_{10} + a_{17} = a_{11} + a_{16} = a_{12} + a_{15} = a_{13} + a_{14} = 0$.

Therefore, $2a_1 + 25d = 0$, i.e. $50 + 25d = 0$. Solving the equation gives $d = -2$.

Since $a_1 > 0$, $d < 0$, $a_{13} + a_{14} = 0$, we get that $a_{13} > 0$, $a_{14} < 0$.

Hence, the sum of the first 13 terms S_{13} reaches the maximum, that is, $n = 13$ and $S_{13} = 13 \times 25 + \dfrac{13 \times 12}{2} \times (-2) = 169$.

10. From the given conditions, $a_1 + a_2 + a_3 = 6$, $a_n + a_{n-1} + a_{n-2} = 60$.

Since $a_1 + a_n = a_2 + a_{n-1} = a_3 + a_{n-2}$, we get that $3(a_1 + a_n) = 6 + 60$, i.e. $a_1 + a_n = 22$.

From $S_n = 231$, we know that $\dfrac{n(a_1 + a_n)}{2} = 231$. So $\dfrac{22n}{2} = 231$, i.e. $n = 21$.

11. Since $A_{21} = \dfrac{21(a_1 + a_{21})}{2} = \dfrac{21 \cdot 2a_{11}}{2} = 21a_{11}$, $B_{21} = \dfrac{21(b_1 + b_{21})}{2} = \dfrac{21 \cdot 2b_{11}}{2} = 21b_{11}$,

we get that $\dfrac{A_{21}}{B_{21}} = \dfrac{21a_{11}}{21b_{11}} = \dfrac{a_{11}}{b_{11}}$.

So $\dfrac{a_{11}}{b_{11}} = \dfrac{A_{21}}{B_{21}} = \dfrac{7 \times 21 + 1}{4 \times 21 + 27} = \dfrac{148}{111} = \dfrac{4}{3}$.

12. $a_1 = 500$, $d = 450 - 500 = -50$.

(1) $a_n = 500 + (n-1) \cdot (-50) = -50n + 550$, $1 \leqslant n \leqslant 8$, $n \in \mathbf{N}^*$.

(2) $S_8 = 8 \times 500 + \dfrac{8 \times 7}{2} \times (-50) = 2\,600$.

13. If the company needs to buy n sets of these printers, let the unit price of each set sold in shopping mall A be a_n, and the unit price of each set sold in shopping mall B be b_n.

From the given conditions, $a_n = \begin{cases} 800 - 20n & n \leqslant 18 \\ 440 & n > 18 \end{cases}$ and $b_n = 75\% \times 800 = 600$.

When $n < 10$, $a_n > b_n$, it costs less to go to shopping mall B.

When $n = 10$, $a_n = b_n$, it costs the same to go to these two shopping malls.

When $n > 10$, $a_n < b_n$, it costs less to go to shopping mall A.

7.3 等比数列

1. (1) Yes, $r = 5$.　(2) No.　(3) Yes, $r = 2$.　(4) Yes, $r = -\dfrac{2}{3}$.　(5) No.　(6) Yes, $r = 0.2$.

(7) Yes, $r = -\sqrt{7}$.　(8) Yes, $r = \dfrac{2\sqrt{3}}{3}$.

2. (1) $a_n = 4 \cdot \left(\dfrac{1}{2}\right)^{n-1}$.　(2) $a_n = 5 \cdot \left(\dfrac{7}{2}\right)^{n-1}$.　(3) $a_n = 6 \cdot \left(-\dfrac{1}{3}\right)^{n-1}$.　(4) $a_n = 64 \cdot \left(-\dfrac{1}{4}\right)^{n-1}$.

(5) $a_n = 12 \cdot \left(\dfrac{1}{2}\right)^{n-1}$.　(6) $a_n = -2 \cdot (-3)^{n-1}$.　(7) $a_n = 2 \cdot 2^{n-1} = 2^n$.

(8) $a_n = 512 \cdot \left(\dfrac{1}{2}\right)^{n-1}$ or $a_n = 512 \cdot \left(-\dfrac{1}{2}\right)^{n-1}$.　(9) $a_n = 36 \cdot (-3)^{n-1}$.

(10) $a_n = 60 \cdot (\sqrt{2})^{n-1}$ or $a_n = 60 \cdot (-\sqrt{2})^{n-1}$.

3. (1) $c = 2\sqrt{6}$ or $c = -2\sqrt{6}$.　(2) $a = -36$.

4. From the given condition, $\begin{cases} a_3 + a_6 = 36 \\ a_4 + a_7 = a_3 r + a_6 r = r(a_3 + a_6) = 18 \end{cases}$.

Then we get $r = \dfrac{18}{36} = \dfrac{1}{2}$.

Since $a_3 + a_6 = 36$, we have that $a_1(r^2 + r^5) = a_1\left(\dfrac{1}{4} + \dfrac{1}{32}\right) = 36$. Solving the equation gives $a_1 = 128$.

$a_n = a_1 r^{n-1} = 128 \cdot \left(\dfrac{1}{2}\right)^{n-1} = \left(\dfrac{1}{2}\right)^{n-8}$.

Since $a_n = \dfrac{1}{2}$, we have $\left(\dfrac{1}{2}\right)^{n-8} = \dfrac{1}{2}$. So $n - 8 = 1$, i.e. $n = 9$.

5. (1) Since $a_2 a_4 + 2a_3 a_5 + a_4 a_6 = 25$, we have that $a_3^2 + 2a_3 a_5 + a_5^2 = 25$, i.e. $(a_3 + a_5)^2 = 25$.

So we get that $a_3 + a_5 = 5$ or $a_3 + a_5 = -5$. Since all the terms are positive, we get that $a_3 + a_5 = 5$.

(2) As we know, $a_1 a_{10} = a_2 a_9 = a_3 a_8 = a_4 a_7 = a_5 a_6 = 81$, then

$$\log_3 a_1 + \log_3 a_2 + \log_3 a_3 + \cdots + \log_3 a_{10} = \log_3 (a_1 a_2 a_3 \cdots a_{10}) = \log_3 81^5 = \log_3 3^{20} = 20.$$

6. (1) Since $a_1 = 10$, $r = \dfrac{20}{10} = 2$, $n = 10$, we get that $S_{10} = \dfrac{10 \times (1 - 2^{10})}{1 - 2} = 10\ 230.$

(2) Since $a_1 = 3$, $r = \dfrac{-6}{3} = -2$, $n = 9$, we get that $S_9 = \dfrac{3 \times [1 - (-2)^9]}{1 - (-2)} = 513.$

(3) Since $a_1 = 45$, $r = \dfrac{15}{45} = \dfrac{1}{3}$, $n = 6$, we get that $S_6 = \dfrac{45 \times \left[1 - \left(\dfrac{1}{3}\right)^6\right]}{1 - \left(\dfrac{1}{3}\right)} = \dfrac{1\ 820}{27}.$

(4) Since $a_1 = -2.7$, $r = -\dfrac{1}{3}$, $n = 5$, we get that $S_5 = \dfrac{-2.7 \times \left[1 - \left(-\dfrac{1}{3}\right)^9\right]}{1 - \left(-\dfrac{1}{3}\right)} = -\dfrac{61}{30}.$

(5) Since $r^3 = \dfrac{a_4}{a_1} = \dfrac{\dfrac{3}{4}}{6} = \dfrac{1}{8}$, we get that $r = \dfrac{1}{2}.$

Since $a_1 = 6$, $r = \dfrac{1}{2}$, $n = 7$, we get that $S_7 = \dfrac{6 \times \left[1 - \left(\dfrac{1}{2}\right)^7\right]}{1 - \left(\dfrac{1}{2}\right)} = \dfrac{381}{32}.$

7. (1) Since $a_1 = 10$, $a_n = 7\ 290$, $r = \dfrac{30}{10} = 3$, we get that $S_n = \dfrac{a_1 - a_n r}{1 - r} = \dfrac{10 - 7\ 290 \times 3}{1 - 3} = 10\ 930.$

(2) Since $a_1 = 15$, $a_n = -\dfrac{3}{625}$, $r = \dfrac{-3}{15} = -\dfrac{1}{5}$, we get that $S_n = \dfrac{a_1 - a_n r}{1 - r} = \dfrac{15 - \left(-\dfrac{3}{625}\right) \times \left(-\dfrac{1}{5}\right)}{1 - \left(-\dfrac{1}{5}\right)} = \dfrac{1\ 873}{2\ 500}.$

(3) Since $a_1 = 0.1$, $a_n = 102.4$, $r = \dfrac{0.4}{0.1} = 4$, we get that $S_n = \dfrac{a_1 - a_n r}{1 - r} = \dfrac{0.1 - 102.4 \times 4}{1 - 4} = 136.5.$

(4) Since $a_1 = 32$, $a_n = 10.125$, $r = \dfrac{24}{32} = 0.75$, we get that $S_n = \dfrac{a_1 - a_n r}{1 - r} = \dfrac{32 - 10.125 \times 0.75}{1 - 0.75} = 75.75.$

8. (1) Since $a_{n+1} = \dfrac{2a_n}{a_n + 1}$, we get that $\dfrac{1}{a_{n+1}} = \dfrac{a_n + 1}{2a_n} = \dfrac{1}{2} + \dfrac{1}{2a_n}$, that is, $\dfrac{1}{a_{n+1}} - 1 = \dfrac{1}{2}\left(\dfrac{1}{a_n} - 1\right).$

Since $a_1 = \dfrac{2}{3}$, we have that $\dfrac{1}{a_1} - 1 = \dfrac{3}{2} - 1 = \dfrac{1}{2}.$

Hence, the sequence $\left\{\dfrac{1}{a_n} - 1\right\}$ is a geometric sequence whose first term is $\dfrac{1}{2}$ and whose common ratio is $\dfrac{1}{2}$.

(2) From question (1), we get that $\dfrac{1}{a_n} - 1 = \dfrac{1}{2} \cdot \left(\dfrac{1}{2}\right)^{n-1} = \dfrac{1}{2^n}$, then $\dfrac{n}{a_n} = \dfrac{n}{2^n} + n.$

Let the sum of the first n terms of the sequence $\left\{\dfrac{n}{2^n}\right\}$ be T_n. Then we have that

$$T_n = \dfrac{1}{2} + \dfrac{2}{2^2} + \dfrac{3}{2^3} + \dfrac{4}{2^4} + \cdots + \dfrac{n}{2^n} \quad ①.$$

Multiply the series for T_n by $\dfrac{1}{2}$, we get that

$$\dfrac{1}{2}T_n = \dfrac{1}{2^2} + \dfrac{2}{2^3} + \dfrac{3}{2^4} + \dfrac{4}{2^5} + \cdots + \dfrac{n}{2^{n+1}} \quad ②.$$

From ① $-$ ②, we obtain that

$$\dfrac{1}{2}T_n = \dfrac{1}{2} + \dfrac{1}{2^2} + \dfrac{1}{2^3} + \dfrac{1}{2^4} + \cdots + \dfrac{1}{2^n} - \dfrac{n}{2^{n+1}}$$

$$T_n = 2\left[\frac{\frac{1}{2}\left(1-\frac{1}{2^n}\right)}{1-\frac{1}{2}} - \frac{n}{2^{n+1}}\right] = 2\left(1-\frac{1}{2^n} - \frac{n}{2^{n+1}}\right) = 2 - \frac{1}{2^{n-1}} - \frac{n}{2^n}.$$

Hence, the sum of the first n terms of the sequence $\left\{\frac{n}{a_n}\right\}$ should be

$$S_n = 2 - \frac{1}{2^{n-1}} - \frac{n}{2^n} + \frac{n(n+1)}{2} = \frac{n^2+n+4}{2} - \frac{n+2}{2^n}.$$

9. (1) From the given condition, $S_{n+1} = 4a_n + 2$, then we get that $S_n = 4a_{n-1} + 2$.

Since $a_{n+1} = S_{n+1} - S_n = (4a_n + 2) - (4a_{n-1} + 2) = 4a_n - 4a_{n-1}$, we have that

$$a_{n+1} - 2a_n = 2(a_n - 2a_{n-1}),$$

that is, $b_n = 2b_{n-1}$.

Hence, the sequence $\{b_n\}$ is a geometric sequence whose common ratio is 2.

Since $a_1 = 1$, $S_2 = 4a_1 + 2 = 4 \times 1 + 2 = 6$, we obtain that $a_2 = S_2 - a_1 = 6 - 1 = 5$.

Then we get that $b_1 = a_2 - 2a_1 = 5 - 2 \times 1 = 3$.

So a formula for the nth term of the sequence $\{b_n\}$ is $b_n = 3 \cdot 2^{n-1}$.

(2) From question (1), $a_{n+1} - 2a_n = 3 \cdot 2^{n-1}$, then we get that $\frac{a_{n+1}}{2^{n+1}} - \frac{a_n}{2^n} = \frac{3}{4}$, that is,

$$c_{n+1} - c_n = \frac{3}{4}.$$

So the sequence $\{c_n\}$ is an arithmetic sequence whose common difference is $\frac{3}{4}$.

Since $a_1 = 1$, we get that $c_1 = \frac{a_1}{2} = \frac{1}{2}$.

Hence, a formula for the nth term of the sequence $\{c_n\}$ is $c_n = \frac{1}{2} + \frac{3}{4}(n-1) = \frac{3}{4}n - \frac{1}{4}$.

(3) From question (2), we know that a formula for the nth term of the sequence $\{a_n\}$ is

$$a_n = 2^n c_n = 2^n\left(\frac{3}{4}n - \frac{1}{4}\right) = (3n-1) \cdot 2^{n-2}.$$

Let the sum of the first n terms of the sequence $\{a_n\}$ be S_n. Then we have that

$$S_n = 2 \times 2^{-1} + 5 \times 2^0 + 8 \times 2^1 + 11 \times 2^2 + \cdots + (3n-1) \cdot 2^{n-2} \quad ①.$$

Multiply the series for S_n by 2, we get that

$$2S_n = 2 \times 2^0 + 5 \times 2^1 + 8 \times 2^2 + 11 \times 2^3 + \cdots + (3n-1) \cdot 2^{n-1} \quad ②.$$

From ① − ②, we obtain that

$$-S_n = 2 \times 2^{-1} + 3 \times 2^0 + 3 \times 2^1 + 3 \times 2^2 + \cdots + 3 \cdot 2^{n-2} - (3n-1) \cdot 2^{n-1}$$
$$= 1 + 3 \times \frac{1-2^{n-1}}{1-2} - (3n-1) \cdot 2^{n-1}$$
$$= 1 + 3 \cdot 2^{n-1} - 3 - (3n-1) \cdot 2^{n-1}$$
$$= -2 + (4-3n) \cdot 2^{n-1}.$$

Hence, $S_n = 2 + (3n-4) \cdot 2^{n-1}$.

10. Let the total number of people who know the good news after the nth hour be S_n. Then we have that $S_n = 1 + 2 + 2^2 + 2^3 + \cdots + 2^n = 2^{n+1} - 1$.

Since the total number of people in the small town is 2 047, we get that $S_n = 2^{n+1} - 1 = 2\,047$.

Solving the equation gives $2^{n+1} = 2\,048$. That is, $n = 10$.

So the time required to spread the good news to a small town with 2 047 people is 10 hours.

11. (1) $a_n = 800 + 800 \times \left(1 - \frac{1}{5}\right) + 800 \times \left(1 - \frac{1}{5}\right)^2 + \cdots + 800 \times \left(1 - \frac{1}{5}\right)^{n-1} = 4\,000 \left[1 - \left(\frac{4}{5}\right)^n\right]$.

$b_n = 400 + 400 \times \left(1 + \frac{1}{4}\right) + 400 \times \left(1 + \frac{1}{4}\right)^2 + \cdots + 400 \times \left(1 + \frac{1}{4}\right)^{n-1} = 1\,600 \left[\left(\frac{5}{4}\right)^n - 1\right]$.

(2) From the given condition, $b_n > a_n$, that is, $1\,600 \left[\left(\frac{5}{4}\right)^n - 1\right] - 4\,000 \left[1 - \left(\frac{4}{5}\right)^n\right] > 0$.

Solving the inequality gives $n \geqslant 5$.

Hence, it takes at least 5 years that the total revenue of tourism exceeds the total investment.

7.4　数学归纳法

1. (1) Hint：
$$1^3 + 2^3 + 3^3 + \cdots + k^3 + (k+1)^3$$
$$= \frac{k^2 (k+1)^2}{4} + (k+1)^3$$
$$= \frac{(k+1)^2 (k^2 + 4k + 4)}{4}$$
$$= \frac{(k+1)^2 (k+2)^2}{4}.$$

(2) Hint：
$$1^2 + 3^2 + 5^2 + \cdots + (2k-1)^2 + [2(k+1) - 1]^2$$
$$= \frac{k(2k-1)(2k+1)}{3} + (2k+1)^2$$
$$= \frac{(2k+1)[k(2k-1) + 3(2k+1)]}{3}$$
$$= \frac{(2k+1)(2k^2 + 5k + 3)}{3}$$
$$= \frac{(2k+1)(k+1)(2k+3)}{3}$$
$$= \frac{(k+1)[2(k+1) - 1][2(k+1) + 1]}{3}.$$

(3) Hint：
$$[(k+1) + 1][(k+1) + 2][(k+1) + 3] \cdots [(k+1) + (k-1)][(k+1) + k][(k+1) + (k+1)]$$
$$= (k+1)(k+2)(k+3) \cdots (k+k) \cdot \frac{(2k+1)(2k+2)}{(k+1)}$$
$$= 2^k \cdot 1 \cdot 3 \cdots (2k-1) \cdot \frac{2(2k+1)(k+1)}{(k+1)}$$
$$= 2^{k+1} \cdot 1 \cdot 3 \cdots (2k-1)(2k+1).$$

(4) Hint：
$$\sum_{i=1}^{k+1} i(i+1)$$
$$= \sum_{i=1}^{k} i(i+1) + (k+1)(k+2)$$
$$= \frac{k(k+1)(k+2)}{3} + (k+1)(k+2)$$
$$= \frac{(k+1)(k+2)(k+3)}{3}.$$

2. (1) Hint：
$$\frac{1}{\sqrt{1}} + \frac{1}{\sqrt{2}} + \frac{1}{\sqrt{3}} + \cdots + \frac{1}{\sqrt{k}} + \frac{1}{\sqrt{k+1}}$$
$$> \sqrt{k} + \frac{1}{\sqrt{k+1}} = \frac{\sqrt{k(k+1)} + 1}{\sqrt{k+1}} > \frac{k+1}{\sqrt{k+1}} = \sqrt{k+1}.$$

(2) Hint：

$$\frac{1}{(k+1)+1}+\frac{1}{(k+1)+2}+\frac{1}{(k+1)+3}+\cdots+\frac{1}{2(k+1)}$$

$$=\frac{1}{k+1}+\frac{1}{k+2}+\frac{1}{k+3}+\cdots+\frac{1}{2k}+\frac{1}{2k+1}+\frac{1}{2k+2}-\frac{1}{k+1}$$

$$>\frac{13}{24}+\frac{1}{2k+1}+\frac{1}{2k+2}-\frac{1}{k+1}>\frac{13}{24}+\frac{1}{2k+2}+\frac{1}{2k+2}-\frac{1}{k+1}=\frac{13}{24}.$$

(3) Hint：

$$1+\frac{1}{2}+\frac{1}{3}+\cdots+\frac{1}{2^{k+1}}$$

$$=1+\frac{1}{2}+\frac{1}{3}+\cdots+\frac{1}{2^{k}}+\frac{1}{2^{k}+1}+\frac{1}{2^{k}+2}+\cdots+\frac{1}{2^{k}+2^{k}}$$

$$\leqslant\frac{1}{2}+k+\frac{1}{2^{k}+1}+\frac{1}{2^{k}+2}+\cdots+\frac{1}{2^{k}+2^{k}}$$

$$\leqslant\frac{1}{2}+k+\underbrace{\frac{1}{2^{k}}+\frac{1}{2^{k}}+\cdots+\frac{1}{2^{k}}}_{2^{k}}$$

$$\leqslant\frac{1}{2}+k+1.$$

(4) Hint：

$$|\sin(k+1)x|$$

$$=|\sin kx\cos x+\cos kx\sin x|$$

$$\leqslant|\sin kx\cos x|+|\cos kx\sin x|$$

$$\leqslant|\sin kx|+|\sin x|$$

$$\leqslant k|\sin x|+|\sin x|$$

$$\leqslant(k+1)|\sin x|.$$

3. (1) Hint：$(k+1)^3+3(k+1)^2+2(k+1)=(k^3+3k^2+2k)+3k^2+9k+6.$

(2) Hint：$2^{2(k+1)+1}+3^{2(k+1)-1}=4\cdot2^{2k+1}+9\cdot3^{2k-1}=4(2^{2k+1}+3^{2k-1})+5\cdot3^{2k-1}.$

(3) Hint：$[3(k+1)+1]\cdot7^{k+1}-1=(3k+1+3)\cdot7\cdot7^k-1=7\cdot[7^k(3k+1)-1]+3(7^{k+1}+2).$

(4) Hint：

$$x^{(k+1)+2}+(x+1)^{2(k+1)+1}$$

$$=x\cdot x^{k+2}+(x+1)^2(x+1)^{2k+1}$$

$$=x[x^{k+2}+(x+1)^{2k+1}]+(x^2+x+1)(x+1)^{2k+1}.$$

4. Hint：Since $\tan\alpha=\tan[(k+1)\alpha-k\alpha]=\dfrac{\tan(k+1)\alpha-\tan k\alpha}{1+\tan k\alpha\tan(k+1)\alpha}$, we get that

$$\tan k\alpha\tan(k+1)\alpha=\frac{\tan(k+1)\alpha-\tan k\alpha}{\tan\alpha}-1. \text{ So we have that}$$

$$\tan\alpha\cdot\tan2\alpha+\tan2\alpha\cdot\tan3\alpha+\cdots+\tan(k-1)\alpha\cdot\tan k\alpha+\tan k\alpha\tan(k+1)\alpha$$

$$=\frac{\tan k\alpha}{\tan\alpha}-k+\tan k\alpha\tan(k+1)\alpha$$

$$=\frac{\tan k\alpha}{\tan\alpha}-k+\frac{\tan(k+1)\alpha-\tan k\alpha}{\tan\alpha}-1$$

$$=\frac{\tan(k+1)\alpha}{\tan\alpha}-(k+1).$$

5. Hint：

Assuming $h(k)=k^2-k+2$, we must show $h(k+1)=(k+1)^2-(k+1)+2$.

As the $(k+1)$ th circle is divided into $2k$ regions，and each of the arc segments divides the region of the plane containing it，we have that

$$h(k+1)=h(k)+2k=k^2-k+2+2k=(k+1)^2-(k+1)+2.$$

6. Hint：

(1) $a_1=\dfrac{1}{2}$, $a_2=\dfrac{1}{8}$, $a_3=\dfrac{1}{26}$, $a_4=\dfrac{1}{80}$.

(2) $a_n = \dfrac{1}{3^n - 1}$. Hint of proof: $a_{k+1} = \dfrac{a_k}{2a_k + 3} = \dfrac{\dfrac{1}{3^k - 1}}{\dfrac{2}{3^k - 1} + 3} = \dfrac{1}{2 + 3(3^k - 1)} = \dfrac{1}{3^{k+1} - 1}$.

7. (1) $a_1 = 1$, $a_2 = \sqrt{2} - 1$, $a_3 = \sqrt{3} - \sqrt{2}$, $a_4 = 2 - \sqrt{3}$.

(2) $a_n = \sqrt{n} - \sqrt{n-1}$.

Hint of proof:

Since $S_{k+1} = S_k + a_{k+1} = \dfrac{1}{2}\left(a_k + \dfrac{1}{a_k}\right) + a_{k+1} = \dfrac{1}{2}\left(\sqrt{k} - \sqrt{k-1} + \dfrac{1}{\sqrt{k} - \sqrt{k-1}}\right) + a_{k+1} = \sqrt{k} + a_{k+1}$,

and $S_{k+1} = \dfrac{1}{2}\left(a_{k+1} + \dfrac{1}{a_{k+1}}\right)$,

we have that $\sqrt{k} + a_{k+1} = \dfrac{1}{2}\left(a_{k+1} + \dfrac{1}{a_{k+1}}\right)$, $a_{k+1}^2 + 2\sqrt{k}\,a_{k+1} - 1 = 0$.

Solving the equation gives $a_{k+1} = \sqrt{k+1} - \sqrt{k}$.

8. For $n = 1, 2, 3$, we have that

$$1 \cdot 2^2 = \frac{1(1+1)}{12}(a + b + c),$$

$$1 \cdot 2^2 + 2 \cdot 3^2 = \frac{2(2+1)}{12}(4a + 2b + c),$$

$$1 \cdot 2^2 + 2 \cdot 3^2 + 3 \cdot 4^2 = \frac{3(3+1)}{12}(9a + 3b + c).$$

Solving the system of equations $\begin{cases} a + b + c = 24 \\ 4a + 2b + c = 44 \\ 9a + 3b + c = 70 \end{cases}$ gives $\begin{cases} a = 3 \\ b = 11. \\ c = 10 \end{cases}$

Now we need to use mathematical induction to prove that the formula $1 \cdot 2^2 + 2 \cdot 3^2 + 3 \cdot 4^2 + \cdots + n\,(n+1)^2 = \dfrac{n(n+1)}{12}(3n^2 + 11n + 10)$ holds for all positive integers n.

Hint of proof:

$$1 \cdot 2^2 + 2 \cdot 3^2 + 3 \cdot 4^2 + \cdots + k\,(k+1)^2 + (k+1)\,(k+2)^2$$

$$= \frac{k(k+1)}{12}(3k^2 + 11k + 10) + (k+1)\,(k+2)^2$$

$$= \frac{(k+1)}{12}\left[k(3k^2 + 11k + 10) + 12\,(k+2)^2\right]$$

$$= \frac{(k+1)}{12}(3k^3 + 23k^2 + 58k + 48)$$

$$= \frac{(k+1)(k+2)}{12}(3k^2 + 17k + 24)$$

$$= \frac{(k+1)(k+2)}{12}\left[3\,(k+1)^2 + 11(k+1) + 10\right]$$

9. For $n = 1, 2, 3$, we have that

$$\frac{1}{1+2} = \frac{p+q+r}{4(1+1)(1+2)},$$

$$\frac{1}{1+2} + \frac{1}{2+6} = \frac{4p+2q+r}{4(2+1)(2+2)},$$

$$\frac{1}{1+2} + \frac{1}{2+6} + \frac{1}{3+12} = \frac{9p+3q+r}{4(3+1)(3+2)}.$$

Solving the system of equations $\begin{cases} p + q + r = 8 \\ 4p + 2q + r = 22 \\ 9p + 3q + r = 42 \end{cases}$ gives $\begin{cases} p = 3 \\ q = 5. \\ r = 0 \end{cases}$

Now we need to use mathematical induction to prove that the formula $\dfrac{1}{1+a_1} + \dfrac{1}{2+a_2} + \cdots + \dfrac{1}{n+a_n} =$

$\dfrac{3n^2+5n}{4(n+1)(n+2)}$ holds for all positive integers n.

Hint of proof:

$$\frac{1}{1+a_1}+\frac{1}{2+a_2}+\cdots+\frac{1}{k+a_k}+\frac{1}{k+1+a_{k+1}}$$

$$=\frac{3k^2+5k}{4(k+1)(k+2)}+\frac{1}{k+1+(k+1)+(k+1)^2}$$

$$=\frac{3k^2+5k}{4(k+1)(k+2)}+\frac{1}{(k+1)(k+3)}$$

$$=\frac{(3k^2+5k)(k+3)+4(k+2)}{4(k+1)(k+2)(k+3)}$$

$$=\frac{3k^3+14k^2+19k+8}{4(k+1)(k+2)(k+3)}$$

$$=\frac{(k+1)(3k^2+11k+8)}{4(k+1)(k+2)(k+3)}$$

$$=\frac{[3(k+1)^2+5(k+1)]}{4(k+2)(k+3)}$$

10. $a_n=(n+1)^2$, $b_n=2^n-1$. For $1\leqslant n\leqslant 5$, $a_n>b_n$. For $n\geqslant 6$, $a_n<b_n$.

7.5 数列的极限

1. (1) $\displaystyle\lim_{n\to\infty}\frac{1}{n+1}=0$.　(2) $\displaystyle\lim_{n\to\infty}\frac{3n-1}{n}=3$.　(3) $\displaystyle\lim_{n\to\infty}\left(-\frac{1}{2}\right)^n=0$.　(4) not exsit.

2. (1) $\displaystyle\lim_{n\to\infty}\frac{4n-3}{2n+1}=2$.　(2) $\displaystyle\lim_{n\to\infty}\frac{n^2+1}{2n^2}=\frac{1}{2}$.　(3) $\displaystyle\lim_{n\to\infty}\frac{2n^4}{6n^5+7}=0$.　(4) $\displaystyle\lim_{n\to\infty}\frac{\sqrt{n}}{n+1}=0$.

3. (1) $\displaystyle\lim_{n\to\infty}\frac{(2n+1)(3n^2-2)}{4n^3-5n^2+6n-7}=\frac{3}{2}$.

(2) $\displaystyle\lim_{n\to\infty}\left(\frac{1}{n^2+1}+\frac{2}{n^2+1}+\frac{3}{n^2+1}+\cdots+\frac{2n}{n^2+1}\right)=\lim_{n\to\infty}\frac{2n^2+n}{n^2+1}=2$.

(3) $\displaystyle\lim_{n\to\infty}\left(1+\frac{1}{1+2}+\frac{1}{1+2+3}+\cdots+\frac{1}{1+2+3+\cdots+n}\right)=\lim_{n\to\infty}\frac{2n}{n+1}=2$.

(4) $\displaystyle\lim_{n\to\infty}\left(1-\frac{1}{2^2}\right)\left(1-\frac{1}{3^2}\right)\left(1-\frac{1}{4^2}\right)\cdots\left(1-\frac{1}{n^2}\right)=\lim_{n\to\infty}\frac{n+1}{2n}=\frac{1}{2}$.

(5) $\displaystyle\lim_{n\to\infty}n^2\left[\frac{100}{n}-\left(\frac{1}{n+1}+\frac{1}{n+2}+\cdots+\frac{1}{n+100}\right)\right]=5\,050$.

4. (1) $\displaystyle\lim_{n\to\infty}\frac{2^{n+2}+3^{n+3}}{3^n-2^{n+1}}=27$.　(2) $\displaystyle\lim_{n\to\infty}\frac{(-2)^{n+1}+(-3)^{n-1}}{(-2)^{n+4}+(-3)^{n+1}}=\frac{1}{9}$.

(3) $\displaystyle\lim_{n\to\infty}\frac{(\sqrt{3}+\sqrt{2})^{n+1}+(\sqrt{3}-\sqrt{2})^{n+2}}{(\sqrt{3}+\sqrt{2})^n-(\sqrt{3}-\sqrt{2})^{n+1}}=\sqrt{3}+\sqrt{2}$.　(4) $\displaystyle\lim_{n\to\infty}\frac{1+3+3^2+\cdots+3^n}{3^n+a^{n+1}}=\begin{cases}\dfrac{3}{2},\ |a|<3\\[4pt]0,\ |a|>3\\[4pt]\dfrac{3}{8},\ a=3\\[4pt]\text{doesn't exsit},\ a=-3.\end{cases}$

5. (1) $\displaystyle\lim_{n\to\infty}\left(1+\frac{1}{n}\right)^{n+2}=e$.　(2) $\displaystyle\lim_{n\to\infty}\left(1-\frac{1}{n}\right)^n=\frac{1}{e}$.　(3) $\displaystyle\lim_{n\to\infty}\left(\frac{2n-1}{2n-4}\right)^{n+1}=e^{\frac{3}{2}}$.　(4) $\displaystyle\lim_{n\to\infty}\left(\frac{2n+3}{2n+1}\right)^{4n-1}=e^4$.

6. (1) Since $\displaystyle\lim_{n\to\infty}\frac{4^n}{4^{n+2}+(m+2)^n}=\lim_{n\to\infty}\frac{1}{16+\left(\frac{m+2}{4}\right)^n}=\frac{1}{16}$, so $\left|\dfrac{m+2}{4}\right|<1$, so $-6<m<2$.

(2) $\displaystyle\lim_{n\to\infty}(2n-\sqrt{4n^2+kn+3})=\lim_{n\to\infty}\frac{-kn-3}{2n+\sqrt{4n^2+kn+3}}=\lim_{n\to\infty}\frac{-k-\frac{3}{n}}{2+\sqrt{4+\frac{k}{n}+\frac{3}{n^2}}}=\frac{-k}{4}=1$, So $k=-4$.

7. (1) $0.\dot{4}=\dfrac{4}{10}+\dfrac{4}{10^2}+\dfrac{4}{10^3}+\cdots+\dfrac{4}{10^n}\cdots=\displaystyle\lim_{n\to\infty}\frac{\frac{4}{10}\left(1-\frac{1}{10^n}\right)}{1-\frac{1}{10}}=\frac{\frac{4}{10}}{1-\frac{1}{10}}=\frac{4}{9}$.

(2) $2.3\dot{8} = 2 + \dfrac{38}{100} + \dfrac{38}{10^4} + \dfrac{38}{10^6} + \cdots + \dfrac{38}{10^{2n}} \cdots = 2 + \lim\limits_{n \to \infty} \dfrac{\dfrac{38}{100}\left(1 - \dfrac{1}{10^{2n}}\right)}{1 - \dfrac{1}{100}} = 2 + \dfrac{\dfrac{38}{100}}{1 - \dfrac{1}{100}} = 2\dfrac{38}{99}.$

(3) $2.2\dot{3}\dot{4} = 2.2 + \dfrac{34}{1\,000} + \dfrac{34}{10^5} + \dfrac{34}{10^7} + \cdots + \dfrac{34}{10^{2n+1}} \cdots = 2.2 + \lim\limits_{n \to \infty} \dfrac{\dfrac{34}{10^3}\left(1 - \dfrac{1}{10^{2n}}\right)}{1 - \dfrac{1}{100}} = 2.2 + \dfrac{\dfrac{34}{1\,000}}{1 - \dfrac{1}{100}} = 2\dfrac{116}{495}.$

(4) $3.7\dot{2}1\dot{5} = 3.7 + \dfrac{215}{10^4} + \dfrac{215}{10^7} + \dfrac{215}{10^{10}} + \cdots + \dfrac{215}{10^{3n+1}} \cdots = 3.7 + \lim\limits_{n \to \infty} \dfrac{\dfrac{215}{10^4}\left(1 - \dfrac{1}{10^{3n}}\right)}{1 - \dfrac{1}{10^3}} = 3.7 + \dfrac{\dfrac{215}{10^4}}{1 - \dfrac{1}{10^3}} = 3\dfrac{3\,604}{4\,995}.$

8. (1) $\lim\limits_{n \to \infty} \dfrac{1 + \dfrac{1}{2} + \dfrac{1}{2^2} + \cdots + \dfrac{1}{2^n}}{1 - \dfrac{1}{2} + \dfrac{1}{2^2} + \cdots + (-1)^n \dfrac{1}{2^n}} = 3.$ (2) $\lim\limits_{n \to \infty}\left(\dfrac{2+3}{6} + \dfrac{2^2 + 3^2}{6^2} + \cdots + \dfrac{2^n + 3^n}{6^n}\right) = \dfrac{3}{2}.$

9. $|q| < 1 \Leftrightarrow -1 < q < 0$ or $0 < q < 1.$ Since $\dfrac{a_1}{1-q} = 4,$ we get that $a_1 \in (0, 4) \bigcup (4, 8).$

10. From the given conditions, $S_1 = \dfrac{\sqrt{3}}{4}a^2;$ $S_2 = \dfrac{1}{2} \cdot 2r \cdot \sqrt{3}r.$

Since $(3 + \sqrt{3})r = \dfrac{\sqrt{3}}{2}a,$ we get that $r = \dfrac{\sqrt{3} - 1}{4}a.$

Therefore, $S_2 = \sqrt{3} \cdot \left(\dfrac{\sqrt{3} - 1}{4}\right)^2 \cdot a^2 = \dfrac{\sqrt{3}}{4}a^2 \cdot \dfrac{2 - \sqrt{3}}{2}.$

So $q = \dfrac{2 - \sqrt{3}}{2},$

$S = \dfrac{\dfrac{\sqrt{3}}{4}a^2}{1 - \dfrac{2 - \sqrt{3}}{2}} = \dfrac{a^2}{2}.$

11. Since $q = \dfrac{3}{4},$ we get that $S = \dfrac{6}{1 - \dfrac{3}{4}} = 24.$

12. (1) Let the area enclosed by the snowflake cure after n-times transformations be $a_n.$

Then we know that

$a_0 = \dfrac{\sqrt{3}}{4},$

$a_n = a_0 + \left(3 \times \dfrac{a_0}{9} + 3 \times 4 \times \dfrac{a_0}{9^2} + 3 \times 4^2 \times \dfrac{a_0}{9^3} + \cdots + 3 \times 4^{n-1} \times \dfrac{a_0}{9^n}\right)$

$= a_0 + \dfrac{a_0}{3}\left[1 + \dfrac{4}{9} + \left(\dfrac{4}{9}\right)^2 + \cdots + \left(\dfrac{4}{9}\right)^{n-1}\right]$

$= a_0 + \dfrac{a_0}{3} \cdot \dfrac{1 - \left(\dfrac{4}{9}\right)^n}{1 - \dfrac{4}{9}}$

$= a_0 + \dfrac{3}{5}a_0\left[1 - \left(\dfrac{4}{9}\right)^n\right]$

$= \dfrac{\sqrt{3}}{4} + \dfrac{3}{5} \cdot \dfrac{\sqrt{3}}{4} \cdot \left[1 - \left(\dfrac{4}{9}\right)^n\right]$

$= \dfrac{2\sqrt{3}}{5} - \dfrac{3\sqrt{3}}{20} \cdot \left(\dfrac{4}{9}\right)^n.$

Hence, the area enclosed by the snowflake cure is

$$\lim_{n\to\infty} a_n \subset \lim_{n\to\infty}\left[\frac{2\sqrt{3}}{5} - \frac{3\sqrt{3}}{20}\cdot\left(\frac{4}{9}\right)^n\right] = \frac{2\sqrt{3}}{5}.$$

(2) Let the perimeters of the snowflake cure after n-times transformations be b_n.

Then we know that

$$b_0 = 3,\ b_n = \frac{4}{3}b_{n-1}.$$

Hence, the sequence $\{b_n\}$ is a geometric sequence whose first term is 3 and whose common ratio is $\frac{4}{3}$.

Since the common ratio is bigger than 1, we get that the limit of the sequence of perimeters of the snowflake curve is infinite.